ANTHROPOLOGICAL PAPERS OF
THE UNIVERSITY OF ARIZONA
NUMBER 80

Reframing the Northern Rio Grande Pueblo Economy

Edited by Scott G. Ortman

THE UNIVERSITY OF
ARIZONA PRESS
TUCSON

The University of Arizona Press
www.uapress.arizona.edu

Printed in the United States of America.

24 23 22 21 20 19   6 5 4 3 2 1

ISBN-13: 978-0-8165-3931-4 (paper)

Editing and indexing by Linda Gregonis.
InDesign layout by Douglas Goewey.

Library of Congress Cataloging-in-Publication Data
are available at the Library of Congress.

♾ This paper meets the requirements of
ANSI/NISO Z39.48-1992 (Permanence of Paper).

Cover: Idealized settlement pattern showing the relationship of towns, villages, hamlets, and houses along a drainage (from Eiselt, Chapter 2); and *Buffalo Man, Buffalo Dance* by Awa Tsireh, courtesy of the Smithsonian American Art Museum, Corbin-Henderson Collection, gift of Alice H. Rossin.

About the Authors

KURT F. ANSCHUETZ received his PhD from the University of Michigan in 1998 and is the program director for Rio del Oso Anthropological Services, LLC, in Albuquerque. His research focuses on late Prehispanic and early Historic period Pueblo agricultural land use, cultural landscapes, and social organization. He also prepares expert testimony for land and water cases either directly for various pueblos or on their behalf through their government-to-government relationships with the US Department of Justice.

FUMI ARAKAWA is director of the University Museum and an associate professor of anthropology at New Mexico State University in Las Cruces. He is also a research associate with the Crow Canyon Archaeological Center. Arakawa obtained his PhD in anthropology from Washington State University. His primary interest is reconstructing sociopolitical organization in the Mesa Verde and Mogollon regions.

CHRISTOPHER BANET is water resources manager at the Southwest Regional Office of the Bureau of Indian Affairs in Albuquerque. He earned a master's degree in soil science from the University of Tennessee, focusing of characteristics of loess soils. Chris's interests are irrigation and water manipulation technologies in the American Southwest prior to and immediately following European contact. He works with data related to Indian water rights as needed for litigation and negotiated settlements.

EILEEN L. CAMILLI received her PhD from the University of New Mexico in 1983 and is a principal of Ebert & Associates, Inc., in Albuquerque. Her research includes Prehispanic agricultural land use, with a focus on the collection of technical data for demonstrating precontact period irrigation practices. She specializes in the photo-identification and mapping of twentieth century and modern agricultural lands. Her work chronicles irrigation practices to support indigenous water rights litigation and settlements.

GRANT D. COFFEY is a GIS archaeologist at the Crow Canyon Archaeological Center. He has authored or co-authored several articles on Pueblo archaeology. He earned his master's degree at Northern Arizona University studying population movements among early Pueblo peoples in southwestern Colorado.

PATRICK CRUZ is a doctoral student in the archaeology program at the University of Colorado, Boulder. His primary research interests focus on precontact Pueblo communities in southwest Colorado and on precontact to present Pueblo communities in northern New Mexico.

KAITLYN DAVIS is a doctoral student in the archaeology program at the University of Colorado, Boulder (CU). She earned her master's degree in anthropology (archaeology) at CU studying the social mechanisms that facilitated Protohistoric Plains-Pueblo economic interaction. Her dissertation work focuses on how Pueblo people adapted their agricultural and land use practices in response to socioeconomic changes brought about by Spanish colonization.

SAMUEL DUWE is an assistant professor in the Department of Anthropology at the University of Oklahoma. His research focuses on Pueblo communities in northern New Mexico, specifically on histories of the Tewa Pueblos. His current work addresses migration, ethnogenesis, colonial encounters, and the challenges and opportunities of contemporary collaborative archaeology.

B. SUNDAY EISELT is an associate professor of anthropology at Southern Methodist University. Her research focuses on the Jicarilla and Hispanic societies of New Mexico, Hohokam and O'Odham ceramic production, ceramic source geochemistry, and community-based and engaged approaches in archaeology. She has studied in numerous geographic regions including New Mexico, Arizona, California, and the Great Basin.

DOUGLAS HARRO is a principal archaeologist and lithic analyst at Paleo Analytics, LLC, based in Idaho. He earned his master's degree in anthropology at Washington State University studying the conveyance of lithic raw materials among the ancestral Puebloan populations of northern New Mexico. Since then his work has focused on the technological adaptations made by early hunter-gatherer-fishers of the California coast.

JOSÉ LOBO is on the faculty of the School of Sustainability at Arizona State University in Tempe. Trained in physics and urban economics, with a PhD from Cornell University, his main research efforts revolve around building an empirically robust theory of settlement formation spanning the very first human settlements to ancient cities to contemporary urban systems

CHRIS NICHOLSON is the director of the Wyoming State Climate Office and Water Resources Data System, and adjunct assistant professor in the Department of Anthropology at the University of Wyoming. He obtained his PhD in anthropology from the University of Wyoming, focusing on behavioral responses to climate change during the late Pleistocene and Mid-Holocene in western Eurasia. His primary interests are in human paleoecology, paleoclimatology, environmental archaeology, and GIS applications in anthropology.

SCOTT G. ORTMAN is an assistant professor of anthropology at the University of Colorado, Boulder, a research affiliate of the Crow Canyon Archaeological Center, and an external professor at the Santa Fe Institute. His research focuses on ancestral Pueblo historical anthropology and on complex systems approaches in archaeology.

PASCALE MEEHAN is a PhD candidate in anthropology at the University of Colorado, Boulder. Her research focuses on rural responses to political collapse in Oaxaca, Mexico. Her other interests include prehistoric migration, colonization, and social memory. She has been involved in archaeological projects throughout the Americas including Peru, Mexico, and the Pacific Northwest.

KARI SCHLEHER has a PhD in anthropology from the University of New Mexico. She is the laboratory manager at the Crow Canyon Archaeological Center and an adjunct assistant professor of anthropology at the University of New Mexico. Using pottery analysis as a tool, her primary research interest is in social relationships as a means of understanding connections among individuals and communities in the past.

ANNA SCHNEIDER earned master's degrees in anthropology and business administration from the University of Colorado, Boulder. Her primary research area is southern Arizona, where her interests include frontiers and borderlands, military and historic archaeology, collaborative and community-based archaeology, and museums. Currently, she is a consultant with Heritage Business International and a staff member at the Amerind Museum in Dragoon, Arizona.

SUSAN SMITH began specializing in palynology in 1985 after completing a bachelor's degree in geology at Humboldt State University, California, and a Quaternary studies master's from Northern Arizona University in Flagstaff. Her current research interest is prehistoric agriculture in the arid Southwest and the potential for these ancient, low-tech systems to help farmers mediate modern environmental challenges.

Contents

TABLES

FIGURES

Economic Growth in the Pueblos?

Scott G. Ortman and Kaitlyn E. Davis

Archaeologists working in the Northern Rio Grande region of New Mexico have long recognized that in the centuries preceding Spanish contact Pueblo people coalesced into larger settlements (Adams and Duff, editors, 2004; Marshall and Walt 1984; Spielmann 1998); produced and exchanged pottery more widely (Cordell and Habicht-Mauche, editors, 2012; Habicht-Mauche, Eckert, and Huntley, editors, 2006); and developed substantial trade networks with peoples to the east (Snow 1981; Spielmann 1991; Wilcox 1981). These big patterns in Northern Rio Grande archaeology suggest that Pueblo people of the region experienced an extended period of social and economic development between about 1300 and 1600 CE. This conclusion is not surprising to archaeologists who work in the region. The purpose of this book is to highlight just how interesting and potentially important this conclusion is in a larger context.

In economic history and related fields there is long-standing debate regarding the extent to which human societies experienced economic growth—in the general sense of increasing material output per unit time—prior to the industrial revolution. For archaeologists, this question raises a whole host of issues, from formalist/substantivist debates to the differences between contemporary and past economies to the value judgments that often accompany such discussions in economics and contemporary politics. These and other issues are taken up in greater detail by Jose Lobo in his contribution to this volume (Chapter 12). Here, we echo Lobo's conclusion that, fundamentally, the question of whether the material outputs of ancient societies changed over time is an empirical one.

Of course, there are several straightforward ways in which the total material output of a society can increase over time. For example, it can increase simply through population growth: so long as the output per person remains constant, more people will produce (and consume) proportionately more food, clothing, pottery, tools, housing, etc. Of course, as Malthus noted, an economy can also grow despite *declining* output per person when the population grows more rapidly than the supply of food and other resources. In this case, total output may still increase, but its growth rate will be slower than the population growth rate, and the output per person will actually shrink. Both these scenarios have been documented in the ethnographic literature (Boserup 1965; Netting 1993; Stone 1996) and have undoubtedly occurred in the past as well. But in many ways these scenarios are not as interesting, or potentially helpful, as the one we focus on in this book: the situation where increases in material outputs outpace population growth due to increases in productivity.

The literature in economic history tends to argue that this type of productivity-driven growth is dependent on technological innovations related to the capture and transformation of energy, and thus was rare to nonexistent prior to the Industrial Revolution (Galor 2005; Mokyr 2005; Wrigley 2013). However, as empirical data have accumulated it has become clear that many past societies—from Prehispanic Mesoamerica to ancient Greece—did in fact generate substantial *per capita* increases in material outputs (Allen 2009; Fouquet and Broadberry 2015; Pryor 2005; Scheidel and Friesen 2009; Stark and others 2016), energy capture rates (Morris 2010, 2013), farming surpluses (Sanders, Parsons, and Santley 1979), consumption rates (Jongman 2014a, 2014b), and wealth accumulation (Morris 2004; Ober 2010; Ortman, Davis, Lobo, Smith, and Cabaniss 2016). Technological progress has been offered as an explanation for these trends as well (Greene 2000; Kander, Malanima, and Warde 2014; Smil 2008), but a wider range of explanations have also been offered, from institutional structures (Acemoglu and Robinson 2012; North, Wallis, and Weingast 2009; Ober 2010) to urbanization (Bowman and Wilson 2011) and expanding trade networks (Algaze 2008; Scheidel 2008; Temin 2012). Thus far, research in this area has been confined primarily to the ancient and medieval societies of Europe (Bosker and others 2008; De Long and Schleifer 1993; Hanson 2016; Hanson, Ortman, and Lobo 2017; Harper 2017; Jongman 2014a, 2014b, 2014c; Malanima 2005; Ober 2010; Temin 2006, 2012). In this volume we argue that the Prehispanic Northern Rio Grande Pueblos should also be considered as a case of sustained economic growth driven by productivity increases, but in this case in a nonindustrial, noncapitalist, and relatively egalitarian society.

It is important to emphasize that in arguing for increased attention by archaeologists to socioeconomic development in the past we are not seeking to impose the specific values of Western capitalism on Pueblo history. Indeed, Pueblo culture itself places value on improving the quality of life for community members, including material conditions. Tewa prayers, for example, often refer to "seeking a life of abundance" as an important goal of personal and community efforts (Laski 1959; Sweet 2004). Given this, what is so interesting, and potentially important, is that Pueblo people created an economic system that accomplished this using distinctively Pueblo ideas, values, and institutions. The exchanges at the center of this economy probably involved far more barter and gift-giving than is typical of capitalist economies (Ford 1972a, 1972b), but the material effects of these transfers are nevertheless apparent. Thus, in this book we seek to reframe the study of Pueblo economic history as the study of long-term changes in the material conditions of life in a system characterized by Pueblo ideas, values, institutions, and technology.

In the remainder of this introduction, we first review several misconceptions that may have discouraged archaeologists from framing Northern Rio Grande Pueblo economic history the way we envision it. Then, we review current demographic and economic measures that illustrate several key properties of the Northern Rio Grande Pueblo economy to set the table for the chapters that follow. Finally, we provide an overview of the topics covered in the remainder of the volume.

MISCONCEPTIONS AND REALITIES

It is obvious from the archaeological record that the material outputs of past societies changed over time, but in our view several misconceptions have kept archaeologists from appreciating the relevance of such patterns for understanding economic growth as a general process. The first misconception is a conflation of the *level* of material outputs with *the rate of change* in that level. It is obvious that per capita rates of material output were quite a bit lower in the past than they are today (Morris 2013; Wrigley 2016). However, the archaeological record shows that there were changes in these rates over time in many societies. It is this rate of change in material output, and not the level of output itself, that is of greatest interest for understanding how societies can improve (or undermine) the material conditions of life for their participants. Thus, the archaeological record of economic development, even in middle-range societies, is potentially relevant for a more general understanding of how and why this process occurs.

A second misconception is that the basic determinants of economic growth are different in present-day societies than they were in the past. For example, it is well-known that as societies increase in scale new properties emerge that are related to social differentiation, integration, and complexity (Blanton and others 1993; Johnson and Earle 2000; Peregrine, Ember, and Ember 2004). This pattern is often taken to imply that the factors that govern growth change with scale. If so, studies of middle-range societies would not be relevant for understanding economic change in the modern world, since modern societies are several orders of magnitude larger than those of the past. However, recent research in complex systems has discovered several properties of human societies that are *scale-free* in the sense that they accumulate in a consistent way as population increases (Bettencourt 2013, 2014; Ortman and Coffey 2017; Smil 2008). This suggests that a basic determinant of economic growth is agglomeration effects that are *open-ended* with respect to population size. The archaeological record of the Rio Grande Pueblos clearly shows increasing agglomeration through time. This book examines the variety of changes that accompanied this process.

A third misconception is the notion that the primary constraint on economic development lies in the realm of physical technology. Although the ability to harness and transform energy and information has progressed at an unprecedented pace since the onset of the Industrial Revolution, Adam Smith recognized long ago that divisions of labor and human networks are also important drivers of development. Technology clearly plays a role, but the ethnographic literature suggests that the more fundamental constraints are psychological, social, and cultural (Ortman 2016a; Pinker 2011; Sahlins 1972; Singer 1981; Walker and Hill 2014). Human societies have, of course, come up with a variety of coercive mechanisms for increasing the scale of organization of human labor, from slavery to serfdom to tribute to corvée. But they have also developed institutions that support increases in the division of labor on a more voluntaristic basis. Following Adam Smith's famous aphorism that "the division of labor is set by the extent of the market," the economist Kenneth Arrow (1994) adds that the extent of this market, or the size of the social network within which goods and services are exchanged, is set by the size of the group to which "a shared sense of justice" is applied. This view suggests that the most fundamental drivers of economic development are ideas, institutions, and rituals that support mutually beneficial interactions among individuals who are not close friends or family. The archaeological record provides a rich record of the development of such ideas and institutions in native North America (Abbott, Smith, and Gallaga 2007; Kohler and others 2014; Ortman 2016a). This book provides additional examples of the connections among cultures, institutions, human securities, and archaeological measures of economic development.

A fourth misconception is that, because many contemporary economies are based on the market mechanism, economic growth also requires formal markets, money, and prices. Although economic growth does require increasing flows of goods and services among individuals, the market mechanism is just one means by which these flows are generated. In many non-western societies, for example, exchanges occur in the form of gifts that incur obligations between the receiver and the giver (Wilk and Cliggett 2007). These exchanges are a form of delayed reciprocity in the absence of a fixed price. It is also important to note that markets need not be "free" for an economy to grow, as is demonstrated by the recent history of the People's Republic of China, which has a mixed market-command economy. The implication of all this is that archaeologists do not need to identify markets or market exchange to discuss economic growth, because its fundamental determinants do not lie in the market mechanism (Abbott, Smith, and Gallaga 2007; Garraty and Stark, editors, 2010). This book uses archaeological data from the Northern Rio Grande to illustrate some of the characteristics of a nonmarket production and exchange system.

A fifth misconception is that preindustrial economies could not develop much beyond the level of mere subsistence (Finley 1973). Archaeologists in the US Southwest have played into this view by focusing almost exclusively on food in quantitative treatments of production (Benson, Petersen, and Stein 2007; Bocinsky and Kohler 2014; Van West 1994; Varien and others 2007). In the Northern Rio Grande, for example, researchers have often focused on relationships among agricultural features, site locations, and ecological factors regarding subsistence-level food production (Anschuetz 2007; Eiselt and others 2017; Hill and Trierweiler 1986; Trierweiler 1990). Food production is essential, of course, but as a society's economy grows its people become increasingly interdependent, with some farmers producing food surpluses and others spending more time doing other things, with the economic system serving to distribute the results of differentiated labor across the population. Initially this process occurs within communities, but with continued development, it becomes regional or even interregional. As a result, one would expect spatial relationships between people and primary production to loosen as part of this process. In other words, a disjunction between the distribution of people and the distribution of agricultural land may itself be a measure of economic growth. The only way to see this archaeologically is to estimate the distribution of population independent of food production resources. Sunday Eiselt begins this process for the Northern Rio Grande in her contribution to this volume (Chapter 2).

It is also important to note that food is not the only thing farmers can produce. In the Northern Rio Grande, Pueblo people raised turkeys, grew cotton, and procured hides for making a variety of clothing products (Kohler, Powers, and Orcutt 2004). Cotton textiles in particular were almost certainly a highly valued trade item for Plains peoples, but until very recently there has been no real attention given to the archaeological record of textile production and exchange. The chapters in this volume by Meehan and Camilli and others (Chapters 4 and 3 respectively) begin to address this gap.

A final misconception derives from the fact that in both historical and archaeological records, developing economies are often associated with increases in material inequality (Johnson and Earle 2000; Picketty 2014). In light of this one could be forgiven for presuming that economic growth can only occur in the context of coercive social institutions and increasing social inequality. This has certainly been the case with regard to the kinds of societies we label "early civilizations" (Flannery and Marcus 2012; Kohler and others 2017; Trigger 2003). But one of the most interesting and potentially important aspects of Northern Rio Grande archaeology is that it presents a record of economic development in a context where there is little to no evidence of coercive institutions or political inequality at the regional level (see Cruz and Ortman, Chapter 5), or of increasing material inequality at the household level. How exactly was this accomplished? This volume addresses this question using evidence ranging from agricultural production, to interethnic ritual and exchange, to community and intercommunity organization.

In our view, and as the chapters in this volume show, the archaeological record of the Northern Rio Grande pueblos addresses many of these misconceptions regarding economic development, thus raising the possibility that the economic history of the Pueblos may inform on a uniformitarian growth process that has operated the same way in the past as it does in the present. In the following sections we reinforce these arguments by summarizing current understandings of Northern Rio Grande demography and by developing and analyzing a series of proxy measures for economic performance at the level of the region, the settlement, and the household.

DEMOGRAPHIC IMPERATIVES

Population is perhaps the single most important variable for assessing economic change. The changing size and density of regional populations are clearly important for food production and several studies have shown that settlement population in particular is closely linked to social complexity (Carneiro 1962, 1967, 2000; Chick 1997; Feinman 2011; Gell-Mann 2011; Henrich 2004; Kline and Boyd 2010; Naroll 1956; Ortman, Blair, and Peregrine 2018; Peregrine, Ember, and Ember 2004) and individual productivity (Bettencourt 2013; Henderson 2003; Ortman and others 2016; Quigley 2009). Indeed, the number of people engaged in production is a fundamental variable in all attempts to explain economic performance (Bettencourt 2013; Glaeser 2011; Jones 2013; Jones and Romer 2010). Estimating the momentary populations and population histories of archaeological sites and regions is difficult and the associated challenges have led some to view all such estimates with skepticism (Drennan, Berrey, and Peterson 2015; Ortman 2016c). Fortunately, recent advances in methodology have led to marked improvement in such estimates for the Northern Rio Grande, and these estimates allow us, and many of the contributors to this volume, to incorporate population into the analysis.

The first innovation has come through the application of unmanned aerial vehicle (UAV) mapping, which allows archaeologists to efficiently measure the amount of melted adobe present in ancestral Pueblo room blocks. Studies of these measurements by Sam Duwe and others at sites where room outlines are also apparent in surface vegetation have shown that there are strong relationships between the areal extent of melted adobe and room counts, and between the height of adobe mounds and the number of stories present (Duwe and others 2016). As a result, it is possible to estimate the total number of rooms in Northern Rio Grande sites, even from traditional plan maps, much more accurately and precisely than it has been in the past.

The second innovation is a method for translating surface pottery assemblages from these sites into curves representing the relative intensity of occupation over time. This method, which improves upon mean ceramic dating in a number of ways, involves (a) cumulating uniform distributions representing the production span of specific pottery types in accordance with their occurrence in an assemblage, and (b) applying Bayes' Theorem to adjust the resulting summed probability distribution based on the likelihood of obtaining the observed mixtures at a site that was inhabited during each of a series of pottery periods (Ortman 2016b, 2017). The resulting probability distributions are estimates of the relative intensity of occupation through time. These can be combined with architectural footprints to estimate the momentary population of a site during each time period.

These methods do not solve all the problems inherent in estimating population. An important outstanding question, for example, is the extent to which the architectural footprints of Northern Rio Grande sites were ever fully occupied (see Anschuetz 2007). Nevertheless, these methods represent the state of the art in estimating population archaeologically, and several chapters in this volume take advantage of these estimates to bring the demographic realm into focus. Here we summarize the application of these approaches to a database of information on Northern Rio Grande archaeological sites developed for phase two of the Village Ecodynamics Project (VEP II). The project is an interdisciplinary effort to understand relationships between ancestral Pueblo society and its environment through a combination of computer modeling and big-data synthesis (Kohler and others 2012; Kohler and Varien 2012; Ortman 2016b). The VEP II study area, shown in Figure 1.1, roughly corresponds to the region known as

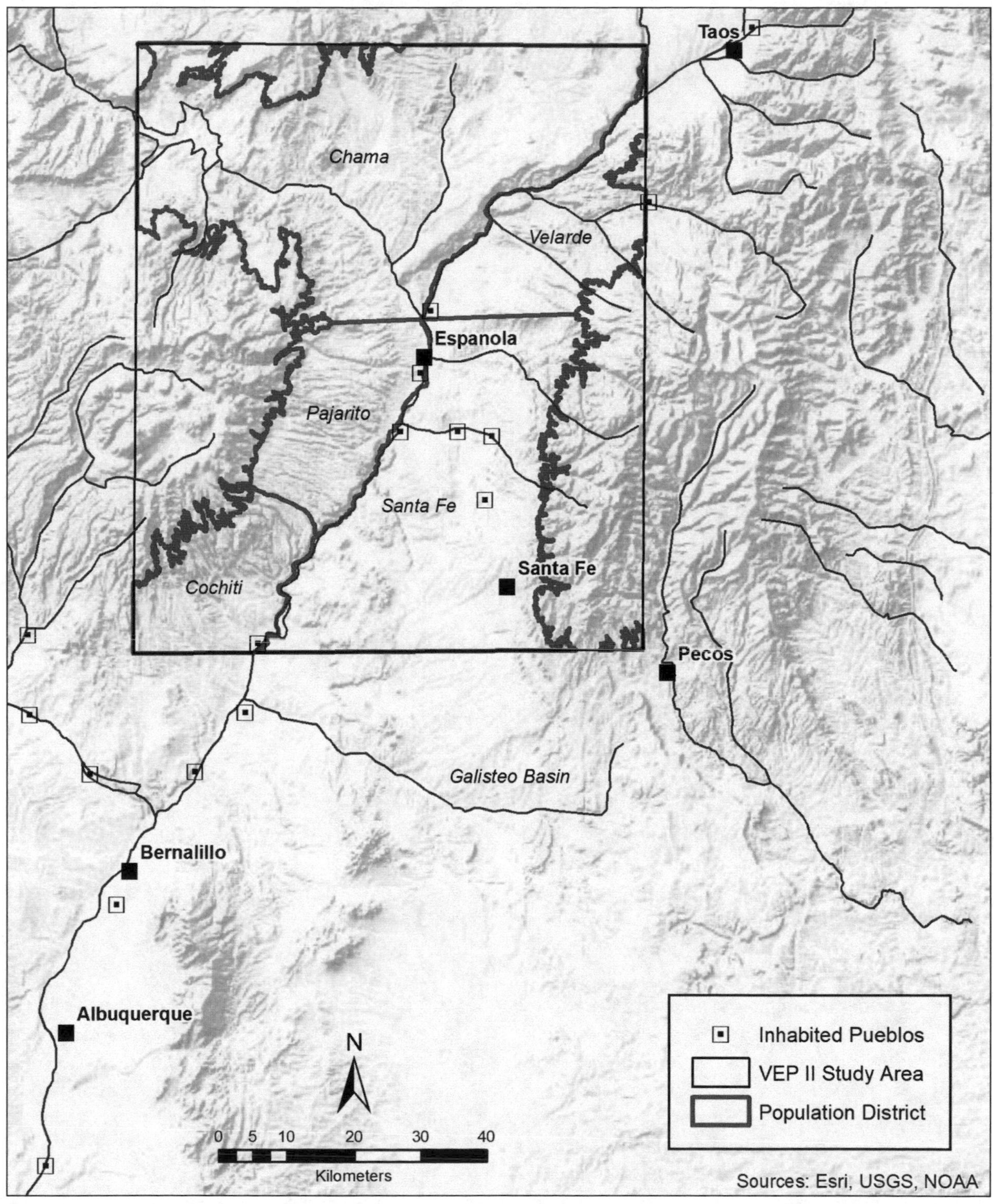

Figure 1.1. The Northern Rio Grande region, contemporary Pueblos, and the VEP II study area. Prepared by authors.

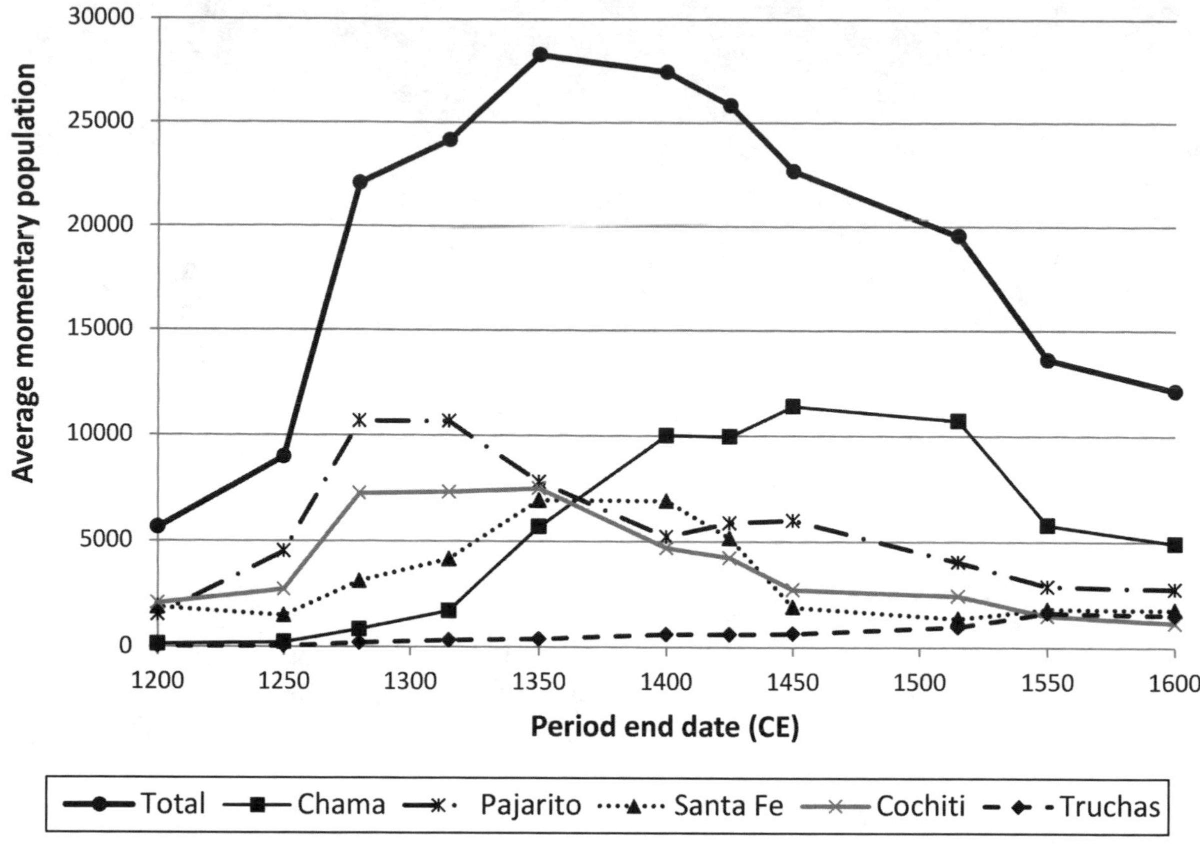

Figure 1.2. Population history of the VEP II study area, by district (after Ortman 2016: Figure 4).

the Tewa Basin after its primary inhabitants at the time of Spanish contact (Anschuetz 2005, 2007).

When grouped by district, these estimates (Figure 1.2) show that between 1200 and 1600 CE Pueblo populations ebbed and flowed across the landscape to a remarkable degree. On the Pajarito Plateau (Cochiti and Pajarito districts) population grew dramatically between 1200 and 1280 as in-migration from the San Juan drainage increased from a trickle to a flood, and then began a long-term decline. In contrast, along the eastern tributaries of the Rio Grande (the Santa Fe district) population growth was most pronounced during the 1300s, declining more rapidly between 1400 and 1450. Finally, in the Chama drainage (the Chama district) population was low until after 1300, at which time a long-term growth process began and continued into the 1500s before declining substantially in the mid-1500s.

Although the total population trajectory in Figure 1.2 suggests long-term decline after about 1400 CE, this curve does not include the Galisteo and Santo Domingo basins to the south. Based on current knowledge, it seems likely that the populations of those areas followed a similar trend to that of the Chama (Snead, Creamer, and Van Zandt 2004; Toll and Badner 2008). If so, it would seem reasonable to conclude that the Northern Rio Grande Pueblo population overall was fairly stable between about 1300 and the mid-1500s. If so, the district-level trends shown in Figure 1.2 are the result of people moving within the Northern Rio Grande region over time. This is important in that it implies that Northern Rio Grande Pueblo society did not impose restrictions on individuals moving between districts, presumably at least partly in response to changing economic opportunities. This is an essential precondition for the development of a regional division of labor. Contributions to this volume by Schleher (Chapter 7), Arakawa and others (Chapter 9), and Davis (Chapter 11) bring this regional division of labor into greater focus.

Figure 1.3 illustrates that the district-level population trends are also apparent at the level of individual settlements. The chart summarizes the population histories of 22 settlements within the VEP II study area that have architectural footprints of at least 500 rooms and are associated with a surface pottery assemblage. Although

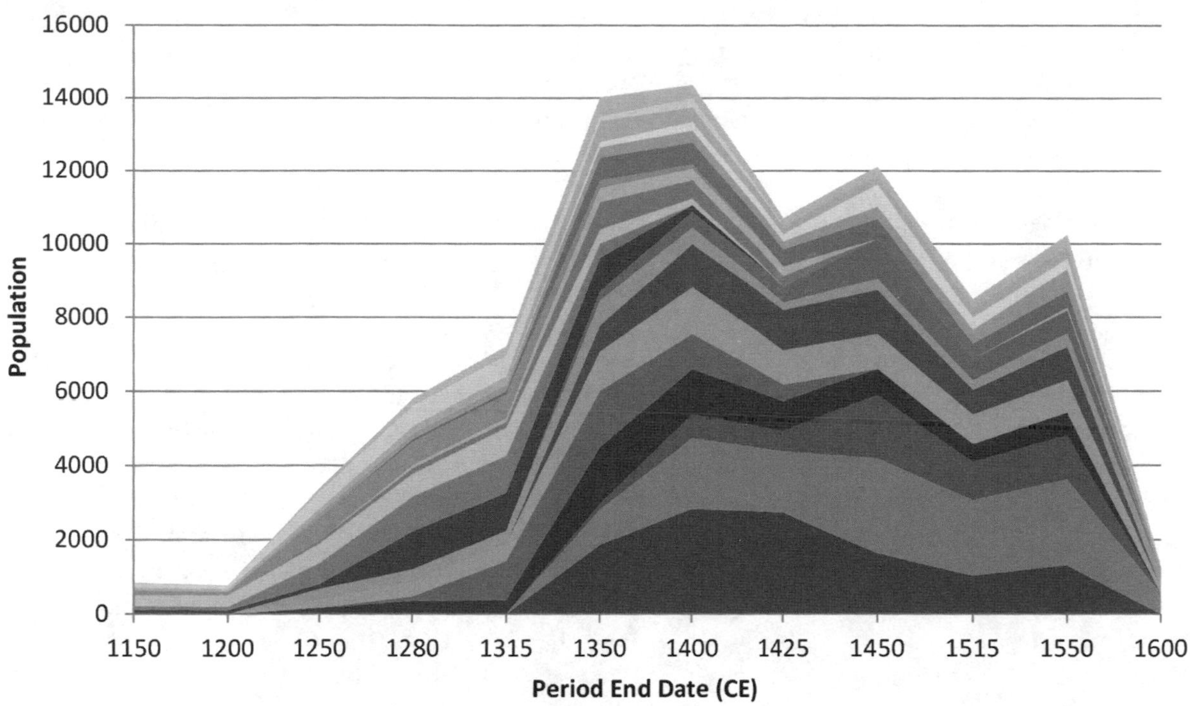

Figure 1.3. Population histories of 22 settlements in the VEP II study area (data from Ortman 2016).

the curve is a bit jagged due to details of the estimation process, it nevertheless shows that the population histories of specific settlements were remarkably diverse, with some settlements remaining small for long periods, others starting large and dwindling over time, and still others being established in the 1300s and growing rapidly. These diverse settlement-level population histories, in the context of a stable regional population, imply substantial levels of internal migration among settlements over time. This reality is reflected in Pueblo stories, in which physical movement from one place to another and the movement that characterizes life itself are prominent (Naranjo 2008). This is also important because one of the basic requirements for growth in a regional economy is something economists call an integrated labor market, which in the ancestral Pueblo context is simply a population that is able to move to where the economic opportunities are (Glaeser, Scheinkman, and Shleifer 1995; Henderson 2013; Jones 2013). This could only develop in the context of regional-scale identities, perhaps reflected in the distributions of major pottery wares (glaze, biscuit, etc.) that are the focus of chapters by Duwe (Chapter 8) and Schleher (Chapter 9) in this volume.

The fact that Northern Rio Grande settlements did not grow and decline in concert with the regional population is good evidence for relatively low barriers to movement from place to place. In this light, it is important to note that Pueblo people place value on movement even today. According to Naranjo (1995:248), "[m]ovement is one of the big ideological concepts of Pueblo thought because it is necessary for the perpetuation of life. Movement, clouds, wind, and rain are one. Movement must be emulated by the people." Anschuetz (2007) has applied these ideas in developing a model in which Pueblo people flowed across the landscape in response to decadal-scale changes in climate. We suggest these data indicate that Pueblo people flowed across the Northern Rio Grande landscape over longer periods as well, and in response to local economic conditions construed broadly.

ECONOMIC INDICATORS FOR THE PUEBLO WORLD

The VEP II project has compiled several additional types of data that are widely available in excavation and survey reports including architectural footprints, room area measurements, and artifact assemblage data. In addition to their use for demographic analysis, these data can be used to construct economic indicators for the region. Several investigators have examined changes in site size, room size, and pottery ratios over time, and all have shown consistent trends in these measures (Fowles 2004; Graves and Spielmann 2000; Hill, Trierweiler, and Preucel 1996; Kohler, Herr, and Root 2004; Snead 2008; Snead, Creamer, and Van Zandt 2004). In Figure 1.4, we present several time series that utilize the VEP II data to summarize changes in the Northern Rio Grande Pueblo economy.

Figure 1.4A presents the total population of the study area. Figure 1.4B presents the mean settlement population based on the population histories of all sites in the database. This measure captures changes in agglomeration, or the spatial aggregation of population in settlements through time. The time series likely over-states the degree of agglomeration early in the sequence because prior to 1400 CE much of the Pueblo population lived in small settlements that would only be in the database if they fell within a surveyed area. For the period after 1400 the series is fairly accurate because by that time most people lived in one of the large settlements known to archaeologists. Thus, the time series suggests a minimum of a three-fold increase in the degree of agglomeration in Pueblo society between 1200 and 1500 CE. Notice also that agglomeration grew consistently over time despite the suggested stable population discussed earlier. This is evidence that agglomeration was driven by social and economic benefits of proximity and not by population pressure.

Figure 1.4C presents the mean area of rooms that have been measured due to excavation or surface visibility. These data encompass nearly 4,000 rooms from 150 different sites. In this case all rooms associated with a given occupational component are associated with the end date of that component based on associated pottery and absolute dates. This time series suggests a roughly 25 percent increase in the floor area of the average room between 1300 and 1500 CE. Several studies have shown that house area is related to household possessions and food stores, and that the distribution of house sizes is a reasonable proxy for "income" and "wealth" distributions (Abul-Megd 2002; Morris 2004; Ortman and others 2015; Smith 1987; Smith and others 2014). Although it is difficult to distinguish house boundaries in Northern Rio Grande sites, the data in Figure 1.4C suggest that the sizes of living spaces followed agglomeration trends over time. This increase in average room size implies increases in average household-level abundance.

Finally, Figure 1.4D presents the average ratio of service (matte-painted and glaze-painted) ware to cooking (indented-corrugated, micaceous, etc.) ware sherds across settlements in the VEP II study area. The series is calculated using pottery tallies that contain service ware sherds and at least 10 cooking ware sherds; these were available for 192 sites in the VEP II database. The measure itself builds from research on artifact accumulations, which emphasizes connections between accumulations, people, and time (Lightfoot 1993; Pauketat 1989; Schiffer 1987; Varien and Mills 1997; Varien and Ortman 2005). Such studies have generally concluded that cooking potsherds accumulate at consistent rates per household in a variety of contexts, and thus provide a useful index of person-years of occupation at a site. This is the denominator of the ratio. The numerator is the number of service ware sherds from the same contexts. Since the denominator is an index of person-years and the numerator represents the same interval of time, variation in the ratio of service wares to cooking wares reflects differences in the per capita accumulation rate of service wares. And since these accumulations are of broken pots, the accumulation rate is also a consumption rate.

Economists have long recognized that consumption rates of material goods vary for a given income level, and they have labeled the difference as being between "low-elasticity" and "high-elasticity" goods (Jongman 2014b). Low-elasticity goods are things for which per capita demand doesn't change much with material living standards. High-elasticity goods, on the other hand, are things for which per capita demand does change with living standards. Examples of low-elasticity goods are salt, hammers, and can-openers, whereas examples of high-elasticity goods include clothing, household space, and artwork. In this framework, cooking pottery falls into the low-elasticity category because in aggregate people only need to cook so much food, regardless of their material standard of living; but decorated pottery falls into the high-elasticity category because it is used primarily for *serving* food and one might expect this activity to become more frequent and elaborate in aggregate as living standards increase. Ratios of the accumulation of high-elasticity goods to low-elasticity goods can thus reveal changes in living standards (Jongman 2014b:81). Accordingly, the ratio of decorated potsherds to cooking potsherds can be viewed as a per capita socioeconomic rate. In this context, the time series in Figure 1.4D suggests a roughly five-fold increase in the service-ware consumption rate per capita between 1300 and 1550 CE. This suggests a substantial increase in household inventories and in the rate of socializing with food.

The overall pattern in Figure 1.4 is of a society where population was stable but population agglomeration, house size, household possessions, and rates of social interaction involving food all increased over the centuries. These patterns demonstrate that Pueblo people achieved lives of increasing material abundance in the centuries preceding

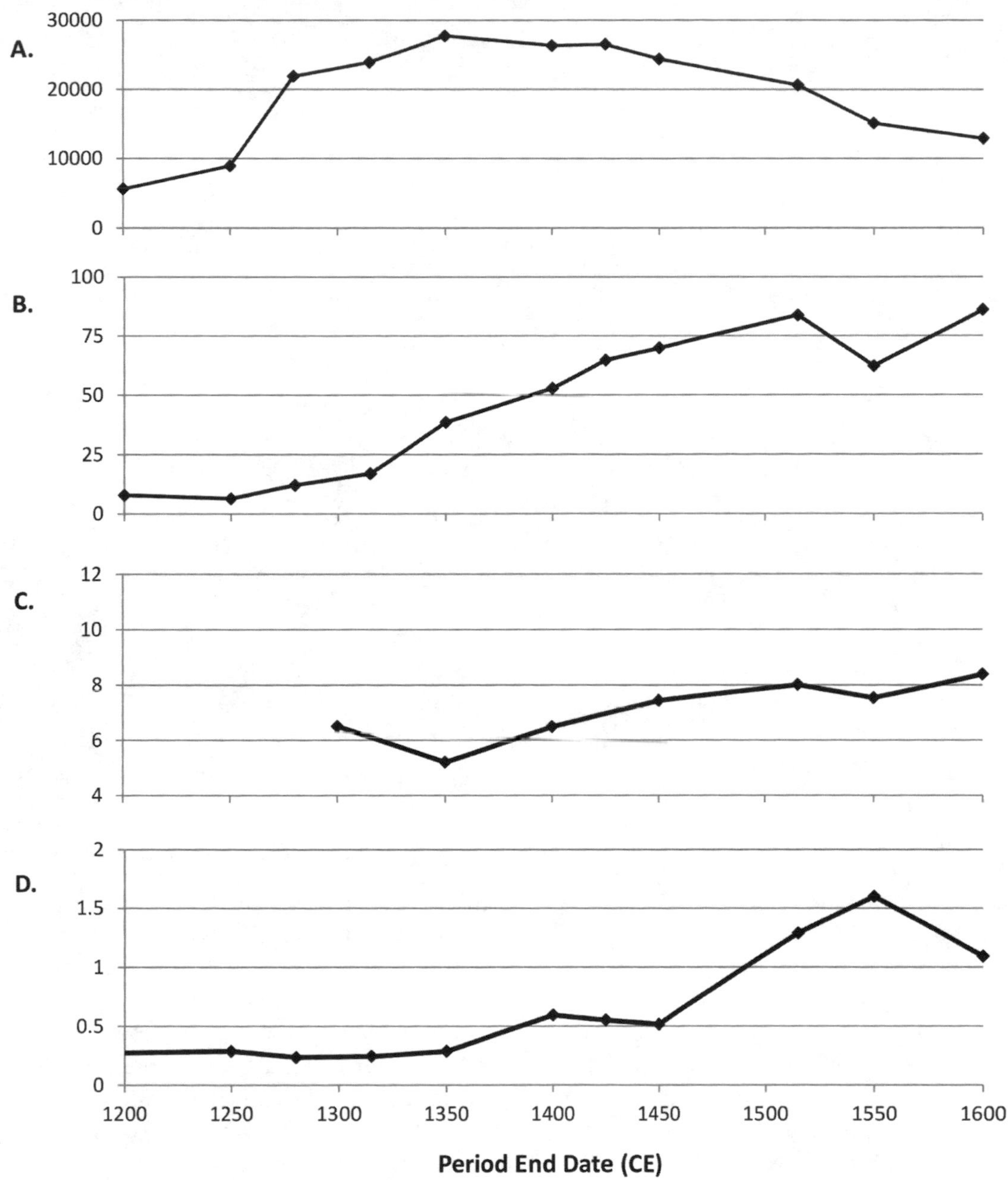

Figure 1.4. Changes in the Northern Rio Grande Pueblo economy through time, using VEP II data: (A) total population in persons; (B) mean settlement population in persons; (C) mean room area in square meters; and (D) the ratio of service ware to cooking ware sherd counts.

Spanish contact. In fact, one can translate these proxies into time series representing the growth rates of various measures that connect directly to discussions regarding growth in the modern world. For example, Figure 1.5 translates the service-ware to cooking-ware time series (Figure 1.4D) into growth rates. These estimates suggest the Northern Rio Grande Pueblo economy grew at as much as 1.5 percent per year during the latter half of the 1300s and the latter half of the 1400s, and it experienced negative growth of somewhat less than 1 percent during the population influx of the late 1200s and the period of excessive drought and initial Spanish contact during the late 1500s. The positive growth rates are somewhat lower than those experienced by industrial societies of recent centuries, but they are far

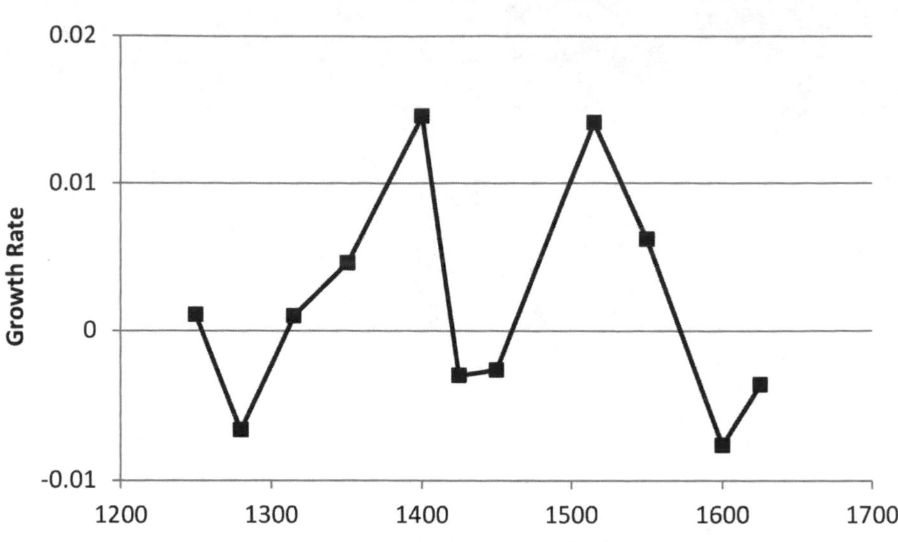

Figure 1.5. Annual per capita growth rate (service ware/cooking ware) through time in the VEP II study area.

from trivial. Indeed, the highest rates imply a doubling time in the consumption rate of service wares of about 50 years, meaning that individuals who lived long enough would have noticed the change during their lifetimes. That Pueblo people, with their communal values and a nonmonetized economy, could have created conditions that improved living conditions fast enough for individuals to notice the change over their lifetimes is a striking thought.

But perhaps the most surprising aspect of this history is the evidence that rising living standards did not lead to a rise in material inequality. Figure 1.6, for example, compares the distributions of room areas (in m^2) across sites, with a break point at 1450 CE. These distributions likely underestimate the actual degree of inequality in house floor areas since people can create larger houses by building more rooms in addition to larger rooms. But it is, nevertheless, quite interesting that both the coefficient of variation for room size and the Gini coefficient of room sizes actually *decreased* over time, even though the average size of rooms increased by about 25 percent during that period. These changes are statistically significant (*ANOVA* $F = 627.55$; $P < .0001$). Archaeologists who study "early civilizations" are accustomed to seeing dramatic increases in the inequality of housing as the scale of a society increases. Indeed, such a correlation is typical across a large sample of post-Neolithic societies (Kohler and others 2017). In this context, the economic history of the Northern Rio Grande Pueblos truly stands out and suggests that it is possible to increase material living standards and decrease material inequality at the same time. It seems to us that everyone should be interested in how Pueblo people accomplished this.

AGGLOMERATION EFFECTS ARE CENTRAL

Of course, documenting the basic patterns of Northern Rio Grande Pueblo economic history is only the first step in a much longer process of investigating why and how it happened. The chapters in this volume examine a variety of factors that seem to have played a role, from extending the geographic and social scale of identity groups to the emergence of diplomatic and intervillage rituals, increasing specialization and exchange, and the growth of communal, nonkin-based institutions. We begin the conversation here by using scaling analysis to show that many of the basic changes documented in the preceding discussion were agglomeration effects. Economists recognize agglomeration as a major driver of economic growth today, as the spatial clustering of population is linked to increased interaction rates, knowledge flows and the division of labor, and decreases in transport costs (Bettencourt 2013; Glaeser and Gottlieb 2009; Henderson 2003; Quigley 2009; Youn and others 2016). It is increasingly apparent that the same "social reactor" process is characteristic of smaller-scale societies known through archaeology. The theory and evidence behind this work have been developed in several studies (Cesaretti and others 2016; Hanson, Ortman, and

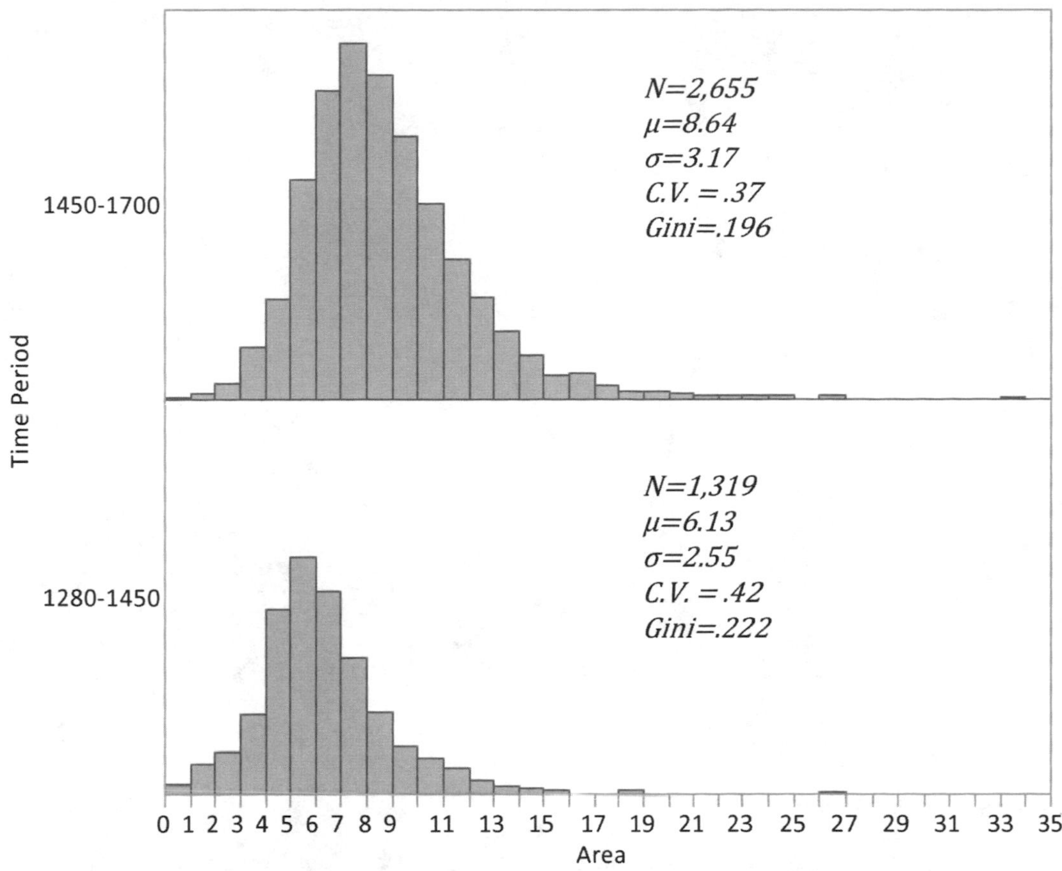

Figure 1.6. Room size distributions (in square meters) for the Northern Rio Grande through time.

Lobo 2017; Ortman and others 2014, 2015; Ortman and Coffey 2017; Ortman, Davis, Lobo, Smith, and Cabaniss 2016) and are discussed further by Ortman and Coffey in Chapter 6. Here, we illustrate how these ideas apply to the Northern Rio Grande Pueblo context.

The basic finding of this research is that a variety of average properties of settlements scale systematically with population, with the form of the relationship being given by the power function $Y = Y_0 N^{\beta}$, where Y is the property of interest, Y_0 is a baseline value, N is the settlement population, and β is an exponent. When Y reflects a socioeconomic or social interaction rate $\beta = 1 + \delta$; and when Y is a measure of the division of labor or resource use $\beta = 1 - \delta$. In both cases $1/6 \leq \delta \leq 1/3$, with the value of δ being determined by the total social connections that can be sustained in a group per unit time given the frictional effects of distance, the way in which the settlement area is measured, and the degree to which paths across the settlement are straight vs. circuitous (Bettencourt 2013, 2014). Both theoretical considerations and empirical evidence suggest these relationships are systematic, open-ended, and predictable, such that on average social interaction and socioeconomic rates increase faster than settlement population, whereas the division of labor and resource use increase at a slower, but still positive rate. In short, agglomeration is inextricably linked to gains in both productivity and efficiency.

One can observe these effects empirically by fitting a power function to measures of N and Y for groups of settlements in a system. The exponent of the fit line is an estimate of β. In Figure 1.7, we provide a scaling analysis of the ways in which three aggregate properties of Northern Rio Grande settlements vary with population using data from the VEP II database. (The data involved in these analyses are available at: https://core.tdar.org/project/392021/social-reactors-project-datasets.) The population proxy in these analyses is the estimated room count, which reflects the maximum possible momentary population of a site.

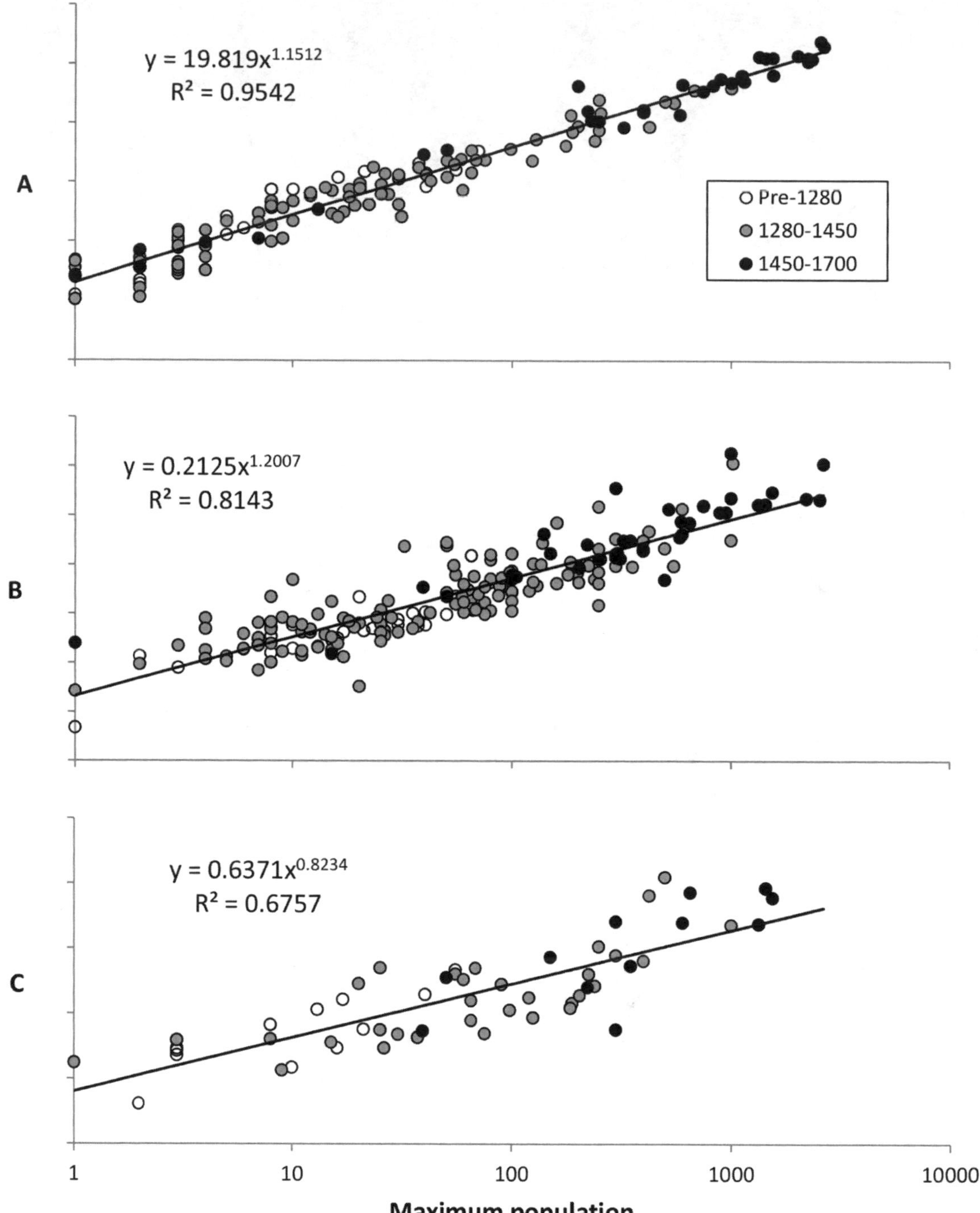

Figure 1.7. Relationships between maximum settlement population and (A) housing index, (B) service-ware consumption, and (C) chipped-stone tool production for settlements in the Northern Rio Grande. Scales are logarithmic.

The actual populations may have been smaller in some cases, but so long as the proportional relationship between architectural footprints and momentary population is independent of site size this should not affect the results.

Figure 1.7A compares the population estimate to a housing index, constructed by squaring the mean room area and multiplying this figure by the maximum population. The first step in calculating this index follows from the assumption that house size is a reasonable proxy for material living standards. We further assume that, with economic growth, half of the associated increase in house size will be translated into larger rooms and the other half will be translated into additional rooms. Thus, squaring the average room size produces a measure that takes both dimensions into account. The second step converts this to an aggregate measure that is proportional to the total roofed area of a site. We calculated this index for 165 sites with room area measurements. Settlement scaling theory predicts the exponent of the best-fit line for the relationship between population and the housing index (or any other aggregate socioeconomic quantity) will be 7/6, or 1.167 (Ortman and Coffey 2017). The observed exponent is 1.151 (*SE* = .020), within one standard error of the expected value for this relationship. Potential explanations aside, this result indicates that, on average, house areas increased faster than settlement population and exhibited increasing returns to scale. The high r-squared value of the regression is due to the role of population in the housing index, but this does not determine the observed deviation of the exponent from one, which is what one would expect if total house area increased proportionately to settlement population. Notice also that we have shaded the symbols for individual sites based on their occupation period, and that sites dating to different periods appear to follow the same relationship. This suggests that increases in mean room area over time (Figure 1.4C) derive primarily from increases in the average populations of settlements over the same period. Basically, both house area and settlement population were part of a single scaling relationship, such that change in one led to change in the other.

Figure 1.7B provides another comparison, this time between settlement population and the total service ware consumption rate. The latter is calculated by multiplying the ratio of service wares to cooking wares by the settlement population. This converts the ratio from a per capita measure to an aggregate measure. The required data are available for 224 sites in the database. Once again, the expected value of the exponent of the best-fit line for the relationship between population and the service-ware consumption rate is 7/6, or 1.167. And again, despite collinearity effects, the observed exponent is 1.201 (*SE* = .038), within one standard error of the expected value. This result indicates that, on average, the service-ware consumption rate also increased faster than population and exhibited increasing returns to scale. Also note that the exponent of this relationship is nearly identical to that of the population to house area relationship shown in Figure 1.7A. And once again, sites dating to different time periods follow a single scaling relation. These results suggest changes in the service-ware consumption rate shown in Figure 1.4D were also systematically related to changes in the average size of settlements through time. Changes in the rate of socializing with food seem to follow directly from changes in the size and density of the social networks manifest in settlements.

Finally, Figure 1.7C compares population to the chipped-stone tool production rate, measured as the ratio of chipped-stone debris to cooking potsherds, multiplied by the population. We possess these data for 64 sites in the database. Unlike service wares, which accumulate because of *consumption*, chipped-stone debris accumulates as a by-product of the *production* of chipped-stone tools. This is a measure of the division of labor. In a society where households are self-sufficient, there is no division of labor above the household level. As a result, each household must produce all the tools they need to use themselves. As these households become more connected, however, individuals have more opportunity to get the tools they need through their social contacts. As a result, the tools that exist can be shared and used more intensively, and fewer tools are needed overall. In turn, this implies that the average individual will not need to spend as much time making stone tools, and the community's tool needs can be met by a decreasing fraction of people producing such tools. The net result will be a stone tool production rate that still increases but does so more slowly than the population (Bettencourt 2014).

Settlement scaling theory predicts that the exponent of the best-fit line for the relationship between population and the chipped-stone tool production rate will be 5/6, or .83. The observed exponent is .823 (*SE* = .072), very close to the expected value. This indicates that on average the chipped-stone tool production rate increased more slowly than population and exhibits an economy of scale. And once again, all sites appear to follow a single scaling relation regardless of their habitation date. Another way of saying this is that the per capita rate of chipped-stone tool production actually declined with agglomeration, but presumably the community's need for chipped-stone tools was still met through people using the tools that were made more intensively. In other words, the inventory of unused tools at any given moment may have decreased as agglomeration created more opportunities for people to borrow tools from their neighbors. This scenario suggests Northern Rio Grande settlements not only became more productive, but also more efficient, as agglomeration levels changed over time.

The most important message from these analyses is that they suggest a wide range of changes in the Northern Rio Grande Pueblo economy derive ultimately from the expansion of human connectivity brought about through agglomeration. (For a popular discussion of these processes in a modern context, see Glaeser 2011.) So, although the time-series patterns in Figure 1.4 are not new, what the scaling analyses in Figure 1.7 add to the discussion is the idea that all of these patterns are linked to a single process related to the changing size, density, and connectivity of human networks. Notice, also, that the scaling results for house areas and service ware consumption (Figures 1.7A and 1.7B) indicate that these measures of socioeconomic output increased at a faster rate than the population of settlements in a context where the overall regional population was relatively constant. This is a striking demonstration of increase in per capita material outputs—that is, productivity—in the absence of technological advances in energy capture or conversion. It is hard to imagine that the physical abilities of individual human beings changed much between 1300 and 1600 CE. The more likely scenario is that individuals became more productive on average due to the increasing opportunities for specialization enabled by increasingly dense social networks. This mechanism, which is commonly referred to as "Smithian Growth," is discussed in greater detail by Ortman and Coffey in Chapter 6, and by Lobo in Chapter 12. We believe this was the primary driving force behind the gains in productivity and material standards of living Pueblo people enjoyed in the centuries preceding Spanish contact.

THE CONTRIBUTIONS IN THIS VOLUME

The demographic patterns, economic indicators, and agglomeration effects highlighted here suggest that the key factors that promoted economic growth in Northern Rio Grande Pueblo society were social, cultural, and political innovations that promoted intercommunity mobility and made it possible for Pueblo people to live in larger communities. The chapters that follow address several dimensions of this process.

In Chapter 2, Sunday Eiselt examines the agricultural resources surrounding a series of major settlements in the Rio Chama drainage and analyzes constructed field areas based on aerial photography to argue that gravel-mulch fields, despite having higher archaeological visibility, could not have been the primary food production areas in these communities. Instead, she argues that floodplains were the most important for food production and that differences in the amount of floodplain per resident from place to place imply that there were substantial flows of food among communities. She also finds evidence that cotton fiber effectively substituted for food production shortfalls in specific localities via a regional "big subsistence" economy. Based on her results, Eiselt argues the large ancestral Pueblo communities of the Chama valley were energetically interdependent.

In Chapter 3, Eileen Camilli, Kurt Anschuetz, Susan Smith, and Christopher Banet provide a summary of the pollen evidence of crops that were grown in the gravel-mulch fields that surround many Rio Grande Pueblo settlements. Their conclusion is inescapable—these fields represent a technology for growing cotton in the cool, high desert. This likelihood, combined with the widespread occurrence of gravel-mulch fields in the Rio Grande, is transformative regarding our views of the Rio Grande Pueblo economy. Their results suggest that the most visible and widespread agricultural features of the Northern Rio Grande archaeological landscape do not index maize agriculture, but instead represent traces of textile production. This implies that Rio Grande Pueblo farmers put substantial effort into nonsubsistence pursuits and suggests that additional study of gravel-mulch fields will be critical for measuring economic development over time.

Chapter 4, by Pascale Meehan, continues this focus on the Rio Grande textile industry by considering the contexts of textile production itself. Her findings show that textiles were produced across the larger Rio Grande region, primarily by men working in kivas, and that the technological style of these articles transcended the ethnic areas documented in the ethnohistoric literature. This pattern contrasts markedly with the regional diversity in technologies and styles of pottery and suggests differences in male versus female social networks and the resulting communities of practice.

In Chapter 5, Patrick Cruz and Scott Ortman look more closely at the distribution and built environments of ancestral Tewa settlements in the Chama drainage to distinguish patterns of relationships among them. Their analysis suggests that Rio Chama settlements did form local settlement clusters, but the internal structure of these clusters is highly diverse. Some local clusters exhibit evidence of a settlement hierarchy while others are more consistent with alliances or confederacies. This seems to be another expression of the fact that, in the Northern Rio Grande, increases in scale did not necessarily lead to increases in inequality. This diversity also suggests that it may be a mistake to view the Northern Rio Grande pueblos as having had any overarching type of political organization. Variation seems to have been the general rule.

In Chapter 6, Scott Ortman and Grant Coffey investigate the evolution and economic significance of plaza-based ceremonies. By analyzing relationships between plaza space, resident populations, and neighborhood populations through time, Ortman and Coffey conclude that "feast-day-type" ceremonies similar to what one can experience at a Pueblo today emerged in Prehispanic times and are apparent in Pueblo built environments beginning around 1450 CE. Based on settlement scaling theory, they also argue that this distinctive type of ceremonialism, which involves regular visiting between villages, was an important driver of economic growth. Their argument is that feast-day-type ceremonies encouraged periodic gathering of the entire social networks of communities, and these gatherings expanded the scope of exchange and stimulated community specialization. In many ways this study is an expansion of and elaboration on the ideas first developed by Graves and Spielmann in their work in the Salinas Pueblos to the south (Graves and Spielmann 2000; Spielmann 2002).

In Chapter 7, Fumi Arakawa, Chris Nicholson, and Douglas Harro examine changing distributions of chipped-stone tool raw materials across the Northern Rio Grande. Based on spatial analyses of raw material frequencies, they argue for the emergence of territorial circumscription and commodity exchange at the level of the ethnolinguistic group by the fifteenth century. An interesting aspect of their analysis is the finding that boundaries between ethnic groups became more strongly marked through time. One might interpret this pattern as reflecting the emergence of barriers to interaction, but the reason one can see these barriers is because of increasing deviation from a simple distance decay model, and this in turn implies more intensive interaction *within* these groups. This pattern thus suggests, somewhat counterintuitively, that the geographic and thus demographic scale of social in-groups expanded over time.

In Chapter 8, Sam Duwe presents a compositional study of matte-painted pottery from the Pajarito Plateau and Rio Chama drainage. His results show substantial flows of Pajarito-made pottery to the Chama during the 1300s, and of Chama-made pottery to the Pajarito during the 1400s and 1500s. These changing flows suggest that fourteenth-century population growth in the Chama was primarily due to northward migration from the Pajarito. They also suggest return visits to the Pajarito over subsequent generations. Duwe's findings strengthen our interpretation of the demographic data with regard to intraregional migration flows.

In Chapter 9, Kari Schleher interrogates the extent to which increasing specialization in pottery manufacture is reflected through increasing standardization of the finished product. Ethnoarchaeological studies demonstrate that pots become more standardized as output per potter increases, and this has led archaeologists to attempt to measure specialization through standardization of pottery assemblages. Schleher examines glaze-painted bowls from San Marcos Pueblo, a major production center in the Galisteo Basin, to show that one can perceive a correlation between standardization measures and production levels if one controls for the number of producers during various periods. This result highlights the fact that controlling for population is critical for studies of craft specialization.

In Chapter 10, Anna Schneider considers an important factor behind economic development—internal peace—with respect to the fascinating disjunction archaeologists have noted between physical evidence of interpersonal violence on skeletal remains and expressions of militarism in art. Her analysis suggests that the scale of group identification increased over time and that an important means of increasing internal peace was to project social unity, in the form of military defenses, to outsiders. These results echo those of Arakawa and others and are also notable in that they represent a first attempt at an interregional quantitative analysis of rock art motifs. Many of the patterns Schneider discusses have been noted on a qualitative level in previous studies, but to our knowledge this is the first attempt at demonstrating these using numbers.

Chapter 11, by Kaitlyn Davis, establishes smoking pipes as an important line of evidence for investigating Plains-Pueblo interaction. Archaeologists have long been aware of the dramatic increase in Plains-Pueblo exchange that began around 1450 CE, but what have not received as much attention, until now, are the social technologies that made this new level of economic integration possible. Davis builds a case that Pueblo people developed pipe-smoking rituals, perhaps precursors to ethnohistoric calumet ceremonies, to sanctify trade negotiations and encourage fair behavior. In doing so, Davis establishes a new proxy for monitoring interethnic exchange and suggests that etiquette and diplomacy, and the institutions that support them, were a critical component of Northern Rio Grande Pueblo economic development.

Finally, Chapter 12, by José Lobo, provides commentary on these chapters from the perspective of an economist who sees the archaeological record as a key source of information for expanding economic theory. Economics has developed a bad reputation within anthropology, primarily due to its historical focus on rational actor theory and the mathematical framework of utility functions. What archaeologists may not be aware of is that in recent decades there has been an opening up of economic theory—partly in response to critiques of neoclassical approaches and partly due to the realities of the empirical evidence—such that today there are several streams of thought within the discipline that are much more consistent with what anthropologists and archaeologists know about human societies. Lobo provides helpful guidance for archaeologists wishing to explore these newer streams of economic thought.

There are increasing calls for archaeology to make a greater contribution to the public discourse regarding issues of contemporary concern (Altschul and others 2017; Kintigh and others 2014; Sabloff 2008, 2010; Smith and others 2012). Archaeologists have begun to take up this challenge with respect to environmental change (d'Alpoim Guedes and others 2016; Fisher, Hill, and Feinman 2009; Schwindt and others 2016; Turner and Sabloff 2012) and the forces behind the growth of Western civilization (Morris 2010, 2013; Ober 2015). In our view, the Northern Rio Grande Pueblos address an additional important issue—alternative pathways to economic development—that archaeologists have been slow to recognize. This is emphatically *not* to say that ancestral Pueblo people were capitalists, utility maximizers, or "rational" economic agents. Rather, it suggests Rio Grande Pueblo people figured out how to create an economy that provided for human needs increasingly well *and* was consistent with traditional Pueblo values of egalitarianism, generosity, community responsibility, and hard work.

We hope these studies will be of interest to students, professionals, and academics in southwestern archaeology, as well as to economic anthropologists, economic historians, and archaeologists who work on middle-range societies elsewhere. We also hope this book will stimulate a new conversation in southwestern archaeology regarding alternative paths toward a life of material abundance and shared prosperity. To engage with this conversation, one must be willing to consider the findings of archaeology in light of contemporary issues, and one must also accept that past societies varied in the extent to which they provided for human needs. These philosophical commitments have not been central to the anthropological project, but we suspect that if we are willing to adopt these commitments archaeology in the Northern Rio Grande and elsewhere may have quite a lot to contribute to conversations regarding social and economic development. Not just in the developing world, but in general.

Acknowledgments. Portions of this research were supported by grants from the National Science Foundation (CNH-0816400) and the James S. McDonnell Foundation (#220020438). The editor wishes to thank the chapter authors for engaging with the ideas at the core of this volume and for being so diligent in meeting various deadlines in the publication process. He also thanks three anonymous peer reviewers for many helpful comments on earlier versions of the manuscript, the Arizona Archaeological and Historical Society for defraying some of the publication costs, and the editors and staff of the University of Arizona Press for shepherding this volume to publication.

CHAPTER TWO

Economic Development and Big Subsistence in the Regional Agricultural Economy of the Ohkay Owingeh Homeland

B. Sunday Eiselt

BIG SUBSISTENCE

This chapter considers the premise laid out in the introduction to this volume by Ortman and Davis that "as a society's economy grows its people become increasingly interdependent . . . with the economic system serving to distribute the results of differentiated labor across the population." Fundamental to the arguments presented here is the relationship between those resources in the environment that provide for the basic necessities of life and their uneven distribution in a landscape. As population grows, extraregional demands fuel economic growth that becomes regional or interregional in scale in order to sustain large settlements or highly populated subregions. I call this *big subsistence*, not in an attempt to coin yet another catch phrase, but as a way of describing the ancestral Tewa agricultural economy of the Classic period (1350–1600 CE) in the Rio Chama watershed in terms of multiple, economically interdependent villages and towns.

Big subsistence not only considers population growth relative to the capacities of an environment to provide for the growing population, it also emphasizes the adaptive brilliance of ancestral Tewa farmers for developing sustainable prehistoric land-use systems that are derived from principles in nature and which persist to this day. Recently subsumed by Ford and Swentzell (2015:354; see also Anschuetz and Hena 1999) under the rubric of "permaculture," the concept serves to explain the diversity of designs and techniques used by prehistoric farmers to cultivate broad areas. It also downplays the role of risk minimization and uncertainty, which is often portrayed as a driving force for agricultural expansion and diversification in the American Southwest. Risk minimization in this sense generally relies on *over*production (surplus) as a means for combating unpredictable, short-term agricultural shortfalls.

Sustainability in the permaculture sense incorporates risk (due to *under*production) into an expansive agricultural theory and economic approach based on observable natural processes with which ancestral farmers would undoubtedly have been very familiar. This contrasts greatly with intensive agricultural approaches that seek to modify existing natural conditions by taking on greater risk and higher labor costs required to enhance production through the development of irrigation and farming infrastructure. Such approaches to farming do not appear until the arrival of the Spanish, who also brought wooly livestock that quickly transformed the Pueblo textile industry and the surrounding natural environment.

Fundamental to the notion of big subsistence as I envision it for the ancestral Ohkay Owingeh people of the Chama Valley is the constant, regional circulation of food, clothing, craft items, and people (including religious or other specialists) through socioeconomic and religious gift exchanges, feasting, and ceremony. Permaculture systems that are land extensive rather than land intensive in terms of food and textile production are the foundation of the regional economy but only succeed through their articulation with the annual flow of agricultural produce, raw materials, finished goods, labor, and services. While such developments may have relieved the pressure on individual households to come up with the basic necessities of survival, they added other, potentially more consequential, social demands on extended families. In other words, although there was less possibility of starvation, failure to fulfill the needs of the larger society constituted a significant risk. Big subsistence was the economically developed system of supply, labor, and demand that was regulated by socioeconomic structures, institutions, and practices that integrated the aggregated settlements and fueled the development and growth of economic systems during the Classic Period in the Rio Chama watershed.

Elements of the economic system as expressed by demand for agricultural production, land, water, and labor in the Ohkay Owingeh homeland reveal key aspects of economic development that are unique to middle-range societies. These, in turn, are based on the corporate organization of production in small family units and the regular redistribution of food and fiber among villages. The data speak to a regional economy in which production and redistribution of cultivated products are tied to supply (the availability of land and water resources on terraces and in the floodplain), demand (subsistence needs relative to population size), and labor (local ability to work in agricultural production) with emphasis on a mobile work force that traveled to and from higher- and lower-order population centers in order to access agricultural fields and redistribute cultivated products to consumers.

This agricultural economy was based not only on supplying the nutritional needs of the burgeoning population in the form of corn, beans, and squash. At least one other staple crop—cotton—must have served as a principal source of fiber required to clothe a regional population exceeding 10,000 individuals (see Chapter 3). The conclusion is fairly obvious: Without the development of an agricultural economy that could integrate the resources of multiple villages distributed among the Rio Chama's tributary drainages, it seems unlikely that the artistic and cultural achievements of the ancestral Ohkay Owingeh people would have been achieved.

The following analysis introduces these concepts based in part on calculations of built agricultural space above the floodplain using pedestrian survey using low-elevation aerial photography in combination with GIS data derived from spectral (color)-based, supervised classification of satellite imagery of ancient fields. Two previous publications, Duwe and others (2016) and Eiselt and others (2017), have examined the architectural evidence for demographic ascendance in the lower Chama Valley manifested by 10 principal villages or towns comprising 1,000 or more persons at their maximum. The former presents a technique for deriving room counts from three-dimensional models of mound volume, which in turn are converted into estimates of population. The latter presents an argument that compares population size (interpreted as a measure of relative demand on the subsistence economy) with the capacity of agricultural fields (defined as a per person requirement of cultivated field area for subsistence). Eiselt and others (2017) conclude that previous studies of prehistoric agriculture in the Chama Valley have significantly underestimated the role of the floodplain in the production of staple crops.

METHODS

In an area characterized by diverse agricultural strategies, the challenge faced by all studies of Prehispanic agriculture in the American Southwest is how to quantify what you cannot see (or at least what has yet to be recorded). This study is based on pedestrian survey, low-elevation imaging using unmanned aerial vehicles (UAVs), satellite imagery (Google Earth Pro or GE), and the supervised classification of aerial imagery to locate fields and obtain field area calculations in terrace and floodplain settings.[1] Fieldwork demonstrated that Prehispanic gravel-mulch gardens, cobble-bordered grid gardens, and cobble terraces in the Rio Chama watershed can be readily identified using GE in certain landscape contexts because their borders are well-defined and they present anomalous shapes and color changes that are readily identifiable from above.

As outlined in Eiselt and others (2017), the borders of terrace and grid garden features that were evident on GE imagery were digitized to create individual, georeferenced polygons. We then used georeferenced fields to generate a supervised classification of unknown field areas, filtered by catchment radii around major Classic period towns. We derived population counts for major towns and villages from Duwe (2011; see also Eiselt and Darling 2013; Duwe and others 2016). Additional site information included data from the Archaeological Records Management System (ARMS) of the Laboratory of Anthropology in Santa Fe. The population estimates presented here are based on 23 towns and villages, which represent all of the known architectural sites in the study area that contain 50 or more rooms (Table 2.1; Figure 2.1). For further discussion of the methods used for agriculture prospection in GE and UAV imaging of fields see Eiselt and others (2017).

Supervised classification of aerial imagery helped to identify terraced fields that may not be readily visible

[1] A supervised classification is one in which the user deliberately teaches or "trains" the image processing software to recognize unique spectral signatures by selecting features in an image that represent predefined classes of interest.

Table 2.1. Architectural Sites Included in This Study Identified by Drainage Location and Site Size Designation

Drainage	*LA#*	*Site Name*	*Site Designation*	*Room Counts*
Lower Chama	274	Poshu'owingeh	Town	1,144
Lower Chama	908	Tsama'owingeh (I, II)	Town	1,355
Lower Chama	301	Tsipin'owingeh	Village	500
Lower Chama	275	Abiquiú Ruin	Village	100
Lower Chama	300	Kapo'owingeh	Village	140
Lower Chama	806	Santa Rosa de Lima	Village	250
Lower Chama	911	LA 911	Village	160
Lower Chama	3505	Palisade Ruin	Village	42
El Rito	306	Sapa'owingeh	Town	2,541
El Rito	307	Cerro Colorado	Village	550
Ojo Caliente	71	Howidi'owingeh	Town	1,697
Ojo Caliente	297	Ponshipa'akedi'owingeh	Town	1,536
Ojo Caliente	380	Hupovi'owingeh	Town	1,209
Ojo Caliente	632	Posi'owingeh	Town	2,410
Ojo Caliente	298	Nuute'owingeh	Village	140
Ojo Caliente	66288	Hilltop Pueblo	Village	153
Ojo Caliente	98319	Sandoval Pueblo	Village	141
Rio del Oso	252	Te'ewi'owingeh	Town	892
Rio del Oso	253	Ku'owingeh	Town	600
Rio del Oso	299	Pesede'owingeh	Town	631
Rio del Oso	6584	LA 6584	Village	405
Rio del Oso	65197	LA 65197	Village	70
Rio del Oso	90844	Maestas Pueblo	Village	43
Total Rooms				**16,709**

Key: Towns = 500 or more rooms; villages = 50 to 499 rooms, with the exception of Cerro Colorado (after Duwe 2011 and Ortman 2010).

in GE. Hudspeth (2013) used a set of the gravel-mulch fields, identified using GE and subsequently verified with pedestrian survey, to train his supervised classification to identify additional fields in areas above the floodplain. He also digitized training areas for four additional landscape classes—piñon-juniper woodland, modern valley agriculture, grassland, and scrubland—to further separate prehistoric, anthropogenically modified areas from the surrounding landscape. For the supervised classification, he used the red, blue, and green visible wavelength bands from aerial imagery distributed as part of the National Agricultural Imagery Program (NAIP) archive for 2011. Following supervised classification, all pixels belonging to separate classes were converted into a polygon vector format so that class-specific areas could be calculated.

The supervised classification located areas of potential fields as pixels that have spectral signatures that are statistically more similar to the hand-selected grid garden pixels than they are to other classes. The technique was improved by limiting the classification to landforms with a 10-degree or lower slope, consistent with known locations of archaeologically identified gravel-mulch fields and cobble bordered grid gardens (see also Hill 1998; Bugé 1984:19; Tjaden 1979:12 for similar slope values in other areas). To standardize the allocation of land, areas examined in the vicinity of prehistoric towns were defined

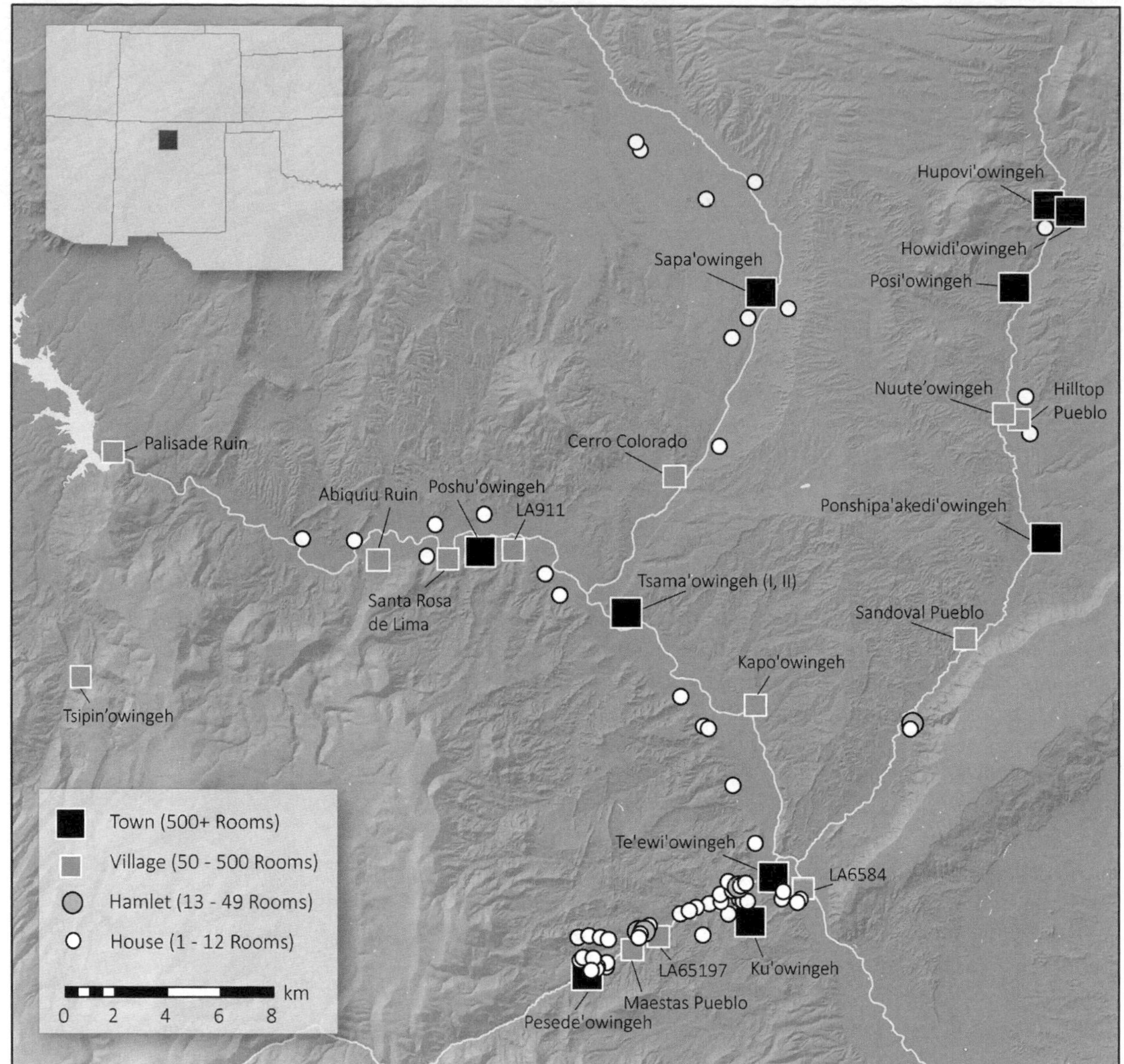

Figure 2.1. Habitation sites in the study area coded by site size designation, following Duwe (2011) and Ortman (2010). Houses have 1 to 12 rooms; hamlets, 13 to 49 rooms; villages, 50 to 499 rooms; and towns, 500 or more rooms. Prepared by author.

by a fixed catchment radii of 2 km to 5 km based on cross-cultural ethnographic data regarding the distances farmers typically walk to their fields (Arnold 1985:32; Chisholm 1970:131; Roper 1979:120; Stone 1996; Varien 1999:153–155). Hudspeth assigned a 2-km radius to villages or towns having 1,000 or fewer rooms, a 3.5-km radius to towns having 1,000 to 2,000 rooms, and a 5-km radius to towns with 2,000 or more rooms assuming that larger villages would require greater amounts of land to support the population. The radii encompass the major ancestral town sites in the study area. Figure 2.2 illustrates the results of the GE and supervised classification survey.

STANDARDS FOR MODELING ARABLE LAND REQUIREMENTS AND MOMENTARY POPULATION

Researchers working in the American Southwest utilize a variety of standards for modeling arable land requirements and momentary population. These are based on different assumptions regarding energy and living space

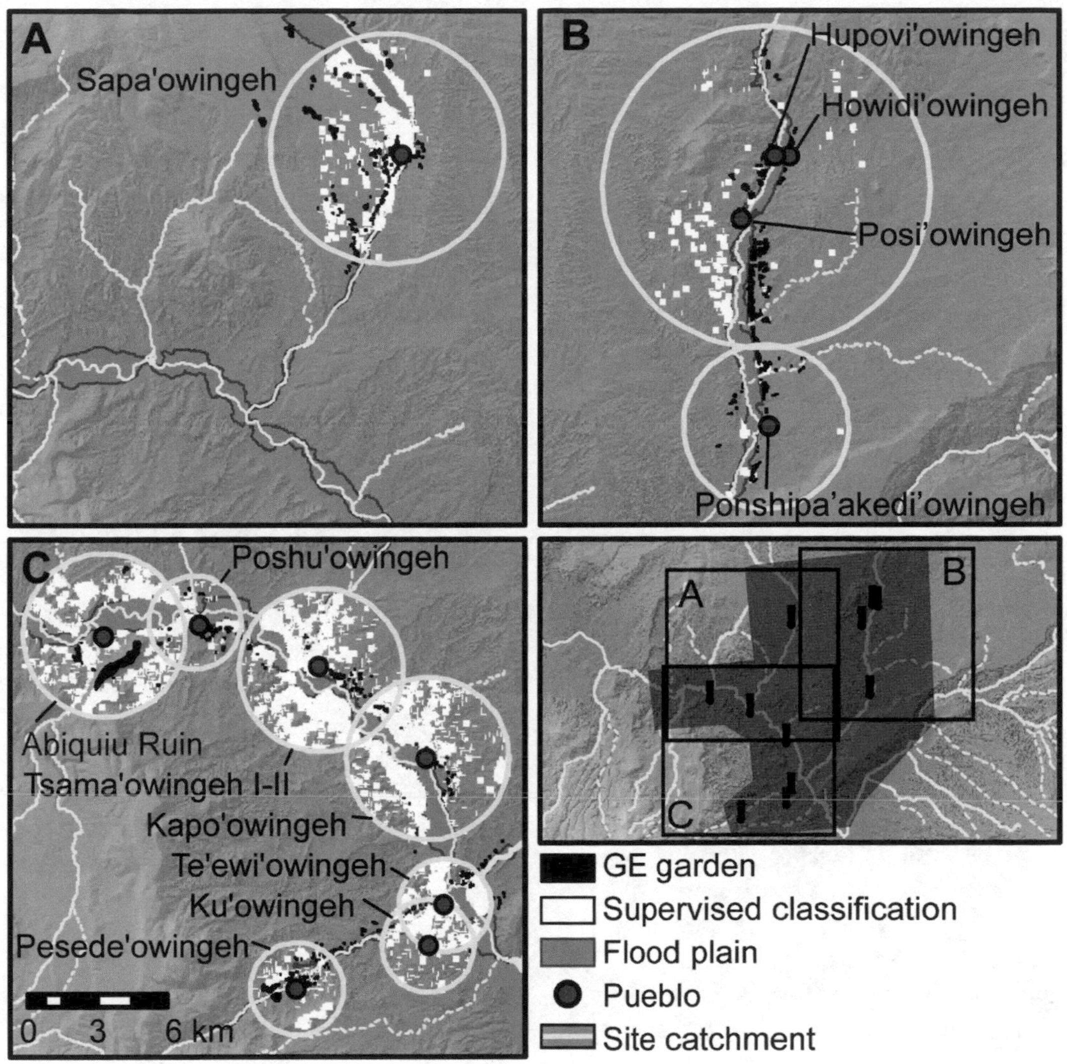

Figure 2.2. GE dry-farming areas (in black) versus *potential* dry farming areas (in white) identified using the GIS supervised classification technique filtered by a 10-degree or lower slope (Hudspeth 2013). GIS search areas were constrained by catchments associated with each of the Classic period ancestral towns (pueblos) shown. Boundaries for the GE survey are shown in gray (bottom right). Prepared by author.

requirements as well as village growth and occupational histories for specific locales. I include all of them in this study in order to explore the range of values that best balance the apparent constraints on arable land and population growth for the Chama Valley.

Arable land calculations of per capita field cultivation are based on constants available in the ethnographic literature on the Rio Grande Pueblo Communities. The figures reported in Lange (1959:426, 438) for Cochiti Pueblo indicate an annual average of 0.31 ha per capita for maize and 0.45 ha (just over one acre) for maize and wheat combined (see also Wetterstrom 1976:191; Spielmann 1982:144). Ford (1992:156) provides information for Ohkay Owingeh from around 1890 CE that indicates an average of 0.46 ha in maize and wheat combined. Anschuetz (1998:405–407) utilized Ford's estimate of 0.46 ha and added productivity measures for beans, pumpkins, and squash as well as nonfood cultigens such as cotton, succulents, pot herbs, ornamentals, and medicinal and ceremonial plants, leading to a revised per capita calculation of 0.47 ha to meet the basic, short-term subsistence requirements of Prehispanic Tewa populations. Anschuetz's final calculation of 0.71 ha was based on the assumption that Pueblo farmers had to nearly double the amount of cultivated land in order to buffer against crop failures and field fallowing and to generate sufficient excess production for other social and cultural needs. Minnis (1985:186) reached a similar figure of 0.6 ha per person in the Mimbres region to account for all crops plus additional cultivated land to account for subsequent bad years. Hill (1998b) used Bradfield's (1971) estimate of 1.01 ha per person for Hopi farmers for his Central New Mexico estimates.

Architectural capacity has been used most commonly as a measure of population. Duwe (2011:705–707, see also Duwe and others 2016; Eiselt and Darling 2013) assembled momentary room count estimations for the known habitation sites in the Rio Chama watershed from a variety of data sources. Following Ortman (2010), he divided sites into four size classes. Multiroom houses range from 1 to 12 rooms in size and were likely occupied by one or two households on a seasonal basis for specialized activities such as farming. Hamlets range from 13 to 49 rooms. Villages are small unit pueblo sites containing 50 to 500 rooms, and towns are large sites exceeding 500 rooms. Duwe estimated momentary population counts using room counts, mound volume, mean ceramic and dendrochronology dates, and a logistic regression formula developed by Ortman (2010) to apportion rooms (and therefore roofed over space) in 50-year periods from 1250 to 1650 CE. Additional refinements to Ortman's (2012) approach are possible, but the estimates presented here (generated by Duwe and presented in his 2011 dissertation and elsewhere) are sufficient to establish regional population growth trends relative to demands for agricultural production (Ortman 2012; Duwe and others 2016; Eiselt and Darling 2013).

Following Creamer's (1993:152) suggestion for Arroyo Hondo Pueblo, Ortman's regression formula sets the maximum proportion of occupied rooms at 90 percent in the prehistoric towns. Other researchers have employed a variety of calculations to estimate maximum room occupation based on surface survey data, including 50 percent occupation for the pueblo of Hawikuh (Smith, Woodbury, and Woodbury 1966:12), 65 percent for settlements in the Zuni area (Kintigh 1985:22), 69 percent at Picuris Pueblo (Crown 1991), 75 percent for Grasshopper Pueblo (Longacre 1976:181), and 78 percent for southwestern ethnographic populations (Hill 1970:75–77; Plog 1975:98). These figures attempt to account for unoccupied architecture, remodeled rooms, and fluctuations in occupation (Liebmann and others 2016; Schacht 1984).

A final consideration is the conversion of roofed space to numbers of individuals expressed as area divided by a per-person constant (a per-capita investment in architecture). Archaeologists working in the American Southwest use one of four constants: 3 m^2 (Clarke 1971), 5.3 m^2 (Hill 1970), 6 m^2 (Casselberry 1974), and 10 m^2 (Naroll 1962; see also Anschuetz 1998; Maxwell 1994) or they assume one person per room if average room sizes are in the range of 4 to 10 m^2 (Duwe 2011; Ortman 2012). Liebmann and others (2016) developed an estimate of 5.57 m^2 per person from historical and archaeological data at Kotyiti, a Jemez area refugee pueblo dating to the Reconquest period.

RESULTS

Per Capita Investments in Agriculture and Floodplain Farming

The GE survey resulted in the discovery of 900 gravel mulch, cobble terrace, and cobble border fields including 660 new fields (approximately three times the number that are currently known through pedestrian survey). Total area represented by GE-defined fields is 348 ha. The supervised classification of NAIP aerial photos identified an additional 554 ha of unverified agricultural fields or plots above the floodplain within the defined radii for all ancestral towns and villages. When combined, the two techniques (GE and supervised classification) identified 897 ha of potential and actual fields. Assuming that all crops were planted at a value of .47 ha per person, these areas would have supported only 1,908 people. The lowest constant of .31 ha would have supported only slightly more at 2,890 people for the Chama as a whole. These totals are far below estimated populations thought to have occupied Chama valley towns.

Some additional upland agricultural sites may as yet be undiscovered, but it is clear from the data that groundwater and irrigation farming below the mesas must have contributed the majority of agricultural production needed to support ancestral Tewa residents. To evaluate this finding, I estimated total floodplain area (in hectares) within the fixed radii identified around major village sites. In each case, the fixed radii encompassed contiguous stretches of the floodplain between villages such that nearly all floodplain areas associated with settled areas were included in this calculation (see catchment radii in Figure 2.2). The total area represented by the floodplains is 3,899 ha, which would have supported 8,296 people using the 0.47 ha per person constant. This underscores an important conclusion about Precolumbian land and water

Table 2.2. Total Hectares Identified by Drainage and Total Individuals Supported Assuming Different Per Capita Constants

Drainage	*Visual GEP (in hectares)*	*Supervised Classification (in hectares)*	*Floodplain (in hectares)*	*Total Hectares*	*Total Individuals Supported Per Capita Constant*				
					.31 ha	*.47 ha*	*.6 ha*	*.71 ha*	*1.1 ha*
Lower Chama	115	369	1,550	2,034	6,562	4,328	3,390	2,865	1,849
El Rito	87	46	1,083	1,216	3,922	2,587	2,026	1,712	1,105
Ojo Caliente	101	32	868	1,002	3,232	2,132	1,670	1,411	911
Rio del Oso	44	102	397	543	1,752	1,156	905	765	494
Total	**347**	**549**	**3,899**	**4,795**	**15,468**	**10,202**	**7,992**	**6,754**	**4,359**

utilization in the Rio Chama basin. In order to support populations in excess of 2,000 individuals, well below any estimate of Classic period population in the study area, the floodplains and bottomlands of the Rio Chama and its tributaries must have been cultivated during the Classic period (Eiselt and others 2017). Depending upon the constant, the Rio Chama watershed had the potential to support up to 15,468 people when floodplain and terrace farming are considered together (Table 2.2). This implies that Chama farmers utilized the entire floodplain and that some villages may not have been economically self-sufficient due to a general lack of floodplain areas in certain drainage systems.

Agricultural Demand: Momentary Population

To explore this further, the per capita investments in agriculture can be compared to momentary population counts to arrive at a reasonable range within which the population may have fluctuated. Table 2.3 includes Coalition and Classic period population counts from the towns and villages provided in Table 2.1, apportioned by 50-year increments for each of the per capita investments in architecture and different village occupancy rates over time (See also Duwe 2011; Eiselt and Darling 2013). It also includes the total hectares of fields and floodplain identified by GE and supervised techniques, as well as the numbers of individuals that could be supported by this amount of land assuming the four previously mentioned constants for agriculture.

The largest estimate derived from the 3 m^2 architectural constant (Clark 1971) can be eliminated because it produces populations that far exceed the agricultural capacity of the Rio Chama throughout most of the Classic period based on any of the four constants for agricultural productivity. The 5.3 m^2 constant also exceeds the carrying capacity for most of the Classic period unless we consider that no more than 50 percent of the rooms were occupied simultaneously and that individuals could farm only .31 ha of land at peak population (1400 to 1450 CE). In this scenario, more agricultural land would be needed to produce other food and fiber staples, as well as surplus to be stored.

The more conservative constant of 1 person per 10 m^2 of architectural space produces a range of population figures that fit within the margin of available land at maximum population from 1400 to 1500 CE. Of these, the 78 percent and 69 percent occupancy figures yield populations that could farm the 0.47 ha per individual to meet short-term demands for food and fiber at peak population. Therefore, it is reasonable to assume that the regional population ranged anywhere from 10,000 to 13,000 people during the Classic period and that it likely fluctuated between these densities over time and space depending on climatic or demographic variables, seasonal requirements for farming and hunting, and mobility. This regional population estimate is also consistent with Ortman's (2016) more recent series, which incorporates occupational intensity curves derived from pottery assemblages, and is reproduced in the introduction to this volume (Figure 1.2).

Agricultural Supply: Arable Land

Economic systems arise, in part, as individuals work to redress imbalances in supply and demand. This can be assessed by the distribution of arable lands relative to population. Table 2.4 provides the momentary population within each of the four drainages (Ojo Caliente, El Rito, Rio del Oso, and Rio Chama) apportioned by drainage in 50-year increments, assuming a population estimate calculated on the basis of one person per 10 m^2 and a 90 percent occupancy rate. Table 2.4 also lists the number of individuals that could be supported within each of the

Table 2.3. Coalition and Classic Period Population Counts for the Rio Chama Watershed

Parameters	*Population Counts by Time Period (CE) and Phase Designation*							
	1250–1300	*1300–1350*	*1350–1400*	*1400–1450*	*1450–1500*	*1500–1550*	*1550–1600*	*1600–1680*
	Coalition Wiyo Phase	*Early Classic*	*Middle Classic*	*Middle Classic*	*Late Classic*	*Proto-historic*	*Colonial*	
1 person/ 3m²								
90% Occupancy	745	3,800	37,001	43,629	42,208	23,782	12,355	0
78% Occupancy	507	3,306	32,191	37,958	36,721	20,691	10,749	0
69% Occupancy	440	2,926	28,491	33,595	32,500	18,312	9,514	0
50% Occupancy	298	2,128	20,721	24,432	23,637	13,318	6,919	0
1 person/ 5.3m²								
90% Occupancy	422	2,151	20,944	24,696	23,891	13,462	6,994	0
78% Occupancy	367	1,871	18,221	21,485	20,786	11,712	6,084	0
69% Occupancy	325	1,656	16,127	19,016	18,396	10,365	5,385	0
50% Occupancy	236	1,205	11,729	13,830	13,379	7,539	3,916	0
1 person/ 10m²								
90% Occupancy	224	1,140	11,100	13,089	12,662	7,135	3,707	0
78% Occupancy	195	992	9,657	11,387	11,016	6,207	3,225	0
69% Occupancy	172	878	8,547	10,078	9,750	5,494	2,854	0
50% Occupancy	125	638	6,216	7,330	7,091	3,995	2,076	0
4,795 Total Hectares (GE, supervised classification, and floodplain)								
Agricultural Per capita Constant	*Total Individuals*							
0.31	15,468							
0.47	10,202							
0.6	7,992							
0.71	6,754							

Note: Phase designations are based on Duwe 2011.

drainages given different per capita constants for agriculture. These figures include GE, supervised classification, and floodplain calculations combined. Grouping the data by drainage is warranted, given that the villages and towns within them lie in close proximity to each other and that the distributions of agricultural fields are nearly continuous between them. Duwe (2011) and Anschuetz (1998) also argue that the proto-Tewa likely conceptualized social identity based on their association with shared watercourses. Much like population, the per capita investments in agriculture probably fluctuated through time based on climatic and demographic variables as well as the seasonal requirements of farming and hunting.

The gray cells in Table 2.4 represent the periods of time during which the population (based on architectural evidence) exceeded local agricultural capacity under different per capita assumptions. The 0.31 and 0.47 estimates come the closest to meeting the requirements of the reconstructed population maximum, and although the 0.47 per capita estimate falls short of the maximum architectural capacity, this shortfall can be attributed to adjustments in momentary (rather than maximum) population or

Table 2.4. Momentary Population Grouped by Drainage Relative to Five Commonly Employed Constants for Per Capita Investments in Agriculture

	Population by Time Period (CE)						
Drainage	*1250-1300*	*1300-1350*	*1350-1400*	*1400-1450*	*1450-1500*	*1500-1550*	*1550-1600*
Lower Chama	176	755	2,286	2,621	2,485	960	140
El Rito	0	0	1,617	2,341	2,131	2,205	2,230
Ojo Caliente	0	104	5,707	6,117	6,249	2,122	0
Rio del Oso	47	281	1,490	2,010	1,798	1,848	1,336
Total	**224**	**1,140**	**11,100**	**13,089**	**12,662**	**7,135**	**3,707**
A. Basic energetic requirements based on corn only							
Lower Chama (.31 per capita)	6,562	6,562	6,562	6,562	6,562	6,562	6,562
El Rito (.31 per capita)	3,922	3,922	3,922	3,922	3,922	3,922	3,922
Ojo Caliente (.31 per capita)	3,232	3,232	3,232	3,232	3,232	3,232	3,232
Rio del Oso (.31 per capita)	1,752	1,752	1,752	1,752	1,752	1,752	1,752
Total (.31 per capita)	**15,468**	**15,468**	**15,468**	**15,468**	**15,468**	**15,468**	**15,468**
B. Basic energetic requirements based on corn, beans, squash, pot herbs, medicinal plants, and fiber							
Lower Chama (.47 per capita)	4,328	4,328	4,328	4,328	4,328	4,328	4,328
El Rito (.47 per capita)	2,587	2,587	2,587	2,587	2,587	2,587	2,587
Ojo Caliente (.47 per capita)	2,132	2,132	2,132	2,132	2,132	2,132	2,132
Rio del Oso (.47 per capita)	1,156	1,156	1,156	1,156	1,156	1,156	1,156
Total (.47 per capita)	**10,202**	**10,202**	**10,202**	**10,202**	**10,202**	**10,202**	**10,202**
C. Basic energetic requirements with sufficient surplus for storage and trade							
Lower Chama (.60 per capita)	3,390	3,390	3,390	3,390	3,390	3,390	3,390
El Rito (.60 per capita)	2,026	2,026	2,026	2,026	2,026	2,026	2,026
Ojo Caliente (.60 per capita)	1,670	1,670	1,670	1,670	1,670	1,670	1,670
Rio del Oso (.60 per capita)	905	905	905	905	905	905	905
Total (.60 per capita)	**7,992**	**7,992**	**7,992**	**7,992**	**7,992**	**7,992**	**7,992**
D. Basic energetic requirements with sufficient surplus for storage and trade							
Lower Chama (.71 per capita)	2,865	2,865	2,865	2,865	2,865	2,865	2,865
El Rito (.71 per capita)	1,712	1,712	1,712	1,712	1,712	1,712	1,712
Ojo Caliente (.71 per capita)	1,411	1,411	1,411	1,411	1,411	1,411	1,411
Rio del Oso (.71 per capita)	765	765	765	765	765	765	765
Total (.71 per capita)	**6,754**	**6,754**	**6,754**	**6,754**	**6,754**	**6,754**	**6,754**
E. Basic energetic requirements with excess surplus for storage and trade							
Lower Chama (1.1 per capita)	1,849	1,849	1,849	1,849	1,849	1,849	1,849
El Rito (1.1 per capita)	1,105	1,105	1,105	1,105	1,105	1,105	1,105
Ojo Caliente (1.1 per capita)	911	911	911	911	911	911	911
Rio del Oso (1.1 per capita)	494	494	494	494	494	494	494
Total (1.1 per capita)	**4,359**	**4,359**	**4,359**	**4,359**	**4,359**	**4,359**	**4,359**

Key: Gray cells indicate periods where the population supported by available land falls below the predicted momentary population based on architecture.
Note: Population estimate based on 1 person per m^2, 90 percent occupancy.

total arable land area in groundwater and terrace farming areas.

Of greater interest is the Ojo Caliente drainage, which contains 46 percent of the total population and only 21 percent of the total arable land derived from GE, supervised classification, and floodplain calculations combined. When apportioned by time, even the lowest population estimate based on architecture would exceed what could be supported by the lowest (.31 hectares per person) agricultural constant. Moreover, this was not a temporary economic imbalance, but a condition that persisted for well over 150 years. In other words, the Ojo Caliente was the center of population for most of the Classic period based on the architectural capacity of the towns located there, even though it lacked sufficient farmland and must have relied on food supplies that were redistributed from other areas in the Chama Valley. This is significant since most models of food redistribution in the American Southwest contend that the circulation of subsistence items helped to offset risks associated with farming, not to supply or re-supply segments of the population occupying areas that were unable to support themselves (Hill 1998b; Herhahn and Hill 1998; Lightfoot 1979; P. Reed 1990; Spielmann 1983). The Ojo Caliente data demonstrate that agricultural products from other areas were fundamental to the maintenance of larger settlements in this drainage, which in terms of their size were on par with other towns in the Ohkay Owingeh homeland. The opposite also is evident along the main reach of the Lower Chama River, where 24 percent of the total population occupied an area with 42 percent of the potential arable land. The El Rito drainage was similarly positioned with surplus land, but at a lower level, while the Rio del Oso could have been relatively self-reliant at the 0.47 per capita level.

The implications are straightforward and illustrate the importance of a regionally based agricultural economy. The Ojo Caliente and possibly the Rio del Oso settlements would have depended at certain times of the year on agricultural products that were cultivated in the Lower Chama and El Rito drainages and transported to the towns and villages located there. The general implication is that food and fiber (and possibly labor) circulated through the settlements in order to address subsistence shortfalls resulting from unequal distribution of land and water resources. Given that shortfalls in arable land can be balanced within the watershed overall, it is unlikely that the Chama area produced sufficient food for interregional exchange. Fiber for cotton is, however, another matter.

Camilli and her colleagues make the case that cotton was the principle crop grown on gravel-mulch fields and they argue that such features were key parts of an indigenous cotton textile industry (Camilli, Banet, and Smith 2010; Camilli and others 2012; see also Chapter 3). If this was the case, then the Ojo Caliente was the center of cotton production for the Chama. Fifty-four percent of all hectares in gravel-mulch fields that were visually identified in GE occur in this drainage, followed at a distance by El Rito at 24 percent. The total area of gravel-mulch fields in the Ojo Caliente is 90 hectares. Using Huckell's (1993:174) estimate of 7.2 blankets per hectare for the Hopi, this amount of land could yield enough cotton to produce up to 650 mantas per year and the Chama as a whole could yield close to 1,200.

Although more work is needed to establish sound productivity measures for cotton in the Chama, this crop undeniably was a major component of the economy, particularly in the Ojo Caliente. Given that lands devoted to cotton reduce overall availability for other crops and that land was already in short supply in the Ojo Caliente drainage, residents may have chosen to make greater investments in cotton in order to balance economic returns in food received from agricultural fields located elsewhere in the watershed. This correlates with the apparent pattern along the Lower Chama where terrace and floodplain are large relative to gravel-mulch fields and where residents may have invested more in the production of food.

Agricultural Redistribution and Big Subsistence

Large towns dominate current thinking about socioeconomic exchange and other interactions in clustered settlements of the Protohistoric era (Adams and Duff 2004; Creamer 1996; Graves and Spielman 2000; Duwe 2011), but from the perspective of production and labor, a broader understanding of the economy is achieved when the settlement system is considered as a whole (Anschuetz 2007). Examination of momentary population, site sizes, and site distributions reveals the network of residential arrangements (houses, hamlets, villages, and towns) making up settlement clusters. These residential arrangements provide insights into how farm labor and products were pooled and exchanged and how the economy of the Chama developed during the first half of the Classic period (1350–1450 CE) when population was on the rise.

Land use would have reached maximum extent during the middle Classic (1400–1500 CE), presenting challenges to the maintenance of fields and the transport of

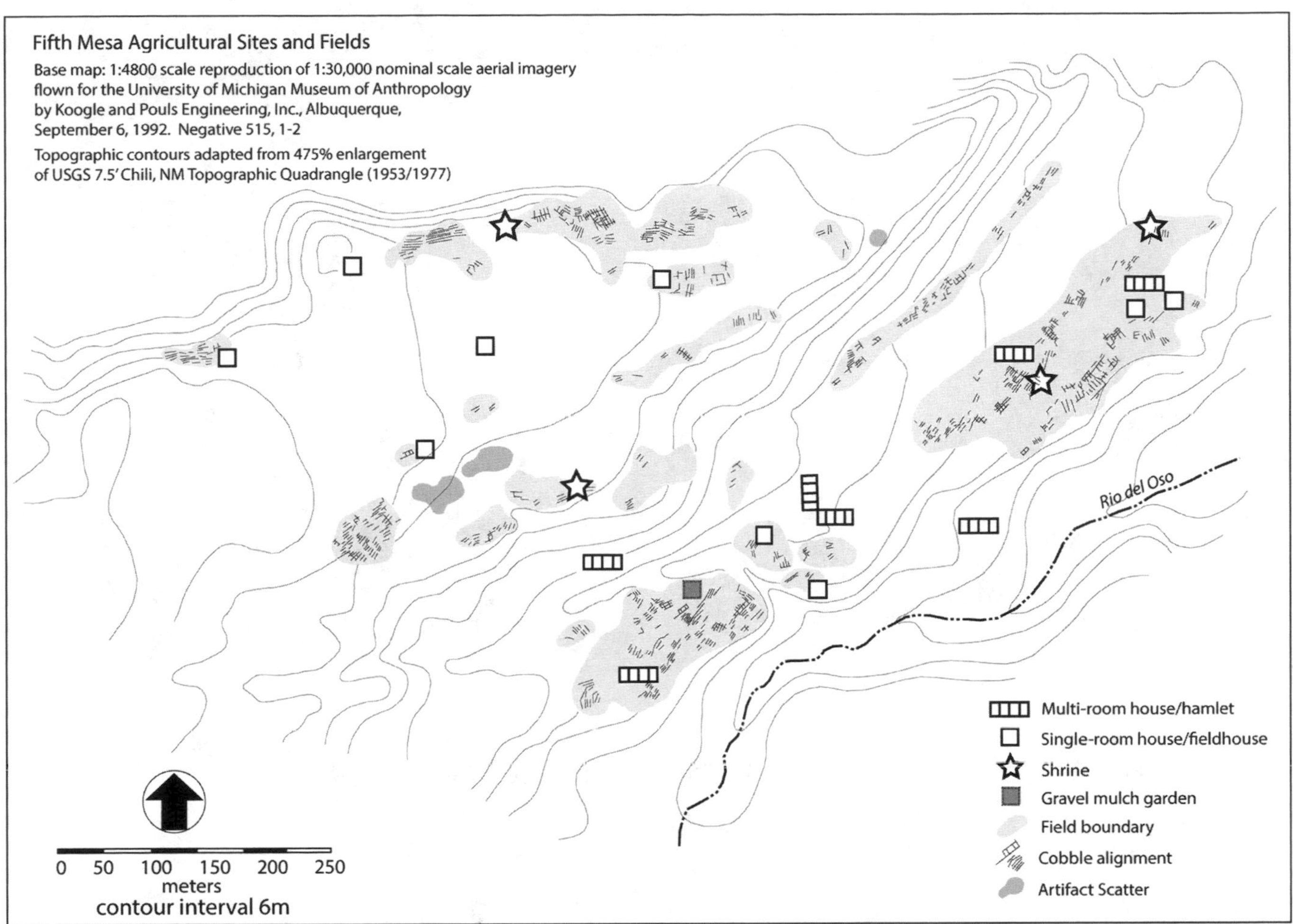

Figure 2.3. An area of agricultural fields and settlements associated with Pesede'owingeh (LA 299). Redrawn by author from Anschuetz (1998:307).

agricultural products. Moreover, while up to 90 percent of the population could have assembled into large towns seasonally or for annual gatherings or special occasions, at other times people were undoubtedly living in smaller villages scattered among larger ones on the same drainage system. Based on prevailing dates (Duwe 2011), these villages outnumbered towns until 1450 CE (see Table 2.1). Occupation of settlements also likely varied according to the agricultural calendar, with the bulk of the working population moving into successively smaller residences during planting and harvesting seasons in order to be closer to the fields. The combination of large and small settlements (towns and villages) and a system of trails provided the necessary infrastructure to facilitate seasonal movement, as well as the redistribution of cultivated food and fiber throughout the regional agricultural economy.

Seasonally occupied hamlets and houses were more numerous than towns and villages. They were located within field complexes and agricultural settings on and above the floodplain. In addition to croplands, field complexes included short-term residential facilities, storage structures, field shrines, and field markers. Anschuetz (1998:416–417) considers these features to be necessary cultural markers of land tenure. Figure 2.3 shows the internal structure of one Classic period field complex located in the Rio del Oso Valley; it is only 500 meters north of Pesede'owingeh (LA 299). Recorded by Anschuetz (1998:307), this complex contains one multi-structure residence (a small hamlet), five multi-room houses, nine single room field houses, four shrines, and 24 visible fields covering a terrace area of roughly 47 ha. Although it is unclear whether the habitations were occupied simultaneously, the

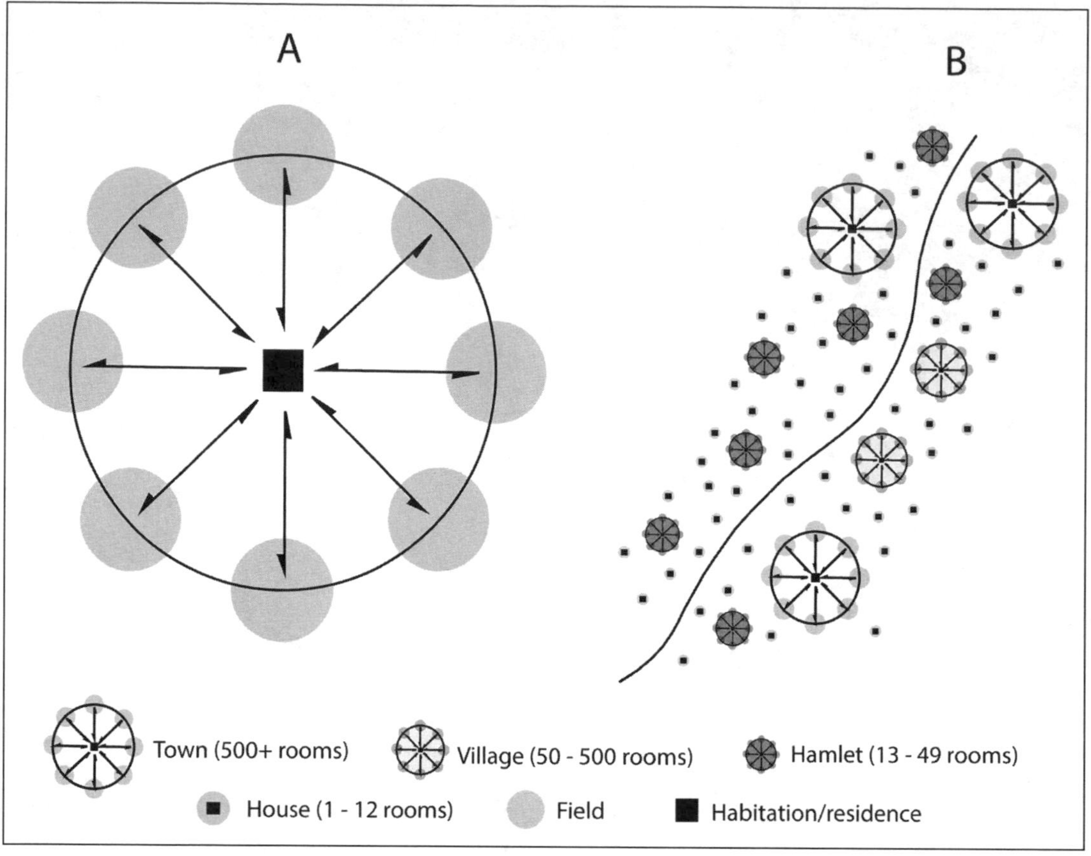

Figure 2.4. Idealized settlement pattern for drainage systems. Prepared by author.

organization of features within the complex suggests that agricultural production was structured through corporate (likely kin-based) collaboration within family groups (Adler 1996, Anschuetz 1998:417–419; Snead 2008:76–80).

As shown in Figure 2.1, settlements within drainages can be seen as integrated economic units comprised of towns, villages, hamlets, and houses dispersed along a waterway and adjoining agricultural terraces. This can be rendered graphically as a settlement pattern made up of a series of nested sites connected by the common use of a drainage system (Figure 2.4). Figure 2.4A represents the idealized movement between a residence and its fields that was likely replicated at different scales. Figure 2.4B shows how residential sites of different sizes were arranged to create a network of intersecting communities embedded within a land-extensive agricultural setting, and the manner in which population was distributed on a seasonal basis to access fields.

This seasonally decomposable settlement pattern structures the pooling of labor resources into residences of different sizes for the efficient extraction, transport, and storage of agricultural products. It assumes that all settlements are connected to each other through economic ties, and that individuals and subsistence items flowed among them. No single village or entity controlled production. Rather, the larger villages and towns likely served as "central places" for full and part-time residents with the ability to host collective economic and other social activities (Hill, Trierweiler, and Preucel 1996:118). Also implied is an economic structure that enables access to land and water resources, housing, and agricultural products regardless of settlement size or position within the settlement system. Interconnectivity, not hierarchy and the sociocultural baggage it implies, is key to understanding how clustered settlements participated in a regional agricultural economy that sustained long-term population growth and the development of towns that at certain times of the year had the potential to house the entire population (see Chapter One).

Regional variation in the settlement system of the Chama Valley and its tributary drainages awaits further study, but variations on this basic theme can be seen in the demographic trends of villages and towns. Such trends also reveal the timing of population decline and changes in settlement pattern that would have affected the economy. For example, settlements along the Lower Chama had the potential to be major suppliers of agricultural crops produced on the broad floodplain and in extensive terrace and alluvial fan complexes on either side of the river. This area also contains higher numbers of occupied villages and a more dispersed settlement pattern than other drainages up through 1450 CE, when most are in decline. The presence of more villages implies greater capacity for pooling resources at lower-order sites consistent with the expanded scale in agricultural production t along major waterways. The Rio del Oso area reveals a similar pattern, but at a smaller scale and with lower capacity residences overall.

The El Rito drainage also has a large floodplain and is bordered on the west by an uninterrupted and expansive Quaternary piedmont alluvium terrace (the El Rito Valley) on which Sapa'ouwingeh (Sapawe) and most of its visible fields are situated. Here the settlement pattern is more centralized and lacks a substantial village component, although numerous field houses have been recorded on the terrace (Skinner 1965; Tjaden 1979; Lawrence 2005, 2009). The large open landscape of the El Rito Valley enabled the concentration of population, and therefore labor, into one "mega-town," the footprint of which covers seven hectares (18 acres). Mobilization of labor is most consistent with diagram Figure 2.4A. This contrasts with the Ojo Caliente drainage where more numerous large capacity towns are separated by only a few small-capacity villages. Field houses are nonexistent in this area, although artifact scatters associated with mulch gardens have been interpreted as temporary agricultural camps (Marshall 1995; Moore 2009; Snead 2008:65; Ware and Mensel 1992; Wiseman and Ware 1996).

Uneven survey coverage and modern development in most drainage systems impede a more complete understanding of hamlet and household distributions relative to the larger, well-known sites in every drainage, but this does not diminish the overall conclusion. The availability and distribution of arable land in floodplain and terrace settings conditioned the arrangement of settlements, the agricultural potential of drainage systems, and, consequently, the organization of labor, resource extraction, and the redistribution of food in the regional economy. It also appears that on a regional scale some settlements shared a common history of development and decline such as the Ojo Caliente and Lower Chama villages and towns, which were largely depopulated by 1550 to 1600 CE. Occupation of the El Rito and Rio del Oso persisted well into the Contact era. As coalescence continued after 1450 CE, the smaller villages dropped out of the settlement system as the larger towns grew and the overall population declined (Duwe 2011). The impacts of this shift in settlement and demography on the regional economy are unknown but have been attributed to drought (Beal 1987; Duwe 2011; Ellis 1968; Hudspeth 2000; Towner and Salzer 2013). This resulted in a steady contraction of the system that coincides with progressive depopulation of villages and towns prior to European contact.

DISCUSSION AND CONCLUSIONS

Researchers working in the Northern Rio Grande and elsewhere have employed models of cooperation and competition to explain large-scale aggregation and settlement into clusters. These models rest on assumptions about how economic systems are organized to reduce the risks associated with farming. Risk avoidance also is invoked to describe the wide variety of techniques employed to intercept, impound, divert, or otherwise distribute water to fields (Bugé 1984:34; Cordell, Earls, and Binford 1984; Dickson 1975, 1979; Glassow 1980; Kulisheck 2005; Maxwell 2000; Minnis 1985; Moore 1981; Woosley 1980). Risk avoidance is clearly endemic to all economies that rely on the cultivation of crops, but does not in itself explain the structure of a fully developed agricultural economy (in terms of supply, demand, labor and redistribution), different socioeconomic orientations that ensure agricultural sustainability and successful land-use design (permaculture), or the large population levels in the Chama Valley, which greatly exceeded those of neighboring areas during the Classic period (Ortman 2016). The idea of big subsistence is introduced here as a way of reorienting the discussion away from the per capita concerns of individuals and fields to the ways in which regional subsistence economies operate. Risk in big-subsistence economies depends on the relative success of individuals and households in marshalling the larger network of social relations that condition the circulation of food and staple products.

With these thoughts in mind, the regional economy of the Prehispanic Chama Valley can be summarized as follows: Classic period residents developed a regional economy that relied upon a diverse set of agricultural strategies that included floodplain farming as an essential component. Farming was based, in part, on agricultural facilities and strategies that were indigenous to the area prior to the onset of large villages, but the agricultural economy grew exponentially. Over a short, 50-year period certain tributary areas exceeded the local land base and relied on regional production for subsistence. By the end of the early Classic period (circa 1400 CE), the regional economy reached maximum capacity. This implies levels of coordination that could only be achieved through preexisting and widely agreed upon institutions and practices operating at different levels of social inclusivity (family, corporate, settlement, and region).

The unequal distribution of land and water resources suggests that certain communities, particularly in the Ojo Caliente drainage, were unable to sustain themselves with local agricultural production. This implies that a regional economy based on the near constant circulation of agricultural products must have existed to ensure adequate supplies of food and fiber and to maintain a balance in certain areas where high investments in cotton production offset a lower capacity for food production in the floodplain. Population movements from large towns to agricultural occupations and fields were not random. As in modern pueblos, they were probably organized on the basis of kinship and corporate principles that governed access to land, water, and cultivated products. Membership in corporate organizations would have guaranteed personal, economic, and reproductive security as well as defense against physical and socioeconomic hardship.

Ford (1972b) suggests that food redistribution in ethnographic Pueblos is governed in one of three ways: (1) through generalized reciprocity, (2) through nonperiodic critical events, and (3) through time-dependent rituals that occur throughout the year. During the recent past, these mechanisms ensured the circulation of food between households whose productive capacities might have varied from year to year. Time-dependent rituals involved especially large quantities of food and people. Ortman and Coffey explore the extent to which this type of redistribution also governed Prehispanic Tewa society in Chapter 6.

Similar social customs likely facilitated the redistribution of food in the Prehispanic Chama Valley given the lack of centralized storage facilities and other markers of elite management of production and distribution in the archaeological record. If this is the case, then Sapa'owingeh (Sapawe), with its plazas that can be measured in acres, had the capacity to host huge integrative rituals that drew from multiple villages. This implies that the social mechanisms compelling food redistribution *within* individual Pueblos also pertained to resource distribution among them from the earliest phases of the Classic period.

The success of big subsistence in the Chama Valley was based on principles of interdependence and the assumption that social norms existed to guarantee the movement of people and agricultural products throughout the system. The development of this economy, in turn, was fundamental to the emergence of proto-Tewa culture and to a distinctively Ohkay Owingeh food and subsistence heritage with deep roots in the lands of the Rio Chama watershed.

CHAPTER THREE

Prehispanic Pueblo Cotton Cultivation with Gravel-Mulch Technology in the Northern Rio Grande Region

Eileen L. Camilli, Kurt F. Anschuetz, Susan J. Smith, and Christopher D. Banet

More than a century ago, anthropologists recognized the association of cobble-bordered and gravel-mulched agricultural fields with the remnants of large, Classic period (1300–1450/1500 CE) Pueblo villages in the northern Rio Grande region of New Mexico (e.g., Bandelier 1892:41–57). The high archaeological visibility of these fields, coupled with the dramatic appearance of some field complexes when viewed from the air, has led to the portrayal of these stone-filled plots as a labor-intensive technology. A variety of agronomic studies, ethnographic analogy, and observations of recent experimental gardens have suggested that gravel-mulch technologies would have enabled agriculture in cool upland settings (Anschuetz 1998; Dominguez 2000a; Lightfoot 1990; Maxwell 2000; White, Loftin, and Aguilar 1995). The chief benefits of gravel mulching are identified as soil moisture conservation and amelioration of soil temperatures to protect crops from frosts early and late in the growing season. Excavations revealing a variety of sinuous partitions; punctuated grids made of large, flat-topped cobbles; and striking waffle-like stone grids led to the initial identification of some of these features as the functional equivalents of gardens in which succulent vegetables, herbs, and medicines were grown (Maxwell and Anschuetz 1992:61). Following identification of maize pollen in gravel-mulched field sediments in the late 1980s and early 1990s, archaeologists suggested that gravel-mulch technologies were a significant component of the agricultural base of the Pueblo populations occupying high, cool settings during late Prehispanic times (Clary 1987; Dean 1991, 1994a, 1994b; Maxwell 1997). This component was thought to have functioned to enable large numbers of people to colonize upland locales, thus easing economic and social pressures that would otherwise have been felt along the floodplains (e.g., Anschuetz 1998; Maxwell and Anschuetz 1992). Investigators ascribed the ubiquity of stone-mulched plots to the short time spans of their use due to soil nutrient depletion and the loss of moisture conservation properties due to the aeolian deposition of finer materials in the gravelly matrix (Lightfoot 1993; Maxwell and Anschuetz 1992).

Two recent interdisciplinary investigations of gravel-mulched agricultural landscapes offer compelling evidence that mulching with local gravels was a method for germinating cotton seed.[1] Studies of gravel mulches in the Yunge Hills near the Pueblo of Yunge Owingeh (LA 59) along the north-central margin of the San Juan Pueblo Grant, and on the San Ildefonso Pueblo Grant northeast of Tunyo (Black Mesa Pueblo [LA 23]) have each identified cultigen pollen rain in gravel mulch that is dominated by cotton (Camilli and others 2012; Anschuetz, Camilli, and Banet 2016). Comparison of pollen in gravel-mulched fields sampled by these two studies with pollen collected from mulched and unmulched contexts documented by other studies within the region also suggests that, although gravel-mulch complexes were probably polycropped, they were associated primarily with cotton cultivation. These findings tend to support archaeological survey observations that rock-mulched fields had longer use-life histories than initially anticipated (Anschuetz 1998). Excavations in the Yunge Hills and on the San Ildefonso Pueblo Grant examined how field positioning aided in providing supplemental surface water for cultivation in gravel mulch. Features identified at gravel-mulched fields include those used to divert, convey,

[1] This work was supported by the Bureau of Indian Affairs, Southwest Regional Office to conduct research into Prehispanic Puebloan agricultural water management technologies in the northern Rio Grande region.

and distribute channelized surface flow to crops, indicating that early Tewa farmers engineered facilities to harvest, as well as conserve, periodic runoff on a greater scale than had previously been recognized.

NATURAL ENVIRONMENTAL AND CULTURAL-HISTORICAL CONTEXTS

The distribution and co-occurrence of readily visible archaeological remnants of old gravel-mulched fields and large Prehispanic Pueblo villages within the Española Basin provide valuable insights into the organization of a key technological component of the early Tewa agricultural system. With some exceptions (e.g., LA 75106 and LA 90671; Anschuetz 1998), early Tewa farmers showed a preference for flat to gently sloping surfaces for their mulched fields. Although gravel mulches comprise an artificial mantle placed over the natural ground surface, this technology depends on relatively gravel-free alluvium for seed beds and plant rooting. Sandy loam or loamy sand sediments with lesser quantities of clay and silt offer textures and nutrients favorable for producing domesticated crops (Anschuetz and Banet 2012). Given the need for large quantities of gravel and cobbles for field construction, it is unsurprising that Tewa farmers focused on settings where naturally occurring rock was locally abundant. Simply put, the quantity and weight of stone required for building gravel mulches prohibited significant field construction more than a few tens of meters from a rock source.

The Española Basin is one of several regions of subsidence along the Rio Grande Rift in Northern New Mexico. Pleistocene riverine terrace remnants within the basin formed during the entrenchment of the ancestral Rio Grande and its tributaries, which cut through the basin's sedimentary Santa Fe Formation. The entrenchment produced ample rock, loamy and sandy soils, and gently sloping surfaces along the margins of the present-day valleys (Figure 3.1). The terraces' elevated positions are thought to have provided gravel-mulched fields protection from late spring and early fall frost damage associated with cold air drainage patterns in the narrow valleys (Anschuetz 1998). These locations also protected the fields from damage during Spring runoff, which can last from March until late June in the Española Basin's main valleys. Figure 3.1 illustrates the distribution of Classic period pueblos and cobble terraces, cobble-bordered grids, and gravel-mulch locations in an inventory of more than 1,000 agricultural sites and features including site locations with cultigen pollen discussed in Tables 3.1 and 3.2.

The same Pleistocene terraces that protected Tewa farmers' gravel-mulched fields from floods and frosts were also favored locations for the construction of residential complexes throughout much of the Classic period (1300–1600 CE). The complexes range in size from several hundred to several thousand rooms. A few large residential settlements, including Ohkay Owingeh (San Juan Pueblo [LA 874]), Tunyo (Black Mesa Pueblo [LA 23]), Cuyamungue (LA 38), and Pohwogeh (San Ildefonso Pueblo [LA 6188]) persisted at least through the late seventeenth century as Tewa residences. Ceramics found among gravel-mulched fields around those sites indicate that these planting beds share life histories resembling those of the nearby towns: both fields and villages were the locations of sustained use and modification across several centuries. Since most gravel-mulched fields occur within a 5-km radius of major habitations and many large pueblos occur less than 8 to 10 km apart along the valley edges, temporary features that could be used as sun shades, windbreaks, overnight shelters, or short-term storage areas are uncommon.

Considering their long histories of use and proximity to large, permanent residences, the distribution of gravel mulches suggests their use as infields within the early Tewa agricultural system. Characteristically, these types of fields are cultivated more frequently and intensively than outfields (Turner 1992:266–367). Agricultural assemblages within the region include scores of gravel-mulched features and associated pits dug for construction materials (Camilli and others 2012: Table 3.2). The documented Yunge Hills agricultural complex covers a 4.4-km length of dissected Pleistocene terrace. The field assemblage includes preserved loci of gravel-mulched surfaces at 116 locations (total 5.7 ha), 99 pits excavated to procure construction materials, and 16 groups of cobble terraces. The San Ildefonso Pueblo Grant assemblage, located on a 0.90-km length of dissected Pleistocene terrace, includes 25 loci of preserved gravel-mulched surfaces (total 3.7 ha), 49 pits, and 10 tanks. The latter are large, pit-like features that were excavated through gravel deposits to expose cultivable soils; they were positioned to receive and retain runoff.

Pottery assemblages, which include a late variant of Santa Fe Black-on-white (1250–1350 CE), Wiyo Black-on-white (1300–1400 CE), Sankawi Black-on-cream (1500–1700 CE), and all of the Tewa wares between, attest that gravel-mulch technology saw its initial application during the late 1200s CE (Anschuetz 1998). These data further indicate that gravel-mulched facilities were used into the seventeenth century. Although the San Ildefonso Pueblo

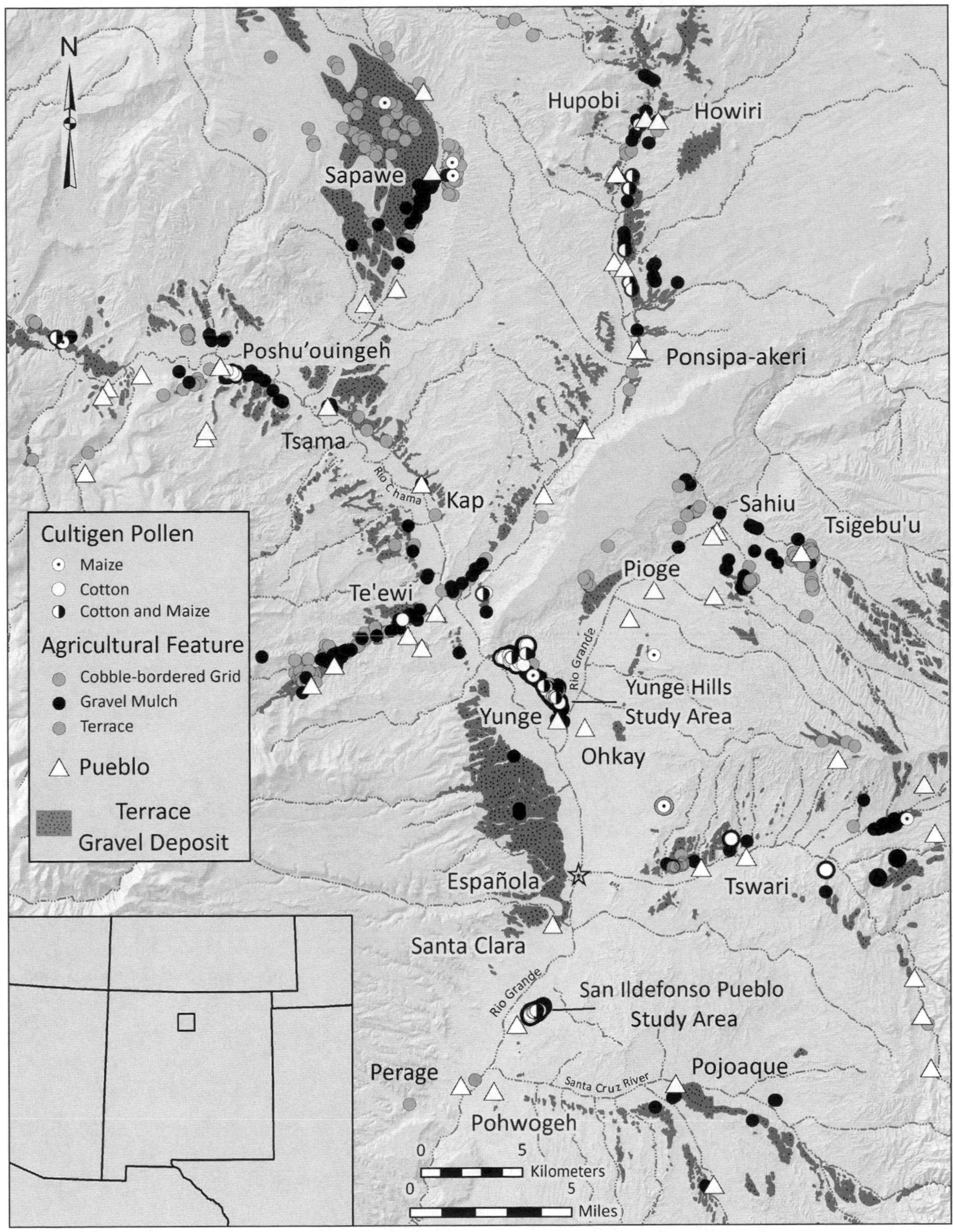

Figure 3.1. Known Prehispanic and early Colonial period agricultural fields, associated cultigen pollen, and contemporary Tewa Pueblos. Prepared by authors.

Table 3.1. Cultigen Pollen in Gravel-Mulched Field Features at Sites in Northern New Mexico

Site and Project Area	*Number of Samples*[a]	*Cultigen-Positive Samples*		*ISM*[b] *Range (gr/gm)*		*Reference*
		Maize	*Cotton*	*Maize*	*Cotton*	
LA 75288 Abiquiu West	5	1	1	1.0	2.0	Dean 1991
LA 71506 Rio del Oso Valley	13	0	2	—	1.0	Dean 1994a
LA 105703, LA 105704, LA 105708, LA 105709, LA 118547 Rio Ojo Caliente Valley[c]	10	7	7	1.0–2.2	1.0–5.7	Smith and others 2012
LA 39537 Rio Ojo Caliente Valley	5	1	1	1.25	0.6	Dean 1997b
LA 105013 LA 105018 El Rito Valley	2	1	0	1.41	0.0	Dean 1997b
LA 48679 Medanales	47	5	9[d]	not available		Clary 1987
Yunge Hills Rio Chama/Rio Grande confluence	65	16	39	0.5–2.4	0.5–15.7	Smith 2012
San Ildefonso Pueblo Grant Rio Grande Valley	37	7	20	0.6–4.0	0.4–9.2	Smith 2009
LA 138467 LA 138468 LA 125767 Santa Cruz River Valley	31	1	6	—	0.5–2.7	Camilli and others 2004a, 2004b; Anschuetz et al. 1999
Totals and Averages	215	39 (18% Ubiquity)[e]	85 (40% Ubiquity)	Average ISM Conc. gr/gm (n = 168)[f] 0.23	0.94	

Notes:

a. Number of samples excludes samples evaluated as pollen-sterile, control samples, and samples collected from unmulched agricultural features (e.g., terraces, pits).

b. ISM is the abbreviation for Intensive Scanning Microscopy (Dean 1998). Data displayed are pollen concentrations expressed as grains/gram (gr/gm).

c. Five of the Rio Ojo Caliente Valley sites investigated by Moore (2009) were resampled during the Yunge Hills field investigation to obtain a regionally comparable analysis.

d. Clary (1987) documented a Malvaceae category as possible cotton, which was later confirmed as cotton pollen by Dean (1991).

e. Ubiquity as a percent of samples.

f. Average ISM concentration excludes Clary's (1987) 47 Medanales samples, which were not analyzed by the ISM method.

Table 3.2. Cultigen Pollen in Unmulched Field Features at Sites in Northern New Mexico

Site and Project Area	*Number of Samples*[a]	*Cultigen-Positive Samples*		*ISM*[b] *Range (gr/gm)*		*Reference*
		Maize	*Cotton*	*Maize*	*Cotton*	
LA 6599 LA 59659 Rio Chama Valley	19	0	0	—	—	Dean 1989
LA 75287 Abiquiu West	4	1	0	3.0	—	Dean 1991
LA 71506 Rio del Oso Valley	4	0	0	—	—	Dean 1994a
LA 101348 LA 101346 Rio del Oso Valley	9	0	0	—	—	Dean 1997a
LA 111597 Rio Ojo Caliente Valley LA 105000, LA 105003, LA 105005, LA 105006, LA 105006, LA 105010, LA 105011, LA 105012, LA 105016, LA 105017, LA 105169 El Rito Valley	16	1	0	2.9	—	Dean 1997b
LA 111461 El Rito Valley	10	7	0	1.3–2.7	—	Smith 1998
Yunge Hills Rio Chama/Rio Grande confluence	6	1	0	0.9	—	Smith 2012
San Juan Airport Ohkay Owingeh	10	4	0	0.6–1.3	—	Smith 2006
Totals and Averages	78	14 (18% ubiquity)[c]	0	0.29 Average ISM Conc. gr/gm (n = 78)		

Notes:

a. Number of samples excludes samples evaluated as pollen-sterile, control samples, and samples collected from gravel-mulched agricultural features.

b. ISM is the abbreviation for Intensive Scanning Microscopy (Dean 1998). Data displayed are pollen concentrations expressed as grains/gram (gr/gm).

c. Ubiquity as a percent of samples.

Grant complex occurs in an area with small, temporary late Developmental period (900–1200 CE) limited activity sites, ceramic types associated with the gravel mulches, along with radiocarbon dates on materials collected from farming soil horizons, indicate that a significant cotton textile industry did not exist here before the second half of the thirteenth century. The near absence of later Tewa Polychrome in mulch-associated ceramic assemblages throughout the region shows that Tewa farmers rapidly reduced their reliance on cotton for blankets and other domestic textiles following Spanish contact.

GRAVEL-MULCH PEDOLOGY

Description of gravel mulches from several locales in the northern Rio Grande region using USDA methods enables diagnostic identification of mulch and provides an understanding of potential beneficial agronomic properties that accrue with gravel mulching (Schoeneberger and others 2002). Gravel mulches are often conspicuous on the present-day ground surface, especially in comparison to adjacent unmulched field areas (Figure 3.2). Nonetheless, burial by aeolian or sheet-washed sediments following a feature's final use or proximity to natural gravel deposits can sometimes complicate identification of culturally applied mulch treatments.

Three parameters lend themselves to a positive identification of gravel mulches: (1) concentrations of gravel, (2) a two-layer morphology, and (3) thickness. These three criteria, along with considerations of context, enable investigators to recognize anthropogenic mulches in the absence of other archaeological evidence. They can also be used to measure the agronomic benefits of gravel mulch. Mulch consists of gravel that ranges in texture from moderately fine (8–16 mm diameter) to coarse (32–64 mm diameter). The closest natural condition is a soil surface with a concentrated lag gravel, amounting to 5 to 10 percent of the soil by volume. Such natural lag gravel is fine (2–8 mm) and most commonly underlain by soil horizons with only a few rock fragments.

Gravel mulching results in a soil horizon that exceeds 15 percent gravel and includes both the natural lag gravel surface and the purposefully placed coarse elements. As a result, a gravelly soil horizon comprised of two subhorizons defines mulch treatments. The upper subhorizon consists wholly of placed gravels that subsequently intermix with aeolian and waterborne fine sediments. The lower subhorizon consists of the native lag gravel horizon, which existed prior to field development and is intermixed with gravel laid down during field construction. Mixing in the lower subhorizon results from a combination of tillage, bioturbation, and freeze-thaw cycles. Generally, the two subhorizons can be equal in thickness or the upper horizon can be slightly thicker. Using the USDA system of soil classification (Schoeneberger and others 2002), the upper subhorizon approximates very gravelly sandy loam, while the lower subhorizon approximates gravelly sandy loam. In some situations, the two layers might be sufficiently mixed through field use and natural pedologic processes to render the two subhorizons indistinguishable.

Combining the two subhorizons, the thickness of gravel mulches ranges between 8 and 18 cm (mean = 12 cm, n = 36) at Yunge Hills and between 11 and 19 cm (mean = 15, n = 26) on the San Ildefonso Pueblo Grant. Santa Cruz River Valley gravel mulches at four sites, LA 138467, LA 138468, LA 138469, and LA 138470 (see Camilli and others 2004a, 2004b, 2004c, and 2004d, respectively), range from 11 to 18 cm (mean = 14, n = 15) thick. This difference in mean values is likely due to disparity in coarse fragment sizes available for quarrying at the three locations. Using these characterizations and documented mulch thicknesses within the region, gravelly layers less than 8 cm thick can be considered lag gravels, while gravelly layers exceeding 18 cm in thickness are natural deposits of terrace gravels.

Among the hydrologic advantages of gravel-mulch farming is increased retention time for flows entering the mulched surface. Surface roughness has long been recognized as retarding water flow (Bennet 1939). Construction of a surface with large pores increases the soil infiltration rate at initiation of a wetting event (Soil Survey Division Staff 1993). Large pore spaces created by coarse mulch force water into a sinuous path, which, in turn, provides more time for moisture infiltration into lower soil horizons. In addition, a rock mulch layer develops a soil horizon with a very low water-holding capacity. The high gravel content with few fine particles creates large pores that provide little opportunity for capillary moisture to adhere to soil elements. That is, moisture entering the constructed mulch layer will tend to move quickly downward and enter the soil of the actual planting bed.

Quartzite, granite, and basalt gravels predominate among the study areas' constructed mulch, and minerals derived from these rocks also are found in unmulched lag soils. The specific heat of these rocks and minerals ranges from 0.70 to 0.85 Joules per gram per degree Kelvin (J/g K). Water far exceeds this value at 4.2 J/g K (Robertson 1988). A moist, unmulched soil absorbs more heat, which in turn allows moisture to evaporate from the soil. Rock mulch,

Figure 3.2. Cobble-bordered field at Tsimajo Site 1 (LA 138469), heavily mulched with local gravels. Photo by Kurt Anschuetz.

in comparison, regulates heat transfer to the underlying soil by acting as a heat sink. Because it holds little moisture, the mulch inhibits evaporation. In the northern Rio Grande region, the presence of rock mulch establishes a springtime diurnal cycle when surface horizons of soils are generally moist. After sunset, rock mulch conducts heat gained from solar radiation during the day to the moist soil below. During this process some heat transfer from the mulch into the air, primarily through radiation, might protect plants against threatening springtime frosts. Moist soils warm with minimal evaporation owing to a reduction in temperature-driven evaporation during the cool nights. As Whiting (2015) has noted elsewhere, this cycle induces soil horizons beneath gravel mulch to warm earlier in the season than soils lacking mulch treatment.

The utility of treating fields in cool, upland settings with gravel mulch lies in its properties that enable cultivated soils to warm and retain heat, thereby buffering against diurnal temperature swings in the early spring. This buffer would be advantageous for cultivating short-day strains of *Gossypium hirsutum* (see Mauney and Phillips 1963:279), for which the interaction of short-day lengths and cool nights induce flowering. It is not known whether cotton plants cultivated aboriginally were short-day strains. As Wright (2000:99–100) observes, some forms of *Gossypium* in northern latitudes do not have a minimum day-length requirement for the initiation of flowering. Nonetheless, she recognizes that, generally, cool night temperatures influence several physiological processes that lead to flowering (Wright 2000:100).

The latitudes of the northern Rio Grande region make early planting of cotton seed risky. Modern varieties of cotton grown in the US Southwest and those thought to have been used aboriginally require at least 300 to 400 accumulated heat units (HU) to be retained in soils for several days prior to and after planting for successful seed germination (Wright 2000:51). Silvertooth (2001:1) describes this condition as a soil temperature between 60 and 65° F in the planting zone for modern cotton, while Wright (2000:51) identifies the optimum soil temperature for planting cotton seed in the uplands as 65° F at seed depth. Temperatures lower than 60° F (15.5° C) are detrimental to germination, emergence, and seedling growth in modern cotton (Texas A & M Agrilife Research and Extension Center 2016). Treating planting beds with mulch would facilitate germination in the early spring by allowing soil temperatures to attain the appropriate heat unit thresholds. Because gravel mulching also decreases diurnal soil temperature fluctuation (White, Dreesen, and Loftin 1998:266, Figure 6), the required soil temperature could be sustained during the period of germination and seedling emergence.

Planting later in the season to counter the effects of cool spring temperatures on germination and seedling emergence is not a desirable alternative, since higher temperatures in the later spring induce more vegetative growth and less flower and seed production (Silvertooth 2001:2). In this regard, Dean (1997c:61) has observed a significant slowing in boll maturation after June 21 in the Santa Fe area. In the later spring, gravel mulch could have continued to create a temperature buffer that ameliorated adverse effects of higher temperatures on bud set and flowering (Wright 2000:100). Experimentally, at least, soil temperatures in gravel-mulched plots have a cooler daily maximum in excess of 8° C less than bare ground during the hottest periods (White. Dreesen, and Loftin 1998:266).

POLLEN EVIDENCE OF PREHISPANIC AGRICULTURE AND COTTON CULTIVATION

In the southwestern United States, cultigen pollen is rare in Prehispanic field sediment samples, especially from fields that were not canal irrigated. This is typically due to low crop yields. Gardens and fields present open surfaces to natural pollen rain, which dilutes cultural imprints, an effect subsequently compounded following abandonment. Physical and biological processes within field sediments destroy pollen, further fading cultural signals. Even in regions that were farmed for thousands of years, pollen evidence of agriculture can be ambiguous if cultural horizons were missed during sampling or if cultigen pollen is scarce in soils. Palynologists understand that in most cases, field soil samples preserve low levels of cultigen pollen, and have invented various techniques to optimize recovery during laboratory extraction (Clary 1987; Gish and Delanois 1993) or at the microscope (Dean 1998).

The pollen research undertaken for the San Ildefonso Pueblo Grant and Yunge Hills studies is based on the Intensive Scanning Microscopy (ISM) method developed by Glenna Dean (1998). The ISM procedure increases the probability of finding rare pollen by scanning more than one microscope slide, but the great advantage of this technique is that the level of analysis is standardized and quantified. The abundance (or absence) of cultigen pollen relative to the amount of soil sampled is likewise quantified. The resulting estimate of cultigen pollen density within field soils may correlate to crop yields, thereby providing an objective parameter with which to compare productivity among different sites and environments.

The ISM method is made possible by introduction of a known concentration of exotic tracer grains (*Lycopodium*) into each weighed sample. During microscopy, the number of tracer grains relative to the sample weight is determined to observe cultigen pollen occurring at a defined concentration, generally 1.0 grains/gram. Successive microscope slides prepared from each sample are scanned until the target analysis level is reached, while the number of tracers and any cultigen pollen grains encountered are documented. Calculation of the density of recovered cultigen pollen in sample sediments is expressed as concentration or the number of grains relative to the tracer spike and the sample weight, abbreviated as gr/gm.

San Ildefonso Pueblo Grant and Yunge Hills ISM pollen analyses document a stunning amount of cotton pollen in samples collected from gravel-mulched fields. The amount is significantly greater in terms of both sample frequency and abundance than the amount of maize identified. In both study areas and considering all agricultural contexts (pits, gravel mulch, terraces, etc.), cotton pollen was recovered in 51 percent of 154 analyzed samples, at ISM concentrations of 0.4 to 9.0 gr/gm from San Ildefonso Pueblo Grant and 0.5 to 15.7 gr/gm from Yunge Hills. In contrast, maize pollen occurred in 13 percent of 72 San Ildefonso agricultural samples, at ISM concentrations of 0.6 to 4.0 gr/gm and 23 percent of 82 Yunge Hills samples at ISM concentrations of 0.5 to 5.5 gr/gm. These results are even more striking when compared to experimental results from modern cotton and maize fields where concentration calculations of cultigen pollen in soil samples are 7 to 14 gr/gm for cotton and 111 to 520 gr/gm for maize (Dean 1995; Hasbargen 1997).

Understanding the pollination ecology of cotton and maize is important for evaluating the pollen concentrations calculated from San Ildefonso Pueblo and Yunge Hills samples. Cotton is an insect-pollinated plant that produces relatively small amounts of pollen. Individual cotton flowers open, wither, and drop to the ground, all on the same day (Hasbargen 1997; McGregor 1976). Cotton fibers are modified hairs that develop around seeds inside a receptacle called a boll. Because of this biology, the high expression of cotton pollen from San Ildefonso Pueblo Grant and Yunge Hills samples suggests a long farming history. The distinctive gravel-mulch substrates captured and preserved shed cotton flowers and residual pollen. Consideration of cotton biology also raises the question of whether the importance of cotton has been underestimated in archaeological studies where sampling schemes emphasize residential features and neglect fields. Unless cotton flowers or pollen are deposited within residential contexts, there is little chance for the pollen to become part of an archaeological site record. In contrast, maize is a wind-pollinated plant that produces abundant pollen, although the down-wind dispersal distance is generally within 100 meters (Raynor, Ogden, and Hayes 1972). The absolute greater amount of maize pollen produced in a field translates to greater probability for the pollen to be preserved in field soils, as well as to hitchhike on farmers and their tools to residential sites.

ISM results point to application of gravel mulch to farming surfaces on the San Ildefonso Pueblo Grant, Yunge Hills, and other similar Pleistocene terrace settings in the northern Rio Grande region as a specialized technique for cotton farming. The success of the innovative gravel mulch for growing cotton is apparent from regional pollen studies. In Tables 3.1 and 3.2, summary results are compared from nine pollen studies of gravel-mulched agricultural contexts at 16 sites to eight studies of 21 unmulched sites. Maize pollen occurs in both mulched and unmulched fields, but cotton pollen is found exclusively in gravel-mulched fields, and, compared to maize, occurs in a greater number of samples at higher concentrations. If ISM concentrations are accurate estimates of cultigen pollen density in field soils, the data in Table 3.1 indicate that the San Ildefonso Pueblo and Yunge Hills fields produced the highest cotton yields within this compiled data set. Moore's (2009) suggestion that maize was the main crop in Rio Ojo Caliente Valley gravel-mulched fields that he studied, with cotton substituted in some years, is not supported by the data shown in Table 3.1. Moore bases his interpretation, in part, on the extremely high concentrations of maize pollen calculated from field samples compared to other inventories of Prehispanic period cultigen pollen obtained from sites within the region (Camilli, Banet, and Smith. 2010; Dean 1991, 1994a, 1995, 1997b, 1997c; Holloway 1995, 2009; Smith 1998, 2008, 2012). This difference suggests that criteria used for identifying maize at sites sampled by Moore (2009) are inconsistent with those of other researchers.

Archaeobotanical evidence of cotton from sites with elevations greater than 1500 m (5000 ft) near Flagstaff, Arizona (Biddiscombe 2003; Hunter 2005; Smith 2007), above 1970 m (6500 ft) on the Pajarito Plateau in northern New Mexico (Smith 2008:561), and from Yunge Hills where elevations average 1768 m (5800 ft) argues for Prehispanic period cotton cultivation at higher elevations in the Southwest. The prehistoric variety of cotton was probably the Hopi short-stapled variety (Malvaceae Family, *Gossypium hirsutum* var. *hirsutum* [formerly var. *punctatum*]) (Wright 2000). Experimental grow-out plots of Hopi cotton near Flagstaff, at an elevation of 1879 m, (6150 ft) produced nearly mature bolls within 90 days (Wright 2000:90–111). Jones (1936) and Lewton (1912) similarly provide estimates of between 84 and 90 days for cotton bolls to develop. Cotton was apparently grown without canal irrigation near the Hopi village of Orayvi (Lewton 1912:6) and in the Rio Grande Valley (Doolittle 2000:223).

Modern varieties of cotton grown in New Mexico require on average about 10 percent more irrigation water than maize and it is likely that cultivation of aboriginal cotton varieties also required more supplemental moisture than maize (Henderson and Sorensen 1968). Aboriginal and modern cotton seed are planted at depths of less than 5 cm, a practice that necessitates keeping the planting zone moist during the pregermination period (Hill 1998a:213; Wright 2000:50–51). In comparison, maize can be planted at depths of between 10 and 45 cm (Muenchrath and Salvador 1995:321) to take advantage of deeper soil moisture reserves. In addition, half the total root length of cotton is confined to the top 0.60 meters of soil (Texas A & M Agrilife Research and Extension Center 2016), while maize's 1- to 2-m long tap root can seek deeper water reserves.

In addition to their intimate knowledge of how to use and enhance the local physiography and harvest water for cultivation in gravel mulch, ancestral Pueblo farmers had several techniques to shorten the growing season necessary for cotton boll production. Cotton seedlings can be jump-started by presoaking seeds, a Hopi practice, and covering seeds with sand to provide less resistance to emerging plants (Beaglehole 1937:40–41; Wright 2000:51–52). Modern farmers brush-pollinate flowers by hand to increase yields and cross varieties (McGregor 1976:181). Immature bolls can be picked early and will continue to mature off the plant (Bohrer 1962:112; Huckell 1993:170–171). In North America, cotton is typically grown as an annual, but perennial growth can be forced by a practice called ratooning, which involves cutting the plant off at the root crown in the fall and insulating the stump with earth. Second-year flower and boll development may be reduced, however (Huckell 1993:169).

Portions of gravel-mulched terraces were probably much more suited for cotton rather than maize cultivation. On some sections of Quaternary terrace in the Yunge Hills, for example, the thickness of soil horizons between the gravel mulch and buried Quaternary gravel deposits is less than 30 cm. Maize, with its long tap root, would not thrive if cultivated in soils with such shallow rooting depths, but cotton, with its more lateral rooting system, could be planted.

CULTIGEN POLLEN FROM YUNGE HILLS AND SAN ILDEFONSO PUEBLO GRANT

Initial cultigen pollen recovery rates from gravel-mulch contexts obtained without ISM techniques in the northern Rio Grande region are 11 and 19 percent, respectively for maize and cotton (Table 3.1). Advances in archaeopalynology and targeting the cultivated ground surface and the constructed mulch mantle for pedologically informed soil sample collection have increased cultigen pollen recovery rates dramatically. The sampling strategy is effective because the interstitial spaces among the gravels act as a sediment and pollen trap. Samples collected with consistent controls over mulch stratigraphy include those collected from the Santa Cruz River and the Rio Ojo Caliente valleys, as well as the two locales described previously. The collective percentages of samples taken from targeted mulch strata at these four locales are 22 and 50 for maize and cotton, respectively.

Yunge Hills and the San Ildefonso Pueblo Grant gravel mulches exhibit variability in the concentration of cultigen pollen within mulch subhorizons. In the Yunge Hills and San Ildefonso Pueblo Grant sample sets, the highest cotton and maize pollen concentrations occur in the contact zone between the mulch and cultivated soil subhorizons (Table 3.3). The seed planting bed lies within the cultivated soil subhorizon that underlies the mulch. Sixty-five or more percent of the samples collected from within the contact zone in each set of samples yielded cotton pollen. The cotton pollen recovery rate from the upper gravel-mulch zone at the San Ildefonso Pueblo Grant drops to about a third of collected samples, while the Yunge Hills recovery rate for cotton pollen from the upper gravel mulch is about the same as that of the contact zone. Investigation into the distribution of cultigen pollen in gravel-mulch strata is worth pursuing to understand the causes of this variability. Factors influencing pollen concentrations might include cotton production that lasted throughout the period of mulch infilling at Yunge Hills, in addition to other factors including thinner mulch treatments. The number of samples collected from the cultivated soil horizon on the San Ildefonso Pueblo Grant is too small to provide definitive patterns, but the lowest proportion of cultigen-positive samples in the Yunge Hills does come from this stratum.

Cultigen pollen also occurs in agricultural features lacking gravel mulch in both project areas. Samples obtained from tank features on the San Ildefonso Pueblo Grant have an exceptionally high cotton pollen recovery rate, 73 percent (Table 3.3). These pit-like features appear to be unique to the San Ildefonso Pueblo Grant. The tanks might simply have provided a depositional context that favors the accumulation of pollen. If this is the sole cause for high concentrations of cotton pollen, some maize pollen should also occur, but maize is absent from the tank samples. Cotton pollen also occurs in and near fan-shaped cobble terraces constructed on the perimeter of Feature 41, a gravel mulch on the San Ildefonso Pueblo Grant. A single sample from unmulched cobble terraces in the Yunge Hills yielded maize pollen (Table 3.3). The higher percentage of samples yielding maize pollen at Yunge Hills might be a product of that area's proximity to both the Rio Chama floodplain and the pueblo of Yunge Owingeh. Nonetheless, the maize pollen recovery rates from gravel-mulched contexts are low in both locales relative to those of cotton pollen.

GRAVEL-MULCH WATER MANAGEMENT TECHNOLOGY

Irrigation technologies documented in the Yunge Hills and San Ildefonso Pueblo Grant study areas included both interception and diversion of water from slopes and intermittent streams to supplement moisture for cultivation in gravel mulch (Camilli 2012a). This practice commonly required advantageous field positioning as well as the use of a porous field border to redirect and spread surface flow. Channel diversion in both locales relied on field borders and canals. Natural processes have eroded loci where water from larger streams could have been diverted. Significant aggradation has also occurred where gravel-mulched surfaces were constructed to receive flow from smaller drainage channels. Examples of gravel-mulch irrigation technology are, as a result, best preserved where aggrading alluvial fans have buried canals and other irrigation fieldworks on upslope field perimeters. Perimeter testing to determine the configuration of constructed field borders along with excavations directed toward exposing upslope loci of gravel-mulched field systems have revealed complex sets of structures engineered to divert surface flow.

In both locales, constructed field borders oriented to intercept flow from small channels served as one type of diversion. Field edges in this context are generally perpendicular to the direction of channel flow and border clasts are large, functioning somewhat like terraces. Constructed cobble borders that intercepted drainage channels range from 2 m to 24 m long and consist of abutting cobbles with their long-axes laid parallel to the field edge. Ovoid cobbles, mined from nearby borrow pits in alluvial gravel

Table 3.3. Cultigen Pollen in Project Gravel-Mulch, Tank, and Cobble-Terrace Features

Project	*Gravel-Mulch Soil Horizon/ Feature Type*	*Number of Samples*	*Maize-Positive Samples*				*Cotton-Positive Samples*			
			Count	*Percent*	*ISM (gr/gm)*		*Count*	*Percent*	*ISM (gr/gm)*	
					Average	*Range*			*Average*	*Range*
San Ildefonso Pueblo Grant	Gravel mulch	15	2	13.33	1.25	0.66–1.83	5	33.33	1.86	0.92–3.31
	Gravel mulch/ farming surface contact zone	17	4	23.53	1.65	0.62–3.98	11	64.71	2.92	0.67–9.20
	Cultivated soil	5	1	20.00	0.71	—	4	80.00	1.09	0.42–2.14
	Gravel-mulched feature total	37	7	18.92	0.86	0.62–3.98	20	54.05	2.29	0.42–9.20
	Tanks	15	0	—	—	—	11	73.33	2.67	0.73–7.98
Yunge Hills	Gravel mulch	23	6	26.09	0.84	0.46–1.77	15	65.22	2.03	0.46–6.32
	Gravel mulch/ farming surface contact zone	18	6	33.33	.92	0.53–1.78	12	66.67	2.96	0.58–15.66
	Cultivated soil	24	4	16.67	1.40	0.58–2.35	12	50.00	1.53	0.67–3.30
	Gravel-mulched feature total	65	16	24.62	1.01	0.46–2.35	39	60.00	2.16	0.46–15.66
	Unmulched cobble terraces	6	1	16.67	0.90	—	0	—	—	—

deposits, range in length from about 12 cm to more than 30 cm. Dominguez (2000b:6.69; see also Poesen and Lavee 1991) observes that the rate of water transmission through gaps between border cobbles would increase at a rate proportional to the velocity of flow and the depth of water impounded behind the border; this water could also move laterally along the border. Water spreading was achieved when a sufficient volume of water was conveyed along field borders to allow flow to pass into the mulch through the spaces between cobbles. The amount of water passing through borders was enhanced where alignments were organized with larger spaces between cobbles or sections of abutted cobbles.

The other diversion mechanisms are canals along field borders, which occur at both the San Ildefonso Pueblo Grant and Yunge Hills gravel-mulched field complexes (Anschuetz, Camilli, and Banet 2016; Camilli 2012a). Within these complexes, cobble field borders aligned at angles oblique to the direction of channel flow served to facilitate diversion into a ditch by creating a reinforced barrier to the water. The field's cobble border formed one bank of a ditch and the natural slope the other. U-shaped field perimeters and short, rectangular inlets aided in concentrating and directing ditch flow. Gravel-mulch perimeters lacking formal borders had similar functions, but they appear to have been restricted to guiding slope wash and flow from very small channels. Canals neither aligned nor connected to a field border also occur. A well-preserved gravel-bermed ditch segment in the San Ildefonso Pueblo Grant agricultural feature assemblage is one example (see Feature 41 discussion).

Evidence for irrigation at upslope perimeters of gravel-mulched fields is better preserved on the San Ildefonso Pueblo Grant than in the Yunge Hills because the area is less affected by erosion and mechanical disturbance. Drainage basins above gravel-mulched field complexes at the former average 2,000 square meters, which is larger than the average size of basins above the Yunge Hills gravel-mulched fields (about 600 m^2). While drainage basins contributing surface water to gravel-mulched field remnants are generally smaller in the Yunge Hills, fields with ditch diversions are, on average, almost twice as large as those where channel flow is simply intercepted by the field border. Roughly 20 ha of gently sloping Quaternary terrace surface lies within the 300 ha Yunge Hills study area. Gravel-mulched fields with cobble borders that could facilitate diversion into a ditch include 0.9 ha on Quaternary terraces within 1.6 km of Yunge Owingeh (LA 59) and another 0.3 ha farther to the north. About 1.5 ha of gravel-mulched field complexes within the roughly 10 ha of Quaternary terrace surface surveyed on the San Ildefonso Pueblo Grant have blocky or U-shaped cutouts on upslope field edges. The cutouts are designed to redirect slope wash and flow from small streams into a canal along the field border.

Gravel-mulch soil samples from both locales exhibit some variability in cotton pollen related to the amount of surface water that fields received. Average ISM concentrations of cotton pollen in cotton-positive Yunge Hills and San Ildefonso Pueblo Grant samples are 2.81 gr/gm (n = 15) and 3.28 gr/gm (n = 8), respectively, for a subset of samples in locations where gravel mulches received water from cobble borders aligned to facilitate the diversion of periodic water flows from stream channels that drain basin basins covering a few hectares. In comparison, ISM concentrations of cotton pollen taken from the subset of gravel-mulch features served by slope wash or channels draining much smaller areas average 1.75 gr/gm (n = 24) for Yunge Hills samples and 1.63 gr/gm (n = 12) for those taken from the San Ildefonso fields. The extent to which this difference is statistically significant has yet to be determined.

Excavation at Yunge Hills has documented field borders incorporated into a canal irrigation system (Camilli 2012a). Feature 12-8 in the Yunge Hills is a 0.23 ha gravel-mulched field at the base of ridges formed by terrace deposits of Rio Chama–Rio Grande gravelly alluvium. A portion of the mulched surface, whose overall dimensions are 74 by 62 m, is positioned in a swale where an alignment of large cobbles that runs the 17 m length of the feature's eastern upslope perimeter is partially buried by alluvial sediments (Figure 3.3). The lowest elevation along the cobble border is in the approximate center of the field, at a 40-cm long gap between alignments of large cobbles. A shallow border ditch ran for 10 m from the field's northeast corner to the gap where border cobbles are absent. The cobble border formed one bank of a 30- to 80-cm-wide and 9- to 10-cm-deep ditch along the field edge; the other bank was continuous with the natural ground surface. A second ditch channel running along an unbordered section of the mulched field's southern perimeter served a bell-shaped inlet (Figure 3.3) where a 1-m-wide gap between two perpendicular cobble borders permitted flow to enter the field and travel along an in-field terrace constructed to spread the water within the mulch. This 10- to 15-cm-deep ditch ran along the unbordered field edge to convey flow to the inlet from small channels that drained toward the southeast field edge.

One of the three soil samples collected from gravel mulch at Feature 12-8 yielded cotton pollen. The ISM cotton pollen concentration of 1.78 gr/gm in this sample is slightly less than the average concentration of cotton pollen within Yunge Hills gravel-mulch samples (Table 3.3). Pollen samples taken from Feature 12-8 gravel mulch also include 2 of the 16 maize-positive samples in the Yunge Hills gravel-mulch sample inventory. A Sankawi Black-on-cream rim sherd recovered from between two border cobbles dates the period of field use to between 1500 and 1700 CE.

Feature 41 on the San Ildefonso Pueblo Grant is a 0.26-ha gravel-mulched field with extensive field border terracing that experienced multiple episodes of remodeling in response to post-construction aggradation on the fields' upslope sides (Anschuetz, Camilli, and Banet 2016). The 52- by 100-m gravel-mulched surface straddles a swale and bordering ridge slopes and features a U-shaped 9- by 20-m cutout in the mulched surface centered on the swale (Figure 3.4).

Superimposed diversion features are shown in Figure 3.4. A cobble-bordered gravel-mulched field with a U-shaped perimeter is the earliest constructed feature within the excavation. Calibrated AMS radiocarbon dates on wood charcoal (Beta-259580) collected from the farming soil horizon range between 1310 and 1440 CE. Associated ceramics include Biscuit A pottery. Subsequent remodeling of the west edge of the cutout includes a laddered series of fan-shaped cobble terraces, while the cobble-bordered mulched surface on the opposite edge to the east is flanked by a shallow ditch. The 17-m long section of field border ditch along the east side of the field cutout at Feature 41 replicates the design of the field border ditch at Yunge Hills Feature 12-8. The dimensions of these ditches are also similar. The width of the ditch at Feature 41 is about 78 cm, and its depth is no more than 15 cm where exposed in excavation profiles. Following the burial of this cobble-bordered field edge, more than one shallow ditch was positioned within the newly deposited overburden to water sections of unburied mulched field that remained exposed downslope. The latest ditch is wider, about 1.5 m. Remodeling this ditch involved constructing a 10- to 15-cm high cobble-armored gravel berm on the its downslope side.

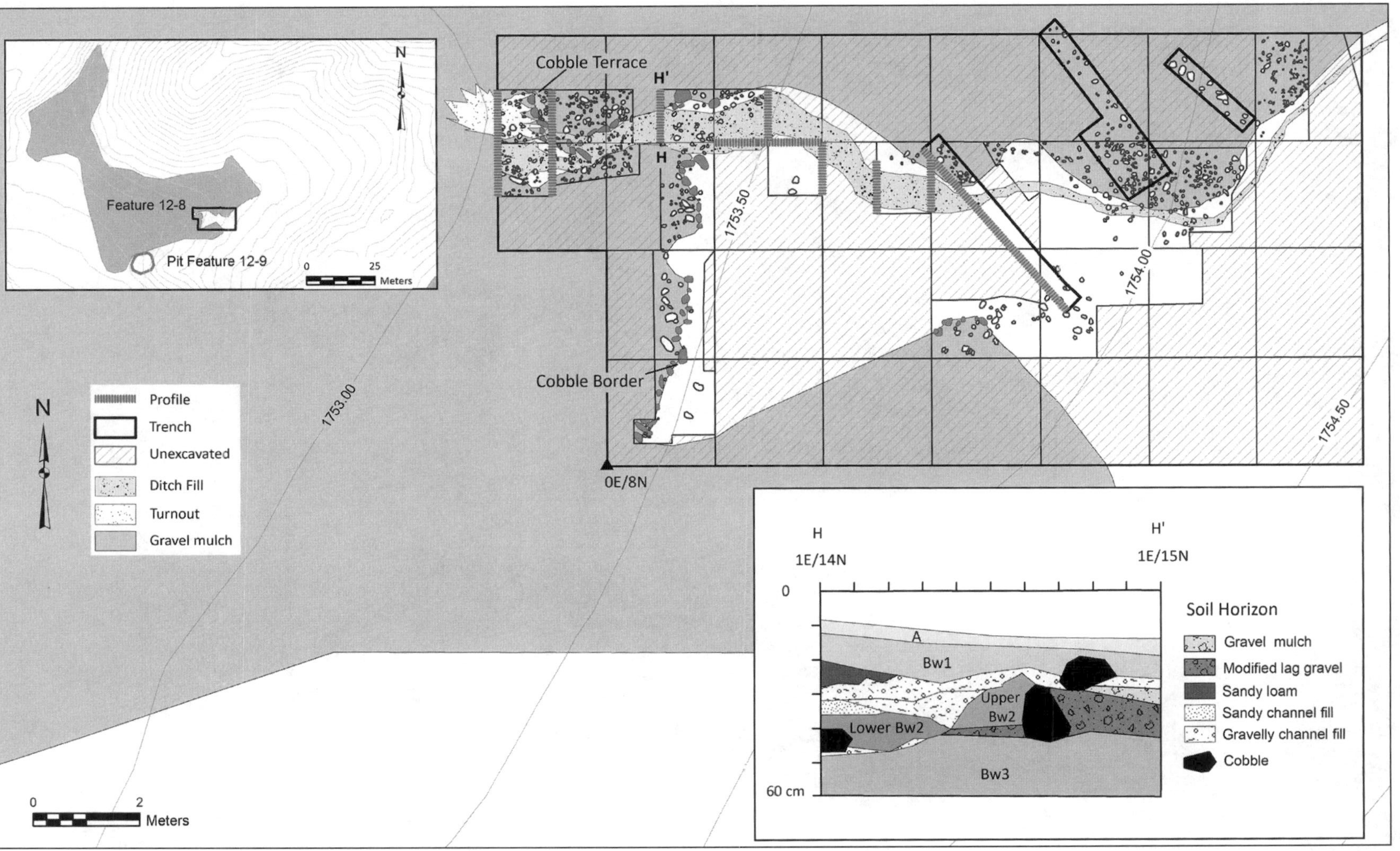

Figure 3.3. Feature 12-8, gravel-mulched field border and ditch inlet stratigraphy in the Yunge Hills east of the Rio Chama. Prepared by authors.

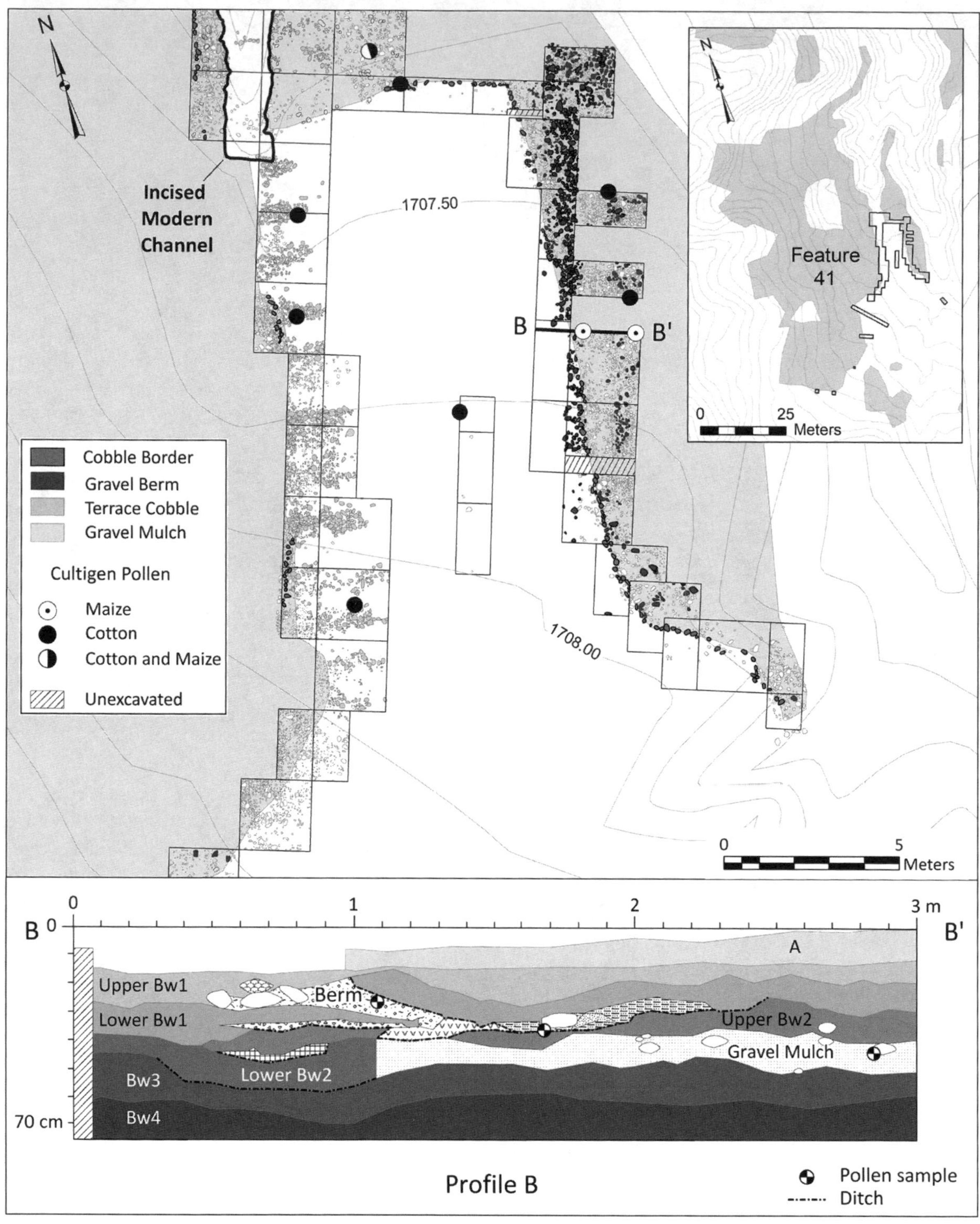

Figure 3.4. Feature 41 on the San Ildefonso Pueblo Grant east of the Rio Grande. The feature consists of a terrace system, gravel-mulched field perimeter, and sequence of ditch construction, shown here in relation to soil horizons. Prepared by authors.

ISM cotton pollen concentrations range from 0.30 to 1.98 gr/gm in 7 of the 20 soil samples collected from bermed and lower ditch fill, deposits within and between cobble terraces, the gravel mulch, and the mulch overburden. Three samples also had maize pollen ISM concentrations between 0.30 and 0.46 gr/gm. AMS radiocarbon analysis of wood charcoal (Beta-259579) dates the latest construction to between cal 1460 and 1640 CE. Associated ceramics include Sankawi and Cuyamungue Black-on-cream wares, while Wiyo Black-on-white sherds found throughout the construction sequence likely represent fragments of a single vessel mixed into alluvial sediments.

SPANISH COLONIAL OBSERVATIONS OF TEWA COTTON PRODUCTION

The regional investigations of gravel-mulch technology described here indicate long-term investment in the practice of gravel mulching to enhance crop production, beginning sometime during the Coalition period (Anschuetz 1995, 1998) and continuing to the time of Hispanic contact. Even with the apparent low productivity of aboriginally grown cotton, ubiquitous cotton cultivation in gravel-mulched fields implies that the northern Rio Grande region Classic Period economy involved textile production with locally grown cotton fiber and possibly inter-regional trade in cotton fiber and cloth. Applying Huckell's (1993:174) yield estimates for Hopi cotton, Yunge Owingeh's occupants could have produced about 42 blankets a year from the 5.74 ha of preserved gravel-mulched field remnants in the Yunge Hills, given simultaneous cultivation of all mulched surfaces. The 3.72 ha of gravel mulches documented within the San Ildefonso Pueblo Grant could have supplied, in turn, enough cotton for about 27 blankets, if farmed in a single annual cycle.

Spanish observations during the early Colonial period provide insights about the production, use, and trade of cotton textiles by Tewa populations. Although his presence in the New Mexican colony was constrained to four months of the winter of 1600 and 1601, Gines de Herrea Horta, one of the Spanish individuals to give testimony at the Valverde Inquest in Mexico City during the summer of 1601, reported that the Tewa grew cotton near the confluence of the Rio Grande and the Rio Chama (Hammond and Rey 1953:645), possibly referring to the Yunge Hills area. By testifying that he had "seen the cotton next to the maize fields of the Indians" (Hammond and Rey 1953:653), Herrea Horta indicated that cotton was not typically intercropped with maize. Gines de Herrea Horta's testimony also highlighted both the need for long storage cycles because of the high degree of agricultural unpredictability in the northern Rio Grande environment and insufficient supplies of cotton textiles to fulfill even the Tewa's own domestic needs for blankets:

> [T]he Indians store the maize of three or four years to make up for the sterility of the land, because it rains very rarely, and instead snows; and the snow serves to moisten the soil so that they can harvest what they sow. And the tribute that the said governor has levied on them is a cotton blanket from every householder every year; and those who do not have blankets give cured hides, which they prepare from the skins of the said cattle of Cíbola or deer. And the reason that there are not many of the said blankets is that so little cotton is harvested there, which this witness has seen by the fields that the said Indians have in the villages that he has visited. And they assured him that if they said that they had no blankets to give, the said soldiers took them from the women, who were left naked [in Carlin and others 2013:26].

Echoing this historical observation of a less than abundant cotton supply, Jesupe Brondat, who served as Juan de Oñate's captain of cavalry from May 1595 until March 1601, attested that the 50,000 to 60,000 Pueblo Indians in the *entirety* of the Spanish Colony "probably gave [Oñate] a total of up to 2,000 cotton blankets a yard and a half long and almost as wide" (Carlin and others 2013:5) during the colony's first few years.

Brondat also provided insight into the Tewa's regional cotton textile production and trade. He wrote,

> [N]o buying or selling or barter, nor any public place where they go to buy or barter, except with the Apaches of Cíbola, who bring them dried meat, fat, and cured skins, which they use for clothing, and in return they give them maize and *cotton blankets dyed in various colors*, which the said Cíbola Indians do not have [in Carlin and others 2013:5, emphasis added].

Not only is it clear that the Tewa Basin's Pueblo residents exchanged textiles with Plains groups for bison products, the fact that the mantas were multicolored implicates the Tewa's use of a mordant in their manufacture, as is required to bind colors onto cotton fiber (Glenna Dean, personal communication ca. 1995).

The use of mordant in Tewa cotton textile manufacture has implications for the technology and culture of manta production that extends beyond the topic of gravel-mulched fields per se. The persistence of mordant use among Tewa groups also offers a possible insight into the significance of the aboriginal cotton industry among the region's Pueblo populations.

The Abiquiu Dam and Ghost Ranch localities are loci of high-grade *piedra alumbre* (rock alum, an aluminum salt), which Tewa weavers used historically as a mordant. Even though wool does not absolutely require use of a mordant and the aboriginal reliance on cotton textiles was dramatically reduced during the first years of the Spanish colony, Tewa groups continued to risk conflict with Athapaskans to obtain *piedra alumbre* as late as the mid-eighteenth century (Wozniak 1992:51). Given the cultural and economic importance of cotton among Pueblo populations prior to the arrival of Spanish colonists at the end of the sixteenth century (e.g., Parsons 1939), it seems reasonable to suggest that mordant harvesting expeditions represent a residual but meaningful behavior.

Early Spanish accounts about the Tewa population's limited ability to produce surplus cotton goods are underscored by the precipitous decline in the Tewa cotton textile industry during the first years of colonization (1598–1601). Likely several factors were responsible. Sheep, whose fiber is easier to spin and dye, as well as possesses superior thermal properties than cotton, also provide meat and pelts. By the time of colonization, Tewa people appear to have determined the benefits of raising sheep outweighed those of growing cotton.

An additional reason for the decline is illustrated by an oral history shared with us by Ben Chavarria of Santa Clara Pueblo (personal communication 2018). He stated that members of his community substantially reduced cotton production (at least for domestic household consumption and foreign trade) because of the *impuesto* (tax) that each family that produced cotton would have to pay the Spanish colony: a cotton manta per year. In other words, cotton was much too difficult to grow, spin, color, and weave to then relinquish the results to colonial authorities. Finally, it is reasonable to suggest that the Tewa calculus about cotton fiber and finished mantas also affected the value of mantas traded to Plains populations, and the disruption of this trade by the Spanish would have thus removed a primary reason for investing in cotton production. Although the archaeological traces of Tewa-Plains trade remain to be comprehensively and systematically investigated, we anticipate that the Tewa trade of rare and highly valued cotton textiles for bison products was highly asymmetrical in terms of the volume of products exchanged. The challenge to archaeologists is to develop methods for reliably identifying and assessing the material traces of an exchange relationship in which relatively small numbers of perishable cotton mantas were traded for much larger volumes of bison products.

DISCUSSION AND CONCLUSIONS

Pedological and palynological methods have resulted in the recognition that Prehispanic Tewa populations grew cotton in planting beds treated with gravel mulch in the northern Rio Grande region. The agricultural landscapes documented on San Ildefonso and Ohkay Owingeh Pueblo lands, the Rio Ojo Caliente Valley, and at several locales in the Santa Cruz River Valley provide the bulk of palynological evidence for cotton cultivation in gravel mulch. Investigations of other Prehispanic agricultural features within the Tewa ancestral homeland provide corroborative pollen data that support an interpretation of gravel mulching as a technique to facilitate reliable cotton seed germination and promote plant productivity (see Tables 3.1 and 3.2). Not only are cotton pollen sample frequencies comparatively high within the San Ildefonso Pueblo Grant gravel-mulched field inventory, the percentage of cotton pollen in samples from large constructed pits, or tanks, within mulch-treated surfaces indicate these features might have been dedicated to cotton production as well (see Table 3.3).

Some of the variability in the cultigens represented at inventoried gravel-mulched fields further suggests that the size of elements used in the construction of lithic mulch is important for cotton cultivation. One lightly graveled surface at LA 105013 (Table 3.1) on the east side of El Rito Creek that Maxwell (1997) identified as mulched contained maize but no cotton pollen. Gravels there are, in fact, from younger Holocene alluvium rather than Quaternary terrace deposits and might be natural lag deposits unsuitable for cotton cultivation (Koning, Smith, and Aby 2008). Similar conditions appear to hold for the mulched plot at LA 125767 in the Santa Cruz River Valley (Table 3.1), which yielded only maize pollen in 1 of 11 samples. Dominguez (2000b:6.29) notes the mulch in that feature is relatively thin and might not be representative of gravel-mulched plots in the northern Rio Grande region.

The accumulating evidence for cotton cultivation in gravel mulch enhances the ability of archaeologists to evaluate and interpret the technological structure and organization of ancestral Tewa Pueblo farming in both upland and lowland settings. Given the identification of cotton cultivation within multiple settings in the northern

Rio Grande region, the agricultural practice of using gravel mulch in upland settings can be better understood as only marginally directed toward food production. Focusing investigations disproportionately on gravel mulches because of their much greater archaeological visibility, archaeologists have not yet adequately considered the question of major field complexes below and above the relatively narrow band of Quaternary terrace remnants (Anschuetz 1998:176–183). With the annual per capita need for agricultural land of ca. 0.7 ha/person estimated by Anschuetz (1998: Table 7.16), the Yunge Hills gravel-mulched fields for example, if planted in maize and other foodstuffs, could not have fully supplied Yunge Owingeh's population with its subsistence requirements.

The wider Tewa subsistence economy relied on an integrated system of diverse strategies and technologies deployed from the floodplains along the permanent streams to the higher elevations of the greater pinon-juniper woodland habitat (ca. 2130 m) (Anschuetz 1998, 2001). Eiselt (Chapter 2; Eiselt and Darling 2013; Eiselt and others 2017) maintains that Tewa farmers farmed floodplains extensively using irrigation from perennial streams. We suggest floodplains were not necessarily reliably cultivatable or even the principal foci of crop production through history due to (1) lowland settings' propensity to flooding during spring runoff and (2) cold-air drainage. A large body of ethnographic, ethnohistorical, and historical data documents the many practical difficulties that challenged Pueblo and Hispanic farmers in the Española Basin lowlands (Anschuetz 1998:173–174). Floodplain settings have received comparatively little formal study to date because of private land ownership, but hoes have been found along the margins of floodplains (e.g., Anschuetz 1998:485, n. 11). Archaeological surveys within the region also document the widespread planting of upland areas by Tewa farmers using gridded terraces, sand-covered mesa tops that have yielded maize pollen aggregates, and other nonmulched field technologies to produce maize (Anschuetz 1998; Anschuetz, Dominguez, and Camilli 2000; Anschuetz and others 2001; Anschuetz, Camilli, and Banet 2006; Dominguez 2000a; Maxwell 1997; McKenna 2015). Tewa community members can recall large-scale upland tracts used to grow maize and beans on the northern Pajarito Plateau as late as the mid-twentieth century (e.g., Tito Naranjo, in Anschuetz 2014; see also insightful discussions by Ford 1980; Ford and Swentzell 2015).

Room and kiva loom holes and finds of stored, cleaned cotton bolls together with cotton garments indicate fabrication of cotton products within the northern Rio Grande region during the Prehispanic era (Chapter 4; Camilli and others 2012). Within the uplands of the lower Rio Chama watershed, examples of cotton products and weaving rooms are few. Nonetheless, the available information appears to represent a well-established textile industry. The most remarkable set of cotton materials recovered through excavation includes cordage, two-ply thread wound on a spindle fragment, and a mass of plain weave cotton cloth woven from the same spindle thread recovered from the floor of Kiva 1 at Te'ewi (LA 252) (Emery 1953). Tree-ring dates on beams recovered from the kiva floor, which hosts four sets of looms holes, are concentrated between 1410 and 1411 CE (Robinson and Warren 1971:27; Wendorf 1953:92). Two other villages offer evidence of cotton weaving. Duwe (2011:456) ascribes a mean occupation date of 1414 CE to the Middle Plaza at Tsama (LA 909), where the loom holes were found in the floor of Kiva 4 (Windes and McKenna 2006). At Poshu'ouingeh (LA 274) unprovenienced tree-ring dates cluster around 1421 CE (Robinson and Warren 1971:28–29). Jeançon (1923:10) excavated loom holes there in the floor of Room 2.

Although indirect evidence of cotton cloth fabrication is meager within the lower Rio Chama Basin, the direct evidence of cotton cultivation in gravel mulches that pollen provides is widespread. The durability of gravel-mulched fields along with their associated ceramics allows identification of the routes by which cotton farming spread across the Española Basin. Surface ceramic assemblages associated with gravel mulches date the inception of a cotton economy within the Rio Chama basin to more than 100 years earlier than occupations from which cotton products and related materials have been recovered. Anschuetz (1995:30–32, 1998) recorded Santa Fe Black-on-white at almost two-thirds of gravel-mulched agricultural features and Wiyo Black-on-white, or an earlier variant thereof, at about one-third of features he surveyed in the Rio del Oso Valley. Small adobe pueblos and one-room field houses in the valley have similar ceramic associations, indicating inception of gravel-mulch technology in this locale sometime during the late thirteenth century, during an increase in population in this portion of the Rio Chama basin.

Gravel-mulch technology accompanied settlement expansion into other parts of the lower Rio Chama watershed, with some cotton fields apparently remaining in use after the arrival of Spanish colonists in 1598. Santa Fe and Wiyo phase ceramics are common at agricultural features near Kap (LA 300), which dates to the fourteenth century and is at the south end of extensive mulched surfaces (most not formally documented) that extend upstream from the confluence of the Rio del Oso with the Rio Chama (Beal 1987:60; Duwe 2011:481). Use of gravel mulching expanded somewhat later into higher elevations of the El Rito Creek and Rio Ojo Caliente valleys, major tributaries of the Rio Chama that drain southern portions of the basin. In these locations ceramic types in gravel-mulch surface assemblages correspond to those found at nearby Classic period villages that were occupied into the mid-1500s (see Camilli 2012b; Moore 2009). Sankawi Black-on-cream ceramics (1500–1700 CE) found in Yunge Hills gravel-mulch surfaces indicate that cotton was cultivated into the early historical era. Tsama (LA 908/909), an upstream settlement with more than 1,200 rooms, appears to have been occupied sporadically into the early seventeenth century (Duwe 2011). The fact that, according to current site records, Protohistoric period ceramics have not been identified in association with nearby labor-intensive gravel mulches reinforces the observation that this pueblo was not in continuous use during the early Spanish Colonial period.

Further work to document gravel-mulch technology will provide a basis for studying the spatial and temporal dynamics of Tewa cotton fiber production for local household and ritual consumption, as well as for the trade of finished textiles to other groups. To date, field investigations of gravel-mulched landscapes have analyzed soils and soil fertility within gravel mulches, identified differences in vegetation cover between mulched and unmulched surfaces, and measured the moisture and heat retention properties of gravel-mulched surfaces relative to bare plots (see White, Dreesen, and Loftin 1998). One valuable investigation of the feasibility of cotton cultivation on the southern Colorado Plateau (Wright 2000) has used experimental cotton grow-out plots. Further experimental work to evaluate interrelationships between day length, temperature, soil moisture and cotton productivity is needed. More archaeological examination of field perimeters could be expected to identify the range of auxiliary structures used to divert and convey intermittent surface flow into gravel mulches. Such work would also benefit study of the Galisteo Basin in north-central New Mexico, which was occupied prehistorically, in part, by a Southern Tewa people, the Tano, and is the only other archaeological district where gravel-mulch technology is known to have been used on a significant scale.

CHAPTER FOUR

Cotton, Community, and Entanglement: Prehispanic Cotton Growth and Textile Production among the Rio Grande Pueblos

Pascale Meehan

In addition to cultivating a range of edible foodstuffs, the inhabitants of the Classic period Rio Grande Pueblos also invested in the agricultural production of cotton and the processing, weaving, and wearing of cotton fiber. Cotton played an important role in Pueblo dress. Early Spanish accounts describe how Rio Grande Pueblo groups were clothed in both cotton and softened hides. The hides were likely received through trade with Plains peoples (Baugh 1991). One of the most common cotton articles described by the Spanish was the *manta*, or blanket, which Pueblo people wore draped across their shoulders (Hammond and Rey 1953; Webster 1997). Other garments identified from kiva murals show men wearing woven kilts and sashes and women in long dresses (Kent 1983; Webster 2007). In this chapter, I bring together lines of evidence from seven areas along the Northern and Central Rio Grande (the Chama, Pajarito Plateau, Pecos, Galisteo, Santa Fe, Middle Rio Grande, and Salinas districts) to examine the interaction between people and cotton between 1350 and 1600 CE (Figure 4.1). I explore how cotton was both an economic and social good whose production entangled local groups with their landscapes and with each other. Long-standing communities of practice involving cotton growth and the production of textiles were shared among Rio Grande Pueblo groups, which may have promoted economic interdependency between communities and regions.

I begin with a discussion of my methods and then present evidence for various steps in the creation of cotton textiles: growing and harvesting cotton, processing cotton fiber into yarn, and weaving cloth. I then relate these results to the notions of communities of practice and entanglements, arguing for a common Rio Grande Pueblo understanding of the processing and weaving of cotton fiber. Environmental differences between Pueblo areas may have contributed to variations in the way that cotton was grown among different groups, but the techniques for manipulating harvested cotton, especially spinning and weaving, were remarkably consistent throughout the regions I examined. The results suggest that pan-Puebloan understandings and practices surrounding cotton growth and manipulation reinforced economic and social ties among communities. Deep-rooted communities of practice, integrated with cross-group social connections, would have contributed to the interconnectivity of the Northern and Central Rio Grande economy, creating strong interpersonal ties across highly mobile populations.

METHODS

For each district (Chama, Pajarito Plateau, Pecos, Galisteo, Santa Fe, Middle Rio Grande, and Salinas), I examined the archaeological literature for the direct evidence of (1) cotton cultivation (identified through the archaeological presence of cotton pollen in fields and/or ethnohistoric records of cotton fields), (2) cotton preparation and the manipulation of raw material (seen from cotton spinning tools and identified in preserved cotton cloth), and (3) the weaving of cotton cloth (often inferred from loom holes in structure floors). Four of the five areas where textiles were found; the Chama, the Pajarito Plateau, Pecos, and Salinas districts also featured either loom holes or evidence of cotton thread making, or both. For this study, I assumed that textile remains found in a district were locally produced, though this has yet to be demonstrated. Table 4.1 lists the sources examined for data on cotton textile production.

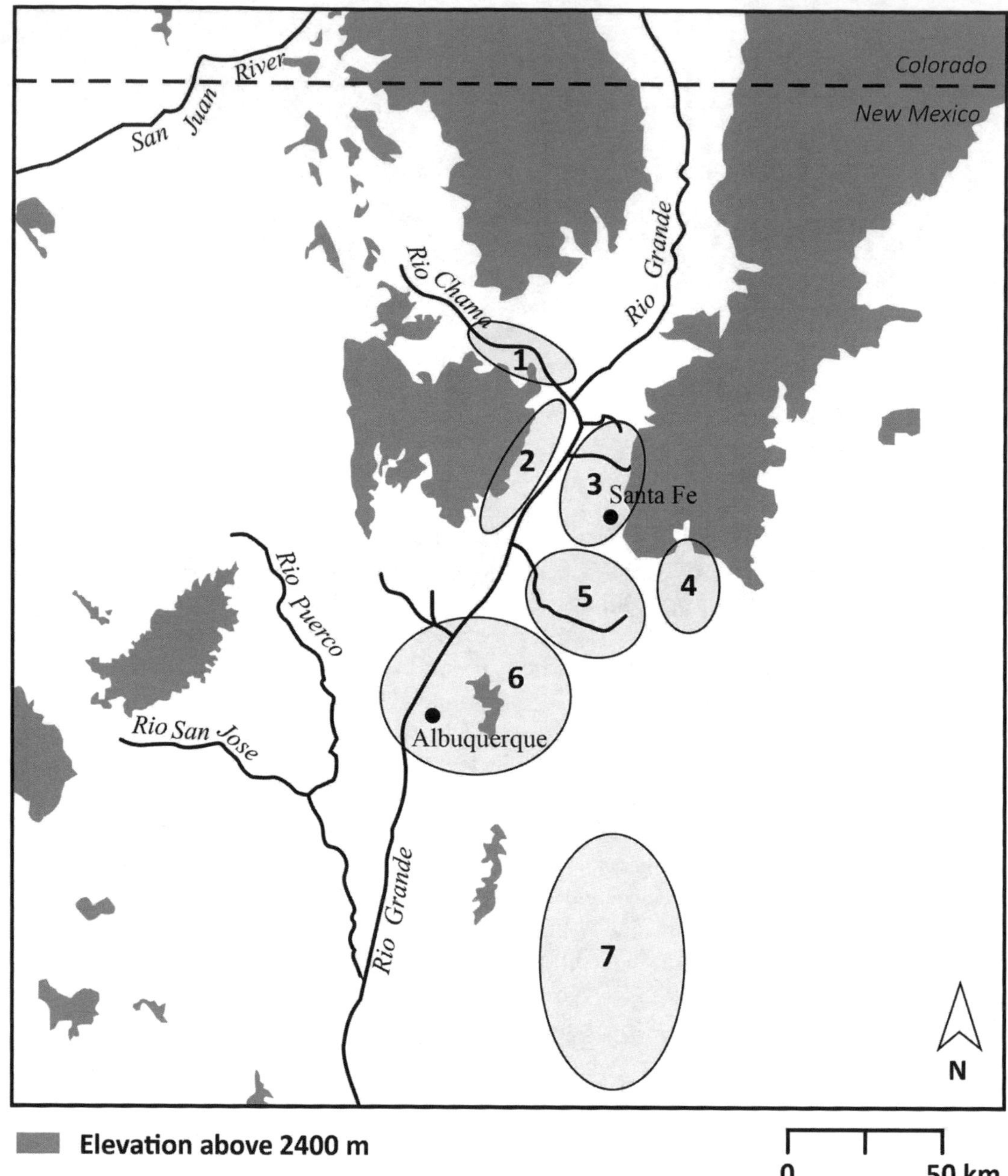

Figure 4.1. Districts discussed in the text: (1) Chama, (2) Pajarito Plateau, (3) Santa Fe, (4) Pecos, (5) Galisteo Basin, (6) Middle Rio Grande, and (7) Salinas. Prepared by author.

The bulk of the evidence for cotton textile weaving comes from structure floors, especially kivas, where loom holes are present. When examining data from kivas, I recorded the size of the kiva as well as the number of loom holes present. I recorded a minimum number of looms (MNL) based on the number of loom-hole rows in each kiva; one row counting for one loom. When feature maps or photographs were unavailable, I estimated the MNL based on written descriptions of kivas. One loom was typically associated with a row of five to six loom-holes (Kidder 1958:252), so in cases were the total number of holes was given but without row information, I calculated MNL by dividing the loom-hole count by six and rounding down to the nearest whole number, yielding conservative estimates. If loom holes were noted but no further details about holes or row counts were given, I identified the MNL

Table 4.1. Sources Examined for Evidence of Cotton Production

District	*Sites*	*Sources*
Chama	Leaf Water site	Luebben 1953
Chama	Poshu'ouingeh	Jeançon 1923
Chama	Te'ewi	Webster 1997; Wendorf 1953
Chama	Tsama	Windes and McKenna 2006
Galisteo Basin	Pueblo Colorado	Nelson 1914
Galisteo Basin	Pueblo Largo	Nelson 1914
Galisteo Basin	Pueblo Shé	Nelson 1914
Galisteo Basin	San Cristobal	Nelson 1914
Middle Rio Grande	Alfred Herrera Site	Peckham 1979; Webster 1997
Middle Rio Grande	Kuaua	Webster 1997
Middle Rio Grande	Pa-ako	Tichy 1937
Middle Rio Grande	Pottery Mound Pueblo	Crotty 1995; Webster 1997; Webster 2007
Middle Rio Grande	Puaray	Webster 1997
Middle Rio Grande	Pueblo del Encierro	Creamer 1993; Webster 1997
Pajarito Plateau	Frijoles Canyon	Toll 1995; van Zandt 1999; Webster 1997
Pajarito Plateau	LA 12609	Steen 1977
Pajarito Plateau	LA 12743	Steen 1977
Pajarito Plateau	Long House (LA 13665)	Powers and Orcutt 1999
Pajarito Plateau	Puye	Webster 1997
Pajarito Plateau	Site 8681 (Fulton 190)	Steen 1977
Pajarito Plateau	Tsankawi	Powers and Orcutt 1999; Toll 1995; Webster 1997
Pajarito Plateau	Tyuonyi	Powers and Orcutt 1999; Toll 1995
Pajarito Plateau	Yapashi Pueblo	Powers and Orcutt 1999
Pecos	Pecos	Kidder 1958; Webster 1997
Pecos	Rowe	Cordell 1998
Salinas	Gran Quivira	Hayes, Young, and Warren 1981; Vivian 2003; Webster 1997
Salinas	Pueblo Pardo	Vivian 2003
Santa Fe	Arroyo Hondo	Creamer 1993; Webster 1997
Santa Fe	Cuyamungue	Wendorf 1952
Santa Fe	Ohkay Owingeh	Chapter 3; Camilli and others 2012
Santa Fe	Pindi Pueblo	Chapter 3; Stubbs and Stallings 1953
Santa Fe	San Ildelfonso	

as one. Because loom holes were concentrated near the centers of kivas, I included only structures that were more than one-quarter excavated in my data set. As always when using data compiled from various sources (including site reports written nearly 100 years ago) the information is imperfect. Some sources cite only those structures with loom holes but are silent on how many other structures lacked them. Other sources do not mention loom holes at all, even when an earlier or later source about the same structure notes them as present. Nonetheless, nearly all the areas examined contained evidence of looms or participation in cotton thread preparation, or both.

RESULTS

Cotton Cultivation

Direct evidence for cotton growing, in the form of cotton pollen in fields, has been found in the Chama district, as well as in fields in the Santa Fe area including at San Ildefonso Pueblo and Ohkay Owingeh (Chapter 3; Hill 1998a: 213; Webster 1997: 418–420). Analysis of pollen and cotton seeds from archaeological contexts indicates that Pueblo farmers grew a variety of cotton similar to Hopi cotton (*Gossypium hopi*). This strain of cotton grows quickly, taking between 84 and 90 days to reach maturity. Compared to the varieties of maize grown in the Rio Grande region, Hopi cotton grows much faster and requires a greater amount of water (Camilli and others 2012; Hill 1998:213). Drawing on early Spanish and later historical accounts of cotton production (Hammond and Rey 1953; Hill 1998), and based on cotton's high water needs, cotton agriculture was initially believed to have been restricted to lowland areas near rivers, where soil temperature was more stable and water more abundant (Hill 1998). It was suggested that cotton production was most frequent in areas in and around Albuquerque, between Cochiti Pueblo and Socorro (Hill 1998; Webster 1997, 2000). However, recent research has expanded the cotton-growing area by showing that gravel-mulched fields[1] in the Chama, Santa Fe, Galisteo, and Middle Rio Grande districts were also used for cotton agriculture (see Chapters 2 and 3). The results from research on gravel-mulched fields alter the long-held image of cotton production in the Rio Grande, as areas previously thought to be unlikely candidates for cotton growth now appear to have been able to supply their own raw cotton (Chapter 3; Gerow and Kurota 2004; Lightfoot and Eddy 1994; Camilli and others 2012).

Although evidence suggests that cotton was grown in four out of the seven areas studied, almost all the districts participated in cotton spinning or weaving, or both (Table 4.2). These results may reflect the fact that cotton remains do not preserve well at open sites and cotton fields are more difficult to identify archaeologically than evidence for textile manufacture such as loom holes. It could also mean, however, that not all communities in the Eastern Pueblo area were growing their own cotton. This is consistent with Webster's view (1997:625) that textile exchange networks in the Eastern Pueblo region probably involved the trade of raw cotton fiber and finished cotton goods from the middle and upper Rio Grande valleys to places such as Pecos and the Salinas Pueblos.[2] In Chapter 3, Camilli and colleagues point to early Spanish accounts that describe the relative scarcity of cotton from an area tentatively identified as the Yunge Hills. Differences could have also existed within districts. In Chapter 2, Eiselt suggests that some Chama settlements may have focused on cotton agriculture and exchanged cotton fiber for plant foods from elsewhere in the Chama Basin where cotton was not being grown. Additional support for the trading of raw cotton comes from the discovery of a Historic period ceramic bowl (Sankawi Black-on-cream) in the Pajarito Plateau that contained cotton bolls, seeds, and lint, indicating that even in areas where there is little evidence for cotton cultivation, raw cotton material was being obtained and manipulated (Camilli and others 2012:8–12; Webster 1997:441–442, 2000:180–181).

Cotton Preparation

In the Pueblo region, cotton would have been ready for harvest around September if planted in July (Spier 1924). Evidence from the Hopi area suggests the bolls were picked early and set out on rooftops to dry and open, as a preemptive measure against early frost (Teague 1998:22). Once open, cotton bolls needed to be picked and cleaned to remove seeds and other plant fibers. This could be done by hand, by rolling bolls up in a blanket so that seeds stuck to the blanket fiber, or by using cotton beaters (Kent

[1] These have been alternatively called lithic-mulched fields (Lightfoot and Eddy 1994), pebble-mulched fields (Lightfoot and Eddy 1994), and cobble-mulched fields (Gerow and Kurota 2004). Despite variations in the name, all refer to the same agricultural practice.

[2] Although Salinas sites like Gran Quivira *do* show evidence of textile production, the data suggest that this developed after the Spanish arrived and introduced sheep as part of the European, wool-based tribute economy (Webster 1997:505). Prehispanic kivas in the area do not contain loom holes, which are features common in other regions including Pecos (Vivian 2003:53).

Table 4.2. Evidence of Cotton and Cotton Textile Production in Each District

Region	*Gravel-Mulched Fields*	*Cotton Seeds*	*Spinning Tools*	*Loom Holes*	*Cloth*
Chama	x	x	x	x	x
Pajarito Plateau			x	x	x
Santa Fe	x		x	x	
Galisteo	x		x		x
Pecos				x	x
Middle Rio Grande	x		x	x	
Salinas					x

1983:29–31; Teague 1998:23). Examples of perishable cotton beaters have been found in the Colorado Plateau, and similar ones might have existed in the Rio Grande Pueblo area.

Once cleaned and organized, cotton fibers were ready to be spun into yarn. There are a variety of ways this could be done including with the fingers (finger twisting), twisting fibers against the thigh (thigh twisting), or spinning using a spindle whorl (Minar 2001:387). In the Pueblo area, spinning was likely carried out using a perishable shaft and a horn or wooden disk-shaped whorl (Teague 1997:48). The Chama, Pajarito Plateau, Santa Fe, and Middle Rio Grande districts have yielded tools associated with spinning and weaving (Table 4.2). These include spindle whorls, possible needles, and battens used for loom weaving (Webster 1997). The identification of spindle whorls in some Pueblo sites indicate that, at least in some areas, spinning involved the use of whorls, although finger and thigh weaving, which do not leave traces in the archaeological record, may have also been used. Historically, cotton working and spinning tools were mostly made of wood, which does not preserve well in the archaeological record. This could explain their absence from areas such as Pecos, where loom holes indicate that weaving was taking place.

Preserved textiles from the Eastern Pueblos provide additional information about the spinning of cotton yarn. When spinning, fibers can either be spun towards the right, where the final slant of the fibers follows the same direction as the middle section of the letter "S," or, towards the left, where the final slant of the fibers follows the same direction as the middle section of the letter "Z." In this way, a yarn can be classified as either S- or Z- spun (Figure 4.2). Once a single strand is created, it can be twisted together with others to form a thicker strand, a process known as plying. To increase the strength of a cord, individual strands are customarily twisted together in the opposite direction from which they were originally spun. Single strands are referred to as "single-ply," two strands twisted together are called two-ply, and so on (Minar 2001:387; Webster 2003:141). In three of the areas where preserved textiles have been found (Chama, Pajarito Plateau, and Salinas), threads were nearly all single-ply with a Z-twist (Webster 1997:50).

Once spun, yarn can be dyed if desired. One of the best indications of the colors and designs used in Rio Grande textiles comes from kiva murals. On murals, black and white appear as the dominant textile colors, with the inclusion of other colors such as yellow, reddish-brown, and lavender in lesser amounts (Kent 1983; Webster 2007). Images from Pottery Mound Pueblo show that textiles displayed intricate patterns and motifs, which may have been created using several techniques. On woven fabrics, these include negative painting, resist-dyeing, and tie-dyeing (Webster 2007:180). Comparing decorative styles and wearing similarities and differences at Pottery Mound, Kawaika'a, and

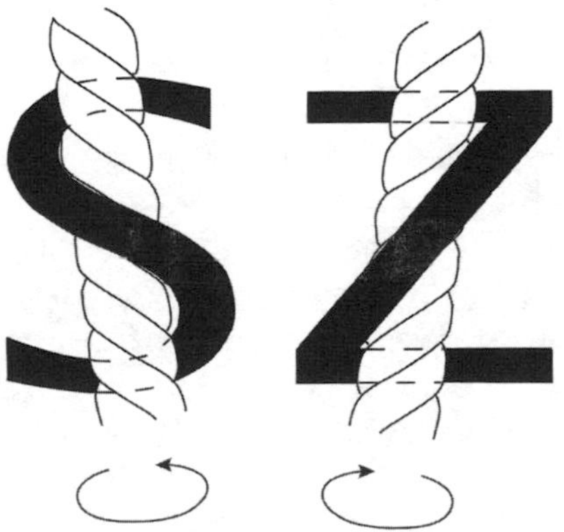

Figure 4.2: Diagram of S and Z twist. Prepared by author.

Table 4.3. Average Number of Looms per Weaving Structure

District	*Total Potential Weaving Structures Examined*	*Total Loom Count (MNL) in Region*	*Average Number of Looms per Examined Weaving Structure*
Chama	10	14	1.40
Pajarito Plateau	17	17	1.00
Santa Fe	16	13	0.81
Galisteo Basin	1	0	0
Pecos	17	17	1.00
Middle Rio Grande	35	71	2.03
Salinas	5	0	0
Total	101	129	1.28

Awat'ovi, Webster (2007) concludes that before 1500 there appeared to have been a shared convention of ceremonial dress, with minor local variation among groups. Although the general form of dress was similar, designs and color schemes varied among the communities. Though they include groups beyond the Rio Grande Pueblos, Webster's analyses hint at a shared stylistic understanding of clothing. Currently, data do not exist that would allow researchers to compare Prehispanic textile patterns among Rio Grande Pueblo groups.

Textile Production

In my analysis, I examined evidence of weaving in two ways. The first was the presence or absence of loom holes in kivas and other structures, and the second was archaeological evidence of preserved textiles. Although most loom holes were found in kivas, not all weaving activities took place in these structures. For example, loom holes have been found in non-kiva structures such as room blocks in Arroyo Hondo (Creamer 1993) and in cavate features on the Pajarito Plateau (Toll 1995). This may have also been the case in the Salinas region, where no loom holes were found in kivas. The data suggest that the Middle Rio Grande district, followed by the Chama and the Pajarito Plateau districts, had the greatest abundance of looms per weaving structure (Table 4.3), but many kivas in places such as Galisteo have not been excavated, leaving us with an incomplete picture.

The length of looms is consistent among the 101 weaving structures for which sufficient data exist.[3] Previous research on looms in Pueblo sites indicate that they measured about 1.5 meters long on average (Kidder 1958:252; Toll 1995:149). The data gathered in this study are consistent with those results, showing an average loom length of 1.6 meters. Although loom size was relatively consistent, the presence of looms varied between areas. On average, there was more than one loom per structure throughout the Rio Grande Pueblo region, but weaving structures in the Middle Rio Grande district had more than twice as many looms as those in the Pajarito Plateau, Pecos, or Santa Fe districts. Some structures at Pueblo del Encierro, for example, had as many as five or six looms each (Webster 1997:469). There was also a great degree of variability in the percentage of possible weaving structures with evidence of looms (Table 4.4). Weaving was most common in the Middle Rio Grande, where 91 percent of the structures examined for this paper contained looms. This contrasts greatly with the Galisteo Basin and Salinas districts, in which no possible weaving structures held looms. Such diversity suggests that, although almost all areas participated in weaving, districts such as the Middle Rio Grande, the Pajarito Plateau, and the Chama were more heavily involved in weaving than others.

The recovery of preserved textiles from sites also allows researchers to determine the weave, shape, and size of cotton materials. The small textile assemblage from Rio Grande Pueblo sites indicate that cotton was used to make clothes, blankets, belts, and bags. Just as loom length and yarn spin was consistent among Pueblo groups, preserved textiles show additional regional similarities including weaving technologies. Most Classic period textiles recovered from Rio Grande Pueblo sites are plain weave, where each weft (or crosswise thread) passes over, then under,

[3] For brevity, I use the term "weaving structures" to describe structures with loom holes. This does not mean that weaving was the only activity carried out in those areas; they likely had multiple uses.

Table 4.4. Percentage of Weaving Structures with Loom Anchors

Region	*Total Potential Weaving Structures Examined*	*Number of Weaving Structures with Loom Anchors*	*Percentage of Weaving Structures with Loom Anchors*
Chama	10	6	60.0
Pajarito Plateau	17	14	82.4
Santa Fe	16	7	43.6
Galisteo Basin	1	0	0
Pecos	17	7	41.2
Middle Rio Grande	35	30	91.4
Salinas	5	0	0
Total	101	64	63.2

one warp (or longitudinal thread) at a time (Figure 4.3). Some of the preserved plain-weave fabrics have a diagonal twill-like appearance, which is caused by combining thick wefts with thin, tightly spun warps. As Webster (1997:502) notes, "although this effect has also been observed in some plain-weave fabrics from Awat'ovi and Hawikuh, it is particularly characteristic of plain weaves found at Eastern Pueblo sites. This suggests that a conventionalized manner of weaving cloth was practiced throughout the region, and that these fabrics were locally produced." This hypothesis is further supported by her analysis of selvage cords and selvage finishes on the textile remains (Webster 1997:504). Selvage finishes are made to reinforce a fabric's edge and prevent it from unraveling. Unlike the single-ply strands that were commonly found within the body of the textile, the 12 selvage cord examples from sites throughout the Eastern Pueblo region were all composed of three strands of Z-spun S-twist yarns twined together in an S-wise direction (Webster 1997:502–503).

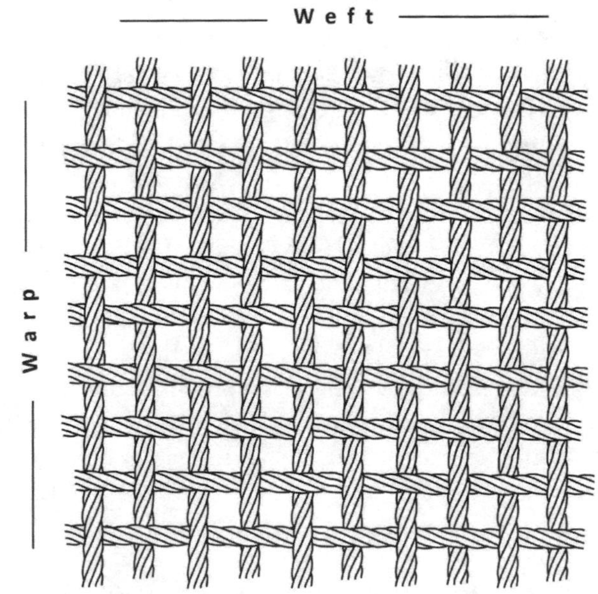

Figure 4.3. Single-ply Z-spun plain weave fabric. Prepared by author.

Although the levels of available data differ among areas and sites, the results show a remarkable consistency in the way that cotton was manipulated among Rio Grande Pueblo groups. Examining the production of cotton goods from cotton growth to the creation of textiles sheds light on some of the shared practices that existed among Puebloan groups. This is especially interesting when one considers that these areas showed important differences in other arenas, including language and ceramic decoration. The Classic period was characterized by migration, community reorganization, and the formation of settlements that incorporated people from different backgrounds (Cordell and Habicht-Mauche 2012). Given this, a pan-Pueblo understanding surrounding cotton growing and textile production may have been one of the factors that facilitated population integration during this dynamic period.

ENTANGLEMENTS AND COMMUNITIES OF PRACTICE

The process of cotton cultivation, harvesting, preparation, and manipulation involved a great deal of organization, time, and effort. The regional consistency shown in spinning and weaving cotton suggests that almost all the Northern and Central Rio Grande areas were involved in cotton farming or processing, or both. This leads to broader questions about how Pueblo people perceived cotton and how this crop was entangled within broader Pueblo community and economic structure.

One way to examine these interactions is through the concepts of entanglement and communities of practice. As understood by Hodder (2012:97), entanglement is based on the "dependencies between humans and things." This perspective focuses on the ways in which individuals and groups are inextricably intertwined with the natural and artificial environments that surround them. The interdependency of people and things enables cultural reproduction but also affects the ways in which cultures change over time. Within this framework, we can understand cotton production and use as one of the many entangled "threads" that formed Rio Grande Pueblo society during the Classic period. As Chapters 2 and 3 show, cotton agriculture and trade served to integrate and connect communities at a regional scale. In addition to cotton growing, yarn production and textile weaving also worked to draw varied groups of people together.

Since cotton manipulation was ubiquitous and relatively uniform throughout the Rio Grande Pueblo area, I use the concept of "communities of practice" to evaluate the cultivation, processing, and weaving of cotton by the Pueblo groups in the sample used in this paper. This concept, especially as it relates to entanglement, is exemplified in Joyce's (2012:150) definition where:

> [a] community of practice is defined as a network of relations among people and objects mediated by actions they conduct, taking place in relation to other communities of practice and continuing over time. . . . A particular way of doing things is learned within a community of practice and reproduced by community members as they enact their own practices.

In other words, a community of practice entails one or more learned behaviors that are held in common and are passed on to new learners. This forms new social relationships between instructors and learners but also creates dependencies among practitioners, their tools, and the materials they manipulate. Because communities of practice "both encompass and cross-cut various social groups and boundaries" (Cordell and Habitch-Mauche 2012:1), they provide a useful interpretive tool to discuss the regional scale of Northern and Central Rio Grande cotton production. Communities of practice are also useful when thinking about economic action. As Ortman and Davis point out in the introduction of this volume, the economic developments of the Classic period are linked to "shared ideas, rituals, and institutions that govern interaction between individuals who are not close friends or family." A communities of practice approach complements this view by examining physical action (how to do things) and mental concepts (why certain things are done the way they are). Overlapping communities of practice, grounded in teachings and lived experience, are embedded in, and help construct, broader "communities of knowing," or "social and cognitive repertoires which guide . . . interpretations of the world" (Boland and Tenkasi 1995:351). These repertoires inform a community's sense of history and belonging and its economic and social relationships with neighboring peoples. Interpreting cotton cultivation, the creation of cotton yarn, and the production of cotton textiles by Rio Grande Pueblo weavers through this view can provide insight into some of the shared understandings that underlie Classic period Puebloan economic change.

COTTON AND COMMUNITIES OF PRACTICE IN THE RIO GRANDE PUEBLOS

The communities of practice related to cotton begin with cotton cultivation. Agricultural investment in the landscape around a settlement would have influenced how the Rio Grande communities saw their place within their inhabited world and would have entangled food and textile production with social and world views. With a growing season of less than 100 days, the rhythm of cotton production would have been different from that of other crops, including maize (Hill 1998:213). Gravel-mulched fields, used to grow cotton in various districts, required high amounts of care. The gravel had to be quarried and spread across the field bed, as well as regularly maintained (Camilli and others 2012:8.9; Gerow and Kurota 2004:221). People using floodplain agriculture would also have needed to prepare fields for planting, although with different techniques than those using gravel mulch. Whichever methods were used, agricultural techniques formed part of conscious decisions made within local Pueblos to work with their environment and obtain high yields. Knowledge and understanding of water sources, temperature changes, and soil depletion informed Pueblo decisions as to where, when, and how to plant crops.

A study of agriculture and worldview in the Tewa world has shown that:

> Water in its various material and ethereal forms unifies the contrasting seasons of the annual cycle and reaffirms the interdependency of people and their cultigens, especially maize. . . . Among Pueblo people more generally, large harvests of corn and other cultivars throughout the summer and fall stand as irrefutable evidence that the movement of life energy, as it flows between the natural and supernatural worlds, is unimpeded. . . . In this sense, agricultural work stands as the day-to-day practice of Pueblo religion because it embodies both physical and mental energies [Anschuetz 2006:65].

In this way, growing cotton would have been part of a community of practice that brought together people and their environment. In Pueblos where cotton was grown, individuals would have associated the cotton crop cycle with the growth and harvest of other cultigens. In the case of gravel-mulched fields, they would have invested care not only during the planting and growing season, but also in field construction and preparation. The growth of cotton and the effort it involved would have been part of a larger understanding of world order in which cotton-growing communities were a part. In places where there is no evidence for cotton agriculture, such as Salinas and the Pajarito Plateau, cotton would have entered the community through trade and exchange relationships. The movement of surplus cotton from cotton producing regions to non-producing areas created social entanglements beyond locally based communities of practice surrounding cotton agriculture.

Just as cotton cultivation involved specific practices and knowledge bases, so, too, did cotton preparation and spinning methods. An experimental study by Minar (2001) showed that yarn spin direction (S- or Z-) is not impacted by factors such as handedness, fiber texture, or spinning technique. Rather, the direction of the spin is determined by how spinners are taught to work the fiber. When spinners were asked why they spun yarn in a certain direction, many responded that "it was the 'traditional' way to spin" (Minar 2001:388). These data indicate that spinning is a learned practice where an apprentice's skills develop over time until performing actions become second-nature and are part of an accepted "natural order" of things (Bourdieu 1977:93, 164–166). Although these concepts have been criticized as not allowing for individual agency and social change (Joyce 2012; Smith 2001), the ideas of embodied social action are important to understanding how Rio Grande Pueblo spinning and weaving techniques indicate a widely shared community of practice. Spinning is an embodied practice; the method of holding the thread and spindle, and the manipulation of the spinning tools are imitated and learned by the student. When learning to spin, students watch "the teacher's position and actions . . . making choices that will affect the outcome, often before realizing that there are choices to be made" (Minar 2001:394). Through increased practice, the motor skills that are required for spinning become mentally entrenched and, as a result, more resistant to change. Textile examples from the examined regions show a consistent spinning twist and archaeological data suggest the use of a common spinning technology (spindle and whorl) throughout the Rio Grande Pueblo region, demonstrating that spinning methods were a shared practice that existed throughout Pueblo communities.

Dyeing cotton yarn would have constituted an additional set of knowledge and practices that included obtaining the mineral and plant pigments necessary to make the dye, mixing components in the right amounts, and carrying out the color fixing process. While some dye elements were locally available, other components may have been difficult, and even dangerous, to access. For example, Kent (1983:31) reports that lavender colors were extracted from ritually important purple corn, but Camilli and others in Chapter 3 note that into the 1700s, Tewa groups ventured into potentially hostile Athapaskan territory to obtain rock alum, a mordant used in the dyeing process. In discussions of pottery production, Huntley and others (2012) and Curewitz and Goff (2012) note that Puebloan potters took technological, social, and ideological reasons into account when obtaining lead for glaze paint. Despite being sometimes farther from home, potters favored certain lead sources due to their established history of use and proximity to sacred landscapes or to other ritually important resources. It is likely that textile producers considered similar aspects when sourcing ingredients for dye, further embedding textile production within larger communities of knowing involving belief, memory, and movement across landscapes.

In addition to finished textiles being consistent in spin, weave, and selvage across Rio Grande Pueblo groups, how and where weaving was conducted was also similar. The bulk of the data indicate that weaving was carried out in kivas. As discussed earlier, the loom hole data from this region show a remarkable consistency in loom width and the number of looms per kiva. Most looms were probably vertical and attached to the ceiling and the floor. Early Spanish accounts mention that weaving was a gendered activity, conducted by men within kivas (Hammond and Rey 1953; Webster 1997:617). Among the early Historic period Hopi, women participated in cotton cultivation and growing, but the task of cleaning and preparing cotton for spinning was specifically carried out by men working in kivas, often within a ritual context (Jolie 2014:385; Kent 1983:29). Circular kivas appear in Rio Grande Pueblo communities in greater numbers around the beginning of the Classic period and have often been considered ritual structures strongly associated with the Katsina Cult (van Zandt 1999:378). In the historical period, kivas were described as multipurpose structures:

> They are places of social resort for the men, especially during the winter, when they occupy themselves with the arts common among them. The same kiva thus serves as a temple during a ritual feast, at other times as a council house for the discussion of public affairs. It is also used as a workshop by the industrious and as a lounging place by the idle [Mindeleff 1891:130].

Written in the late 1800s, Mindeleff's account does not necessarily represent kiva use in the late 1400s, but it does suggest that kivas were associated with a myriad of activities, which, during the Classic period, included cotton textile production. That men wove textiles in the winter is also consistent with the timing of cotton cultivation, as the crop would have been harvested in the fall. The location of looms in kivas places weaving within a restricted space, separate from the home and outside of public view. Within the kiva, weaving techniques would have been taught to young apprentices by more seasoned experts, creating a community of practice based on face-to-face interactions. The idea that there was a community of practice centered around weaving is also supported by the fact that, in some cases, old loom holes in kivas seem to have been replaced with a fresh set, placed to allow a loom of similar length and in almost precisely the same location as the old one (Kidder 1958). Given the closed contexts within which cotton cloth was created, textiles have been more directly associated with certain members of the population, especially men, even if everyone or nearly everyone wore finished textiles.

ECONOMIES, TEXTILES, AND COMMUNITIES OF PRACTICE

The Classic period in the Rio Grande is characterized by population movement, agglomeration, and economic development. The variability in ceramic decoration (Adams and Duff 2004; Eckert and Cordell 2004), language (Fowles 2004; Ortman 2012), and lithic sourcing (Chapter 7) among the Rio Grande Pueblos serve as examples of the diversity that existed among these groups during the Classic period. Nevertheless, the similarities in cotton manipulation techniques among the Rio Grande Pueblos suggest that these groups shared a common understanding of how cotton yarn should be spun (single-ply, Z-twist), how textiles should be woven (most often plain weave), how selvages should be added on, how wide looms should be (~1.6m), where these should be located (predominantly in kivas), and who should be weaving (most likely men).

The cotton manipulation techniques identified here have antecedents throughout the Southwest. Early examples of gravel-mulched fields from between 850 and 1300 CE have been found in the Hohokam area, and fields dated to between 1150 and 1250 CE have been identified in Sinagua culture areas in Northern Arizona (Lightfoot 1996). Examples of plain-weave textiles have been found on the Colorado Plateau that date to around 1000 CE and evidence of looms, battens, and spinning tools begin to appear in that area between 900 and 1100 CE (Teague 1998:117). Similar weaving practices were also present during the Pueblo III period. Kiva E at Long House on Mesa Verde, for example, contained three sets of loom holes (Hall 2007:51). Loom weaving was also practiced in the Eastern Pueblos during the Coalition (Pueblo III) period, identified by examples including loom holes at Pueblo Alamo in the Galisteo Basin (Webster 1997:485). Kent (1983:35) notes that almost all the loom-woven textiles from Prehispanic contexts are single-ply Z spun, the same style found at Classic period Eastern Rio Grande sites. That similar spinning and weaving methods were established during the Coalition period speaks to the longevity of these practices. It is unclear whether population growth in the Eastern Pueblos during the Late Coalition period is due to a boom in the local population or an influx of immigrants from elsewhere including the northern San Juan drainage (Habicht-Mauche 1993; Ortman 2012) and the Western Pueblos (Eckert 2007). Nevertheless, movement and migration were common among Puebloan communities and, as populations shifted, fragmented, and coalesced within the Rio Grande region, established practices related to cotton manipulation persisted (Cordell and Habicht-Mauche 2012; Eckert 2007; Ortman 2012). In new settlements, gravel-mulched fields were constructed, and knowledgeable community members with the memory of past textile work recreated spaces in which they could carry on cleaning, spinning, and weaving activities, as well as instruct new learners. Communities of practice involving cotton production and manipulation intersected and overlapped with other local and nonlocal communities of practice in different arenas including mineral and plant procurement for dyes and ceramic manufacture. Similarities in decorative elements between textile design and iconography on pottery have been noted throughout the Southwest (Webster 1997) and it is possible that, following population influx and settlement changes, the new decorative styles developed for Pueblo IV ceramic wares had parallels in textile production (Eckert and Cordell 2004; Eckert 2007). Despite possible changes to textile decorations, common understandings of how to grow, spin, and weave cotton would have been part of the suite of shared communities of knowing that enabled people to come together and contribute to the economies of the Classic period.

Ethnohistorical and ethnological sources recount that the manipulation of cotton and the creation of cotton textiles was a gendered practice associated with men. This differs from pottery production, which is most frequently tied to women (Cordell and Habicht-Mauche 2012). This suggests that gendered groups made different kinds of goods and participated in communities of practice that were, at least in part, spatially, socially, and economically distinct. The production of textiles in kivas suggests that weaving was conceptually linked to ritual activities and may have been the task of specific ritual organizations. John Ware (2014:37) writes that ritually based Eastern Pueblo sodalities cross-cut regional linguistic differences and may "extend their rituals beyond their home communities." If a similar ritual organization existed in the past, where sodality membership was kept low and exchange of information and specialized religious knowledge was passed along down sodality lines, it is possible that cotton weaving would have been an exclusive activity (Ortiz 1994; Ware 2014). If true, this may help explain the persistence of interregional similarities seen in cotton weaving techniques among the Rio Grande Pueblos. The links among ceremonial activities, intergroup relationships, and trade are further emphasized by Ortman and Coffey (Chapter 6), who describe how regular interactions among villages for ceremonies spurred important economic interactions and community specialization.

Having weavers within a community may have been ritually important among all Pueblo groups, but pueblos such as those along the Middle Rio Grande appear to have been much more invested in weaving than others. Although most areas averaged around one loom per weaving structure, at Middle Rio Grande sites like Pueblo del Encierro, kivas had as many as five or six rows of loom homes (Webster 2007:469). It is possible that this variation reflects a greater local need for textiles compared to other areas, but it may also hint at specialization and regional exchange networks. The Middle Rio Grande area is just north of Salinas, where completed cloth was found but no evidence of cotton manufacture was identified. It is also adjacent to the Pecos region, which served as a gateway to trading with Plains communities, and where no evidence of cotton agriculture has yet been found. Middle Rio Grande sites may have provided finished cloth to Salinas Pueblos in exchange for goods such as salt and they may have traded raw and/or spun cotton to Pecos for agricultural products or hides from the Plains (Kraemer 1976; Baugh 1991). Raiding, warfare, intergroup marriage, trade fairs, and the establishment of long-term exchange partners have all been suggested as methods of Plains-Pueblo exchange. In contrast, inter-Pueblo exchange was likely mediated through a variety of social networks across communities including corporate kin-based relationships and sodality membership. Pueblo groups created networks of economic interdependence while also reinforcing communities of practice and knowing that bonded distant groups.

Entanglements related to cotton exchange and production were also affected by the life-span of these objects (Hodder 2012; Olsen 2010). A long-lived item, worn or used on multiple occasions, would have become associated with memories of past events, bringing people and things together across time and space. At the same time, cotton textiles can easily be destroyed, frayed, torn, or worn out, requiring patching or replacement. The perishable nature of cotton played a role in the long-term interactions among groups, because economic and social ties were required to maintain supplies of this good.

The growth and production of cotton were intimately tied to agricultural practices and seasonality, while the manipulation of the cotton fiber brought community members together through shared patterns of learning and doing. These patterns have a long history in the US Southwest. Common methods of cotton manipulation and weaving were found in nearly all Rio Grande regions. These commonalities point to a shared Puebloan understanding related to cotton production and speak to the importance of cotton weaving as a social and ritual activity. As trade items, raw cotton, spun yarn, and completed textiles would have tied Pueblo communities to each other and to the people of the southern Plains. The embodied practices of planting, harvesting, spinning, and weaving, together with the notions of personhood that accompany bodily adornment, would have connected individual and social identities. As populations shifted and communities aggregated over the course of the Classic period, the continued demand for textiles would have drawn on networks of exchange, production, practice, and knowledge that spanned local and regional Pueblo communities.

Acknowledgments. I would like to thank Scott Ortman for the invitation to participate in this volume and for his constructive comments on previous drafts. I owe great thanks to Laurie Webster who kindly reviewed initial drafts of this document and offered many helpful insights. Additional thanks to two anonymous reviewers who provided detailed, thorough feedback and many productive suggestions.

CHAPTER FIVE

Revisiting Settlement Clusters: Political Organization and Economic Cooperation

Patrick Cruz and Scott G. Ortman

One of the characteristic features of Late Prehispanic Pueblo spatial organization in the US Southwest is settlement clustering (Adams and Duff 2004). Several authors have suggested that the emergence of such clustering was connected to the increase in long-distance trade that characterized the Classic Period Northern Rio Grande (Spielmann 1994; Wilcox 1991). In recent decades, several different interpretations of the political organization implied by settlement clusters have been proposed. In this chapter, we examine the available evidence for Classic period (1350–1600 CE) settlement clusters in one portion of the Northern Rio Grande to determine the extent to which patterns among these sites correspond to these various models. We also discuss the implications of these patterns for the ultimate drivers of socioeconomic development in the centuries preceding Spanish contact.

We consider three possibilities regarding the political organization implied by settlement clusters. First, the clustering of villages might reflect a two-tiered settlement hierarchy, or what we call a "community cluster." In this scenario, one might expect to find evidence that one of the villages in a cluster is a "mother" village that had administrative authority over the others, as might occur in the development of independent local polities. This model is well-represented in the literature from the US Southwest and beyond. Upham (1982), for example, interpreted settlement clusters in the Western Pueblo area as "politically united villages acting in concert in local and extra-local affairs with resident elites managing formal alliances between regions." In a similar vein, Wilcox (1981, 1991) suggested settlement clustering in the Rio Grande region reflects the emergence of centralized, two-tiered political organization. Farther afield, Anderson (1994) has argued for two-tiered settlement hierarchies as an indicator of chiefdoms in the Late Prehistoric US Southeast, and Marcus and Flannery (1996) consider it an indicator of emergent rank society in Formative Oaxaca. Under this model one would expect to see groups of smaller and younger settlements in proximity to a dominant central settlement that likely provided political, social, and economic functions for the satellite villages. We refer to such a dominant settlement as a "mother village," and other peripheral settlements within the cluster as "daughter villages." We use this kin-based terminology because it is occasionally used by Pueblo people themselves in describing relationships among villages, and because it captures our sense that such relationships likely developed as communities grew and divided over time. In other words, we do not view the mother-daughter relationship as necessarily resulting from a previously independent settlement being subjugated by a neighboring settlement, as is often implied in studies of political evolution elsewhere.

A second possibility is that clusters of villages reflect the existence of ethnic alliances or confederacies, what Johnson (1982) and Spielmann (1994) have labeled "sequential hierarchies." Continuing with our kin-based terminology, one might consider such villages to be "sibling" villages. In this type of organization, decision-making occurred through a series of increasingly inclusive representative councils that met periodically to maintain internal peace and provide for a common defense against external enemies. Under this model, one would expect clusters to contain two or more villages of relatively equal age and size, with replicated civic features in each community. A settlement cluster would contain sibling villages that were allied with each other as opposed to a single community that was administered from a mother village.

Finally, a third possibility builds from the fact that ethnographic accounts of the Pueblos (e.g., Dozier 1970) emphasize their economic independence and political autonomy. If this was also the situation in the past, then perhaps settlement clustering has nothing to do with social or political organization, but instead reflects resource distributions or some other aspect of local geography such as suitable building locations. Under this political autonomy model, one would expect the location and size of settlements to derive from specific local conditions, such as the distribution of agricultural land, as opposed to variation in intercommunity relations.

We evaluate these various possibilities using the location, size, architectural traits, and associated floodplain areas of Classic Period settlements in the Rio Chama valley of the Northern Rio Grande (Dougherty 1980; Duwe 2011, 2013; Duwe and others 2016; Eiselt and others 2017; Fowles 2004). Settlements first appeared in this area during the thirteenth century. They gradually formed into localized clusters during the fourteenth and fifteenth centuries. During the Classic period (1350–1600 CE) the Rio Chama was characterized by increases in the number and size of settlements and the emergence of diagnostic material culture associated with the historical Tewa people (Duwe 2011:217). Plan maps of most of the sites we consider are presented in Figure 5.1. The questions we address here revolve around relationships between groups of adjacent ancestral Tewa sites. Were some villages connected to others socially, politically, religiously, and economically? What implications might these connections have had on levels of social inequality? What were the mechanisms behind the demographic growth of communities? We hope the answers to these questions for the Rio Chama region will help clarify social, economic and political processes that were at play throughout the wider Pueblo world at this time.

SETTLEMENT CLUSTERS VS. COMMUNITY CLUSTERS

A settlement cluster is a group of two or more settlements that are notably closer to each other than they are to other settlements. In defining settlement clusters for the Rio Chama, it is important to acknowledge that all the major ancestral Tewa settlements in this region are located adjacent to floodplains. Eiselt (Chapter 2) also presents evidence that the floodplains of the Rio Chama and its tributaries were the primary food producing areas for these sites. As a result, settlement clusters in this area take the form of linear groups of settlements along watercourses as opposed to groups that cluster in two-dimensional areas.

Distances between adjacent settlements are important in determining which sites to include in a settlement cluster. Using cross-cultural data for smallholder agriculturalists and cost-distance analysis, Varien (1999) defined three catchment zones that map onto characteristic types of movement and interaction. These catchment zones are regions emanating outward from a village that likely represent differing intensities of use and types of resource access rights. The first zone is a radius of up to 2 km from a village; it represents the zone of most intensive agricultural production and daily face-to-face interaction. It is the exclusive domain of a specific village. The second zone occurs between 2 and 7 km away from a village and is part of the settlement's land use area but does not entail the same exclusivity or intensity of use as the first zone. This zone may overlap with the secondary catchment zones of neighboring villages and in such cases can be used to suggest their inclusion as part of a single community, since such villages are in close proximity and maintain shared access to resources (Varien 1999). The third catchment zone has a radius of between 7 and 18 km from a village. It represents open space that is not claimed exclusively by any community. Varien (1999:173) notes that as villages grow, they require more land resources. As they concentrate in space their catchment zones overlap more extensively, creating a greater necessity for multi-settlement political institutions to facilitate interactions and resolve disputes.

Given this background, we define a community cluster as a type of settlement cluster in which settlements are within the first two catchment zones and one of the villages in the group stands out as dominant. We refer to this dominant village using the traditional Pueblo idiom of a "mother village" and the nondominant villages as "daughter" villages.

What Is a Mother Village?

Our conception of a mother village builds on previous discussions of "community centers" in the northern Southwest (Glowacki and Ortman 2012; Varien 1999; Varien and others 2007). Although the community center concept was developed in a setting where most settlements are dispersed single-family farmsteads, the concept can be scaled up to apply to clusters of villages. In these sources, community centers are defined as the largest settlements in a local cluster. They often have longer occupational histories and contain forms of civic-ceremonial architecture that are not present in other sites. Such settlements are

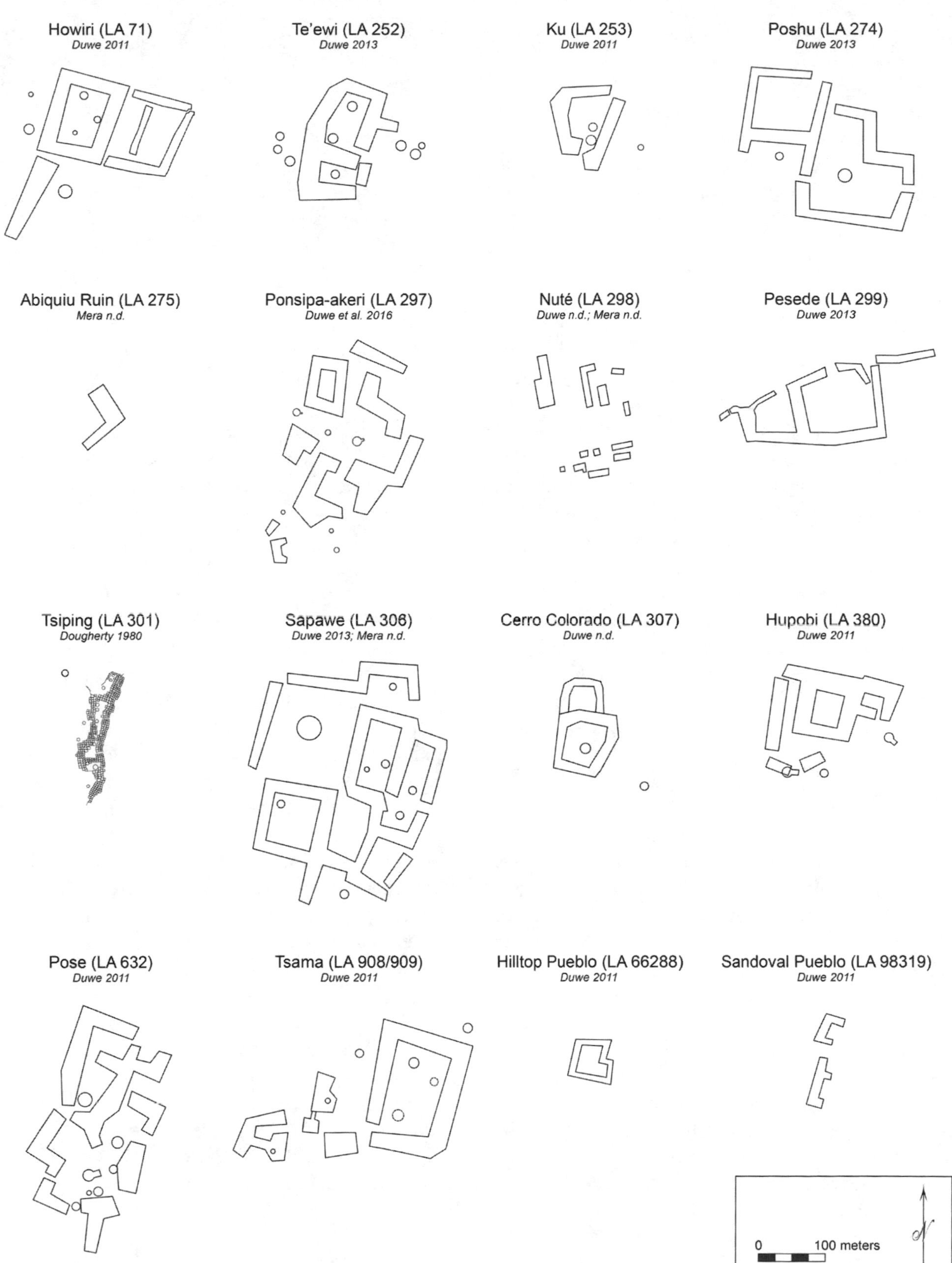

Figure 5.1. Plan maps of Rio Chama sites. Courtesy of Sam Duwe.

also presumed to have played a central role in structuring social, economic, and political interactions among communities. Translated to the context of the Rio Chama, we would expect the mother village of a settlement cluster to have similar relative properties to a community center. We would expect it to be the oldest and largest settlement in a cluster and would expect it to contain more or larger architectural civic-ceremonial features than are present in satellite villages.

One way of identifying a mother village is by its size, as reflected in room counts. A mother village would also likely have more kiva area and/or plaza area than other villages in the cluster in order to accommodate ritual participants from surrounding daughter villages. Such a village might also have an especially large kiva or plaza that signaled a stronger sense of centralization within that village. Finally, it is possible that the earliest village established in an area became the mother village as a community cluster emerged over time. As the pioneering settlement, such villages would have the dominant voice in regulating access rights to surrounding lands. This would affect the establishment of daughter villages within its sphere of influence. One would also expect the first-established village in an area to have had a complete set of ceremonies that would not necessarily be replicated in daughter villages. As a result, daughter villages would be ritually dependent upon the mother village.

Expectations for Different Types of Political Organization

In this chapter we use these concepts to investigate three possible, but not necessarily mutually exclusive, forms of political organization in the Classic Period Rio Chama: (1) politically independent villages with no intervillage organization; (2) alliances of sibling villages who shared resources; and (3) community clusters containing a dominant mother village and subordinate daughter villages. Under Model 1 we would expect larger villages to have more kivas and plaza space simply because of their internal needs. We would expect any tendency toward spatial clustering to be explainable by relationships between village size and the adjacent floodplain. Villages that are smaller or are associated with broader floodplains should be closer together than villages that are larger or occur along narrower floodplains. Under Model 2 we would expect to find little difference in village age, size, total plaza area, and total kiva area among settlements in a cluster, but we would expect to find evidence for overlapping agricultural catchments. This would imply that adjacent settlements must have developed means of regulating access to the lands between them. Finally, under Model 3, we would also expect overlapping catchments, but in addition we would expect people, plaza area and kiva area to be concentrated in a dominant settlement. A strong mother village would likely serve as a gathering space for people from surrounding daughter villages to accommodate their participation in community events. As such, we expect to find plaza and/or kiva space concentrated at the community center.

Based on our analyses (described next), what we see is that all three of these models apply to various settlements and settlement clusters in the Rio Chama. Thus, as Fowles (2004) and Spielmann (2004) have pointed out, it may be a mistake to consider ancestral Tewa political organization as having had a single form. Rather, it may have varied substantially from place to place, perhaps suggesting that the Classic period was an era of experimentation in various forms of multisettlement political organization.

DATA AND ANALYSES

To assess these various models, we utilize a dataset of site locations, room counts, kiva areas, plaza areas, and establishment dates compiled by several recent projects (Duwe 2011, 2013; Duwe and others 2016; Ortman 2016; see also Chapter 6). The site-level data we examine are summarized in Table 5.1; the distribution of settlements considered is shown in Figure 5.2; and distances between settlements within clusters are presented in Table 5.2. Careful readers will notice that our room count estimates are slightly different than those utilized by Eiselt in Chapter 2. These differences derive from the use of data from different recordings of these sites. The first step we followed in identifying settlement clusters was to consider the locations of settlements along shared waterways: the Rio Ojo Caliente, the Rio Del Oso, the Rio Chama, and the Rio El Rito. Second, we identified the largest villages along each waterway as potential mother villages. Third, we identified smaller villages near potential community centers. This process led to the identification of six settlement clusters, and potential community clusters, centered on the villages of Ponsipa-akeri, Pose, Sapawe, Tsama, Ku, and Tsiping. Each of these is described in detail.

Ponsipa-akeri Cluster

The first settlement cluster—Ponispa-akeri—is located at the southern end of the Rio Ojo Caliente. This group presents the strongest evidence for Model 3, or mother-

Table 5.1. Settlement Data

Site Name	*Cluster*	*Initial Date*	*Room Count*	*Kiva Count*	*Total Kiva Area (m²)*	*Largest Kiva Area (m²)*	*Plaza Count*	*Total Plaza Area (m²)*	*Largest Plaza Area (m²)*
Ponsipa-akeri	Ponsipa	1250	1533	7	436.01	139.13	6	18038	11931
Nuté	Ponsipa	1400	140	—	—	—	1	1056	1056
Hilltop	Ponsipa	1350	140	—	—	—	1	1393	1393
Sandoval	Ponsipa	1250	136	—	—	—	2	620	349
Pose	Pose	1350	2833	7	1225.64	346.57	4	17937	12244
Howiri	Pose	1350	1697	6	735.22	298.11	3	12661	5040
Hupobi	Pose	1350	1202	5	560.54	181.01	3	6799	4097
Sapawe	Sapawe	1350	2560	10	1250.75	340.11	7	53612	24698
Tsama	Tsama	1250	1274	6	848.55	221.44	2	16022	10969
Poshu	Tsama	1350	1088	3	181.03	104.25	5	31929	14507
Cerro Colorado	Tsama	1280	550	2	222.76	113.48	1	2102	2102
Abiquiu	Tsama	1350	150	1	?	?	?	—	—
Ku	Ku	1280	627	3	363.99	176.14	1	4042	4042
Te'ewi	Ku	1350	600	12	477.79	73.16	2	6320	4143
Pesede	Ku	1280	593	—	—	—	2	9975	7365
Ku II	Ku	1280	50	—	—	—	3	?	?
Tsiping	Tsiping	1200	500	13	411.79	117.52	1	1079	1079

daughter community organization. This proposed community cluster was dominated by the village of Ponsipa-akeri based on its size and establishment dates relative to neighboring sites. Ponsipa-akeri was established in the late thirteenth century and grew to be a large village with more than 1500 rooms at its height. In contrast, the other three villages in this cluster each had less than 150 rooms. One was established about the same time as Ponsipa-akeri, whereas the other two were established about a century later. All the proposed daughter villages were less than 5 km from Ponsipa-akeri. This would place them within Varien's second catchment zone, which suggests joint access to natural resources. Given that kivas play important political, social, and religious functions, it is important to note that subterranean kivas are apparent only at Ponsipa-akeri. This suggests that inhabitants of the smaller villages in this community traveled to Ponsipa-akeri and utilized the kivas there. In addition, two of the kivas at Ponsipa-akeri have unusually large diameters (10.65m and 13.31m; 7.21m was the mean for other kivas) and are located on either end of the main plaza in conspicuous locations. It is possible that these kivas reflect some level of representative dualism or moiety organization. Finally, Ponsipa-akeri has the largest plaza-to-room ratio of the sites in this cluster, which suggests that proportionately it had a larger plaza than any of its neighboring villages after adjusting for size. This is probably an indication that more public functions took place at Ponsipa-akeri.

Ponsipa-akeri was centrally located between two daughter villages to the north (Nute and Hilltop) and another village to the south (Sandoval Pueblo) along a shared waterway, and it had far more plaza space (85%) than all the other villages in this cluster combined. One plaza in particular was 11,931 m^2, whereas the combined area of the other five plazas at the site is only 6,107m^2. In short, all the available data seem consistent with the notion that this settlement cluster was a community cluster in which Ponsipa-akeri was the mother village and there was a two-tiered settlement hierarchy.

Pose Cluster

The Pose cluster consists of Pose and two other large villages, Hupobi and Howiri. It is located along the Rio Ojo Caliente north of Ponsipa-akeri. All three have more than 1,000 rooms, and all three were established around the same time in the fourteenth century. Hupobi and

Table 5.2. Distances (in kilometers) between Sites in Settlement Clusters

	Pose	*Howiri*	*Hopobi*	
Pose	—	3.2	2.9	
Howiri	3.2	—	0.5	
Hopobi	2.9	0.5	—	
	Ponsipa-akeri	*Sandoval*	*Hilltop*	*Nute*
Ponsipa-akeri	—	4.6	4.0	4.4
Sandoval	4.6	—	8.2	8.3
Hilltop	4.0	8.2	—	0.5
Nute	4.4	8.3	0.5	—
	Tsama	*Poshu*	*Abiquiu*	*Cerro Colorado*
Tsama	—	5.5	9.4	5.5
Poshu	5.5	—	3.8	7.8
Abiquiu	9.4	3.8	—	11.5
Cerro Colorado	5.5	7.6	11.5	—
	Ku	*Te'ewi*	*Ku II*	*Pesede*
Ku	—	1.8	0.7	6.4
Te'ewi	1.8	—	1.8	7.7
Ku II	0.7	1.8	—	6.0
Pesede	6.4	7.7	6.0	—

Howiri are separated by 0.5 km, well within the first level catchment zone radius, suggesting that they were paired settlements of a single community. This is also consistent with Tewa oral traditions regarding these sites collected by Harrington (1916). These two, in turn, are approximately 3 km from Pose, suggesting that all three shared access to natural resources. Because Hupobi and Howiri are so close, they could even be considered a single settlement. Combined, they are nearly equal in size to Pose, and this makes it difficult to identify a potential mother village based on size. If there was a mother village Pose would seem most likely due to its size, the fact that it contains the largest plaza in the cluster, and the fact that Pose figures prominently in Tewa oral tradition (Ortiz 1969:16).

Yet, in most respects—total plaza area, kiva area, and room count—Hupobi/Howiri is nearly equivalent to Pose. Of the three largest kivas in the Rio Chama study area, Pose has the largest (21.01m diameter) and Howiri has the third largest (19.48m diameter). The largest plaza at Pose is more than twice as large as the largest plaza at either of the two other villages, but room-to-plaza ratios suggest that Pose does not contain more plaza space per capita than the other sites. Also, of note is that all three villages had a large central plaza that dwarfed the surrounding plazas within each village. The lack of differentiation between Pose and Hupobi/Howiri is surprising given Tewa oral history, which suggests Pose was the mother village for all Tewa people of the region (Harrington 1916). The lack of a larger plaza, as indicated by plaza-to-room ratio, does not support the notion that Pose was a more important gathering place than Hupobi/Howiri. Instead, the very large kivas at Pose and Howiri indicate that important political, social, and religious functions took place in both locations. Overall, this cluster does not exhibit centralization and is most consistent with Model 2. This suggests that the Pose cluster represents an alliance or confederacy of sibling villages with strong, horizontally integrated institutions. Several authors have suggested that when such is the case there is far less opportunity for vertical differentiation and hierarchy to develop (Blanton and Fargher 2008; Blanton and others 1993; Spielmann 1994). The Pose cluster may thus reflect the existence of both strong community institutions and weak top-down leadership. It also indicates some level of cross-community political integration because such

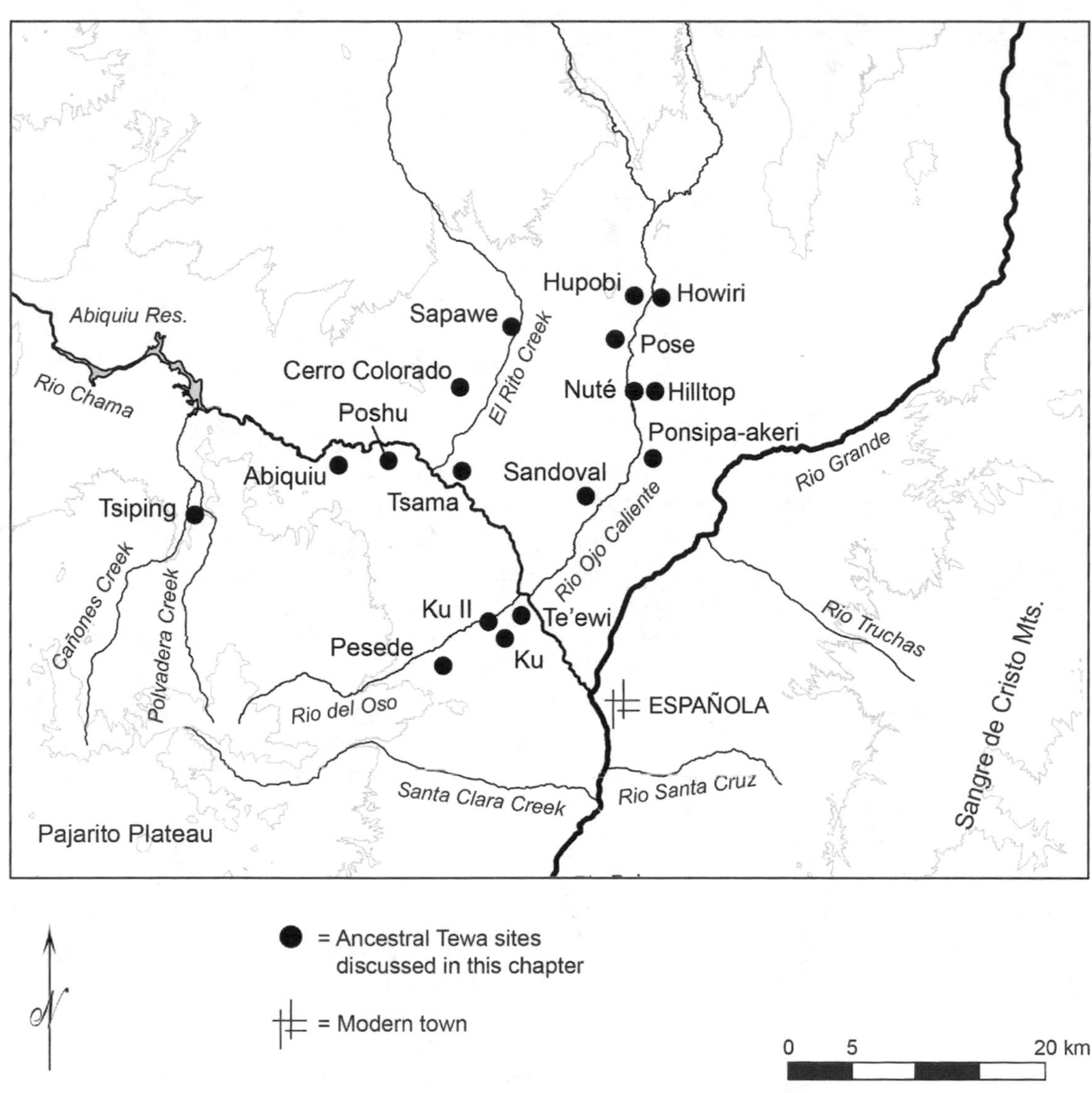

Figure 5.2. Regional map showing the locations of the sites in this analysis. Courtesy of Sam Duwe.

institutions would in some ways act in place of managerial elites but without social hierarchy.

Sapawe

The Sapawe settlement "cluster" is unusual in that it consists of a single village. Nevertheless, the sheer size of Sapawe is on par with the total populations of other community clusters, and Sapawe is located immediately adjacent to an especially large expanse of floodplain. At more than 2,500 rooms, Sapawe is comparable in size to Pose. Originally, we considered the possibility that Cerro Colorado should be considered part of the Sapawe community since Cerro Colorado is the closest neighboring village to Sapawe and it also lies along the El Rito River. Cerro Colorado is, however, closer to Tsama than to Sapawe (5.47 km vs. 7.13 km, respectively). It thus appears that Sapawe was a community cluster unto itself. The size of Sapawe, combined with its adjacent floodplain and distance to other sites, is suggestive of Model 1.

Sapawe has seven plazas including the largest plaza in the study area. The plaza-to-room ratio indicates that this single plaza was not only the largest plaza but was far larger than almost any other plaza in the study area even when adjusted for population. Comparing the two largest sites in the Rio Chama, Sapawe has only slightly fewer estimated rooms than Pose, but has 67 percent more plaza area. Not only is this size difference intriguing, but we must ask why Sapawe, with no satellite villages surrounding it, had so much plaza space. One possibility is that these very large plaza spaces were set aside to accommodate visitors from surrounding villages (see Chapter 6). The data for Sapawe indicate either that Cerro Colorado was a daughter village of Sapawe despite being closer to Tsama, or that Sapawe hosted larger scale gatherings of people from other settlement clusters or even groups from outside the study area. Unlike Pose, there is no recorded oral tradition, which may indicate that Sapawe played a unique role in the region.

Tsama Cluster

This cluster contains four villages: Tsama and Cerro Colorado on the north bank of the Rio Chama, and Poshu and Abiquiu on the south bank. There are two villages that could potentially be the mother village of this cluster. Tsama was chosen because it was established as much as a century before Poshu and was nearly a third larger. This conclusion is ambiguous, however, because Tsama and Poshu both have more than 1,000 rooms and are only 5.5 km apart. This distance puts them outside the first catchment zone that would indicate they were part of the same settlement, but within the second zone, which indicates that they shared access to productive resources.

A curious aspect of the relationship between Tsama and Poshu is that Tsama has more than double the number of kivas than all other villages in the cluster combined, but Poshu has nearly twice the plaza space as Tsama. Though not the largest plaza in the study area, Poshu has the largest plaza-to-room ratio, which is even greater than Sapawe (29.35m^2/room vs. 20.94m^2/room, respectively). This indicates that large public events that included visitors took place at Poshu. Even when its largest plaza is removed from consideration, Poshu's plaza-to-room ratio is still 16.01m^2/room, which is very high for the region. This leads to a question: If these two villages belonged to the same cluster (Tsama was built earlier and likely lasted longer and Tsama had a larger population and more kiva space), then why does Poshu have so much more plaza space? It may be that Tsama and Poshu were part of an alliance, as specified by Model 2, but this still does not explain the additional plaza area at Poshu. Perhaps this reflects a similar situation to Sapawe, where the inhabitants of Poshu hosted visitors from other clusters or even from beyond the study area. Another possibility is that Tsama and Poshu were mother villages for separate community clusters. Even though these two sites are relatively close, a crucial factor may be that they are located on opposite sides of the Rio Chama. Both villages also seem to have had a single small daughter village located within their secondary catchment zones, Cerro Colorado and Abiquiu, respectively.

Ku Cluster

The villages in this settlement cluster are Ku, Ku II, Te'ewi, and possibly Pesede. This cluster presents a similar puzzle to the Tsama-Poshu cluster, in this case with regard to whether Ku or Te'ewi should be considered a potential mother village. Because these two villages lie only 1.75 km apart, it is likely that they shared resources and may have been part of a single community. Although both villages contain around 600 rooms, Ku is the most likely center because it was established first and has the largest kiva (36% larger than any kiva at Te'ewi). However, Te'ewi has more kivas and more plaza space than Ku. The number of kivas at Te'ewi is large for a village of its size, especially in comparison with Sapawe or Pose. The sizes of Te'ewi kivas are also quite small, however, and thus reflect use by similarly small groups. Te'ewi had four times as many kivas as Ku, but only 24 percent more kiva space than Ku.

The characteristics of the sites in this cluster exhibit a blend of all three models. First, Ku and Te'ewi are of similar size, contain a full suite of civic-ceremonial features, and are in such proximity that they must have shared access to local resources. These are all characteristics of a sibling village alliance (Model 2). On the other hand, Ku II is a small site, lacking kivas, that lies within a kilometer of Ku and fits the model of a daughter village (Model 1). Finally, Pesede is about the same size as Ku and Te'ewi but does not have any identifiable kivas. It may therefore be an additional daughter village. This site, however, contains substantial plaza space and the largest single plaza in the Rio del Oso, and it is nearly 7 km away from Ku. So it may also represent a single settlement cluster like Sapawe, consistent with Model 1, at which kivas are not visible on the modern ground surface for some reason.

It is important to mention that the next ancestral Tewa community downstream from the Ku cluster included Yungeh and Ohkay'owingeh, which are located about 7 km from Te'ewi at the confluence of the Rio Chama and Rio Grande. Yungeh contains an estimated 520 rooms, but data regarding the sizes of plazas and kivas are lacking save for an obscure mention in Ellis (1987:20) acknowledging that there had been a plaza at the site. It is also clear that at the time of Spanish contact Yungeh and Ohkay formed a single, paired-village community, where the summer moiety lived at Yungeh and the winter moiety lived at

Ohkay (Ortiz 1979). Architectural data for Classic period Ohkay'owingeh are lacking, but due to the evidence of pairing from Tewa oral tradition it is reasonable to suggest it was of similar size to Yungeh. There is good reason to suggest that during the Classic period an additional cluster with characteristics of a Model 2 (sibling) alliance, and similar demographic scale to the Ku cluster, existed about 7 km downstream. That both the Ku and Yungeh clusters were of similar scale and composition suggests that clusters in the lower reaches of the Rio Chama were not as centralized as those farther upstream.

Tsiping

Except for Sapawe (and possibly Pesede), the only other isolated village community in the study area that persisted into the Classic period was Tsiping. With 500 rooms, 13 kivas, and 1 plaza, Tsiping is located 15.54 km from Poshu and 11.7 km from Abiquiu. This suggests that Tsiping was an isolated community, consistent with Model 1. Tsiping was established early, around 1200 CE, and was inhabited until about 1425 CE based on tree-ring dates and associated pottery (Duwe 2011).

An unusual feature of this village is its elevated and defensible location on top of a steep mesa at some distance from potential farmland. Another unusual feature is the presence of 13 small kivas, most of which are arranged in a row facing toward the west-northwest. The only other village with comparable numbers of kivas is Te'ewi, which was established around 1350 to 1400 CE and has a similar room count. It is tempting to suggest that Tsiping was a precursor to Te'ewi due to these similarities. Except for a single large kiva, the 12 kivas at Tsiping and the 12 from Te'ewi are similarly small, averaging 5.44 m and 6.98 m in diameter, respectively. The fact that Te'ewi was established just as Tsiping was abandoned is also suggestive. More data are needed to assess this potential connection.

DISTRIBUTIONS OF CIVIC FEATURES

One of the assumptions embedded in our analysis is that the floor area of a kiva is related to the size of the group that conducted activities in that space. Thus, one might expect there to be a relationship between the distributions of kiva areas and the types of groups that met in various sites. Figure 5.3, which displays the distribution of kiva areas across the Rio Chama sites, provides some support for this view. The chart shows that most of the kivas in these sites have floor areas of 50 m^2 or less. This is a suitable size for meetings of groups that make decisions by consensus. There is also a second size mode consisting of large kivas with floor areas of between 50 and 150 m^2. There is at least one of these at every site except for Pesede and the other suggested daughter villages, most of which appear to lack kivas all together. Such structures appear to be large enough to host rituals involving both participants and an audience, perhaps reflecting gatherings of ritual specialists analogous to historic Tewa "made people" (Ortiz 1969). Finally, there is a small group of very large kivas that have 150 to 350 m^2 of floor area. These occur only at Howiri, Hupobi, Pose, Sapawe, Tsama, and Ku. These are of comparable size to the great kivas of earlier sites of the San Juan drainage including those in Chaco Canyon and were likely used for ceremonies involving hundreds of people (Adler 1989; Lekson 1984). One possibility is that they were utilized for the preparations of dancers for plaza-based rituals. If so, it would suggest there was substantial ceremonial differentiation among villages, and that certain types of ceremonies only took place in certain sites.

Notice, however, that the numbers and distributions of very large kivas vary across settlement clusters. The Ponsipa-akeri cluster, which exhibits the clearest evidence of a two-tiered settlement hierarchy, does not have a very large kiva at all; but the Pose cluster, which exhibits the clearest evidence of alliance, has at least one very large kiva in each of its constituent sites. There is also one very large kiva at Sapawe, the single-site cluster, and at least two at Tsama and one at Ku. The latter two are potential mother villages that occur in clusters with characteristics of alliances as well. This is another line of evidence that suggests ritual organization in the Classic period Rio Chama varied substantially both within and among clusters.

Another assumption of our analysis is that plaza areas are related to the sizes of the groups that met in those spaces. As a result, one might expect mother villages to have had plaza spaces that could easily accommodate visitors from other sites. This could be judged in terms of the largest plaza area or the largest plaza-to-room ratio in a village. Many sites contain multiple plazas. This may simply reflect long-term aggregation processes, whereas a very large plaza space might suggest stronger village centralization and authority. The distribution of plaza areas across sites and clusters is presented in Figure 5.4. This figure shows that proposed mother villages generally have one or two plazas that are far larger than the others. The extreme size of the largest plaza at Sapawe stands out, as does the concentration of plaza area within a single plaza in the Ponsipa-akeri cluster, which we previously noted exhibits the strongest evidence for a two-tiered settlement

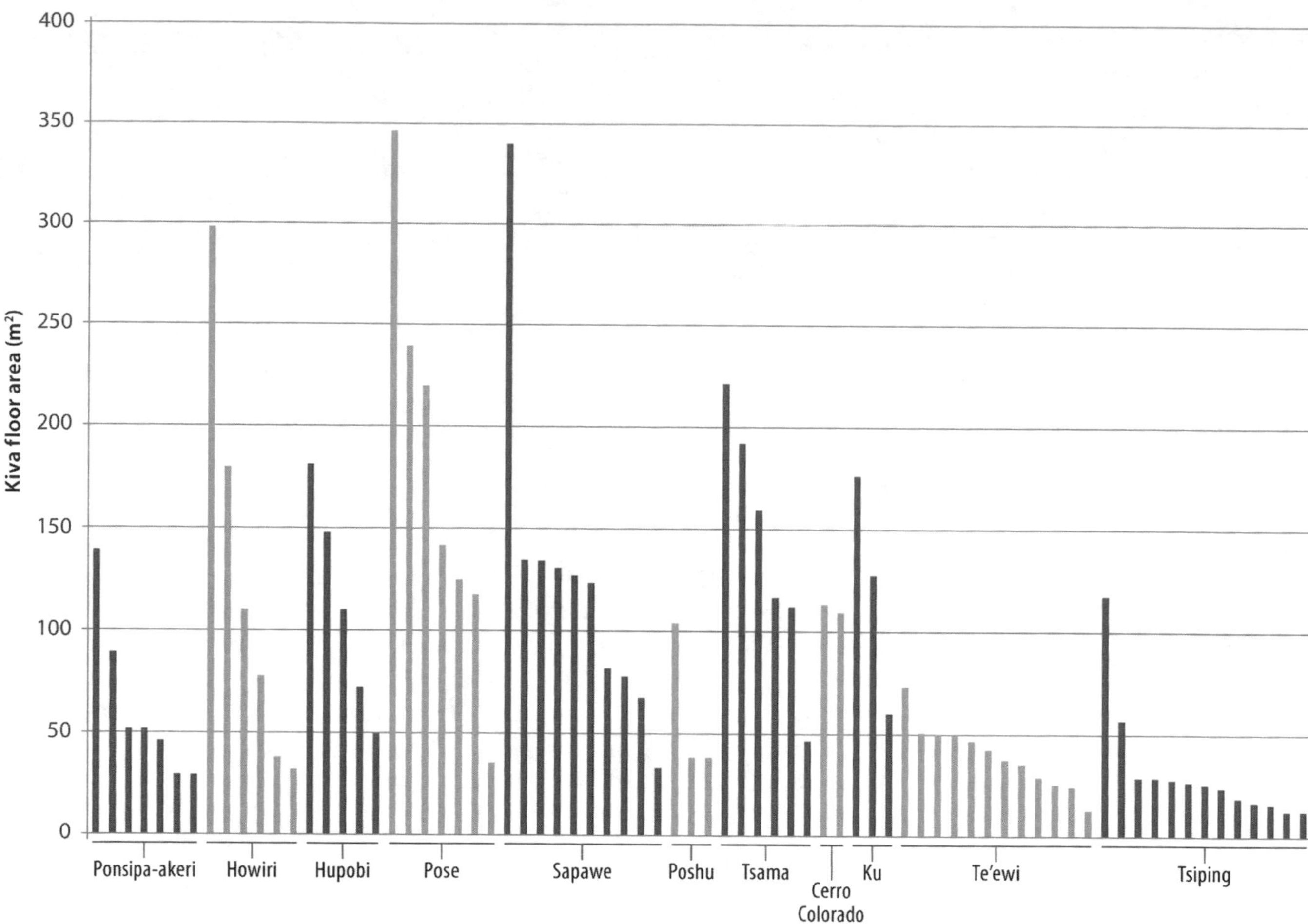

Figure 5.3. Distribution of kiva floor areas by site and cluster. Prepared by authors.

hierarchy. In addition, Poshu also has a very large plaza, which reinforces the suggestion that the Tsama cluster contains two mother-daughter village pairs (Tsama-Cerro Colorado and Poshu-Abiquiu).

The relationship between the number of rooms and the size of the largest plaza at various sites is also helpful for distinguishing potential mother villages. These data are presented in Figure 5.5. The most striking feature of this chart is just how large the largest plazas are relative to the sizes of the sites in which they occur. For example, if one assumes a conversion of one resident per room, the largest plazas at Sapawe and Tsama enclose about 10 square meters per resident, and the largest plaza at Poshu encloses about 15 square meters per resident. The plaza space per resident would be even larger if the architectural footprints of these sites were never completely occupied, as Anschuetz (2007) has suggested. This is far more space than was needed for the sizes of the dance groups and audiences that could have been generated by the residents of these sites. Also, it seems unlikely that a community would have set aside plaza spaces that far exceeded their actual needs due to the increased cost of walking and carrying things around town. These considerations suggest it is reasonable to assume that the entire architectural footprints of these sites were inhabited at some point. In addition, the exceptional size of the Sapawe plaza, a single-site cluster, suggests that this village hosted large numbers of visitors from adjacent settlement clusters. This scenario is not neatly captured by any of the three models (independence, sibling/confederacy, and mother-daughter) we consider in this chapter.

Finally, it is important to note that especially large plazas do occur in settings consistent with a mother-daughter village pattern (Tsama, Poshu and Ponsipa-akeri), but in the cluster most consistent with a sibling/confederacy pattern (Pose, Hupobi/Howiri) plaza space per resident is generally lower. The significance of this difference is unclear at this point, but it does suggest that certain communities put more effort into accommodating visitors

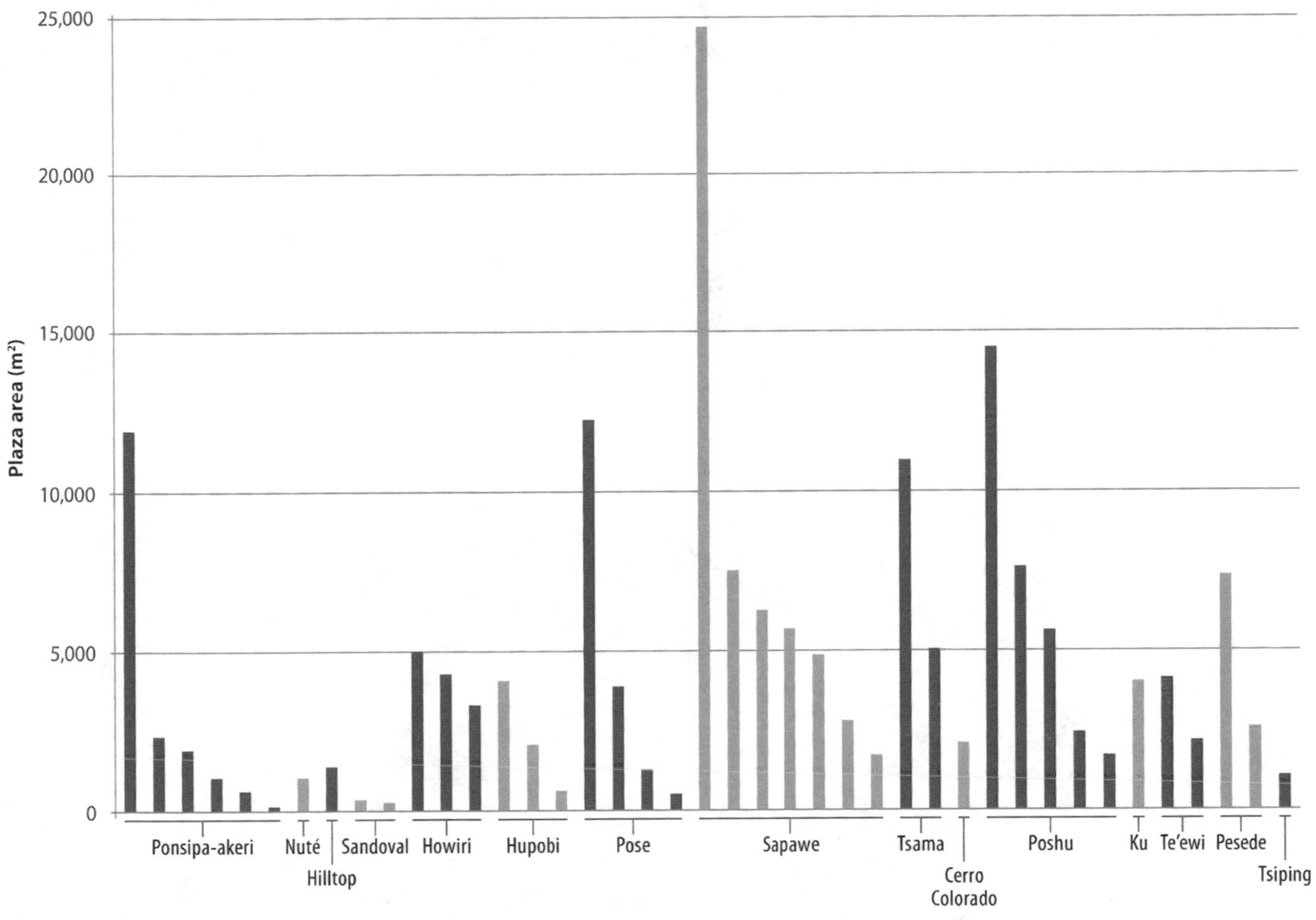

Figure 5.4. Distribution of plaza areas by site and cluster. Prepared by authors.

than others. Ortman and Coffey (Chapter 6) develop the hypothesis that plaza space was set aside in Protohistoric Northern Rio Grande pueblos to accommodate the entire social network of that settlement. This could account for much of the variation seen in Figure 5.5, but differences in the pattern of plaza space across clusters suggests there were additional factors specific to each community that structured the built environments of individual sites.

DISTANCES BETWEEN SETTLEMENT CLUSTERS

The final aspect of the sites that we consider in this chapter is the pattern of distances between clusters, as measured by the distances between proposed mother villages. Table 5.3 presents these data. If Poshu and Tsama were part of different clusters they would have had to have been allied because they are only 5.5 km apart, within the zone of shared resource access (see Table 5.2). Perhaps the organization of this part of the Rio Chama involved two allied mother villages, each of which had a daughter village. This would represent a combination of Models 2 and 3. Among the other clusters, the closest pairs are Ponsipa-akeri and Pose at 8.7 km, and Pose and Sapawe at 9.1 km, followed by Tsama and Sapawe at 12.4 km, Tsama and Ku at 13 km, Sapawe and Poshu at 14.2 km, and Tsama and Ponsipa-akeri at 15.4 km. These distances suggest that adjacent settlement clusters controlled their own territories from 5 to 7 km from their central settlements and were generally within a day's walk of each other. These patterns of distances in combination with patterns in plaza space indicate that residents of clusters generally maintained exclusive access to their surrounding lands, but also regularly hosted visitors from adjacent clusters to their central settlements for ceremonial events. Ortman and Coffey extend these ideas in Chapter 6.

Beyond this, the specific distances between settlement clusters probably relate to a variety of factors including the distribution of suitable building sites, the history and size

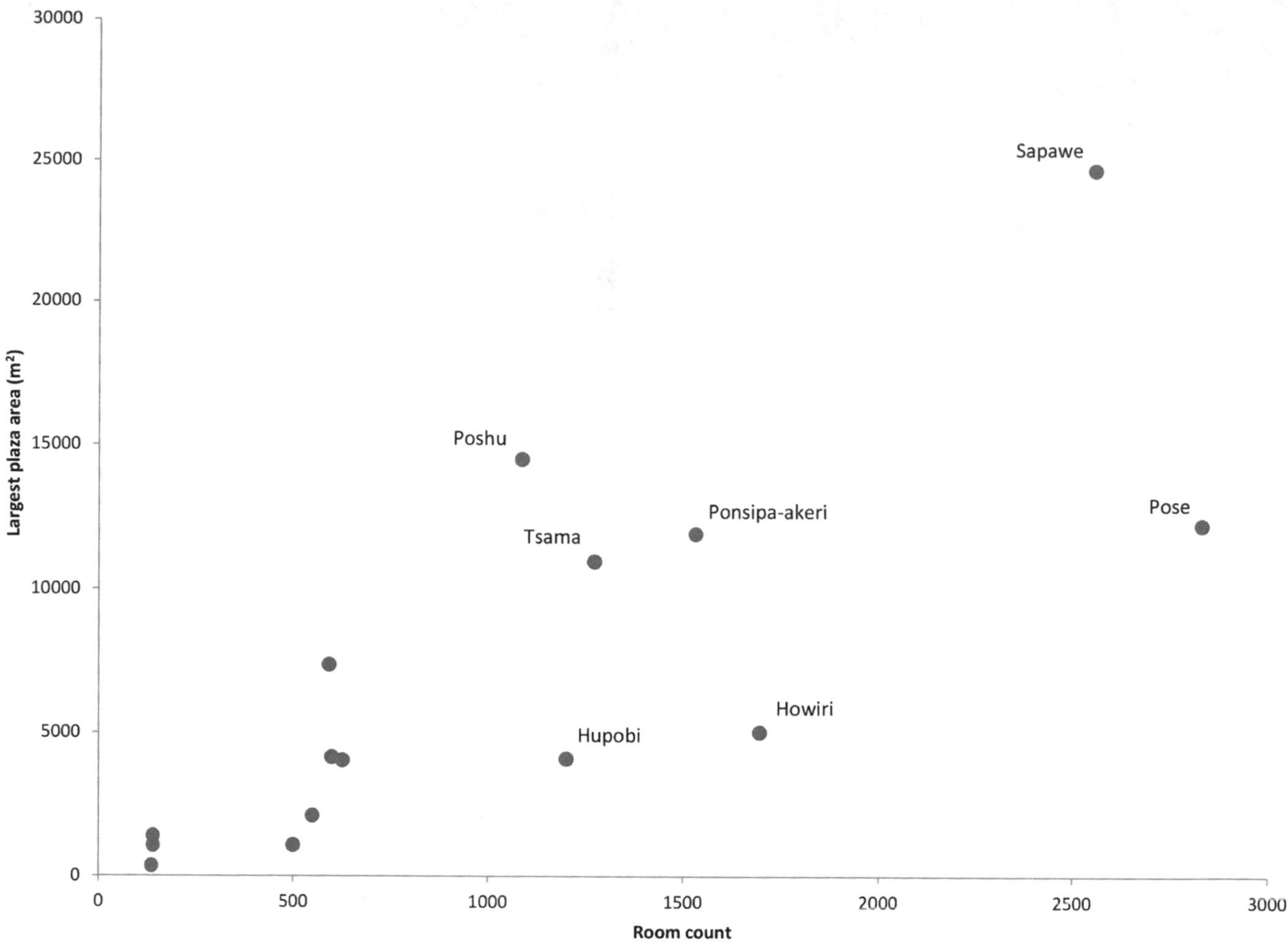

Figure 5.5. Relationship between site size and largest plaza area. Prepared by authors.

of adjacent settlements, and the distribution of irrigable land along watercourses. So, for example, the most likely reason the Pose and Sapawe clusters are so close, despite being the two most populous clusters, is that their centers are along watercourses that run parallel from north to south. In contrast, the Ponsipa-akeri and Ku clusters are farther apart, despite having smaller populations, because there is relatively little irrigable floodplain along the Rio Ojo Caliente below Ponsipa-akeri.

CONCLUSIONS

In this chapter we have examined data from Classic period ancestral Tewa settlements of the Rio Chama drainage to identify community clusters and assess the degree to which they reflect a specific form of social organization. First, we defined settlement clusters and potential mother villages based on the patterns of sizes and distances between sites along shared waterways. We found that room counts generally worked well for determining potential mother villages, and that villages established earlier in time tended to become the largest villages in each cluster. We also used Varien's (1999) ideas about community clusters to establish likely distances for differing levels of community social interaction. Distances of less than 2 km between villages likely represented a shared settlement; villages between 2 and 7 km apart likely were part of a shared larger community; and villages more than 7 km distant likely represented independent communities.

Kiva number and size was also relevant for examining intervillage relations. We initially proposed that the largest kivas would be in mother villages of community clusters, however, the three largest kivas in the region occur at Pose, Howiri, and Sapawe. Pose and Howiri appear to have been

Table 5.3. Distances (in kilometers) between Community Clusters

	Pose	*Ponsipa-akeri*	*Sapawe*	*Poshu*	*Tsama*	*Ku*
Pose	—	8.7	9.1	21.8	18.1	25.2
Ponsipa-akeri	8.7	—	13.5	20.7	15.4	18.4
Sapawe	9.1	13.5	—	14.2	12.4	23.4
Poshu	21.8	20.7	14.2	—	5.5	17.0
Tsama	18.1	15.4	12.4	5.5	—	13.0
Ku	25.1	18.4	23.4	17.0	13.0	—

allied sibling villages, while Sapawe was a single village. Thus, kiva size by itself may reflect village or cluster size more than community organization. We also found several cases where potential daughter villages lacked kivas (or at least evidence of kivas) all together. This is consistent with the notion that civic functions were localized in mother villages in at least some settlement clusters. This in turn is consistent with a two-tiered settlement hierarchy in these specific instances.

Primary plaza size and total plaza area were considered in our analysis. The primary pattern to emerge is that the relationship between room counts and total plaza area is highly variable and plaza area per room is often quite large. This pattern in combination with practical concerns suggests that the architectural footprints of these sites were fully inhabited at some point, and it suggests that plaza space was set aside to accommodate more than just the residents of a given village. Importantly, we found excess plaza space in villages associated with all three types of community organization we considered (isolated, sibling/alliance, and mother-daughter). This indicates that plaza space was involved in intercommunity relations, but that patterns of visitation among villages were somewhat independent of the suggested organization of a settlement cluster. Ortman and Coffey suggest a general interpretation of this pattern in Chapter 6.

The only settlement cluster that exhibits the full range of patterns expected under a hierarchical mother-daughter model is the Ponsipa cluster. This cluster contains a large and long-lived mother village surrounded by smaller and more recently established daughter villages at regular intervals of around 4 km. The largest plaza space, plaza-to-room ratio, and the largest kiva(s) are in the mother village. The Tsama cluster may also contain two sets of mother-daughter villages, but in this case the evidence is less clear, and this cluster could even reflect an alliance of two mother-daughter pairs (Tsama-Cerro Colorado and Poshu-Abiquiu). The Pose cluster exhibits the clearest evidence of a confederacy of sibling/allied villages, whereas Sapawe and Tsiping appear to represent isolated village communities. Finally, the Ku cluster exhibits evidence of all three forms of community organization considered here.

Overall, this analysis suggests that the social and political organization of settlement clusters varies from case to case. It appears that each settlement cluster pursued different strategies and levels of centralization and thus levels of authority. Perhaps these differences are due to the application of a common set of organizational principles rooted in family relationships to local areas with distinct histories. It may also be the case that community groups imported sociopolitical relationships from prior settlement locations as people moved into the Rio Chama drainage from elsewhere in the Northern Rio Grande or even from the Four Corners area. Although it appears likely that Tewa settlement clusters of the Classic Period Rio Chama shared some form of community identity due to close spatial proximity and its implications for land and resources, the type of integration that occurred among villages within clusters seems to have varied from hierarchical to confederate to independent. This suggests there is no single best model for interpreting the sociopolitical significance of settlement clustering in the Northern Rio Grande. Perhaps Pueblo ancestors developed an alternative form of integration for which we still lack the appropriate models.

One conclusion that is clear from this analysis, however, is that the increasing size of Rio Chama communities during the Classic period was not associated with the emergence of coercive sociopolitical institutions. Of the three models of settlement clustering considered here, only the mother-daughter village model, which implies a two-tiered settlement hierarchy, could possibly be construed as a reflection of coercive sociopolitical institutions. The only cluster that fits this model to a reasonable extent is the Ponsipa cluster. Yet, collectively, there are fewer than 2,000 rooms across all the sites in the Ponsipa cluster, and this total is less than the number of rooms at other villages such as Sapawe and Pose, or between pairs of potential sibling villages such as Hupobi and Howiri, and Tsama and Poshu. So even if the organization of the Ponsipa cluster was more hierarchical than the others, it was far from the largest agglomeration of people in the Rio Chama.

In the introductory chapter of this volume, Ortman and Davis suggest that one of the fundamental drivers of socioeconomic development in the Northern Rio Grande was the spatial clustering of population in settlements. Our analysis has provided no evidence that the ultimate sizes of ancestral Tewa communities in the Rio Chama were driven by the emergence of coercive sociopolitical institutions. Thus, if socioeconomic development occurred in the ancestral Tewa world, it seems clear that it occurred in a context where sociopolitical institutions promoted cooperative economic relations within and between communities as opposed to hierarchical relations. In this way, the economic history of the Tewa pueblos appears to provide a model for socioeconomic development that is more consistent with the values and aspirations of contemporary Americans than is true for many other ancient societies known through archaeology.

CHAPTER SIX

The Network Effects of Rio Grande Pueblo Rituals

Scott G. Ortman and Grant L. Coffey

The plaza-based public rituals of the Northern Rio Grande Pueblos are well-known to both anthropologists and tourists (Ford 1972; Kurath and Garcia 1970; Sweet 2004). For visitors, the obvious aspects of these rituals include community members who dance in unison wearing rich regalia, drummers and singers who provide musical accompaniment, an audience of community members and visitors who encircle the dancers around the edges of the plazas, meals or gifts of food for community members and visitors, and vendors who sell traditional craft items. For community members, the ostensible purposes of these events include promoting an abundance of crops and game animals, celebrating natural and agricultural cycles, and commemorating the patron saint of the Pueblo. In the process, they also promote community solidarity, strengthen social relationships, support the maintenance of tradition, attract a lot of visitors, and, most importantly for this chapter, stimulate flows of food, goods, and services among those who attend.

Today, the most widely attended dance in the annual ceremonial calendar of a pueblo is the one that takes place on the feast day of the patron saint of the community (Parsons 1939). Although the origin of these patron saint feast days is murky, what is not as often appreciated is that most traditional dances of the Northern Rio Grande pueblos include all the elements of the feast day (minus the presiding *santo*) including asynchronous timing across villages (Ford 1972b). Archaeologists have also argued that ceremonial feasting associated with plaza-based ceremonies was a stimulus to specialization and exchange in the Rio Grande region during Protohistoric times (Graves and Spielmann 2000; Spielmann 2002). In this chapter, we extend these arguments in suggesting that "feast-day-type" ceremonialism developed in Prehispanic times and was an important driver of the substantial increases in community size, specialization, economic integration, and living standards that Ortman and Davis note in their introduction to this volume.

We build this argument by considering the relationship between settlement population, location, and plaza space in light of an emerging perspective known as *settlement scaling theory*. This perspective argues that human settlements generally function as *social reactors*, concentrating human interactions, and their outcomes, in space and time (Bettencourt 2013, 2014; Ortman and Coffey 2017). It also proposes that this process leads to predictable and measurable patterns in the archaeological record and provides an explanation for emergent properties of human settlements in many contexts (Ortman and others 2014; Ortman and others 2015; Ortman, Davis, Lobo, Smith, and Cabaniss 2016). Important to this framework are mathematical models that derive expected quantitative relationships between settlement population, infrastructure needs, and socioeconomic rates from fundamental processes of movement and interaction. These processes are always present, but the ways in which they are harnessed by societies to meet human needs can and do vary. Here, we show that feast-day-type ceremonies reflect a distinctive form of social networking that leads to unusual, but still predictable, patterns in the archaeological record.

RELATIONSHIPS BETWEEN PEOPLE AND PLAZAS

One can imagine a variety of ways of building a pueblo, and one might expect these different approaches to yield different relationships between people and plaza space across settlements. In the following paragraphs we develop four scenarios that lead to differing expectations regarding this relationship. Obviously, a wide variety of factors conditioned the amount of plaza space that was set aside in any specific village. What these various models do is propose which factors mattered most in this process, spelling out what effect these would have for the overall relationship between people and plaza space in Pueblo built environments.

Scenario 1: Geometry. The first and simplest scenario is one in which plaza space is simply a byproduct of the arrangement of houses around a central square. If all houses face inward and are arranged around the perimeter, the plaza area will be proportional to the square of the number of houses. Since the number of houses and the population will also be proportional to the number of rooms in the pueblo, this relationship can be expressed simply as

$$A_p = \left(l_r \frac{N}{2_p}\right)^2, \tag{1}$$

where A_p is the total plaza area, N the settlement population, p is the number of plazas in the pueblo, and l_r is the length of plaza frontage per capita. In this scenario, there is no intention to set aside plaza space for any particular reason. The amount of plaza space is simply a function of geometry relative to the number of houses arranged around plaza perimeters. Equation 1 suggests the total plaza area in a pueblo would be proportional to $(N / 2p)^2$. One might, however, expect the exponent to decrease as the fraction of houses that do not face any plaza increases.

Scenario 2: Social Mixing. The second scenario is one in which plaza space represents the area through which community members move to interact with each other. In this case, one would expect the spatial arrangement of houses in a pueblo to reflect a balance between the costs of moving around and the benefits of interacting with other community members. This scenario corresponds to the *amorphous settlement model* discussed by Ortman and colleagues (Ortman and others 2014; Ortman and others 2015; Ortman, Davis, Lobo, Smith, and Cabaniss 2016). The average cost for a person to interact with others is set by the distance L across the circumscribing area of the settlement A_s and is given by $c = \varepsilon L = \varepsilon A_s^{1/2}$ (where ε is the energetic cost of movement); and the benefit of the resulting interactions is given by $y = \hat{g} a_0 l N / A_s$ (where $\hat{g}$ is the average productivity of an interaction, a_0 is the interaction distance, l is the average daily path length of an individual, and N / A_s is the population density of the settlement). If one assumes a spatial equilibrium, one can set costs equal to benefits, $c = y$, and thus arrive at

$$A_s(N) = (G/\varepsilon)^{\alpha} N^{\alpha}, \tag{2}$$

where $G = \hat{g} a_0 l$ and $a = 2/3$. Because $(G / \varepsilon)^a$ is a constant in any given context, Equation 2 implies that, if pueblo built-environments developed primarily to facilitate social mixing of the residents, the total area of a pueblo, and thus the total plaza area, would grow more slowly than the resident population. As a result, as settlements grow, houses would get closer together, there would be less plaza space per capita, and plaza space would be used more intensively for travel between houses.

Scenario 3: Accommodating Residents. The third scenario builds from two observations regarding plaza-based ceremonies. First, the primary activities that take place during these ceremonies occur in plazas. Second, during ceremonies plazas function more as theatres containing performers and spectators than as a means of moving between houses (Kurath and Garcia 1970; Ortiz 1972). Given this, a Pueblo would need to set aside enough plaza space to accommodate the resident population as performers and spectators during community rituals. Because in this scenario individuals need to fit in the plazas but not necessarily move independently through them, one would expect the total plaza area to be proportional to the resident population. This can be written as

$$A_p = p_0 N^{\beta}, \tag{3}$$

where p_0 is the plaza space per capita and $\beta \approx 1$. In this scenario, plaza space is itself a proxy for the resident population of a community.

Scenario 4: Accommodating Social Connections. The final scenario incorporates one additional observation. Today, feast-day-type ceremonies typically bring together the entire social network of a pueblo, not just its residents. As a result, a community that hosts such dances would have an incentive to set aside enough plaza space for the entire group to gather simultaneously. One would expect the size of this group to have been somewhat larger than the resident population, but how much larger?

We answer this question by considering the number of social contacts the average individual in a Pueblo community would have had with others in the surrounding area. We first assume that the number of neighbors N_n within a given radius of a person's home community was distributed evenly across that area, and that the average individual moved through this area along a path of length l, coming into contact with others within a given distance a_0 along this path. We do not mean to suggest that individuals move randomly with respect to their local environments, only that there are limits on how far a person can move and people must get close to each other for face-to-face interaction to occur. These simplifications are obviously not true in detail, but it is reasonable to assume the local details average out when one considers the aggregate properties of localized social networks across a settlement system. Under these conditions, the average number of social contacts k made by an individual with people from neighboring communities per unit time would be given by

$$k = a_0 l (N_n/A_n), \tag{4}$$

and the total number of contacts made by the overall population of the settlement, N_s, would be

$$K_s = kN_s = a_0 l (N_s N_n/A_n). \tag{5}$$

In addition, the total number of social ties K_s maintained by a community of size N_s can be estimated, following Bettencourt (2014), as

$$K_s = k_0 N_s^{1+\delta}, \tag{6}$$

where k_0 is the baseline social connectivity and $1/3 \geq \delta \geq 1/6$, depending on the degree to which paths across the local environment are straight or circuitous. The range of potential values for δ derives from models of spatial organization for settlements, including the amorphous settlement model (scenario 2) discussed above, in which individuals arrange themselves in space so as to balance interaction benefits with movement costs (Ortman and others 2014). Equations 5 and 6 can be used to test whether Classic period Rio Grande Pueblo populations were actually arranged spatially to facilitate social mixing at the level of local neighborhoods.

As an aside, it is interesting to note that Equation 6 can also be derived from traditional gravity models by considering the effects of distance for the number of social contacts that can be sustained by a population over a given area (Plog 1976). The gravity model proposes that the total number of interactions between two locations per unit time is given by $I \propto N_1 * N_2/d^2$, where d is the distance between the two locations N_1 and N_2 and are their respective populations. This relation can be rewritten in terms of a single population over an area as $I \propto N * N/A \propto N^2 / A$. Since it is also typical that the area needed for N to make a living increases with $A \propto N^{1-\delta}$ (see Ortman and others 2014), we can simplify this relation further by writing $I \propto N^2 / N^{1-\delta} \propto N^{1+\delta}$. Thus, Equation 6 builds from and is consistent with existing approaches to measuring social interaction in geography and other fields.

How many people were connected in the social network of a pueblo? One would expect this number, and thus the total number of people N_t who attended feast-day-type ceremonies at that village, to have been greater than N_s. We begin by noting that the combination of Equations 5 and 6:

$$(k_0/a_0 l) N_s^{\delta} = (N_n/A_n), \tag{7}$$

implies that the population density surrounding a pueblo is on average proportional to the population of the central settlement raised to the δ power. In other words, a pueblo that hosted plaza-based ceremonies exerted an attractive force on the surrounding population that was proportional to N_s^{δ}.

Next, we assume that, because human effort is bounded, the distance over which regular social contacts are maintained is essentially constant and is limited to the daily commute distance to and from a given pueblo. In cross-cultural studies of pedestrian societies, this distance is about 15 km (Varien 1999). This assumption resolves A_n in Equation 7 into a constant, with the result that the population density of the neighborhood centered on a pueblo becomes proportional to the population of the central settlement raised to the δ power. Because N_s people lived in the settlement itself, the number of neighbors who attended feast-day-type ceremonies in this scenario is given by $N_n = n_0 N_s^{\delta}$, with n_0 a constant of proportionality representing a baseline level of visitation. The total number of attendees would therefore be

$$N_t = N_s + N_n = N_s + n_0 N_s^{\delta} = n_0 N_s^{1+\delta}. \tag{8}$$

Now, we once again incorporate the observation from Scenario 3 that plaza-based ceremonies use plazas as theatres in which performers and spectators gather. Given this, we once again assume that community planners sought to set aside a constant amount of plaza space per participant in these ceremonies, and that the amount of space that was set aside was adjusted as the community population changed over time. Accordingly, we can write

$$A_p = p_0 N_t = p_0 n_0 {N_s}^{1+\delta}, \tag{9}$$

indicating that both plaza area and the total number of participants should scale with the same exponent as the total social contacts of community residents. Finally, we can derive an expectation for the relationship between local connectivity and plaza space by combining Equations 6 and 9:

$$A_p = \frac{p_0 n_0}{k_0} {K_s}^{\gamma}, \text{ where } \gamma \approx 1. \tag{10}$$

Equation 10 indicates that the total plaza space in a pueblo that hosts feast-day-type ceremonies should be proportional to the total social connections maintained by the residents.

The four scenarios developed above lead to distinct expectations regarding the average quantitative relationship between room counts, plaza space, and neighborhood population density across Pueblo settlements. In Scenario 1, simple geometry is the driving force and one would expect plaza space to be proportional to the square of the number of residents divided by the number of plazas times two. In Scenario 2, social mixing of community residents is the driving force, and one would expect plaza space to grow proportionately to the resident population raised to the 2/3 power. In Scenario 3, accommodating community residents as performers and spectators is the driving force, and one would expect plaza space to increase with the resident population in a strictly linear fashion, which is to say, with an exponent of one. Finally, in Scenario 4, accommodating the social network of the community is the driving force, and one would expect plaza space to increase faster than the resident population, with an exponent between 7/6 and 4/3. In this last scenario, one would also expect villages to form spatial clusters due to the attractive force exerted by the population of each settlement across its neighborhood.

DATA AND ANALYSIS

We evaluate these expectations using information for Northern Rio Grande Pueblo settlements within the Village Ecodynamics Project's New Mexico study area (Ortman 2016b), as well as settlements in the Pecos Valley, Galisteo Basin, and Santo Domingo Basin (Figure 6.1). We used pottery, tree-ring dates (when available), and assessments in the literature to assign sites to one of two time periods: 1280 to 1450 CE and 1450 to 1600 CE. The earlier period corresponds to the Late Coalition through Early Classic periods, and the later period to the Middle and Late Classic periods. The latter period is sometimes referred to as the Protohistoric period. We set our break point at 1450 CE so that we could distinguish patterns during the period of most marked economic development from those of earlier periods (Snow 1981; Wilcox 1981). We estimated room counts from house-mound areas and heights using methods devised by Duwe and others (2016), and we assumed that resident populations are proportional to room counts based on the correspondence between roofed space per capita in vernacular architecture and the average size of pueblo rooms (Brown 1987).

We also measured the areas of all plaza spaces for all settlements for which we could obtain a scaled plan map of the architecture. For many sites, the only maps available are the ones created by H. P Mera and archived at the Laboratory of Anthropology. For these maps, we used Duwe's (2008) conversions to translate from feet to meters (feet × .3048), and to convert Mera's pace to meters (paces × .96). We also worked with maps created by Duwe (2011) for sites in the Chama Valley; Marshall and Walt (2007) for the Santa Cruz and Truchas drainages; Nels Nelson and others for sites the Galisteo Basin (Barnett 1969; Nelson 1914; Toll and Badner 2008); and a variety of authors for sites on the Pajarito Plateau (Hewett 1906; Kohler, editor, 2004; Powers and Orcutt, editors, 1999; Steen 1977, 1982; Trierweiler 1990; Vierra, Nordby, and Martinez 2003), the Pecos Valley (Cordell 1998; Head and Orcutt 2002; Kidder 1958), and elsewhere (Creamer 1993; Snead 2008; Stubbs and Stallings 1953; Wendorf 1953). It is important to emphasize that the population estimates we utilize reflect an assumption that the entire architectural footprint of a pueblo was inhabited at some point during the period to which the site is dated. Thus, they reflect the maximum momentary population of each site. We recognize that some researchers might object to this assumption but feel it is appropriate because we are examining the total plaza space in these settlements, which is in turn defined by the total architectural footprint and thus its peak potential population.

Any open space that was defined by house mounds or enclosing walls on three or four sides was considered a plaza, and for all such spaces we measured the area enclosed by these features in square meters. In addition, we considered spaces defined by house mounds on two sides as plazas when it appeared that the houses around the perimeter faced into that space. In these cases, we measured the rectilinear area defined by the extent of the rooms along the length and width of the defined space. When one or more rooms or kivas occurred inside a plaza, we subtracted the floor area of those buildings from the

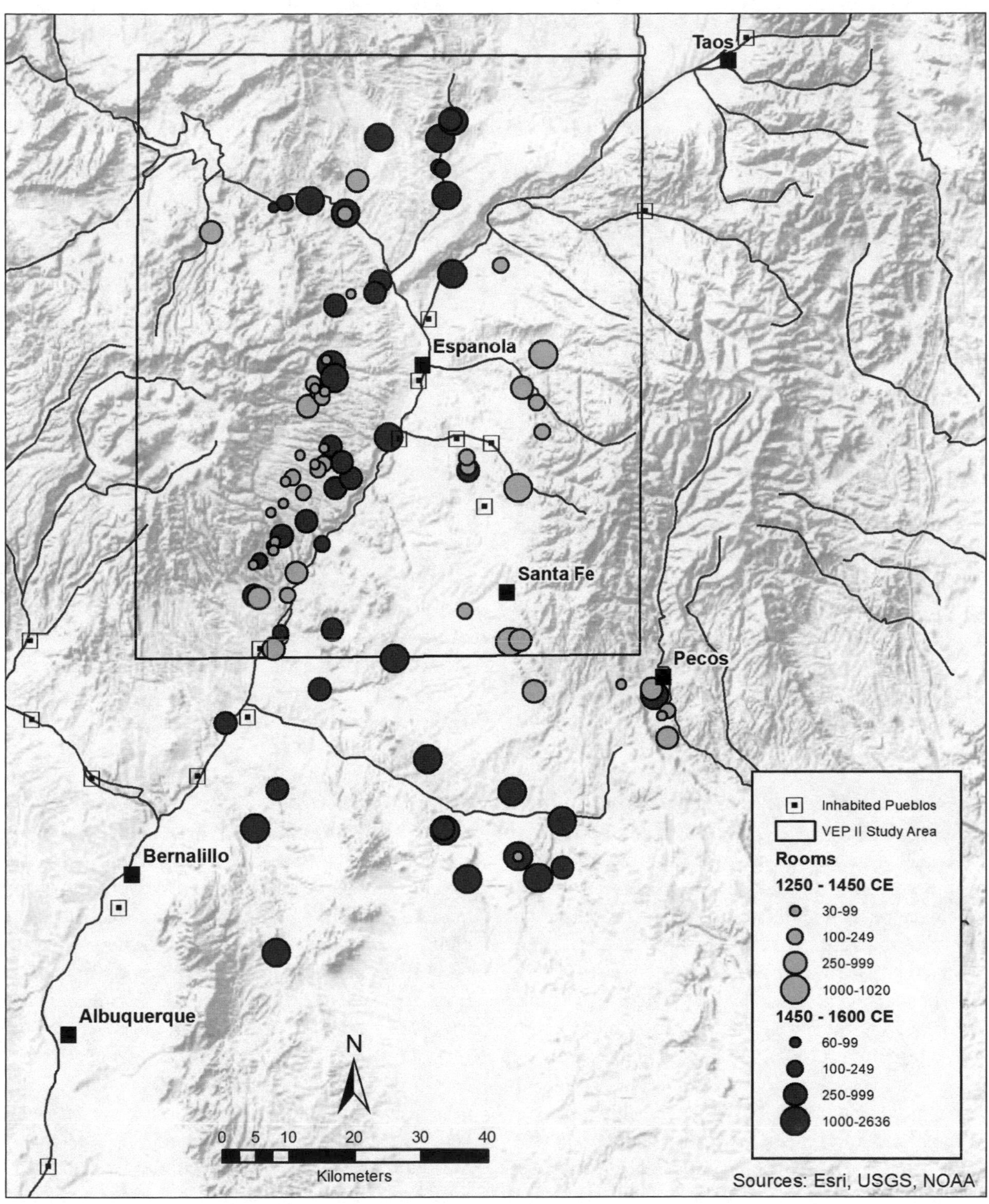

Figure 6.1. Distribution of sites with measured plazas included in the analysis. Prepared by authors.

Table 6.1. Relationship between *N/2p* and Plaza Area through Time

Time Period	1250 to 1450 CE	1450 to 1600 CE
Sample Size	47	47
Pre-factor (95% C.I.)	21.63 (4.53 – 103.22)	1260.75 (102.44 – 15516.4)
Exponent (95% C.I.)	.86 (.48 – 1.24)	.38 (-.14 – .91)
r^2	.30	.04*

Note: *This regression is not significant ($P = .16$).

total area to calculate the net open space within that plaza. In all, we measured plaza areas for 47 sites dating to each of the two time periods.

Finally, we estimated the population of the neighborhood surrounding each site for which we have plaza measurements by adding up the rooms at all sites that: (1) contained 50 or more rooms; (2) were inhabited during the period in question; and (3) were within 15 kilometers of the subject site based on Euclidean distances calculated from UTM coordinates. This analysis involved a total of 94 sites dating from 1250 to 1450 CE and 96 sites dating from 1450 to 1600 CE. Here again, we used room counts, and thus maximum momentary population estimates, in these calculations. It is unlikely that all sites in a neighborhood were fully-occupied at any given moment, but so long as one can characterize the fraction of inhabited rooms across neighborhoods as having a mean and standard deviation this issue should only affect the residuals of the relationship between settlements and neighborhoods. (The resulting dataset is available at: https://core.tdar.org/project/392021/social-reactors-project-datasets.)

We evaluate relationships among these measures of settlement population, plaza area, and neighborhood population density through ordinary least-squares (OLS) regression of the log-transformed data. This is feasible because $Y = aX^{\beta}$ and $\log Y = \beta \log X + \log a$ are equivalent. OLS regression of the log-transformed data provides estimates and standard errors for the prefactors (intercepts) and exponents (slopes) of the relationship between the two compared variables. This allows us to assess the degree to which Rio Grande Pueblo built environments are consistent with the expectations of each of the previously discussed scenarios.

RESULTS

Table 6.1 presents regression results for the relationship between $N/2p$ and A_P for settlements dating to each of the two time periods. These results clearly show that Scenario 1 (geometry) was not the driving force behind plaza space in the Northern Rio Grande Pueblos. If it were, one would expect the exponent of the relationship between these two measures to be about two. In neither case does the 95 percent confidence interval for the estimated exponent even come close, and in the case of the later period there is no significant relationship between the two measures at all.

Table 6.2 presents regression results for the relationship between resident population and plaza space during each period. These analyses are also presented visually in Figure 6.2. These results are more interesting. First, they show that these data do not correspond with Scenario 2 (social mixing) because the 95 percent confidence interval for the exponent of this relationship does not include 2/3 during either period. Second, they suggest that Scenario 3 (accommodating residents) is a plausible explanation for the relationship between population and plaza space in settlements dating prior to 1450 CE. The estimated exponent for this relationship is very close to one, and the 95 percent confidence interval of this estimate comfortably includes one. This result suggests Pueblo settlements inhabited between 1250 and 1450 CE developed in such a way that they contained a consistent amount of plaza space per resident. This is, in turn, consistent with the use of these plazas as theaters for ceremonies that involved the community residents as dancers and spectators. Notice also that the pre-factor (intercept) of this relationship suggests these plazas contained 3.59m^2 of space per resident. This is consistent with the notion that plaza space was set aside to accommodate community residents, as dancers and spectators, during ceremonies. This is inherently plausible given the measurement technologies available to Pueblo leaders, and the formations and movements that characterize Pueblo dances still today.

Third, Table 6.2 suggests Scenario 4 (accommodating social connections) is the most likely scenario for the use of plazas during the 1450 to 1600 CE period. The

Table 6.2. Relationship between Population and Plaza Area through Time

Time Period	1250 to 1450 CE	1450 to 1600 CE
Sample Size	47	47
Pre-factor (95% C.I.)	3.59 (1.06 – 12.18)	2.51 (.57 – 11.07)
Exponent (95% C.I.)	1.04 (.80 – 1.28)	1.23 (1.01 – 1.46)
r^2	.62	.72

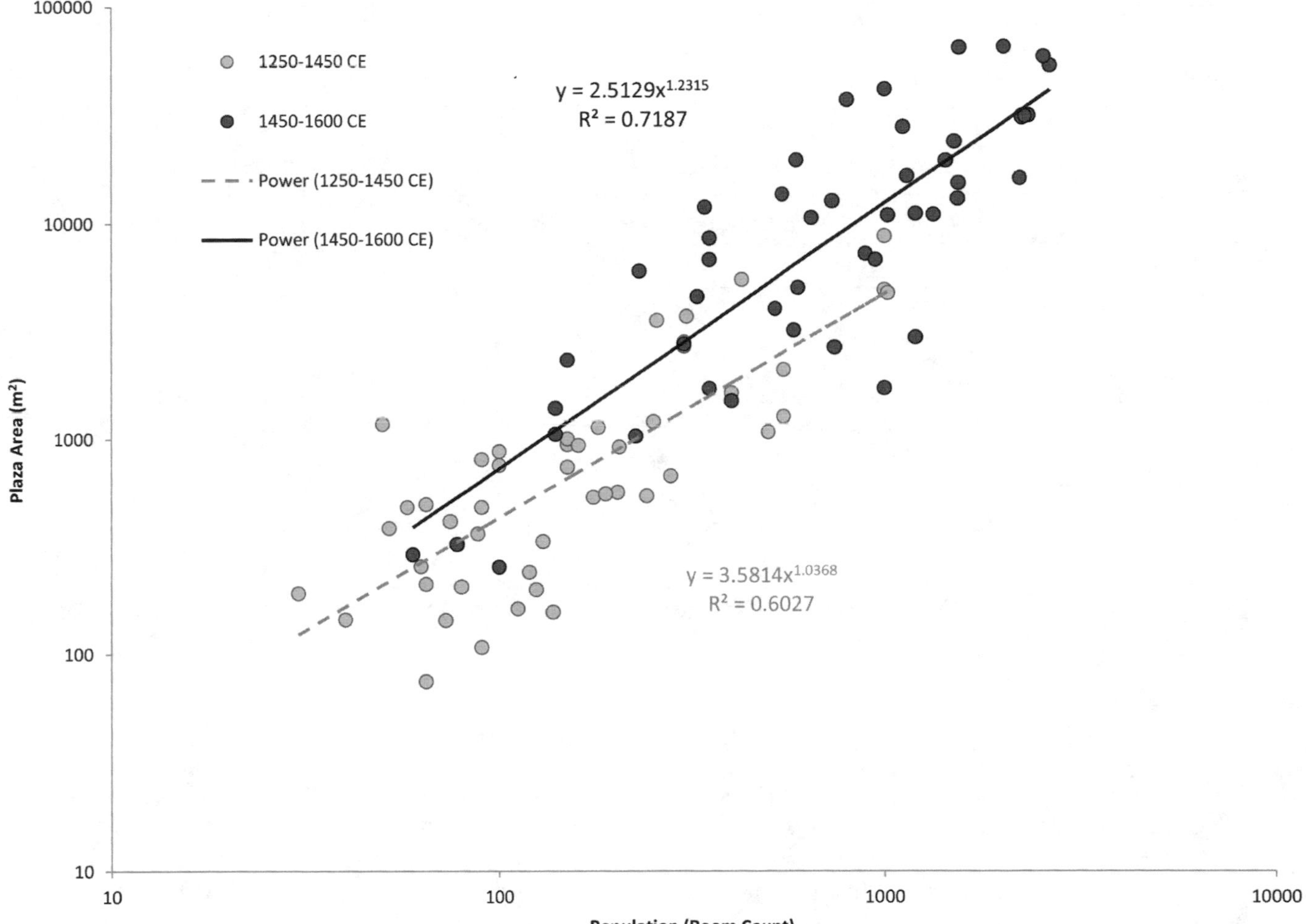

Figure 6.2. Relationship between population (room count) and plaza area for two time periods. Prepared by authors.

exponent for the average relationship between resident population and plaza space is larger than one, and the 95 percent confidence interval for this estimate also does not include one. The estimated value of this exponent (1.23) falls comfortably between 7/6 and 4/3 and is thus consistent with the expectation that $7/6 \leq 1 + \delta \leq 4/3$. This result suggests Northern Rio Grande Pueblo settlements inhabited between 1450 and 1600 developed in such a way that plaza space was set aside to accommodate the entire social network of the community. This in turn suggests that "feast-day-type" ceremonies like those that occur today took place regularly in these communities. Notice also that the pre-factor of this relationship implies that each person who participated in a ceremony only had about

Table 6.3. Relationships between Population, Connectivity, and Plaza Area, 1250 to 1450 CE

Analysis	*Population vs. Connectivity*	*Population vs. Neighbors*	*Connectivity vs. Plaza Area*
Sample Size	47	47	47
Prefactor	$k_0 = 20.1$	$n_0 = 14207$	$\frac{p_0 n_0}{k_0} = 108.75$
(95% C.I.)	(4.07 – 99.04)	(2883 – 70012)	(16.11 – 734.32)
Exponent	$1 + \delta = .672$	$\delta = -.328$	$\gamma = .288$
(95% C.I.)	(.360 – .983)	(–.640 – –.017)	(–.007 – .582)
r^2	.28	.08	.08*

Note: *This regression is not significant (*P*=.062).

Table 6.4. Relationships between Population, Connectivity, and Plaza Area, 1450 to 1600 CE

*Analysis**	*Population vs. Connectivity*	*Population vs. Neighbors*	*Connectivity vs. Plaza Area*
Sample Size	40	40	40
Prefactor	$k_0 = 3.52$	$n_0 = 2487$	$\frac{p_0 n_0}{k_0} = 1.52$**
(95% C.I.)	(1.83 – 6.76)	(1295 – 4776)	(.237 – 9.70)
Exponent	$1 + \delta = 1.15$	$\delta = .153$	$\gamma = .962$
(95% C.I.)	(.1.05 – 1.25)	(0.53 – .252)	(.751 – 1.17)
r^2	.93	.19	.68

Notes:

*For these analyses we excluded: (a) sites in the Santo Domingo Basin due to incomplete survey data for this district and (b) Pecos Pueblo due to the lack of an archaeological signature for the number of Plains people who regularly visited this site.

**The value of this parameter based on the pre-factors from other analyses is 2.5.

2.5 m^2 of space within a plaza on average. This smaller area may reflect the fact that spectators do not require as much space as dancers and, as community populations increased, the ratio of dancers to spectators would decrease, thus reducing the average area needed per participant.

Tables 6.3 and 6.4 add further support to Scenario 4 by comparing relationships between settlement population, neighborhood density, and plaza space during each period. In these analyses, the number of *neighbors* is the total number of rooms in settlements containing at least 50 rooms that are within 15 km of the central site and *connectivity* is measured by dividing the product of residents and neighbors by the area of a circle with a 15km radius. Table 6.3 presents the analysis for the 1250 to 1450 CE period. The results are inconsistent with Scenario 4, as expected given the relationship between population and plaza space noted above for this period. The exponent of the relationship between population and connectivity is less than one, and the 95 percent confidence interval for this estimate does not include one. Also, the exponent for the relationship between population and neighborhood density is negative, and the 95 percent confidence interval for this estimate does not include zero. Finally, there is no significant relationship between social connections and plaza area across settlements dating prior to 1450 CE. These results indicate that as Pueblo settlements grew between 1250 and 1450 CE, the population density of the surrounding neighborhoods actually declined, such that residents had fewer social connections with neighbors on average. This is the kind of settlement pattern one would expect in an economy where communities were self-sufficient in energetic terms. In this scenario the economy of each community would have been redundant. As a result, larger settlements would need larger hinterlands, and this would have the effect of pushing neighboring villages away.

Table 6.4 shows that the situation after 1450 CE was quite different. We believe these differences can be traced to the development of feast-day-type ceremonies. These results show, first, that during this period the population density of the neighborhood surrounding Pueblo settlements increased as the population of the central site grew larger. Consistent with Scenario 4, the exponent (elasticity) of this increase is close to 1/6, and the 95 percent confidence interval for this estimate comfortably includes 1/6. As a result, social connectivity also increased faster than settlement population. Third, Table 6.4 shows that plaza area is proportional to social connectivity across these sites, as specified by Equation 10. The exponent of this relationship is not appreciably different from one and is therefore consistent the expectation of Scenario 4 that plaza space would be set aside proportionately to the entire social network of a community when that community hosted feast-day-type ceremonies on a regular basis.

Finally, it is important to note that the estimated pre-factor for the post-1450 connectivity vs. plaza area relation is reasonably close to the value one obtains by combining the individual pre-factors p_0, n_0, and k_0 in accordance with Equation 10. From these analyses we have

$$\frac{p_0 n_0}{k_0} = 2.51m^2 * \frac{2487\,neighbors}{706.8km^2} \;/\; 3.52\ connections = 2.5,$$

which is of similar magnitude to the value (1.52) derived from the relationship between plaza area and connectivity. The fact that these results are internally-consistent across analyses increases our confidence that Scenario 4 captures fundamental socio-economic implications of feast-day-type ceremonies, and it strengthens our conclusion that Pueblo communities of the 1450 to 1600 period developed in ways that facilitated this type of ceremonial system.

DISCUSSION

In many ways these results are quite surprising. First, there are likely errors in every measurement we worked with, from room counts and populations to plaza counts, plaza areas, and neighborhood population densities. We have also maintained only coarse chronological control and there is no reason to believe that all the rooms dating to a given period were inhabited simultaneously. In addition, there were surely a variety of local factors that influenced the amount of plaza space at each settlement, and our analysis of neighborhood population densities is based solely on straight line distances. That fact that a series of integrated patterns consistent with Scenarios 3 and 4 should emerge from these data, given all these shortcomings, suggests that these errors are unstructured, and that the social forces that generated these patterns were quite strong. In other words, the fact that we can obtain quantitative results that are consistent with expectations when measured on average across the system suggests the models we work with capture the factors that mattered most in structuring Pueblo-built environments over time. There must have been a variety of additional factors that structured the specific relationship between people and plazas at individual sites, but these are captured by the residuals from the average scaling relationship and would seem to be secondary to the factors incorporated into Scenarios 3 and 4.

Second, Scenario 4 involves a series of models derived from first principles that lead to expectations regarding not just the functional form of relationships among population, plaza space, and neighborhood connectivity but the specific values of the parameters of these relationships. It is not self-evident that these parameters should have any particular values, but that is what emerges from the modeling exercise, and it is what the empirically-derived estimates of these values turn out to be (within the range of statistical tolerance). That such exercises in reductionism can lead to specific and nontrivial numerical expectations that are amenable to empirical testing is exciting. Indeed, the exercise suggests that complex systems approaches have real potential for building a quantitative and predictive theory of the structure, function, and evolution of human societies overall.

Third, it is important to emphasize that the relationships between population and area identified in this study are different from patterns that have been observed for many other societies. For example, the relationship between settlement population and area has been investigated for a wide range of societies, including contemporary metropolitan areas in the United States and Sweden, medieval European cities, Roman cities, Prehispanic settlements in the Central Andes and Basin of Mexico, and Native American villages of the Middle Missouri and Mesa Verde regions (Bettencourt 2013; Nordbeck 1971; Cesaretti and others 2016; Hanson and Ortman 2017; Ortman, Davis, Lobo, Smith, and Cabaniss 2016; Ortman and others 2014; Ortman and others 2015; Ortman and Coffey 2017). In all these cases, settled area increases more slowly than population, with an exponent between 2/3 and 5/6, such that settlements generally grow denser as they increase in population. The results presented here, in contrast, indicate that Northern Rio Grande Pueblo settlements had roughly constant population density between 1250 and 1450 CE, and *decreasing* density between 1450 and 1600 CE. Although these relationships derive from the same basic social networking processes found in other societies, the way in which Pueblo people harnessed these processes and the patterns in the built environment that resulted appear to have been quite unusual.

It is also important to mention that a few additional studies of the relationship between settlement population and plaza area have been completed, and these have yielded quite different results from those reported here. For example, Hanson and others (2019) examined the relationship between population and forum areas in ancient Roman cities, finding that the exponent of the relationship is in the neighborhood of .67, consistent with our social mixing model (Scenario 2). This suggests that fora in Roman cities were not used for mass participation ceremonies like those that occurred in Pueblo plazas but were instead part of the infrastructure that supported daily social mixing. In another study, Ossa, Smith, and Lobo (2017) examined the relationship between population and plaza space in Mesoamerican cities and towns, finding exponents in the neighborhood of .4, even smaller than the Roman case. No model that predicts this value has been developed thus far, but it is clear from these results that plazas in Mesoamerican cities and towns were used quite differently than Pueblo plazas. This larger context is important because it demonstrates that human societies create built environments that support social networking in a variety of ways. Even if the functional effects of human networks are universal and impose strong constraints on what can happen, there is still room for variation within these constraints. It seems to us that identifying this range of variation and evaluating its potential and limits is an important way archaeology can contribute to the social sciences.

Toward this end, we note that the decreasing density implied by the Protohistoric population vs. plaza area relationship makes it hard to imagine that this distinctive type of social networking could be scaled up to the level of contemporary cities. When applied to communities at a Pueblo scale, however, this form of social networking has clear advantages, and we suspect it contributed to the marked expansion in community specialization, exchange volume, and material standards of living noted for the Protohistoric period. Consider for a moment what feast day-type ceremonies did at a systemic level. First, they supported the creation and maintenance of mixing populations that were larger than settlement populations. Second, by each village hosting events on different days, the same individual could participate in multiple mixing populations over the course of a year. This would have multiplied social connectivity beyond the level possible in a more typical system where public gatherings occurred primarily in central places of a settlement hierarchy. Finally, these larger and more interconnected mixing populations would have supported a more widespread exchange network and an expanded division of labor, characterized by greater specialization in production relative to what was possible in the earlier system where plaza-based ceremonies were primarily for residents. In short, we suggest the emergence of feast day-type ceremonies around 1450 CE supported a process known to economists as "Smithian" growth that stimulated economic development and the formation of settlement clusters among the Protohistoric Pueblos (Arrow 1994; Kelly 1997; Adams and Duff 2004).

CONCLUSIONS

We have utilized settlement scaling theory to develop and test four models concerning the relationship between plaza space and population across Northern Rio Grande Pueblo settlements. Our results suggest that, initially, these settlements were designed to accommodate community residents as dancers and spectators in plaza-based ceremonies. By the onset of the Protohistoric period around 1450 CE, however, Puebloan built-environments were being designed to accommodate the entire social network of a community for feast day-type ceremonies that appear to have had all the features one can experience today. The correspondence in time between the emergence of feast day-type ceremonialism, the formation of settlement clusters, and other evidence of economic expansion noted by archaeologists suggests that the emergence of this distinctive ceremonial system played a central role in in these developments.

We suggest that feast day-type ceremonies stimulated a form of economic development known as Smithian growth in the following way. By hosting ceremonies for their entire social network of friends and acquaintances, Pueblo communities ensured that this entire network would meet and interact on a regular basis. By each community hosting its events on different days, the system ensured that individuals would participate in several distinct mixing populations over a given period. By giving food to visitors, Pueblo communities ensured that these visitors had free hands to carry things they had in abundance to the pueblo as gifts or trade items, and to carry things the pueblo had in abundance back home at the end of the day. By bringing together larger groups of people, these ceremonies ensured that individuals could satisfy a larger fraction of their material needs through social contact. In this way, they stimulated greater community-level specialization in production and an expanded regional division of labor. The result was an economy that was more efficient, interdependent, and raised living standards for everyone involved. So even though the spiritual and moral purpose of plaza-based ceremonies was to encourage the beneficence of nature and reinforce the values of generosity and industry, the material outcome of these events was an economy that was remarkably productive, given its demographic scale.

These conclusions arise through a style of analysis that has not been commonplace in archaeology. Indeed, we have adopted a natural-science type of reasoning that involves willful reductionism and explicit formalism. We have also adopted a system-wide level of analysis that ignores many interesting details at the level of local communities and their specific histories, but which captures emergent properties of the society overall and yields striking insights concerning the distinctive ways Pueblo culture and society worked to meet human needs. Based on the results presented here, we suggest that this style of research has great potential for generating knowledge that is not only interesting, but useful. In this way, the distinctive form of social networking embodied in Northern Rio Grande Pueblo ceremonies may inspire a larger world to discover new ways of improving the human condition overall.

Acknowledgments. Portions of this research were supported by grants from the National Science Foundation (CNH-0816400) and the James S. McDonnell Foundation (#220020438).

CHAPTER SEVEN

Diachronic Changes in Tool-Stone Raw Material Distributions and Exchange Systems in the Northern Rio Grande

Fumiyasu Arakawa, Christopher Nicholson, and Douglas Harro

The question of how and why discrete populations in the American Southwest shifted tool-stone procurement patterns and use over time is one that we can address from the perspective of a shifting economy. The transition from the Basketmaker to the Pueblo period saw a reduction in residential mobility and an increased reliance on agricultural food. As residential stability increased, there was a coincident rise in territoriality with an attempt to control local tool-stone raw materials (Arakawa 2006). By controlling these resources, communities independently embraced different barter systems where agents exchanged lithic raw materials for other items or resources. As part of a long-term study of resource material use in the American Southwest, this research focuses on tool-stone procurement patterns in the Village Ecodynamics Project (VEP) II South study area during the Coalition (1200–1325 CE) and Classic (1325–1600 CE) periods to address the emergence of commodity-based economies over time. In this research, we attempt to determine whether certain ancient Puebloan village members had control over nonfood resources, particularly lithic raw material types, and hypothesize that the manipulation and dominance of specific lithic raw materials by some villagers is indicative of an emergent commodity-based economy in this region.

We examine the proportion of debitage of three broad raw material types (obsidian, Pedernal chert, and basalt) recovered from 264 Northern Rio Grande sites dating from two sequential time periods (Table 7.1). We assume that, in general, all three flaked stone material types were heavily used and valued relatively equally in each time period. The dominance of specific "highly valued" lithic raw materials at a specific village, however, serves as an indicator of a commodity-based economy for those materials, resulting in an emergence of territoriality and a push for resource control from certain villages that had an interest in craft specialization. We define commodity production and commodity exchange as the process of producing a specific good with the intent of exchanging that good for another product(s).

Early commodity-based economies were likely initiated in Neolithic societies by individuals who recognized an opportunity to take their manufactured products and exchange them for other finished products, commodities, or resources. This process of exchange became more formalized and was carried out more and more often with individuals or groups outside of one's own kin group and community. It was distinctly different from existing forms of reciprocity, sharing, and exchange, with the exchanged objects having different levels of value or functionality. With an increase in population densities, early commodity-based economies also facilitated alliance formation among groups, which further aided in the acquisition of certain natural and cultural resources (Abbott, Smith, and Gallaga 2007; Garraty and Stark 2010; Kohler, Powers, and Orcutt 2004). By embracing a commodity-based economy and moving away from other forms of reciprocity, Classic period populations could regularly exchange resources and goods with local alliances or other ethnic groups. Indeed, during the Classic period, ancestral Pueblo economies changed in part because of the shift toward individuals engaging in specialized production of certain goods along with the emergence of local and regional trade fairs (Spielmann, 1988b, 2002; Ford 1972). This economic transition is a major shift from kin-based economic systems grounded in reciprocity to a more commodity-based economic system focused on the exchange of goods (Kohler, Powers, and Orcutt. 2004; Ortman 2016b).

Table 7.1. Time Periods and Raw Material Percentages at Each Site

Laboratory of Anthropology Site Number	*Site Name*	*Time Period*	*Obsidian %*	*Basalt %*	*Pedernal Chert %*
330		Coalition	8.16	6.10	67.30
350		Coalition	70	5	20
351		Coalition	70	5	20
909	Tsama (West)	Coalition	2.94	3.50	83.1
1051	El Pueblo de Santa Fe/Santa Fe Civic Center	Coalition	11	0	50
3752		Coalition	6.45	41.94	51.61
3752		Coalition	3.33	56.67	40
3755		Coalition	6.67	16.67	76.67
3760		Coalition	30	23.33	46.67
3771		Coalition	3.33	30	63.33
3790		Coalition	3.33	6.67	90
3814		Coalition	10	20	60
3821		Coalition	10.53	45.61	42.11
3842		Coalition	16.67	3.33	73.33
3848		Coalition	15.15	12.12	66.67
3851		Coalition	9.38	18.75	68.75
3852		Coalition	12.5	9.38	68.75
3858		Coalition	15.15	3.03	81.82
4602		Coalition	97	0.5	2
4604		Coalition	93	5	1
4605		Coalition	98	1	1
4606		Coalition	98	1	1
4607		Coalition	75	5	20
4608		Coalition	78	15	5
4609		Coalition	80	10	10
4616		Coalition	40	20	40
4618		Coalition	21.90	10.50	8
4618		Coalition	50	10	40
4619		Coalition	60	5	35
4620		Coalition	45	10	44
4621		Coalition	50	10	40
4622		Coalition	45	10	45
4623		Coalition	65	4	30
4624		Coalition	10.23	25	14.20
4624		Coalition	50	10	35

continued

Table 7.1. (continued)

Laboratory of Anthropology Site Number	*Site Name*	*Time Period*	*Obsidian %*	*Basalt %*	*Pedernal Chert %*
4626		Coalition	16.67	33.30	19.40
4688		Coalition	50	25	25
4690		Coalition	50	25	25
4708		Coalition	50	1	49
6787		Coalition	37.63	8.60	12.90
6788		Coalition	12.50	12.50	50
6789		Coalition	17.24	6.90	44.80
9781		Coalition	28	10	60
9842		Coalition	10	40	40
9845		Coalition	20	10	70
9863		Coalition	10	10	80
12119		Coalition	12.07	6.90	79.31
12211		Coalition	30	15	30
12587		Coalition	16.94	7.10	6.50
12614		Coalition	22.45	4.10	42.90
12641		Coalition	50	35	15
12641		Coalition	18	80	2
12664		Coalition	40	30	30
12685		Coalition	20	20	60
12696		Coalition	2.70	2.70	64.90
12702		Coalition	50	10	40
12706		Coalition	22.22	7.40	40.70
12709		Coalition	14.70	14.70	44.10
15865		Coalition	0	60	40
16036		Coalition	3.23	0	96.77
16036		Coalition	15.63	3.12	78.12
16062		Coalition	3.33	3.33	93.33
16062		Coalition	9.68	6.45	80.65
16062		Coalition	18.75	15.63	62.50
16071		Coalition	22.58	29.03	48.39
16800		Coalition	49	2	49
21285		Coalition	45	10	40
21291		Coalition	65	10	25
21307		Coalition	80	5	14
21312		Coalition	55	5	40
21313		Coalition	10	5	85
21328		Coalition	45	10	45

Table 7.1. (continued)

Laboratory of Anthropology Site Number	*Site Name*	*Time Period*	*Obsidian %*	*Basalt %*	*Pedernal Chert %*
21329		Coalition	70	10	20
21343		Coalition	29	10	60
21345		Coalition	40	1	59
21346		Coalition	85	7	7
21348		Coalition	25	25	49
21351		Coalition	33	33	34
21356		Coalition	81	8	10
21360		Coalition	30	9	70
21366		Coalition	75	1	24
21378		Coalition	15	75	10
21396		Coalition	15	5	80
21398		Coalition	60	9	30
21400		Coalition	45	15	40
21408		Coalition	15	45	40
21422		Coalition	5.66	1.20	89.60
21432		Coalition	10.57	3.10	83.30
21466		Coalition	90	5	5
21469		Coalition	30	60	5
21474		Coalition	70	5	20
21475		Coalition	68	10	20
21478		Coalition	68	2	30
21489		Coalition	80	15	5
21490		Coalition	100	0	0
21498		Coalition	33	66	0
21501		Coalition	70	25	0
21604		Coalition	85	7	6
21674		Coalition	85	8	7
21676		Coalition	60	20	20
21677		Coalition	100	0	0
21679		Coalition	60	25	13
21680		Coalition	78	5	5
21688		Coalition	50	30	30
21689		Coalition	60	20	20
21690		Coalition	60	20	20
29672		Coalition	5	5	90
29682		Coalition	50	10	40
29683		Coalition	7	3	90

continued

Table 7.1. (continued)

Laboratory of Anthropology Site Number	*Site Name*	*Time Period*	*Obsidian %*	*Basalt %*	*Pedernal Chert %*
29691		Coalition	95	1	3
29692		Coalition	88	10	0
29700		Coalition	95	0	5
29701		Coalition	95	5	0
29707		Coalition	90	10	0
29708		Coalition	80	10	5
29709		Coalition	80	10	5
29710		Coalition	85	10	0
29711		Coalition	100	0	0
29712		Coalition	80	5	15
29719		Coalition	50	50	0
29720		Coalition	40	55	5
29738		Coalition	100	0	0
29738		Coalition	97	2	1
29740		Coalition	98	1	1
29743		Coalition	75	23	2
29744		Coalition	90	10	0
29745		Coalition	100	0	0
29746		Coalition	8.24	0.30	88.50
29746		Coalition	90	9	1
29747		Coalition	50	50	0
29751		Coalition	60	38	2
29756		Coalition	35	10	35
29764		Coalition	70	10	10
29765		Coalition	80	5	10
29766		Coalition	70	10	20
29767		Coalition	75	5	10
29769		Coalition	75	5	10
29774		Coalition	89	10	0
29777		Coalition	40	18	40
29783		Coalition	75	15	5
29784		Coalition	80	1	18
29789		Coalition	28	2	70
29795		Coalition	35	3	60
29814		Coalition	45	10	45
29819		Coalition	45	10	45
29823		Coalition	25	15	60

Table 7.1. (continued)

Laboratory of Anthropology Site Number	*Site Name*	*Time Period*	*Obsidian %*	*Basalt %*	*Pedernal Chert %*
29840		Coalition	45	9	45
29867		Coalition	10	65	25
29873		Coalition	10	10	80
50904		Coalition	7.32	70.70	17.10
50908		Coalition	12.50	50	22.50
50912		Coalition	10	60	13.30
50916		Coalition	51.67	28.30	16.70
50917		Coalition	3.08	61.50	24.60
50918		Coalition	10	50	10
50953		Coalition	20.49	11.48	64.75
50955		Coalition	19.35	16.13	64.52
53163		Coalition	13.79	8.05	75.86
53181		Coalition	43.33	0	50
60065		Coalition	13.46	7.69	75
60260		Coalition	10	86.67	3.33
60333		Coalition	6.67	33.33	50
60353		Coalition	6.67	10	83.33
60372	Burnt Mesa Pueblo (Survey)	Coalition	38.89	2.78	50
60372.1	Burnt Mesa Pueblo (Area 1)	Coalition	6.08	44.90	44.50
60372.2	Burnt Mesa Pueblo (Area 2)	Coalition	4.19	78.30	15.10
60481		Coalition	28.21	4.27	64.96
65615		Coalition	16.67	10	63.33
65702		Coalition	75	15	8.33
65731		Coalition	13.79	19.54	66.67
65775		Coalition	31.25	6.25	56.25
65776		Coalition	46.74	5.43	41.30
65788		Coalition	21.59	27.27	51.14
65789		Coalition	27.96	12.90	55.91
65792		Coalition	38.71	12.90	48.39
65809		Coalition	36.67	16.67	46.67
70787		Coalition	3.39	5.08	89.83
70796		Coalition	22.86	5.71	71.43
70840		Coalition	9.38	3.12	87.50
70867		Coalition	32.26	9.68	58.06
70869		Coalition	30	3.33	63.33

continued

Table 7.1. (continued)

Laboratory of Anthropology Site Number	*Site Name*	*Time Period*	*Obsidian %*	*Basalt %*	*Pedernal Chert %*
70886		Coalition	30.3	3.03	60.61
70889		Coalition	18.75	25	43.75
70890		Coalition	11.43	0	77.14
70890		Coalition	11.11	8.33	69.44
70913		Coalition	32.76	10.34	32.76
70995		Coalition	20	10	66.67
71038		Coalition	35.14	2.70	59.46
71041		Coalition	25.95	9.16	64.12
77596		Coalition	5.88	8.82	79.41
77597		Coalition	6.67	13.33	80
77621		Coalition	41.94	12.90	38.71
77647		Coalition	10.94	3.12	82.81
77651		Coalition	12.12	30.30	57.58
77684		Coalition	12.62	20.39	66.99
77744		Coalition	6.67	3.33	86.67
77751		Coalition	10	25	60
84060		Coalition	13.33	0	80
86534		Coalition	9.22	5.30	21.30
135290		Coalition	5.65	8.10	23.60
38.1	Cuyamungue (Component 1)	Classic	6.20	0	53.1
38.2	Cuyamungue (Component 2)	Classic	3.70	1.20	56.10
38.3	Cuyamungue (Component 3)	Classic	9.50	1.70	56
42		Classic	83.87	11.29	0
59	Yunge Owingeh	Classic	6.30	7.70	30.80
61	Pojoaque	Classic	5.40	4.20	22.90
71	Howiri	Classic	1.60	20.70	17.80
78	Frijolito	Classic	11.40	77.10	11.40
78		Classic	12.22	10	76.67
98	San Marcos	Classic	10	24.90	35.60
174	Caja del Rio North	Classic	3.50	30.60	44.50
211	Tsankawi	Classic	21.40	4.30	61.40
250	Yapashi	Classic	40	41.40	15.70
297	Ponsipa-akeri	Classic	2.40	10.40	42.60
301	Tsiping	Classic	0.90	0.10	98.10

Table 7.1. (continued)

Laboratory of Anthropology Site Number	*Site Name*	*Time Period*	*Obsidian %*	*Basalt %*	*Pedernal Chert %*
792	Cuyamungue North	Classic	3	0	30.30
908	Tsama (Central and East)	Classic	10	1.60	77.90
3766		Classic	12.50	15.63	71.87
3768		Classic	15.15	6.06	69.70
3769		Classic	6.67	26.67	66.67
3770		Classic	0	22.58	77.42
3782		Classic	23.33	0	73.33
3783		Classic	22.86	0	74.29
3812		Classic	22.86	11.43	65.71
3838		Classic	6.45	35.48	54.84
3840	Shohakka	Classic	33.40	41.50	11
3840		Classic	16	42.67	38.67
9821		Classic	30	60	10
9849		Classic	15	75	10
9850		Classic	15	65	10
9851		Classic	40	50	10
9856		Classic	0	99	1
10942		Classic	2.78	63.89	33.33
12247		Classic	25	25	45
29659		Classic	40	10	50
29824		Classic	20	10	70
29834		Classic	30	10	60
29835		Classic	35	35	30
29841		Classic	20	10	70
29849		Classic	5	15	80
29853		Classic	60	15	20
29869		Classic	0	80	20
50970		Classic	14.74	47.37	36.84
50971		Classic	6.25	40.63	46.88
50974		Classic	9.52	31.75	34.92
60070		Classic	16.67	10	73.33
60104		Classic	10	6.67	83.33
60229		Classic	13.33	13.33	40
60255		Classic	10.26	5.13	74.36
60258		Classic	23.33	0	70

continued

Table 7.1. (continued)

Laboratory of Anthropology Site Number	*Site Name*	*Time Period*	*Obsidian %*	*Basalt %*	*Pedernal Chert %*
60282		Classic	16.67	6.67	76.67
60415		Classic	3.23	3.23	93.55
60543		Classic	3.33	3.33	70
60550	Tyuonyi Annex (Survey)	Classic	70.90	19.30	8.30
60550	Tyuonyi Annex (Component 1)	Classic	10	76.67	13.33
61049		Classic	66.67	13.33	13.33
65657		Classic	70	6.67	6.67
65748		Classic	73.33	6.67	10
70963		Classic	3.33	53.33	13.33
71000		Classic	20.69	6.90	70.11
71057		Classic	20	8.57	62.86
77691		Classic	27.12	45.76	25.42
77716		Classic	3.33	56.67	40
84146		Classic	5.26	57.89	36.84

Note: There are 13 instances where a site is represented by more than one lithic dataset, where the original researchers analyzed a different component of a site, or a single site is represented both by surface finds from a survey and field excavations. For example, the repeated records for LA 3752, 12641, 16036, 16062, 29738, and 70890 are from different loci at the same site, and several reported percentages from sites—LA 4618, 4624, 29746, 78, 3840, and 60550—are from debitage assemblages documented by both survey and excavations.

Territorial circumscription of resources is an essential ingredient in the development of an emergent commodity-based economic system (Clark and Hirth 2003:33–34; Rathje 1971, 1972). In prehistory, territoriality or land-tenure systems are often defined through empirical inference of social, economic, or ecological restrictions on resource use that are imposed by individuals or groups on other individuals and groups, such as lineages, clans, moieties, or communities. Territoriality can be simply defined as "the system of rights and privileges that human groups use to protect their resources and resource areas from outsiders" (Adler 1996:338). Studies of territoriality or land-tenure systems usually focus on how exploitive uses of local resources within a community are buffered from similar uses by other communities. Thomas Malthus argued for the power of exponential growth. Increasing population density strongly influences resource availability and opportunities for mobility, since rising agricultural production cannot, in general, keep up with human population growth. This effect inevitably leads to competition for resources. Following Malthus, several scholars suggested that territories emerge as a typical response to such competition (Boserup 1965; Brown and Podolefsky 1976; Dyson-Hudson and Smith 1978; Netting 1969). When a sense of territoriality is developed, people who inhabit the same landscape cannot equally procure and use the same resources. Procurement of resources, in this case lithic raw materials, would be controlled by specific groups. Consequently, these groups also controlled the distribution and exchange of these resources within their alliances. This kind of regional barter system is a precondition for the emergence of a commodity-based economy.

Craft specialization, which begins by a voluntary process, is also part of a commodity-based economic system and presumably occurs only after one community either enables or limits access to a valued resource to another communities. We argue that craft specialists began creating projectile points of specific raw materials in the Northern

Rio Grande region during the Classic period and then exchanged their finished products for natural resources or cultural items.

STUDY AREA AND TIME PERIODS

This study examines tool-stone procurement on the Pajarito Plateau and incorporates several sites from the VEP II South study area between 1200 and 1600 CE (Ortman 2010a; Schwindt and others 2016). The VEP is a long-term research program that conducts empirical studies and models the interactions between Puebloans and their environment between 600 and 1600 CE. One of the goals of this project is to use the results of the research to better understand human social evolution. The VEP II South study area has rich collections of lithic assemblages (Figure 7.1). We focus on assemblages that are dated to the Coalition (1200–1325 CE) or Classic (1325–1600 CE) period.

In the Northern Rio Grande, and especially on the Pajarito Plateau, archaeologists have identified a number of changes between the Coalition and Classic periods. During the Coalition period, population increased exponentially in comparison to earlier periods (Boyer and others 2010; Ortman 2016; Schillaci and Lakatos 2016). During the subsequent Classic period, several villages (e.g., Ponsipa-akeri, Howiri, San Marcos, and Tsama) saw major population expansion, as illustrated by the more than 1,000 rooms identified at these sites.

HISTORY OF RESEARCH AND THEORETICAL PERSPECTIVE

In a study of stone tool debitage, Harro (1997) compiled data from several hundred assemblages on the Pajarito Plateau to, among other things, identify whether residents created social boundaries related to procurement activities (see also Walsh 1997, 1998). Harro investigated tool-stone procurement patterns of three raw material types—obsidian, Pedernal chert, and basalt—and examined how procurement patterns related to the proximity of sites to raw material source areas. Obsidian was obtained from various locations in the Jemez Mountains, including Cerro Toledo, the Valles Grande, and Polvadera Peak. Pedernal chert was obtained at or near Cerro Pedernal, located in the northern portion of the study area, while basalt sources are ubiquitous over the southern and eastern perimeter of the Pajarito Plateau along both sides of the Rio Grande (Figure 7.1). Harro identified a social barrier immediately north of Frijoles Canyon that bisects the plateau into north and south sections. This was independently confirmed by Walsh (2000; see also Kohler 1990:151). Data suggest the boundary began forming during the Late Coalition period and was fully in place by the Classic period. Social boundaries such as this are likely indicative of a conscious effort by emerging ethnic groups to control important resources.

In another study of tool-stone procurement patterns, Arakawa and others (2011) investigated obsidian procurement patterns in the VEP I study area in southwestern Colorado using X-ray fluorescence (XRF) analysis. This study analyzed obsidian projectile points and debitage to compare the heterogeneity of procurement patterns between 600–1020 CE and 1020–1280 CE. The results show that ancestral Pueblo people imported more obsidian projectile points from areas close to the Jemez Mountains in the Northern Rio Grande region during the late 1200s CE. The interpretation of these results ties to early migration processes whereby people traveled from the central Mesa Verde region to the Northern Rio Grande region and brought back finished projectile points from areas closer to the Jemez Mountains in New Mexico. One important issue regarding obsidian procurement patterns is determining which villages in or near the Jemez Mountains were responsible for manufacturing the obsidian projectile points. Very few obsidian cores or debitage have been recovered from sites in the VEP I study area, so it appears the obsidian projectile points were manufactured elsewhere, probably in areas close to the Jemez Mountains quarries.

In Chapter 12, José Lobo advocates for the concept of "Smithian" growth to understand and reconstruct socioeconomic developments among the Rio Grande Pueblos. We suggest that tool-stone procurement studies allow us to address three key concepts related to this approach: scale, craft specialization, and emergent commodity-based economies. Anthropologists working in the American Southwest have discussed how increasing scale (e.g., population size) can cause social and cultural upheaval in early agricultural societies (e.g., Arakawa 2012; Bodley 2003; Duff 2002; Duff and Wilshusen 2000). For example, Arakawa (2012) argues that population increases in the central Mesa Verde region set the stage for ancestral Pueblo groups to develop an incipient social hierarchy just prior to the depopulation of the region around 1280 CE. This social stratification was accompanied by population increases in each village and led certain individuals to seek control of, and eventually manipulate, key religious or ceremonial events. In this case, the power possessed by individuals was not economic, rather it was religious, social, and political

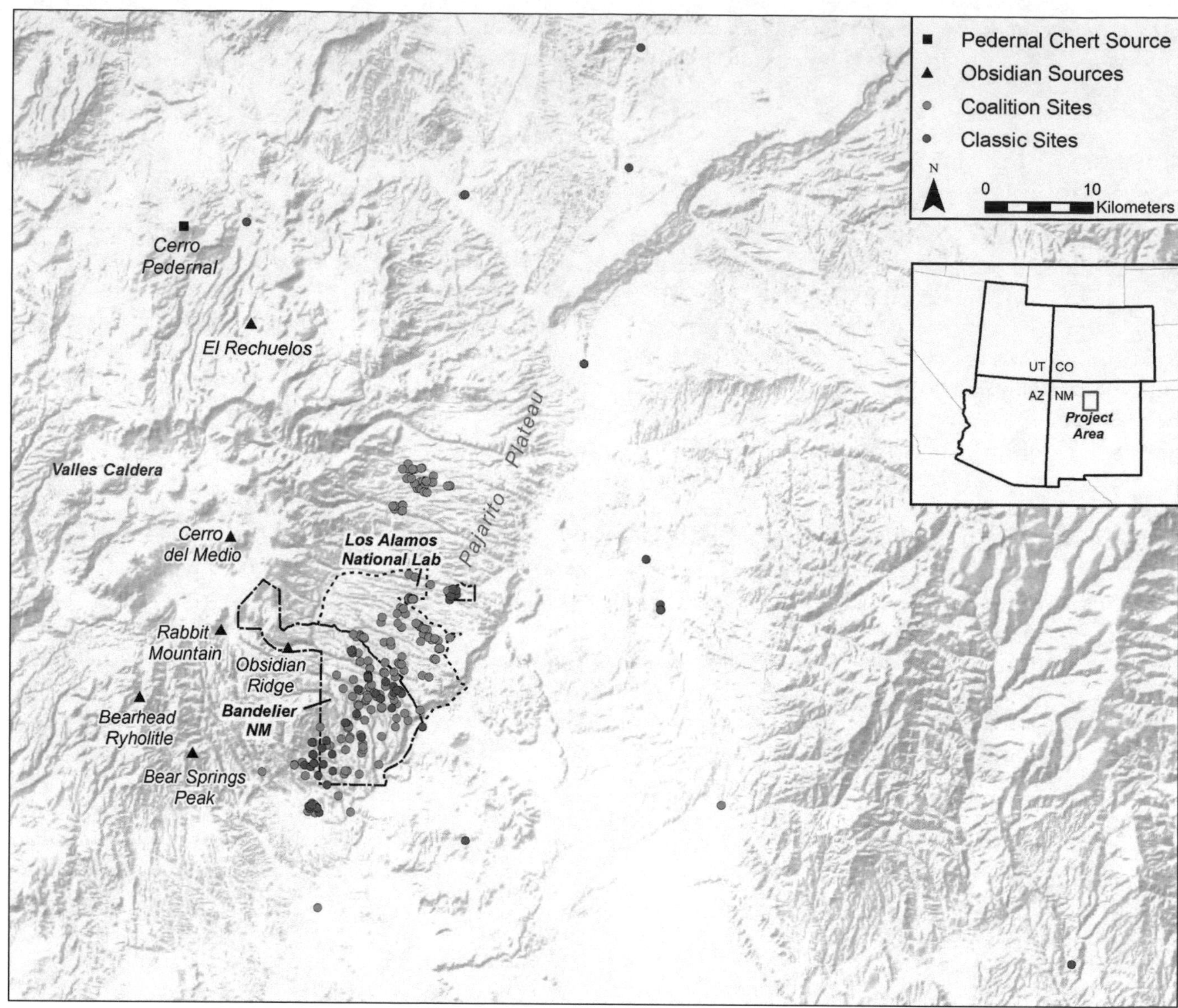

Figure 7.1. Project study area showing sites used for this study. Prominent obsidian sources noted with triangles. Prepared by authors.

(Arakawa 2012). Since specific individuals began dominating these aspects of social life, the structure of village organization would have changed. It is likely that increases in population led some villagers to focus on specific tasks outside of subsistence, such as the manufacture of religious objects for ceremonies.

This type of craft specialization is likely related to the increasing scale of social complexity. Here, we define craft specialization as the "regular, repeated provision of some commodity or service in exchange for some other by a household, community, or social class" that is performed by specialists who make more of something than they need for their household and dependents (Costin 1991:3). This surplus allows for exchange of goods for something needed or desired. Based on this definition, we expect to find that certain forms of craft production were controlled by specific individuals or groups and that their end products were sought after and exchanged for other objects or resources.

Costin (1991) distinguishes between high and low degrees of craft specialization. High-degree specialization is characterized by a high number of consumers, a low number of producers, and high social complexity in large settlements. Low-degree specialization, in contrast, is indicative of having a low number of consumers with a roughly equal number of producers, and low social complexity in smaller settlements (Costin 1991). In the VEP II South study area, although the scale of communities and settlements increased exponentially over time, villages rarely exceeded more than 2,000 people (Arnold 1992:61). These villages most likely exercised a low-degree of specialization but developed an emergent commodity-based economy when scales (i.e., population density) increased from the Coalition to Classic periods (Kohler 2004). In the archaeological record, we can use tangible physical evidence to examine population increases and craft specialization, which might show site clusters with high proportions of specific lithic raw materials. These two aspects allow us to consider the development of early commodity-based economies. To explore this emergence, we test the spatiotemporal distribution of lithic assemblages from several sites for variations in use of raw material types.

METHODS AND MATERIALS

To investigate the emergence of commodity-based economies, we compiled debitage data from 264 sites in the VEP II South study area (Harro 1997; Ortman 2010a). For this study, we examined site reports in the Laboratory of Anthropology at the New Mexico Historic Preservation Division, in Santa Fe. More than 200 site reports from the study area contained data on debitage recovered from test excavations and surface collections. From these reports, we gleaned debitage data from 44 Coalition and Classic period assemblages recovered from medium-sized (more than 10 rooms) to large habitation sites. The proportion of each material type (e.g., obsidian, Pedernal chert, and basalt) was calculated for each sample from each site for the Coalition and Classic periods in an attempt to take sampling error into account. This study focuses on the percent of obsidian, Pedernal chert, and basalt because quarries and sourcing areas of these raw materials can be readily identified. Since CRM site reports often do not differentiate Pedernal chert from general chert, we only use lithic assemblages where Pedernal chert was specifically identified. For obsidian, we aggregate all obsidian types into one category as we did not have opportunity to conduct XRF analysis to source each debitage piece. To ensure statistical significance only datasets containing more than 25 pieces of debitage were used (Arakawa 2006). In addition to the regional scale of 264 sites, we investigated a subset of tool-stone procurement using 220 assemblages from habitation sites surrounding the Pajarito Plateau (Table 7.1). We employed the same procedure for choosing lithic assemblages as the macro-level study. These were derived from the Bandelier Archaeological Survey (BAS) and Pajarito Archaeological Research Project (PARP) data from Harro's (1997) thesis research. Fieldwork for the PARP occurred over a period of nine years between 1977 and 1985 (Hill and Trierweiler 1986); the BAS work took place between 1985 and 1991 (Powers and Orcutt 1999). To examine how tool-stone procurement patterns relate to the development of commodity-based economies, we analyzed the proportion of each debitage material type across the landscape using geographic information system (GIS) tools. The proportion of each raw material type at each site was plotted and interpolated for both time periods (Coalition and Classic), with 200 assemblages dating to the Coalition period and 64 assemblages dating to the Classic period. Using ArcGIS 10.2 with Spatial Analyst, we created six maps using the Inverse Distance Weighting (IDW) tool. The IDW tool is a raster tool that determines a cell's value using a linearly weighted combination of several points in close proximity and assumes that these points share similar traits. The resulting maps highlight spots on the landscape where sites share commonalities, in this case the proportion of each raw material type across time. The proportion of each material type can then be compared for each period, with differences between the time periods illustrating how populations shifted economic strategies. Although the results of the IDW method illustrate general patterns of the proportion of lithic raw material distribution, it is important to acknowledge that areas that lack sites or data points can create skewed results and this is an issue with any interpolation algorithm and output between what is identified on the ground versus what has not been recovered from the archaeological record. In other words, when the spatial coverage of data is insufficient, the results of the IDW method created biases. Although we do not have lithic data at equal intervals across the study area, the existing data are adequate to reveal general patterns of tool-stone procurement patterns by evaluating a series of maps produced using GIS.

For the local scale analysis, we complimented the IDW comparison maps of the proportion of each material type across time periods by adding cost distance maps of obsidian sources, as Pedernal chert resources are located much farther to the north near Cerro Pedernal, whereas basalt source areas seem to be distributed throughout the study area. Four obsidian sources (Polvadera [El Rechuelos domes north of Polvadera Peak], Cerro del Medio [Valles rhyolite], Obsidian Ridge [Cerro Toledo rhyolite], and Bearhead Rhyolite Primary Dome [Paliza Canyon]) were used as source points. Slope derived from 60-meter Digital Elevation Model (DEM) was used as a cost surface in the Cost Distance tool in Spatial Analyst to visualize those areas where it was potentially easier to obtain the respective raw materials.

We hypothesize that sites within the study area where raw materials are more abundant and are farther from their point of origin are areas where territorial circumscription and craft specialization occurred, leading to commodity-based market activities. During the Coalition period, we expect to see higher amounts of obsidian at sites closer to these resource patches and as the distance from the source increases the proportion of that raw material should decrease (Renfrew 1969, 1977). With the inception of craft specialization and a desire to control material types during the Classic period, we expect that people who are farther away from high value resources travel farther to obtain and attempt to control these source materials regionally, which increases the value of goods they manufacture that are designated for exchange.

RESULTS

Regional Patterns

We can begin to see distinct differences in tool-stone material use between the Coalition and Classic periods in the southern portion of the VEP II South study area (Figure 7.2). A regional comparison of the IDW maps during these two time periods reveals several noteworthy patterns. During the Coalition period, there were high concentrations of basalt distributed at several sites around the Pajarito Plateau, with lower amounts trending across the landscape toward the northeast. During the Classic period, concentrated pockets of basalt diminish and are more evenly dispersed throughout the northwest portion of the study area, though there is an area with higher proportions nearest the Pajarito Plateau (Figure 7.2). The northeast portion of the study area continues to have lower amounts of basalt.

There are also major changes in the distribution and concentrations of Pedernal chert from the Coalition to Classic periods (Figure 7.2). Much higher concentrations of Pedernal chert are found in the northern portion of the study area during the Coalition period (Figure 7.2). Lower proportions of Pedernal chert stretch across the remaining portion of the region. This pattern suggests that people who inhabited the areas nearest the Pedernal chert quarries in the northwest traded these materials with people in the northeast. This pattern contrasts with that of the Classic period, which showed an increase in the concentration of Pedernal chert in the northwest and a more equal distribution of the chert across the landscape. There was a high concentration of Pedernal chert at Tsiping (LA 301) and only a slightly more pronounced density along the northern border of Bandelier National Monument. The high concentration of Pedernal chert at Tsiping suggests that the source of this material underwent changes in ownership or control over time. An alternative explanation to this pattern is that obsidian was preferred but the people of Tsiping were blocked from obtaining it, making Pedernal chert the best substitute material.

The results of the regional IDW for obsidian illustrate yet another pattern. During the Coalition period, obsidian was distributed fairly evenly across the region, with only a few areas of greater concentration in the northern part of Bandelier National Monument (Figure 7.2). In contrast, during the Classic period, obsidian became more concentrated at the eastern edge of Frijoles Canyon and in the southwest portion of the study area (Figure 7.2). This southward shift of concentrations of obsidian suggests that during the Classic period, people in those areas were able to procure, use, and discard more obsidian than people who were closer to the sources. In other words, during the Coalition period, a few population centers in the north exploited more obsidian because they were closer to sources like Obsidian Ridge, and those living in the south used very little. A change occurred during the Classic period such that sites in the southern portion of Bandelier National Monument used most of this material. Sites in this area are farther away from Obsidian Ridge and Bearhead Rhyolite Dome than other Classic period sites, but they have a higher percentage of obsidian in their assemblages. Like Pedernal chert, the shift in distribution and concentration of obsidian may be indicative of changes in resource ownership or control.

Local Patterns

At a regional level, obsidian concentrations are highest in areas of the southern Pajarito Plateau. To better understand whether obsidian procurement was dominated by specific settlements we draw in our scale of analysis to the local level and look more closely at patterns on the Pajarito Plateau. Sites in this region are predominantly found within Bandelier National Monument with several sites lying to the northeast and south (Figures 7.1 and 7.3). Using the regional-level IDW maps of each raw material

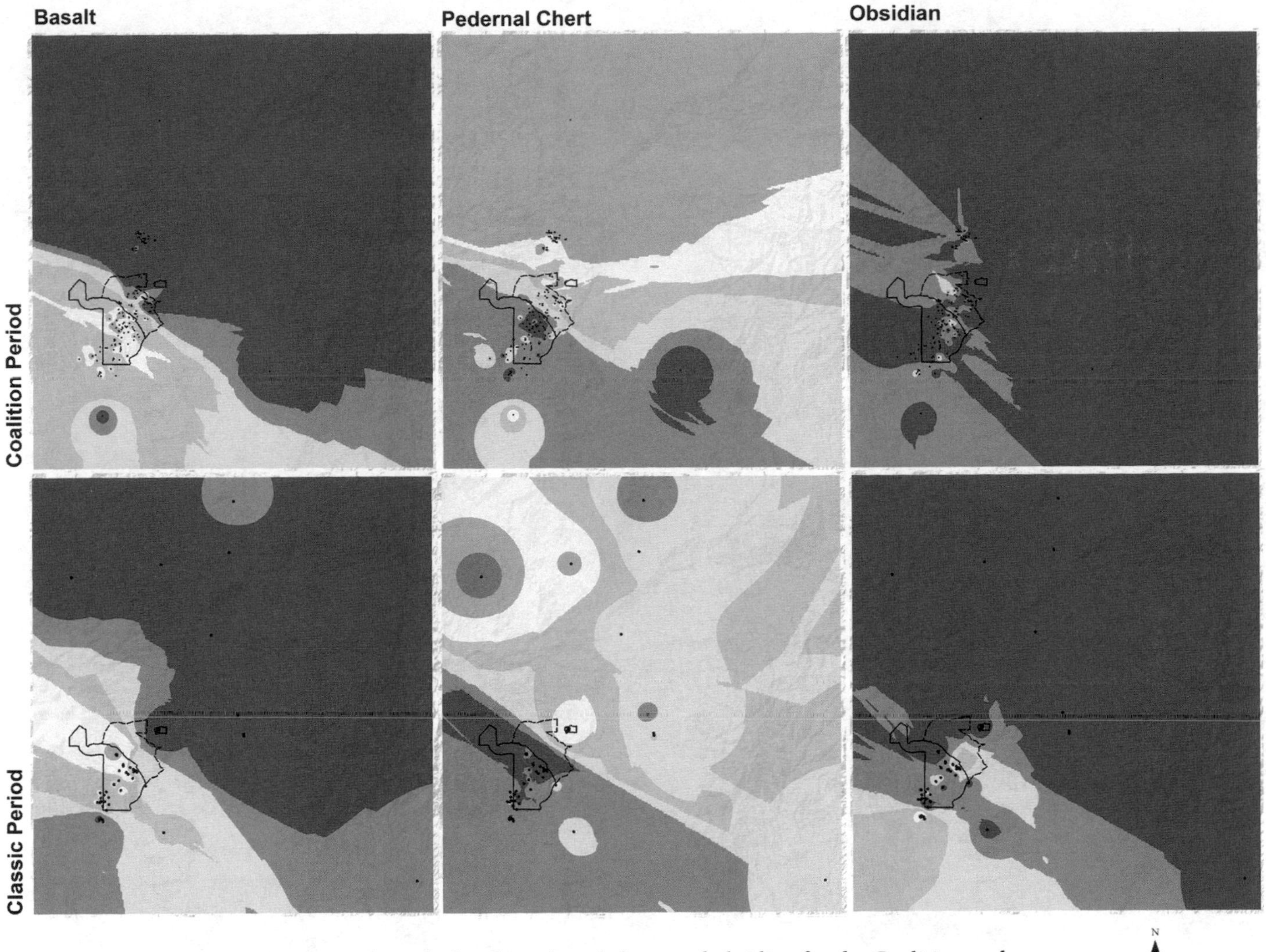

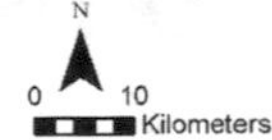

Figure 7.2. The results of IDW analyses for basalt, Pedernal chert, and obsidian for the Coalition and Classic periods. The resulting maps highlight regions where sites share common proportions of each raw material type for each period, with differences between the Coalition and Classic periods illustrating how populations shifted raw material acquisition. Prepared by authors.

type distribution, we generated simple difference maps using the Map Algebra tool in ArcGIS 10.2 to highlight changes in distribution over time. Yellow, orange, and red (with red being the highest) indicate areas where raw material proportions were higher during the Coalition period, whereas light- to dark-blue indicate the inverse where raw material type proportions were higher during the Classic period (Figure 7.3).

There is a noticeable northwest-southeast delineation between sites. People in the southeastern portion of the plateau used more basalt during the Coalition period, with those to the south dominating basalt procurement during the Classic period (Figure 7.3). The opposite pattern occurs for obsidian. Higher obsidian proportions are found in the north during the Coalition period, switching to the south and east during the Classic period (Figure 7.3). The outlier in this role reversal is Pedernal chert, where the distribution is focused in the northeast portion of the study area during the Coalition period, but the chert is found at only a few isolated sites during the Classic period (Figure 7.3).

The local scale IDW difference map shows a pronounced decrease in obsidian use in the northern portion and in sections along the northeast boundary of Bandelier National Monument. Based on earlier research regarding the distribution of basalt and Pedernal chert, Harro (1997) and Walsh (2000) identified regional differences

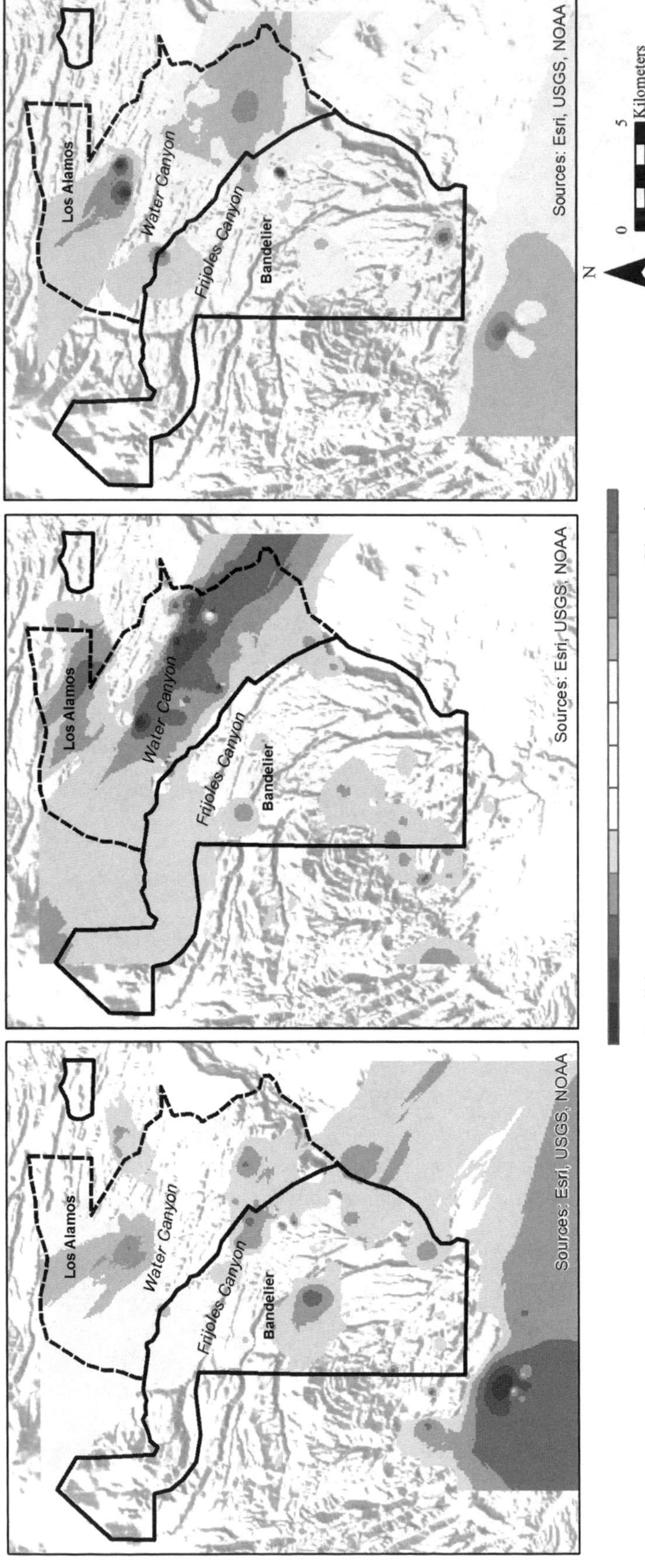

Figure 7.3. Lithic materials use during the Classic and Coalition periods. Inverse Distance Weight maps for basalt (left), Pedernal chert (center), and obsidian (right) between the Classic and Coalition periods. Black to dark gray (with black being the highest) indicates areas where raw material proportions were higher during the Coalition Period, whereas light-gray tones indicate the inverse where raw material type proportions were higher during the Classic period. Prepared by authors.

in raw material procurement along a linear monoclinic feature adjacent to Water Canyon. Harro (1997) argues that this line suggests a strict social barrier developed during the transition from the Coalition to the Classic periods, such that the plateau became divided into northern and southern sections along an east-west line in the vicinity of Frijoles Canyon. Indeed, this boundary line approximates the ethnographic boundary between Tewa and Keres speaking residents of the plateau. The emergence of a social boundary around 1300 CE is an indication of the development of ethnolinguistic group-level territories, which further suggests the emergence of regional relations of production and exchange.

Regarding obsidian tool-stone procurement patterns, it is important to note that LA 6550 in Frijoles Canyon had an unusually high proportion of obsidian bifacial thinning flakes in its debitage collection (Root 1989:77). Root and Harro (1993:58–59) argue that this may be a sign that biface trade blanks were being produced for exchange during Classic times, perhaps with pueblos to the east or with Plains hunter-gatherers. Harro also notes that this site has an unusually high proportion of obsidian relative to the sites around it. In addition, Harro (1997:98) identified hot spots of obsidian abundance in several canyons on the southern Pajarito Plateau; these increased during the Classic period. Harro argues that this is further evidence of production for exchange with other Pueblo and Plains groups. An increase in the procurement of obsidian and reduction of that obsidian into bifacial trade blanks points to a system where groups living in the Pajarito Plateau had easy access to obsidian raw material and they developed a system that allowed them to use the resource for trade with other groups who sought this material type. Future research on the lithic assemblages collected from these sites, including a detailed accounting of projectile points and their material type, can provide crucial information about craft specialists, community specialization, and control over resources during the Classic period.

Using the cost distance surfaces for four major obsidian sources around Bandelier National Monument along with IDW maps, we can begin to see where higher concentrations of obsidian shifted toward sites farther away from their original source (Figure 7.4). During the Coalition period, we expect to see higher amounts of obsidian at sites closer to these resource patches. As the distance from the source increases, the proportion of that raw material should decrease. With the inception of craft specialization and a desire to control key material types, groups who are farther away from high-valued resources would have the incentive to obtain valuable materials through exchange. This appears to be what happened on the Pajarito Plateau between the Coalition and Classic periods.

During the Coalition period, sites in the eastern portion of Frijoles Canyon just east of Obsidian Ridge have the highest proportions of obsidian (Figure 7.4). Sites to the southwest of the Bandelier National Monument boundary also have slightly higher concentrations and likely obtained their materials from Bearhead Rhyolite Dome or other secondary deposits (Arakawa et al. 2011: Figure 6). During the Classic period, sites south of the Bandelier National Monument boundary saw some of the highest densities of obsidian, while those in the eastern portion of Frijoles Canyon diminished in concentration. The shift of the acquisition, use, and discard of obsidian debitage between the Coalition and Classic periods indicates that a few villages controlled and dominated obsidian materials during the Classic period. This supports the notion that craft specialists would have manufactured valuable end products, such as projectile points and bifaces, and exported them to other villagers and possibly other ethnic groups. This further suggests that the tool-stone procurement pattern, particularly obsidian, reflects the development of commodity-based exchange during the Classic period.

DISCUSSION AND CONCLUSIONS

Tool-stone procurement patterns from the VEP II South study area reveal several interesting patterns that allow us to look at the development of commodity-based economies in the American Southwest. Although basalt procurement patterns did not show major shifts from the Coalition to Classic periods, Pedernal chert and obsidian procurement patterns show a well-defined regional difference. This suggests that during the Coalition period villages near the northern margin of Bandelier National Monument procured and controlled basalt materials and that during the Classic period villages near the southern margin of Bandelier National Monument procured and dominated obsidian materials. In addition, Tsiping (LA 301) dominated production using Pedernal chert in the northwest during the early Classic period. In combination with Harro's (1997) primary results, our findings concerning territorial circumscription of obsidian sources and the emergence of the regional barter systems in Frijoles and Cochiti canyons support the view that commodity-based economies emerged during the Classic period in the study area.

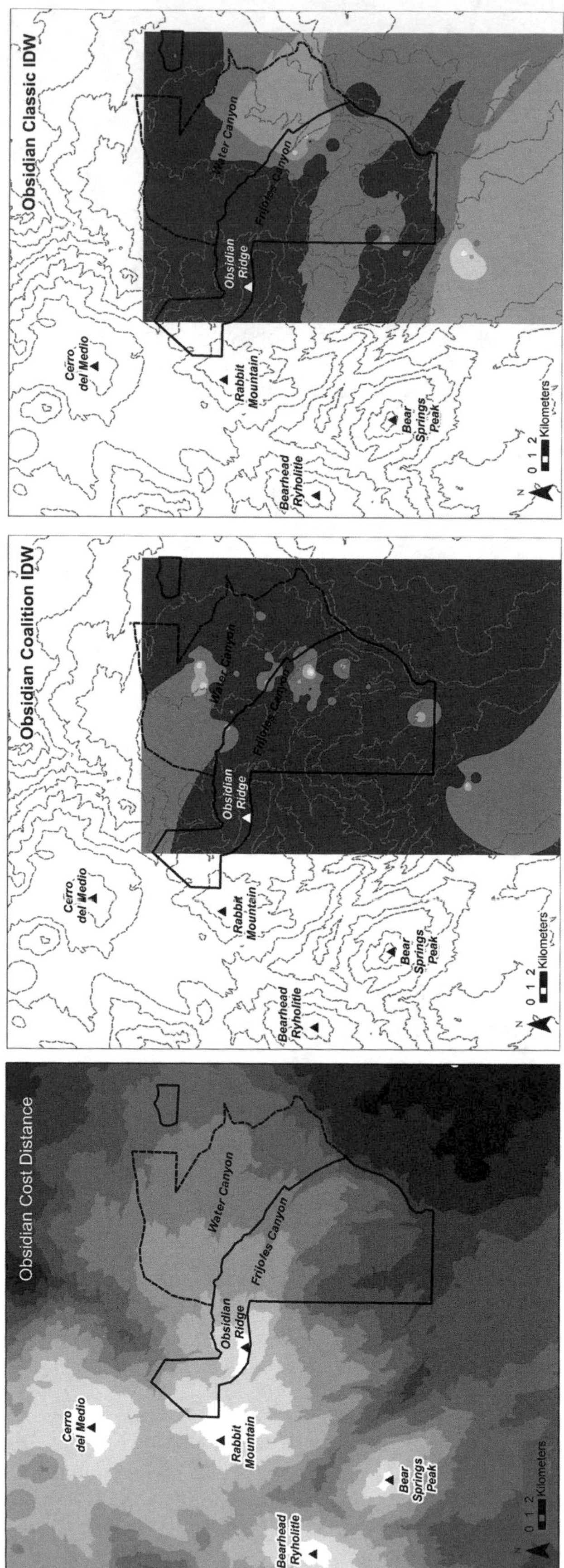

Figure 7.4. Changes in obsidian densities in relation to cost-distance calculations: obsidian cost distance from five obsidian quarries (left) and inverse distance weight (IDW) maps of obsidian proportions during the Coalition (center) and Classic (right) periods. Contour lines on the IDW maps represent the cost distance contours. Prepared by authors.

Although the results of the regional and local study using debitage data revealed much about how tool-stone procurement patterns changed over time, research that will allow us to use this information in a more comprehensive manner still needs to be done. To this end, we propose several directions for future research on lithics in the northern Rio Grande region. First, it is important to identify Classic period sites on the Pajarito Plateau where obsidian tools were produced for exchange. Such studies would extend Harro's (1997) hypothesis of an emerging obsidian exchange with the Great Plains. Second, we need to develop methods for identifying specialists who produced projectile points for exchange. To pinpoint the emergence of craft specialization, it is important to obtain detailed lithic provenience data and conduct geochemical analysis (XRF) and projectile point analysis (i.e., morphology and point attributes). Third, as this research addressed broad trends of tool-stone procurement patterns between the Coalition and Classic periods, it is important to investigate finer temporal patterns (i.e., Early and Late Classic periods) in lithic raw material procurement, use, and discard. Fourth, because the results of our analysis for Pedernal chert show the domination and manipulation of this particular raw material type at Tsiping during the Classic period, it would be worthwhile to reanalyze the lithic assemblage (both tools and debitage) at this site to look for further evidence of resource control related to village-level craft specialization and commodity exchange. Fifth, it is important to add additional lithic data for those portions of the study area that have been neglected by archaeological survey. By so doing, the results of the IDW difference maps of tool-stone procurement can be improved, giving us a more accurate picture of procurement patterns. Finally, it is crucial to obtain detailed data on the distribution of obsidian point frequencies from the study area. The results of the distribution of projectile point frequencies made of obsidian can determine whether obsidian projectile points are distributed evenly across the landscape or are more prevalent at some sites.

In this study we have used basic debitage data as inputs for simplified GIS analytical methods. Thus, our conclusions regarding the emergence of commodity-based economies in the northern Rio Grande region are still preliminary. This research reveals a broad pattern of change in tool-stone procurement from the Coalition to Classic periods, which suggests that when population density and agglomeration increased during the Classic period, tool-stone procurement patterns changed as well. Specifically, obsidian distributions suggest that certain raw materials were controlled and dominated by certain villages around Bandelier National Monument. In addition, a sense of territoriality became visible between the Coalition and Classic periods within and around the Bandelier National Monument. There are a few anomalous sites on the southern end of the Pajarito Plateau that apparently produced obsidian tools for exchange during the Classic period. From this we can hypothesize that these tools were manufactured by particular craftspeople. A similar pattern is observed at Tsiping (LA 301) where Pedernal chert emerged as an important raw material type during the Classic period. The emergence of craft specialists, a broader exchange network, and the development of territoriality all suggest that ancestral Pueblo people developed commodity-based economies during the Classic period through the mechanisms of Smithian growth.

CHAPTER EIGHT

The Economics of Becoming: Population Coalescence and the Production and Distribution of Ancestral Tewa Pottery

Samuel Duwe

The Northern Rio Grande region experienced a dramatic social and residential transformation beginning in the late thirteenth century. Much of the Four Corners region was depopulated due to drought and social unrest and the resulting migrants traveled to the far-flung corners of the American Southwest including northern New Mexico (Ahlstrom, Van West, and Dean 1995; Kuckelman 2008; Ford, Schroeder, and Peckham 1972; Ortman 2012). Migrants and autochthonous people came together and began to coalesce in villages that quickly grew to more than 1,000 rooms. Associated with these new living arrangements was a florescence in novel social, ceremonial, and economic organizations that was a response to, or the catalyst for, coalescence (Adams and Duff 2004). By the mid-fourteenth century these coalescing communities began to express subregionalizations in material culture that suggest the formation of societies like those of contemporary Pueblo people (Mera 1934). This chapter examines the history of one of these peoples, the Tewa, and particularly addresses the relationship between population coalescence, economic relationships, and identity formation.

The broader strokes of Tewa history and its relationship with the larger Rio Grande region have been known for over a century. Kidder (1915) noted distinct geographic distributions of pottery across northern and central New Mexico in the Classic period (1350–1600 CE) and Mera (1934) correlated these patterns with historical Pueblo ethnic and linguistic boundaries as sketched by Harrington (1916). An emerging fourteenth-century Tewa identity was defined by the geographic extent of a distinct white ware tradition found along the Tewa Basin, running along the Rio Grande rift valley as far south as Santa Fe and north past Abiquiu Reservoir. These early arguments have been surprisingly resilient and continue to be supported by modern research that details the archaeology and geographic extent of ancestral Tewa architecture, agriculture, and ritual landscapes (Chapter 2; Anschuetz 1998, 2007; Duwe and Anschuetz 2013; Duwe 2011, 2016).

In recent years, archaeologists have focused much of their attention on the origins of the Tewa people, including their language and society, and have concluded that Tewa history is complex and resulted from the amalgamation of disparate peoples during the thirteenth and fourteenth centuries (Duwe 2011; Duwe and Anschuetz 2013; Ortman 2012). Yet few studies have sought to understand the internal dynamics of the developing Tewa world, particularly how different communities formed, interacted, and diversified to become the modern Pueblos. Although the entire Northern Rio Grande region underwent similar processes of population growth, agglomeration, and economic development—the focus of this volume—I agree with Cruz and Ortman (Chapter 5) that we should not lose sight of the important diversities that arose across communities with unique histories. The Tewa world today is not a monolithic whole but is rather a composite landscape of six villages that, despite claiming a common language and culture, are autonomous and have unique social, political, and economic histories. Although the large-scale patterns of Tewa history are becoming better understood, much less is known about the development of specific communities and their social and economic relationships, within this emerging Tewa world.

One way to begin to address this question is to examine the production and distribution of pottery in and between two well-studied areas of the ancestral Tewa Basin: the Rio Chama watershed and the northern Pajarito Plateau. If we can assume that the movement of pottery is indicative of some sort of social interaction (feasting, exchange, marriage, etc.) then documenting the relative flow of pots between these two areas becomes a proxy for social connectivity. If this connectivity increases or decreases through time it is possible to make preliminary interpretations about the dynamics of Tewa social life. In this chapter I present the results of a provenance study of ancestral Tewa decorated pottery from 13 sites in the Rio Chama watershed and on the northern Pajarito Plateau. Due to the diverse geology of the region it is possible to differentiate between pots that were made locally or imported in both areas, and thus estimate the frequency of nonlocal pottery across sites. In the discussion that follows, my focus is on patterns of decorated pottery production and distribution, or more specifically, on how these patterns changed over time from small, dispersed hamlets in the Coalition period (1200–1350 CE) to large, continuously coalescing villages in the Classic period (1350–1600 CE).

My central observation is that, although Tewa pottery was produced in large quantities in both areas, the Rio Chama watershed and northern Pajarito Plateau exhibit different quantities of local and nonlocal pottery that suggest varying economic and social relationships, as well as histories of movement. By correlating these data with population histories, I argue that unique Tewa identities developed during the Classic period through the process of population coalescence. This process continued through the Historic period and resulted in today's diverse Tewa Pueblos.

HISTORIES OF SETTLEMENT AND COALESCENCE IN THE TEWA WORLD

Although the emerging Tewa world is archaeologically defined by the development of a distinct pottery tradition beginning in the early fourteenth century, the Tewa Basin is diverse both ecologically and culturally. The basin is one of deep contrasts and expansive vistas, from the tall, jagged Sangre de Cristo Mountains in the east to the volcanic summits of the Jemez Mountains and the broken topography of the Pajarito Plateau to the west and south. The varied settlement histories of different portions the Tewa Basin reflects this diverse landscape. Ancestral Tewa settlement occurred along the Rio Grande in the Española valley, in the Santa Cruz, Pojoaque, and Tesuque watersheds, throughout the Rio Chama valley and its tributaries, and on the northern Pajarito Plateau (Anschuetz and Scheick 1996; Beal 1987; Duwe 2011; Crown, Orcutt, and Kohler 1996). I am interested in the social and economic interaction between two highly populated and well-studied areas of the ancestral Tewa world with very different settlement histories: the Rio Chama watershed and the northern Pajarito Plateau.

The Pajarito Plateau, located in the southwestern portion of the Tewa Basin, was unoccupied until the turn of the thirteenth century but quickly became a population center, as thousands of migrants from the Four Corners region settled on its mesa tops (Ortman 2012). Early sites were generally small (fewer than 10 rooms), however, in the late thirteenth and early fourteenth century population size increased rapidly as U-shaped and fully enclosed plaza pueblos were built in the central and northern parts of the plateau north of Frijoles Canyon (Crown, Orcutt, and Kohler 1996), the traditional Tewa ethnic boundary defined by Harrington (1916). Many of these villages continued to grow through the beginning of the Classic period, including the sites of Potsuwi'owingeh and Tshirege'owingeh analyzed in this study (Hewett 1906, 1953; Wilson 1916). The causes for the shift to aggregated settlements may, in part, be climatic considering that relatively high water tables and aggrading floodplains made high-elevation settings more favorable for growing enough crops to feed these expanding populations (Orcutt 1991).

In the early fourteenth century, the sites on the Pajarito Plateau housed more ancestral Tewa people than any other area in the region (Ortman 2016b; See also Chapter 1: Figure 1.3). By the beginning of the Classic period, however, population on the plateau began to drop as people built fewer, but much larger, villages. One such cluster of coalescing communities includes the sites of Potsuwi'owingeh, Tshirege'owingeh, Navawi'owingeh, and Tsankawi'owingeh, located near to and north of the modern town of White Rock. These villages were occupied through the end of the fifteenth century, with Tshirege'owingeh and Tsankawi'owingeh potentially remaining inhabited into the period of Spanish colonization (Duwe 2011; Schroeder and Matson 1965). Drought and floodplain degradation throughout the fourteenth and fifteenth centuries likely contributed to the depopulation of the Pajarito Plateau. Ortman (2016a:78) suggests that the very high population on the plateau would have increased vulnerability to frost and drought and that movement towards other areas was spurred on by environmental and food security considerations. It has been proposed that these people moved to both the Cochiti area to the south and the Rio Chama watershed to the north (Orcutt 1999; Duwe 2011).

The settlement history of the Pajarito Plateau contrasts dramatically with the history of the Rio Chama watershed, which was unoccupied by full-time village agriculturalists until the mid-thirteenth century. The earliest settlements were located along the lower reaches of the Rio Chama and the Rio del Oso valleys, including the upland habitats in between (Beal 1987; Windes and McKenna 2006; Anschuetz 1993; Bremer 1995a, 1995b). The origin of these initial settlers is currently unknown but both architectural and ceramic attributes suggest these people were primarily migrants from the north (Windes and McKenna 2006; Ortman 2012). Population continued to grow through the first half of the fourteenth century as population expansion continued into the Chama. These newly built sites express heterogeneity in material culture, which suggests multiple groups of people with disparate histories and identities settling in the watershed, possibly from multiple areas across the Tewa Basin including the Pajarito Plateau (Duwe 2011:266–272).

The beginning of the Classic period was met with a major transformation in the size, density, and organization of the residential settlements in the Chama. The small hamlets and villages of the Coalition period were depopulated as people coalesced into 10 large villages spaced almost evenly along the Rio Chama, Rio Ojo Caliente, Rio del Oso, and El Rito Creek, with some settlements possessing populations of potentially more than 2,000 people (Chapter 5; Duwe and others 2016). These new villages were most likely built by the diverse communities that previously lived in the watershed. It is also likely, based on regional population histories, that much of this growth can be attributed to settlement by Pajarito villagers (Ortman 2012). By 1400 CE, the Chama had become the population center of the Tewa world and gradually came to support, potentially, 10,000 people by the end of the fifteenth century (Ortman 2016b; Duwe and others 2016). From the late fifteenth to the middle of the sixteenth century the people of the Chama continued to coalesce into a handful of large sites. By the end of the sixteenth century the watershed lay virtually empty as Tewa people coalesced at or near their modern villages along the Rio Grande. The reasons for the depopulation of the Chama are contested but are probably related to climatic instability, increased regional conflict and competition, and disease (Beal 1987; Orcutt 1991; Ramenofsky and Feathers 2004; Jeançon 1912, 1923; Wendorf 1953; Ortiz 1969:16).

In summary, although the ancestral Tewa, particularly those of the Classic period, were participating in the same ideational system represented by a singular pottery tradition, settlement histories and patterns of population coalescence vary greatly between the Rio Chama watershed and the northern Pajarito Plateau (Graves and Eckert 1998). There are also indications that during the Classic period these areas began to form distinct social relationships with the surrounding Rio Grande community, which may have influenced the eventual diversification of Tewa societies. Rio Grande Glaze Ware, produced by ancestral Keres and Tano potters from roughly Albuquerque to Santa Fe and including the central and southern Pajarito Plateau, is found in very low frequencies at sites in the Tewa Basin (Habicht-Mauche 1993:33–36; Shepard 1942; Gauthier 1987; Mera 1934). This is particularly true for the Chama where site ceramic assemblages have 1 to 3 percent glaze ware and little additional nonlocal pottery (Duwe 2011: Appendix B). This indicates that the region was economically and socially isolated. Villagers on the Pajarito Plateau, however, maintained closer ties with glaze ware producers south of the Tewa Basin, as demonstrated by both larger proportions of glaze ware in ceramic assemblages and the high frequencies of Pajarito-produced biscuit ware pottery distributed to sites such as Pecos Pueblo (Duwe 2008; Shepard 1936). Although the differences in regional interaction between the two areas are likely related to geographic proximity (villages on the Pajarito Plateau were closer to glaze ware-producing potters, for example), the correlation with historical ethnic boundaries suggests the possibility of emerging Pueblo identities. This begs two questions: how were these emerging and dissimilar Tewa communities interacting with each other, and what can this tell us about the development of Tewa societies? The remainder of this paper presents the results of a provenance analysis that tracks the production and distribution of six ancestral Tewa pottery types that span the Coalition and Classic periods to understand the changing economic and social relationships between the Chama and the northern Pajarito Plateau.

THE PROVENANCE STUDY

To examine the production and distribution of ancestral Tewa pottery, two types of samples were subjected to chemical compositional analysis: modern clay sources (to understand regional geochemical variability) and archaeological sherds from Coalition and Classic period sites on the Pajarito Plateau and in the Rio Chama watershed.

Clay Sampling in the Tewa Basin

Archaeologists working in the region have assumed that the ancestral Tewa people who resided in villages in the Rio Chama watershed and on the Pajarito Plateau produced much of their own pottery (Gauthier 1987; Curewitz 2008). Because potters rarely travel more than 7 km to a clay source, it is likely that Prehispanic clay sources were located relatively close to villages (Arnold 1985). Fortunately, the ancestral Tewa sites of the Rio Chama watershed and Pajarito Plateau are situated among starkly different geologies (see Duwe 2011:713–717 for a more in-depth discussion). This makes it possible to geochemically differentiate between the two areas to establish locally versus nonlocally produced pottery.

Quaternary period volcanism and erosion define the surface geology in the majority of the Tewa Basin (Figure 8.1). The valley bottoms and terraces of the Chama are comprised primarily of Quaternary gravel and sand deposits that have been weathered from earlier Precambrian and Tertiary deposits (Muehlberger 1960). In particular, the Precambrian deposits are only found in the northern part of the study area in the Rio Ojo Caliente valley. The geology of the Pajarito Plateau, on the other hand, is primarily defined by the eruption of the Valles Caldera volcano between 1.61 and 1.22 Ma ago (Broxton, Goff, and Wohletz 2008). The resulting Bandelier Tuff was deposited across the plateau; deposits up to 3 m thick are found as far as 20 km from the Valles Caldera (Dunbar 2005). Many of the villages were built into or on top of the tuff, which also appears to have been the primary source of clay for Pajarito villagers (Curewitz 2008).

I sampled 25 clays from across the Rio Chama watershed, focusing on possible sources within 3 km of the ancestral Tewa villages selected for this project. These included both residual and redeposited clays from Precambrian, Tertiary, and Quaternary deposits (see Duwe 2011: Appendix B). I collected and analyzed clays that were likely used in the production of decorated ancestral Tewa pottery (white, gray, and tan in color) and had suitable workability (using the generous criteria of being able to be formed into tiles and fired without significant cracking or deformation). Unfortunately, I did not survey the Pajarito Plateau for clays, but I did include one sample eroding from Bandelier Tuff on the northern Pajarito Plateau that was collected by Los Alamos National Laboratory archaeologists. Clay samples were prepared for compositional analysis by crushing and mixing the clay with de-ionized water on a clean surface to avoid contamination. The clay was then formed into 10- by 10-cm tiles and fired in a furnace at 800 degrees Celsius to burn away carbon materials inside the clay and replicate the firing technique used by the ancestral Tewa potters.

Sampling Pottery

To examine the economic and social relationships between the Rio Chama watershed and the northern Pajarito Plateau through time, I selected 874 sherds that encompass as much temporal, spatial, and compositional variability as possible (Table 8.1). The samples are of all the ancestral Tewa pottery types manufactured from 1200 to 1600 CE: Santa Fe Black on-white, Wiyo Black-on-white, Abiquiu Black-on-gray, Bandelier Black-on-gray, Sankawi Black-on-cream, and Potsuwi'i Incised (Table 8.2). This pottery was produced locally within the Tewa Basin, and, with the exception of Santa Fe Black-on-white, which was manufactured widely across the northern Rio Grande in the Coalition period, all can be related to an emerging Tewa identity (Eckert, Schleher, and James 2015; Harlow 1973). As date ranges for the pottery are debated, I chose relatively narrow date ranges for this project based on my knowledge of the local culture history and because these align well with the momentary population history defined by Ortman (2016b) that is used to interpret these data.

Most of these samples originate from 11 late Coalition and Classic period sites across the Rio Chama watershed that cluster along major tributaries of the Chama (Fowles 2004). Analyses of these sub-areas form the basis of my results and interpretations and include sites along the Rio Ojo Caliente, the Rio del Oso, and the Rio Chama proper. Although each of these drainages appear to have their own unique geology, most of these sites are near or adjacent to Precambrian outcrops, Tertiary clastic deposits (the Santa Fe Formation), and Quaternary alluvium. Two sites from the northern Pajarito Plateau that sit directly on Quaternary Bandelier Tuff, the source for biscuit ware clay, were included (Curewitz 2008). Pottery from Tsiping'owingeh (LA 301) was also sampled. Although the site is located on a tributary of the Chama, deposits of Bandelier Tuff and Tertiary igneous rock that are similar to Pajarito Plateau deposits are located nearby. Because of the geology, Tsiping'owingeh is not grouped with sites in either the Chama or the Pajarito Plateau and was analyzed as a separate entity.

All ceramic samples selected for compositional analysis were reanalyzed for stylistic, technological, and typological attributes. Although redundant, this ensured that no two samples originated from the same vessel. The specimens included in this study are not random samples but instead represent an attempt to include a wide range of variability in construction including paste and temper types, as observed through a 40X reflected light microscope analysis.

Procedure

To perform the compositional analysis of clay and pottery samples I employed time of flight-laser ablation-inductively coupled plasma-mass spectrometry (TOF-LA-ICP-MS),

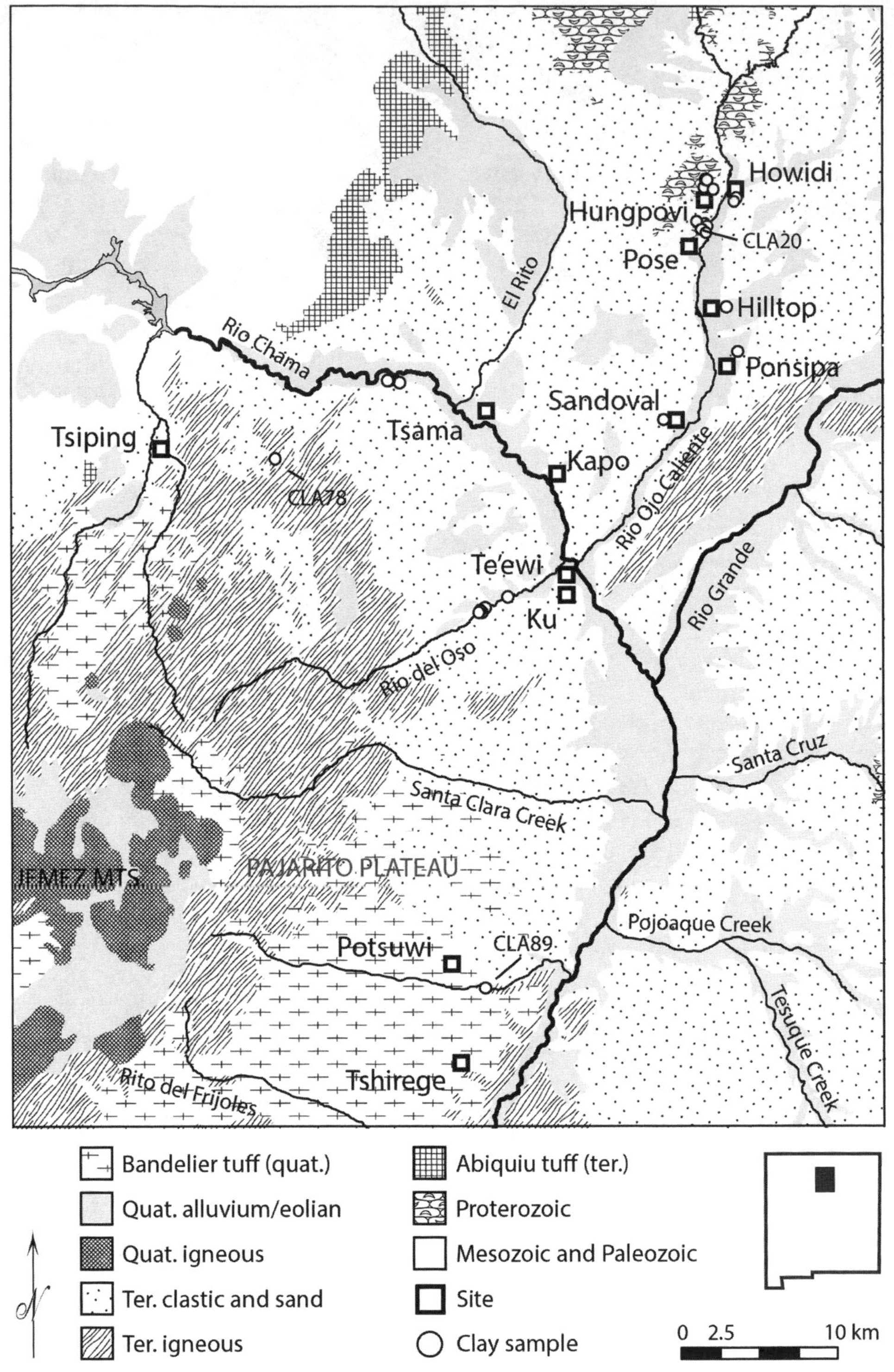

Figure 8.1. Surface geology, clay sample locations, and archaeological sample locations in the study area. Prepared by author.

Table 8.1. Samples of Six Ancestral Tewa Ceramics Analyzed from Coalition and Classic Period Sites in the Rio Chama Watershed and on the Pajarito Plateau

Site Name (LA No.)	*Dates*	*Santa Fe Black-on-white*	*Wiyo Black-on-white*	*Abiquiu Black-on-gray*	*Bandelier Black-on-gray*	*Potsuwi'i Incised*	*Sanakwi Black-on-cream*
Rio Ojo Caliente							
Howiri'owingeh (71)	1377–1537	0	13	30	58	23	23
Ponsipa'akeri (297)	1312–1550	7	16	34	22	11	13
Hungpovi'owingeh (380)	1363–1550	0	10	24	27	15	16
Pose'owingeh (632)	1344–1500	0	7	22	28	14	14
Hilltop Pueblo (66288)	1362–1600	0	0	6	12	0	2
Sandoval Pueblo (98219)	1322–1394	2	9	8	0	0	0
Rio del Oso							
Te'ewi'owingeh (252)	1365–1600	0	0	0	10	13	10
Ku'owingeh (253)	1366–1500	0	11	24	24	2	12
Rio Chama							
Kapo'owingeh (300)	1300–1400	6	6	15	1	0	0
Tsama'owingeh (908/909)	1251–1550	2	10	3	4	0	1
Pajarito Plateau							
Potsuwi'owingeh (169)	1348–1550	0	3	24	23	15	14
Tshirege'owingeh (170)	1357–1600	4	9	24	24	15	17
Tsiping'owingehe	1317–1400	10	40	24	8	0	0
Totals		31	134	238	241	108	122

Note: Occupation dates were derived from a combination of dendrochronology and ceramic mean dating (Duwe 2011, 2013).

which has been demonstrated to be effective in addressing questions regarding pottery provenance (Speakman and Neff 2005). I chose to perform chemical composition analysis because of the geochemical heterogeneity of the region, although petrographic analysis (an ongoing project) will also be important to understand regional geologic source variation (Curewitz 2008; Curewitz and Foit 2018). The use of the laser ablation method is of particular interest because it allowed me to target the paste matrix of each sample and avoid inclusions (temper or naturally occurring rocks and sand). As a result, my analysis differs from bulk chemical analysis in that I am specifically analyzing the paste matrix (and avoiding natural nonplastics in the matrix) and hence the provenance of clay used in pottery manufacture.

I used the California State University-Long Beach GBC OptiMass time-of-flight ICP mass spectrometer with a Nd:YAG laser at 60 percent power to analyze the 899 samples (874 ceramic samples and 25 raw clay source samples). Data for 44 elements were recorded; U, Sc, Cr, Ni, Cu, As, and Lu were discarded because of their preponderance of missing values. Five standards were analyzed between every 15 samples: (1) NIST 1633A, (2) NIST 1633B, (3) NIST SRM612, (4) NIST SRM614, and (5) Ohio Red Clay. Data calibration was performed using standard multivariate procedures and all concentrations were converted into base log 10 values to normalize the distribution for trace elements (Glascock 1992). A discussion of how the sherds were sampled, prepared, and calibrated is detailed elsewhere (Duwe 2011:718–733).

RESULTS

The chemical analyses of the archaeological sherds and modern clay samples resulted in a rich database that permits one to begin to understand economic patterns of pottery production and distribution within the Tewa

Table 8.2. Pottery Produced in the Tewa Basin from 1200 to 1600 CE

Type	*Documented date range*	*Dates used in the analysis*	*Description*	*References*
Santa Fe Black-on-white	1175–1425	1200–1350	Primarily bowl form with dark gray carbon paint. Paste is characteristically blue-gray with sand, siltstone, or tuff temper. Geometric designs are applied to bowl interiors.	Habicht-Mauche 1993; Kidder and Amsden 1931; Sundt 1984
Wiyo Black-on-white	1250–1475	1300–1400	Exclusively bowls with interiors polished and painted with dark, black carbon paint. Soft paste tempered with fine volcanic material. Bold designs with thick lines are applied to bowl interiors.	Habicht-Mauche 1993; McKenna and Miles 1996; Mera 1935; Wendorf 1953
Abiquiu Black-on-gray	1375–1450	1350–1450	Almost exclusively bowls, light porous paste self-tempered with quartz sand and tuff or pumice. Sharp black carbon paint is applied on a thin slip and polished. Designs include zigzags, crosses, checkerboards, and hatched triangles.	Breternitz 1966; Kidder 1931; Mera 1934; Harlow 1973
Bandelier Black-on-gray	1400–1550	1400–1500	Technology identical to Abiquiu Black-on-gray, although also made in jar form. Paint and slip are applied to both the interior and exterior of bowls.	Breternitz 1966; Kidder and Amsden 1931; Mera 1934; Harlow 1973
Potsuwi'i Incised	1450–1650	1500–1600	Primarily jar form. Similar paste as Sanakwi Black-on-cream. Surface decoration entails incised lines in geometric patterns along the mid-section, often with a mica wash.	Harlow 1973; Mera 1932
Sankawi Black-on-cream	1525–1600+	1500–1600	Both bowls and jars. Slip and paste are pink, orange, and tan with sand or pumice temper. Thinner walls compared to earlier types. Designs are more complex than the biscuit wares and lines are thinly painted with carbon paint.	Breternitz 1966; Harlow 1973; Mera 1932; Smiley, Stubbs, and Bannister 1953

Basin. In the discussion that follows I first seek to define initial compositional groups within the total assemblage. By comparing these groups with the chemical profiles of local clay sources I draw preliminary conclusions of the provenience of many of the pottery samples in the database. I then compare the relative frequencies of the two areas by each of the six ceramic types to understand how the economic relationship between the Chama and the northern Pajarito Plateau. Finally, I acknowledge that disparities in population size between the Rio Chama watershed and northern Pajarito Plateau can bias both the counts and relative frequencies of pottery moving from one area to the other (Duff 2002:169–171). I propose and use a model that accounts for this disparity when analyzing changing patterns of ceramic circulation across time and space.

Group Definition and Provenance

Initial examination of the entire decorated ceramic dataset using cluster analysis and examination of elemental bi-plots revealed two primary groups. The calculation of principal components based on 33 elements confirmed these groupings,[1] which were further refined using jackknifed Mahalanobis distance calculations (Davis 1986:485–487). I assigned group membership to samples that had greater than 5 percent probability of belonging to one group and less than 0.1 percent of belonging to any other group, or samples with an order of magnitude difference. Fifty-nine percent (516/874) of the pottery samples can be confidently assigned to one of two core groups based on conservative statistical probabilities. Based on mean elemental concentrations between the two groups, Group 1, the larger of the two groups (n=426), is enriched with high quantities of magnesium and strontium (Duwe 2011:751). Group 2 (n=90) has much higher concentrations of iron, titanium, and vanadium. Elemental bi-plots verify intragroup homogeneity and intergroup separation

[1] Na, Si, Ca, Cs, Ba, and Th were not included in the principal components analysis because of their noted unreliability in this type of analysis (Hector Neff, personal communication, January 2010).

(Figure 8.2). Table 8.3 displays the counts of Group 1 and 2 samples by each site analyzed for this project.

How can we explain the patterning of these two groups? Although ancestral Tewa pottery shares many common technological and stylistic attributes, the various types have distinct differences in temper, paste texture, and firing. These differences could also be representative of the use and availability of a variety of clay sources. Interestingly, Groups 1 and 2 both include all six analyzed ceramic types (Santa Fe Black-on-white, Wiyo Black-on-white, Abiquiu Black-on-gray, Bandelier Black-on-gray, Sankawi Black-on-cream, and Potsuwi'i Incised), suggesting that group separation is not strictly based on differing ceramic material and manufacturing techniques. Rather, group separation appears to be the result of large-scale regional geochemical variability.

To begin to establish the provenance of the archaeological samples from Groups 1 and 2, I classified the raw clay sources collected on survey against both core groups using Mahalanobis distance calculations based on the first six principal components. I employed the same conservative classification method used to assign group membership to the pottery samples. Unfortunately, only three clay samples could be reliably classified, which is likely due to my not being able to locate clays used in the past. It is also possible that the prehistoric potters mixed clays from more than one source during production. The three clay samples are, however, helpful in elucidating regional geochemical variability (clay sample locations are located on Figure 8.1). For example, there is an 18.5 percent probability that CLA89, a gray residual clay eroding from Bandelier Tuff on the Pajarito Plateau, belongs to Group 2. This suggests to me that the provenance of Group 2 pottery is the northern Pajarito Plateau where Bandelier Tuff is prominent and previously shown to be the parent material for locally produced biscuit wares (Curewitz 2008; Curewitz and Foit 2018). In the Rio Chama watershed, CLA20, a light-brown alluvial clay located near Lower Proterozoic felsic metavolcanic and plutonic rock in the Rio Ojo Caliente valley, has a 5.5 percent probability of being in Group 1. These Precambrian deposits are unique to the Rio Ojo Caliente and were heavily eroded as later Quaternary alluvium. Although the group probabilities are low, due to the poorly understood geochemical variability of the groups these help to establish possible provenance. While Group 1 is bigger and more diverse than Group 2, I propose that they were likely made with clays from the Rio Ojo Caliente Valley and surrounding areas, not the Pajarito Plateau. Lastly, CLA78, a tan, alluvial clay eroding from Tertiary clastic deposits near Tertiary basalt and andesite, demonstrated a 55.7 percent probability of belonging to Group 2. CLA78 is located along Abiquiu Creek south of the Rio Chama but is eroding from similar Jemez Mountain parent material as CLA89. Therefore, the extent of Group 2 variability is probably not confined to the Pajarito Plateau proper but extends along the edges of the Jemez Mountains.

The comparison of modern clay sources to archaeological samples begins to paint a picture of the generalized provenance of the two compositional groups: Group 1 represents the Rio Chama watershed, specifically its northern-most tributaries; and Group 2 represents the northern Pajarito Plateau and the flanks of the Jemez Mountains. The provenience of Groups 1 and 2 adds further weight to this interpretation following the "criterion of abundance" (Rands and Bishop 1980:19–20). Group 1 pottery, while found at sites in both the Chama and on the Pajarito Plateau, completely dominates the ceramic assemblages in the Chama watershed. There are no Group 2 samples at sites in the Rio del Oso valley, and only three samples (0.1%) at sites along the Rio Ojo Caliente. Group 2 pottery, besides being almost completely absent in the Chama, comprises the majority (55.3%) of pottery analyzed at sites on the Pajarito Plateau. I can confidently determine local pottery from sites along the tributaries of the Chama and on the Pajarito Plateau, but the geographic and geochemical extents of Groups 1 and 2 are unclear. For example, 57.8 percent of the sampled pottery from Tsiping'owingeh, a site located along a tributary to the Rio Chama, belongs to Group 2. Although the site is nearly 40 km from Potsuwi'owingeh on the Pajarito Plateau, Tsiping'owingeh shares a similar geology because of the eruption of Valles Caldera. Additional sampling of clays in both areas, as well as of the adjoining regions (the Rio Grande Valley and its tributaries to the east), is necessary to conduct a more fine-grained compositional analysis. Regardless, the present data allow me to differentiate local and nonlocal pottery from sites across the region and begin to understand degrees of economic interaction.

Changing Economic Relationships

Although this research is still in its preliminary stages and will eventually incorporate petrographic and stylistic analysis of pottery as well as a more detailed study of the region's geochemical variability, the most important finding is that ancestral Tewa pottery was produced in large amounts on both the Pajarito Plateau and in the Rio Chama watershed during the Coalition and Classic periods (Table 8.3). While previous research has determined that

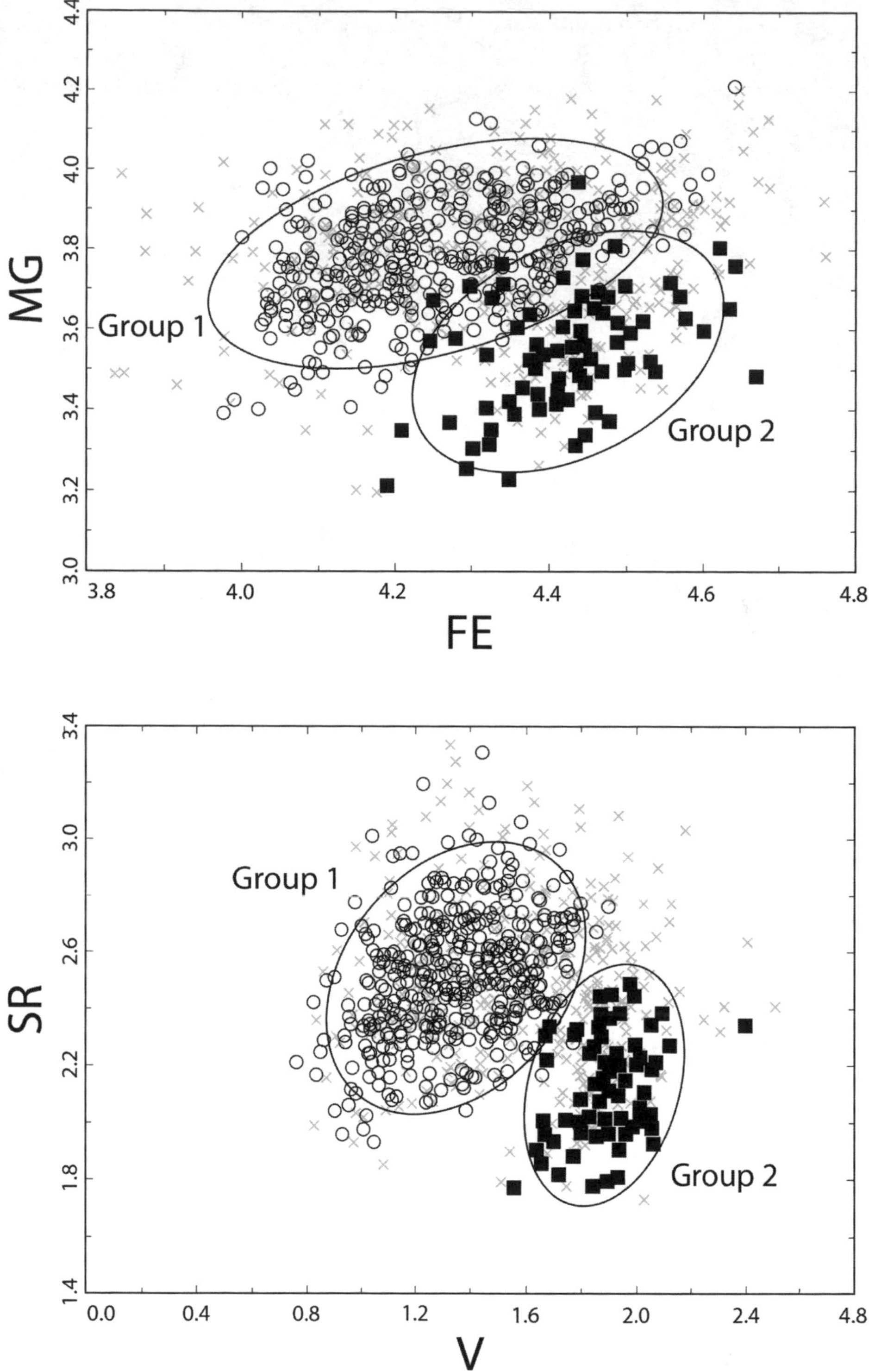

Figure 8.2. Elemental bi-plots of iron by magnesium and vanadium by strontium, demonstrating the distinct grouping between Group 1 and 2 samples of archaeological sherds. Unclassified samples are represented by a gray X.

Table 8.3. Counts of Group 1 and 2 Samples for Each Ancestral Tewa Pottery Type Found at the 13 Sites Analyzed for This Project

Drainage	*Santa Fe Black-on-white (1200–1350)*		*Wiyo Black-on-white (1300–1400)*		*Abiquiu Black-on-gray (1350–1450)*		*Bandelier Black on gray (1400–1500)*		*Potsuwi Incised (1500–1600)*		*Sankawi Black-on-cream (1500–1600)*		*Totals*
	Group 1 (Chama)	*Group 2 (Pajarito)*	*Group 1 (Chama)*	*Group 2 (Pajarito)*	*Group 1 (Chama)*	*Group 2 (Pajarito)*	*Group 1 (Chama)*	*Group 2 (Pajarito)*	*Group 1 (Chama)*	*Group 2 (Pajarito)*	*Group 1 (Chama)*	*Group 2 (Pajarito)*	
Rio Ojo Caliente													
Total samples	1	1	37	1	81	1	92	0	37	0	39	0	290
Total percentage	50.0%	50.0%	97.4%	2.6%	98.8%	1.2%	100.0%	0	100.0%	0	100.0%	0.0%	
Rio del Oso													
Total samples	N/A	N/A	7	0	16	0	21	0	7	0	13	0	64
Total percentage	N/A	N/A	100.0%	0	100.0%	0	100.0%	0	100.0%	0	100.0%	0	
Rio Chama													
Total samples	0	3	2	6	6	0	5	0	N/A	N/A	1	0	23
Total percentage	0	100.0%	25.0%	75.0%	100.0%	0	100.0%	0	N/A	N/A	100.0%	0	
Pajarito Plateau													
Total samples	0	4	0	3	22	12	13	9	6	9	1	15	94
Total percentage	0	100.0%	0	100.0%	64.7%	35.3%	59.1%	40.9%	40.0%	60.0%	6.3%	93.8%	
Tsiping'owingeh													
Total samples	0	3	7	13	9	7	3	3	N/A	N/A	N/A	N/A	45
Total percentage	0	100.0%	35.0%	65.0%	56.3%	43.8%	50.0%	50.0%	N/A	N/A	N/A	N/A	

sites on the Pajarito Plateau produced a great deal of the region's biscuit ware pottery (Abiquiu Black-on-gray and Bandelier Black-on-gray), far less has been known about the scale of pottery production in the Chama (Curewitz 2008). The sheer amount of pottery found at sites in the Chama suggests that much was produced locally and this assertion is supported by the high proportions of Group 1 pottery at sites in the watershed (Gauthier 1987).

An equally surprising result of this analysis is that there appear to have been changing patterns of ceramic circulation between the Pajarito Plateau and the Rio Chama watershed through time. Table 8.4 displays the observed frequencies of Chama-made pottery found at Pajarito Plateau sites and Pajarito-made pottery found at Chama sites for each ceramic period. I reduced the latter data into two groups that reflect the region's geologic and cultural diversity: the Rio Chama watershed (including samples from the Rio Ojo Caliente, Rio del Oso, and Rio Chama) and the Pajarito Plateau. Tsiping'owingeh was removed from this analysis due to its ambiguous association with either area. Because my samples are not random the comparison of the frequencies likely do not represent a quantitative statistical measure of interaction between the two areas. The strong patterns for (and against) ceramic mobility do, however, suggest dramatic and important change through time.

In the Coalition period no Chama-made pottery was observed at sites on the Pajarito Plateau, but a sizable amount of Pajarito-made pottery was found at sites in the Chama suggesting an open flow of pottery—a proxy for social interaction—from south to north. In fact, 80 percent of sampled Santa Fe Black-on-white pottery (1200–1350 CE) from Chama sites originated on the Pajarito Plateau. It is probable that the flow of Pajarito-made pottery into the Chama reflects the thirteenth-century migration into the area as pots were either brought by migrants themselves or were exchanged as part of social networks with their friends and family in the south. These social pathways would have been extended northward as people settled the Chama. These relationships began to change in the fourteenth century with the production of Wiyo Black-on-white (1300–1400 CE). Although Pajarito-made pottery was still circulating into the Chama it was at much lower quantities (13%). Perhaps this change anticipates the emerging economic and social networks of the Classic period.

By the mid-fourteenth century patterns of the production and circulation of pottery between the Pajarito Plateau and Rio Chama watershed dramatically reversed. There is little to no evidence (aside from one sherd of Abiquiu Black-on-gray) of Pajarito-made pottery at sites in the Chama in the Classic period. However, a substantial amount of Chama-made Abiquiu Black-on-gray (65%), Bandelier Black-on-gray (59%), and Potsuwi'i Incised (40%) ended up at sites on the Pajarito Plateau. Although the lack of Pajarito-made pottery observed in the Chama is confounding (and is discussed later in this chapter) the large amounts of Chama-made pottery found on the Pajarito Plateau suggest intense economic relationships between the two areas. The population of the Rio Chama watershed underwent a substantial influx of migration in the mid-fourteenth century, likely from the Pajarito Plateau (Duwe 2011). Perhaps the flow of pottery from the Chama reflects return visits by socially and historically linked individuals.

Table 8.4. Observed Frequencies of Analyzed Pottery from Sites in the Rio Chama Watershed and on the Pajarito Plateau

Pottery Type and Dates	*Chama to Pajarito*	*Pajarito to Chama*
Santa Fe Black-on-white (1200–1350 CE)	NA	0.80
Wiyo Black-on-white (1300–1400 CE)	NA	0.13
Abiquiu Black-on-gray (1350–1450 CE)	0.65	0.01
Bandelier Black-on-gray (1400–1500 CE)	0.59	NA
Potsuwi'i Incised (1500–1600 CE)	0.40	NA
Sankawi Black-on-cream (1500–1600 CE)	0.06	NA

Note: Values labeled NA had no observed samples.

By the end of the Classic period, the Chama and Pajarito Plateau appear to have become isolated from each other. While Pajarito Plateau sites had substantial amounts of Abiquiu Black-on-gray (65%), Bandelier Black-on-gray (59%), Potsuwi'i Incised (40%), and Sankawi Black-on-cream (6%), they show progressively less nonlocal pottery. Although this project presents a preliminary investigation of a single material class, it suggests that by the end of the Classic Period the Rio Chama watershed and the Pajarito Plateau had become economically and socially independent from one another.

Acknowledging Population Disparity

Based on the temporal patterns of observed frequencies of pottery made on the Pajarito Plateau and found in the Rio Chama watershed (and vice versa) there appears to have been significant change in ceramic mobility between the Coalition and Classic periods. It is important, however, to address a factor that introduces bias in these results: the disparity in population size between the Chama and the Pajarito Plateau. To summarize an earlier discussion, the northern Pajarito Plateau had a much larger population in the late Coalition period and this pattern was reversed in the Classic period as the Chama became the population center of the Tewa world.

The size of population can dramatically affect the amount of pottery that is moved across the landscape, even with the same per capita level of production (Duff 2002:169–171). Let us assume that an ancestral Tewa potter exports 10 percent of her pottery. In an area with 1,000 potters this would result in 100 pots being exported; in contrast, an area with 100 potters would export only 10 pots per year, despite the same rate of export per potter. In a random sample the flow of pottery between regions would appear to be an order of magnitude less from the region with fewer potters even though the per capita production is the same.

Therefore, it would be inappropriate to analyze the direction and magnitude of ceramic circulation (as a proxy for social interaction) between the Chama and the Pajarito Plateau without accounting for population disparity. To account for this disparity, I created a null model of ceramic circulation that provides expected relative frequencies of Chama and Pajarito-made pottery that should be found at all sites within the two areas based on relative population sizes if ceramic circulation was completely open and random. The model assumes that (1) pottery was made by people everywhere in the two areas; (2) the amount of pottery produced in a given area is directly proportional to the size of its population; and (3) that all the pottery produced between two regions was perfectly mixed and randomly scattered across sites within the two regions. These assumptions, as well as the resulting model, are not meant to be realistic but offer an important check on interpreting the observed frequency patterns. By comparing the expected frequencies generated by the null model with the observed frequencies (Chama-made pottery found at Pajarito Plateau sites and Pajarito-made pottery found at Chama sites) discussed in the previous section it is possible to better understand the magnitude and directionality of ceramic circulation between and within the areas relative to the population disparity.

The expected values produced by the null model relies solely on the relative frequencies of population size between the Chama and the Pajarito Plateau (Ortman 2016b), while the observed values reflect the results of the provenance analysis (Table 8.5).[2] The null model relies on population estimates to produce expected relative frequencies of Rio Chama and Pajarito Plateau-produced pottery at all sites in the region if ceramic circulation were completely open and not restricted by cultural or geographic variables. For example, based on the null model for Abiquiu Black-on-gray (produced between 1350 and 1450 CE) we should expect 0.72 of Chama-made and 0.28 of Pajarito-made pottery at every site in the two areas. The null model will, rarely, if ever, represent actual ceramic circulation in the past. However, deviations of observed values from the provenance analysis from the expected values under the null hypothesis should provide some control over population disparity both between areas and through time. To return to the example of Abiquiu Black-on-gray, 0.65 of Group 1 (Chama) samples were found at sites on the Pajarito Plateau. This is similar to the expected frequency of 0.72 based on a majority of the region's population residing in the Rio Chama watershed in the late fourteenth century. A deviation (observed–expected values) of -0.07 suggests that there were slightly fewer Chama pots found at sites on the Pajarito Plateau than expected by the null model. This can be contrasted to very few (0.01) Pajarito-made samples observed at sites in the Chama that have an expected value of 0.28. The deviation of -0.27 suggests that significantly less pottery was being moved from the Pajarito Plateau to the Rio Chama than expected by the null model. When compared to the deviation of pottery moving from the Chama to the Pajarito Plateau (-0.07), it becomes apparent that even when taking population disparity between the two areas into account there were likely many more pots moving from the Chama to the Pajarito Plateau than vice versa. This pattern suggests there was some structure to pottery exchange between the two regions and that perhaps some other product flowed in the opposite direction, from the Pajarito to the Chama.

Calculating the deviation between observed and expected relative frequencies is also useful in comparing the magnitude of change in ceramic circulation within an area through time while accounting for changes in population disparities (Table 8.6). For example, during the

[2] I drew from Ortman's (2016b) data to determine the momentary population estimates for both areas during the six time periods when the analyzed pottery was manufactured. Although his counts for the Rio Chama watershed were retained, I only included sites from the Pajarito Plateau between Santa Clara creek and Frijoles Canyon that manufactured ancestral Tewa pottery. To fit Ortman's multiple periods of momentary population estimates to the date ranges of Tewa pottery I averaged multiple periods within each ceramic date range.

Table 8.5. Observed (Provenance Analysis) and Expected (Population Estimates) Relative Frequencies from Sites in the Rio Chama Watershed and on the Pajarito Plateau, including the Deviations between the Two (Observed–Expected Frequencies)

	Santa Fe Black-on-white (1200–1350)		*Wiyo Black-on-white (1300–1350)*		*Abiquiu Black-on-gray (1350–1450)*		*Bandelier Black-on-gray (1400–1500)*		*Potsuwi'i Incised (1500–1600)*		*Sankawi Black-on-cream (1500–1600)*	
	Group 1 (Chama)	*Group 2 (Pajarito)*	*Group 1 (Chama)*	*Group 2 (Pajarito)*	*Group 1 (Chama)*	*Group 2 (Pajarito)*	*Group 1 (Chama)*	*Group 2 (Pajarito)*	*Group 1 (Chama)*	*Group 2 (Pajarito)*	*Group 1 (Chama)*	*Group 2 (Pajarito)*
Observed Counts												
Rio Chama	1	4	46	7	103	1	118	0	44	0	53	0
Pajarito Plateau	0	4	0	3	22	12	13	9	6	9	1	15
Observed Frequencies												
Rio Chama	0.20	0.80	0.87	0.13	0.99	0.01	1.00	0	1.00	0	1.00	0
Pajarito Plateau	0	1.00	0	1.00	0.65	0.35	0.59	0.41	0.40	0.60	0.06	0.94
Population	1577	5535	2800	5611	10891	4253	11867	3664	9332	3226	9332	3326
Expected frequencies	0.22	0.78	0.33	0.67	0.72	0.28	0.76	0.24	0.74	0.26	0.74	0.26
Deviation (Observed—Expected)												
Rio Chama	−0.02	0.02	0.54	−0.54	0.27	−0.27	0.24	NA	0.26	NA	0.26	NA
Pajarito Plateau	NA	0.22	NA	0.33	−0.07	0.07	−0.17	0.17	−0.34	0.34	−0.67	0.67

Note: Deviations labeled NA had no observed samples.

Coalition period a large amount (0.80) of Pajarito-made Santa Fe Black-on-white (1200–1350 CE) was observed at sites in the Chama. In the subsequent years, much less (0.13) Pajarito-made Wiyo Black-on-white (1300–1400 CE) pottery was found at the same sites. A rough comparison of the observed frequencies suggests that there was much less ceramic circulation from the Pajarito Plateau to the Rio Chama watershed in the fourteenth century. However, the relative frequency of the population of the Pajarito Plateau was declining between the time periods (0.78 to 0.67) and hence so were the expected values. Was the decline in observed Pajarito-made pottery at sites in the Chama due to changing social or economic patterns, or just an artifact of changing proportions of population and the production of pottery between the two areas? By calculating and comparing the deviations between Santa Fe Black-on-white (0.02) and Wiyo Black-on-white (-0.54) it appears that there were far fewer Pajarito-made Wiyo Black-on-white pots found in the Chama than expected, even after accounting for changes in population size between the two areas.

Table 8.6. Deviations between Observed (Provenance Analysis) and Expected (Population Estimates) Frequencies from Sites in the Rio Chama Watershed and on the Pajarito Plateau

Pottery Type and Dates	*Chama to Pajarito*	*Pajarito to Chama*
Santa Fe Black-on-white (1200–1350 CE)	NA	0.02
Wiyo Black-on-white (1300–1400 CE)	NA	−0.54
Abiquiu Black-on-gray (1350–1450 CE)	−0.07	−0.27
Bandelier Black-on-gray (1400–1500 CE)	−0.17	NA
Potsuwi'i Incised (1500–1600 CE)	−0.34	NA
Sankawi Black-on-cream (1500–1600 CE)	−0.67	NA

Note: Deviations labeled NA had no observed samples.

DISCUSSION AND CONCLUSIONS

This provenance study demonstrates that ancestral Tewa pottery dating from 1250 to 1600 CE was produced in both the Pajarito Plateau and the Rio Chama watershed using distinct geochemical clay sources. Patterns of production and distribution of this pottery, although preliminary, indicate a fluidity in economic (and social) connectivity between the two areas through time.

In the Coalition period the areas were linked through shared histories; based on similarities between architecture and ritual landscapes at least some of the settlers of the Rio Chama watershed were from the Pajarito Plateau. The provenance study supports this. Although the early settlers of the Chama manufactured their own pots using local clays, substantial quantities of Santa Fe Black-on-white and Wiyo Black-on-white pottery were imported from the Pajarito Plateau. This suggests either direct population movement from the Pajarito to the Chama or some other type of interaction stemming from interconnected social networks.

The close ties between the Pajarito Plateau and the Chama continued into the early years of the Classic period, again likely based on the movement of people between the areas from south to north. Although potters in the Chama were almost exclusively producing and using their own decorated pottery (Abiquiu Black-on-gray, Bandelier Black-on-gray, Sankawi Black-on-cream, and Potsuwi'i Incised), large quantities of Chama-made pottery ended up at sites on the northern Pajarito Plateau, particularly in the fourteenth and fifteenth centuries. Based on my limited, nonrandom sample, nearly half of the biscuit ware (Abiquiu Black-on-gray and Bandelier Black-on-gray) consumed at Pajarito sites of the period was imported from sites in the Rio Chama watershed. This implies a strong economic relationship based on shared settlement histories. Given the evidence of imbalances between population and agricultural lands noted by Eiselt (Chapter 2) for the Classic Period Rio Chama, this pattern may imply increasing flows of other products (foodstuffs or cotton; see Chapter 3) in the opposite direction, from the Pajarito to the Chama.

Later in the Classic period, and particularly in the sixteenth century, economic bonds between the two areas appear to have weakened. While people in the Chama continued to exclusively use locally produced pots, Pajarito villagers imported fewer numbers of Chama-made pots through time, with only 2.3 percent of Sankawi Black-on-cream coming from the north. If we assume that the distribution of pottery reflects social connectedness, by whatever mechanism, this pattern suggests these two areas were becoming increasingly isolated from one another on the eve of the Historic period. This fits well with the idea that unique Tewa identities and social landscapes were forming in the fifteenth and sixteenth centuries.

How can we explain the mechanisms of this diversification? Why do sites in the Chama show increasing isolation while those on the Pajarito Plateau remained economically intertwined with both the Chama and the surrounding Rio Grande region (as evident by higher frequencies of glaze ware)? And why did the flow of pottery from the Chama to the Pajarito Plateau decrease over time? I propose that differences in settlement histories between the two regions, and particularly the process of population coalescence, contributed to these patterns.

By the beginning of the fifteenth century the Rio Chama watershed had become the population center of the Tewa world. Climatic instability encouraged people from the Pajarito Plateau and elsewhere in the Tewa Basin to settle along the relatively fertile river valleys of the watershed. Social and economic systems were developed to provision this large and diverse population (Chapter 5; Duwe 2016; Duwe and Anschuetz 2013), and Chama-wide social networks were necessary for agricultural security (Chapter 2). Chama residents appear to have produced nearly all their pots, including enough surplus to distribute some of this production to people on the Pajarito Plateau. Perhaps this self-sufficiency, spurred on by a sense of economic security and driven by favorable environmental factors and high populations, accounts for the lack of nonlocal pottery found at sites in the Rio Chama watershed (Ortman 2016a). These patterns may also reflect a high level of interdependency, where pots and other manufactured goods such as cotton cloth (possibly) from the Chama flowed to the Pajarito, and other goods such as stone tools, hides, and food flowed in the opposite direction. It is beyond the scope of this discussion to broach the causal factors of coalescence, but it may have been catalyzed by both internal factors such as self-sufficiency and economic security and external forces such as an increasingly competitive and hostile landscape (Fowles 2004; Fowles and others 2007).

The story of the Chama contrasts greatly with that of the Pajarito Plateau. By the beginning of the Classic period population gradually declined on the Pajarito Plateau as people left for other locales. The villages that remained were highly coalesced towns that in comparison with sites in the Chama were much more socially connected with their neighbors. This includes an intense economic relationship with sites in the Rio Chama, particularly in the fourteenth and fifteenth centuries, which likely represented kinship and social ties reflecting Pajarito villagers moving north into the Chama. These ties also extended south, with ancestral Keres and Tano communities represented through higher quantities of glaze ware pottery in Pajarito sites. The correlation of population loss with increased social interaction is a common theme in Pueblo history. Ford (1972) describes how villages hit with epidemics in the nineteenth and twentieth centuries reached out widely to find potential mates and replace the loss of ceremonial leaders and knowledge. The increased cultural contact of the Pajarito Plateau, opposed to the isolation of the Chama, may have contributed to the development of unique Tewa identities.

The second question—regarding the reasons for the decreased economic relationships between the Chama and the Pajarito Plateau through time—is more difficult to answer. By the sixteenth century the population in the Chama began to decline as populations either left the watershed or continued to coalesce into a handful of remaining villages. Although the weakening of these relationships may have begun in the fifteenth century as the Chama became more isolated (as demonstrated by frequencies of Bandelier Black-on-gray pottery), the last years of occupation in the Chama were socially tumultuous. This upheaval may have disrupted the social and economic networks between the two areas. Also, though not as well known, similar processes may have been happening on the Pajarito Plateau where only two villages were occupied to the end of the sixteenth century.

Regardless of the mechanisms that led to the diversification of individual Tewa communities the eventual result was, and is, a composite landscape of six related but distinct Tewa homelands within the Tewa Basin. Although the entire northern Rio Grande experienced unprecedented growth and change in the centuries preceding the arrival of the Spanish, each area had its own unique relationship with its physical and social landscape, which must have been, in part, formed through the process of population coalescence during the Prehispanic era. This project has demonstrated that the Tewa world is not a monolithic entity, either geochemically or culturally, and therefore presents countless opportunities for understanding the many scales of Tewa becoming.

Acknowledgments. These analyses were performed with the financial assistance of the California State University Department of Anthropology Short-Term Visitor Program and the National Science Foundation grant BCS-0228187 (Principle Investigator, Hector Neff). The fieldwork was supported by a National Science Foundation Dissertation Improvement Grant (#0741708).

CHAPTER NINE

Community Specialization and Standardization in the Galisteo Basin: The View from Pueblo San Marcos

Kari L. Schleher

San Marcos Pueblo is one of the few archaeological communities in the US Southwest that exhibits clear evidence of specialized production. A large aggregated town, it is located along the western margin of the Galisteo Basin and was occupied from the late 1200s until the Pueblo Revolt of 1680 (Figure 9.1). San Marcos potters specialized in the production of Northern Rio Grande glaze-painted pottery (Figure 9.2). These beautiful bichrome and polychrome vessels have interested archaeologists for nearly a century and extensive research has been done on their production and distribution (Dyer 2010; Habicht-Mauche 1993, 1995; Herhahn 1995, 2006; Herhahn and Huntley 2017; Huntley and others 2007; Jones 1995; Motsinger 1992, 1997; Nelson and Habicht-Mauche 2006; Reed 1990; Shepard 1942, 1965; Staley 1990; Warren 1969, 1979; Welker 1997). Elsewhere, I have identified great stability in all aspects of glaze ware production at San Marcos Pueblo (Schleher 2010, 2017; Schleher, Huntley, and Herhahn 2012), but in this chapter I introduce a new element into the discussion of specialization in pottery production—a view of production when number of producers is included. I discuss the evidence for specialization in pottery production at San Marcos Pueblo, as well as how specialized production has been identified ethnographically. I then address how morphological standardization in the vessels produced at San Marcos might be used to identify specialized production in other locations across the US Southwest where such possibilities exist, especially when a comparison of population is included. Finally, I consider the implications of community-level specialization at San Marcos for overall interpretations of Rio Grande Pueblo economy.

PUEBLO POTTERY PRODUCTION AND SPECIALIZATION

Specialization, defined as production over the needs of the household, was first documented in the Northern Rio Grande in the form of community-level specialization in the production of Glaze-painted pottery (Shepard 1936, 1942). This discovery, by Anna Shepard in the early 1900s, did not fit with what most archaeologists of the day thought about the Ancestral Pueblo economy, which was seen as household-based (Cordell 1991). Kidder (1936:xxiii, emphasis mine) commented on Shepard's discovery and the drastic realignment this discovery necessitated in understanding the pueblo economy:

> Shepard has now demonstrated that several very important types of pottery contain ingredients which could not possibly have been procured in the valley. *It is her opinion that the thousands of vessels concerned were brought to the pueblo in manufactured form.* If this was actually the case, we are faced by the necessity for a drastic rearrangement of ideas regarding the status of the ceramic industry, not only at Pecos, but throughout the Southwest. It has always been assumed that pottery was one of the regular household tasks of every Pueblo woman; that each town was in that regard self-sufficient. *But if whole classes of pottery, such as Glaze I and Biscuit, were imported, we must postulate an extraordinary volume of trade and allow for a compensating outward flow of other commodities.* Furthermore, we must believe that the production of

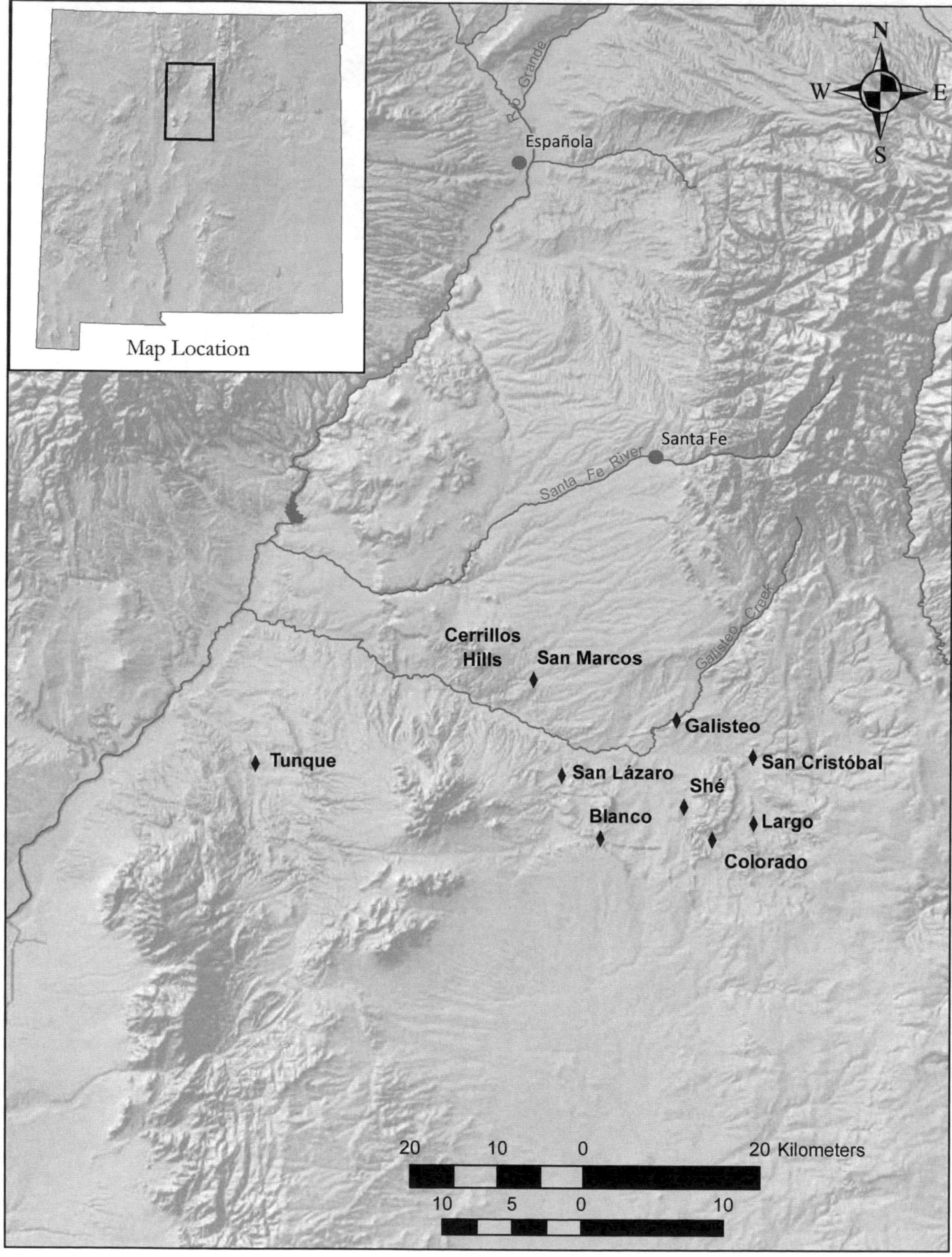

Figure 9.1. Locations of archaeological sites discussed in the text. Courtesy of Grant Coffey.

> vessels at the source of supply was much greater than was needed for home consumption, in other words, that rudimentary commercial manufacturing was practiced.

Evidence for rudimentary commercial manufacturing, or specialized production of pottery, has continued to build over time (Shepard 1942; Reed 1990; Warren 1969). Almost all these studies have built on Shepard's pioneering work and use of mineralogical tests—mostly petrographic analysis of temper—to determine the quantity of vessels produced at specific sites and the spatial extent of their consumption (Habicht-Mauche 1993, 1995; Nelson and Habicht-Mauche 2006; Reed 1990; Warren 1969, 1979). Some analyses have also examined the final products themselves for evidence of craft specialization (Herhahn 1995, 2006; Jones 1995; Motsinger 1997; Schleher 2010; Schleher, Huntley, and Herhahn 2012; Staley 1990; Welker 1995).

Some researchers argue that there was a relatively high level of production in the form of village or community specialization, such that specific villages made more pottery for export than others. Others argue that most villages made their own pottery. This question of specialization in pottery production ties into the overall volume themes presented in Chapter 1. As will be shown, the extent of the role of the Galisteo Basin pueblos in specialized production of glaze ware has been debated, but there is no doubt that there was some level of specialization in glaze ware production and a change in that level of production through time at particular sites. Although the *level* of material output in pottery for particular sites is debated, I argue for a *clear rate of change* in the level of those outputs that is reflected in changes in the degree of specialization through time, especially at the site of San Marcos Pueblo.

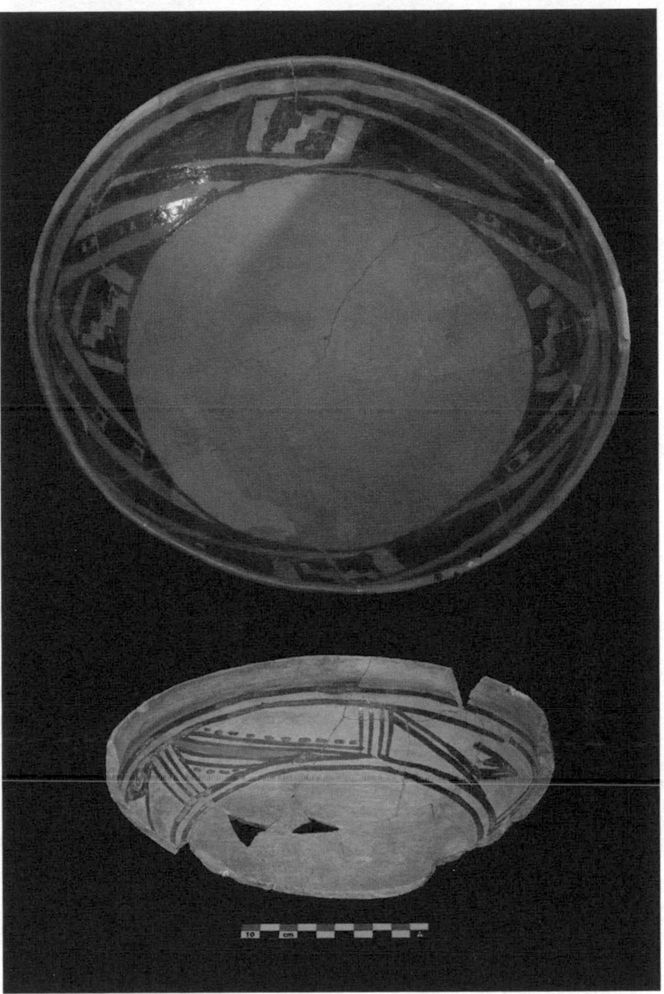

Figure 9.2. Examples of Rio Grande Glaze Ware pottery vessels from San Marcos Pueblo. *Top*: Agua Fria Glaze-on-red (Glaze A), Catalog # 29.0/ 4663 (AMNH). *Bottom*: San Lazaro Glaze Polychrome (Glaze D), Catalog # 29.0/ 4569 (AMNH). Images courtesy of the Division of Anthropology, American Museum of Natural History.

As described previously, Anna Shepard was the first researcher to demonstrate specialization through the examination of Northern Rio Grande Glaze Ware production (Shepard 1936, 1942, 1965). Shepard conducted petrographic analysis on pottery from Pecos and demonstrated that many of the vessels were tempered with nonlocal materials. She then expanded her sample using sherds collected by Mera (1933) from 40 sites and argued for specialized production in several regions including the Galisteo Basin (Habicht-Mauche 2002:53). This larger sample allowed Shepard to use glaze ware pottery types to look at temporal patterns in production. Northern glaze ware types, manufactured from the early 1300s through the late 1600s CE, are organized temporally in an alphabetical sequence, from Glaze A through Glaze F, based on changes in rim form and design (Eckert 2006). Using the glaze ware types for temporal control, Shepard found that potters living in the Galisteo Basin dominated production during the middle period of glaze ware production, especially for glaze types C and D. The earlier (Glaze A and B) and later (Glaze E and F) pottery production periods, in contrast, saw local centers of production over many areas. These results had implications for archaeologists' interpretations of Pueblo society. Instead of the prevailing assumption of Pueblo household self-sufficiency, Shepard inferred that Pueblo people participated in complex systems of craft specialization and exchange (Cordell 1991; Habicht-Mauche 2002:52).

Shepard included San Marcos Pueblo in the Galisteo Basin District and grouped the temper used by San Marcos potters with her general andesite rock temper category. Andesite-tempered vessels were exported out of the Galisteo in larger proportions during the middle period of glaze ware production, with the production of Glaze C and D types, while local ceramics recovered within the Galisteo were also locally made. During the late part of the glaze ware series, with the production of Glaze E and F pottery, dominance in Galisteo production declined—many more temper types began to be used, and many areas produced most of their own pots. This view of sites in the Galisteo Basin as major ceramic producers continued with the work of Helene Warren.

Warren's (1969, 1979) research took Shepard's study of centralized production further and suggested that centralized production occurred at specific sites in and near the Galisteo Basin during the middle period of Glaze Ware production. Warren argued that San Marcos Pueblo was a major production center during the fifteenth century, with the production of Glaze A and Glaze C pottery. Tunque, a village just to the west of the Galisteo, peaked in production somewhat later than San Marcos and dominated production of Glaze C and D vessels. Warren's view was that these two sites were production centers for Glaze Ware pottery and that the intensity of production at these sites changed over time (Warren 1969, 1976, 1979).

Research in the 1980s and 1990s continued to support the view of the Galisteo Basin region as a production center, but also expanded the number of areas that may have been important producers at different times (Schleher 2010, 2017). Habicht-Mauche (1993, 1995) examined pottery production at Arroyo Hondo Pueblo and found a regional system of production and exchange indicating community specialization in three districts: Albuquerque, Galisteo Basin, and Santo Domingo.

Other recent studies suggest a slightly different picture of glaze ware production. These studies represent the accumulation of knowledge on glaze ware production and, thus, present a significantly more complex picture of production than the earlier studies of Shepard and Warren. For example, Reed (1990) examined pottery from six villages in the Galisteo Basin and suggested that San Marcos was just one of several villages that specialized in glaze ware production. In contrast, Morales (1997:699) found that there was extensive production evidence at Tunque Pueblo and that Tunque exported relatively large quantities of Glaze D pottery. Nevertheless Morales (1997:929) noted, as did Creamer and Renken (1994) and Reed (1990), that pottery production was very widespread, even small sites had some evidence of pottery production.

Nelson and Habicht-Mauche (2006) used petrographic analysis to argue that, although San Marcos was an "important Glaze Ware production center," the distribution of wares made at the pueblo was primarily focused within the Galisteo Basin and at a few specific sites outside of the basin. Schleher and Boyd (2005) also used petrographic analysis of Glaze A through Glaze D sherds from field house sites near Cieneguilla to support the tie between this site and San Marcos—approximately 50 percent of the sherds examined came from San Marcos.

These more recent investigations, conducted on a finer scale than those of Shepard (1942) and Warren (1969, 1976, 1979), suggest complex patterns of manufacture and exchange. All continue to support San Marcos as *one* location of specialized production for export to other sites, especially during the period of production of Glaze A through Glaze D. Although studies do not lead to a consensus on the *degree of specialization* in glaze ware production, all studies indicate that glaze ware vessels were produced in the Galisteo Basin and specifically at San Marcos. Many villages manufactured pottery for their own use and exchange, but certain villages, including San Marcos and Tunque, produced and exchanged more than others, showing that, even without a market mechanism, economic development is reflected in the complexities of pottery production in the region (see Chapter 1). With this background I turn to an evaluation of the extent to which specialized production is manifested archaeologically in the pottery produced at San Marcos.

THE ORGANIZATION OF PRODUCTION AND SPECIALIZATION

Archaeologists consider the organization of production to be an important component of economic, technological, political, and social organization (Chavez 1992; Clark and Parry 1990). The organization of production is frequently examined in the context of complex societies and the maintenance of hierarchy in those societies (Brumfiel and Earle 1987; Costin and Hagstrum 1995). Because of this emphasis, most organization of production models focus exclusively on complex, market-based societies. Development of theoretical models to address the organization of production in middle-range societies has lagged behind (Mills and Crown 1995).

Specialization is simply one way to organize production. Craft production may or may not be specialized. Using the simple definition of specialization as production over the needs of the household, a specialist is someone who produces more objects than she or he uses in the immediate household and thus has extra objects to gift, barter, or exchange (Costin 2001:276).

Numerous typologies and classifications exist for characterizing the organization of production (Costin 1991; Peacock 1982; Rice 1987; Santley, Arnold, and Pool 1989; Sinopoli 1988; van der Leeuw 1977). For the current research, I use the four-parameter approach developed by Costin (1991). These four parameters—context, concentration, scale, and intensity—describe the degree of specialization in the organization of craft production. Although each parameter can be analyzed using ceramics from San Marcos Pueblo (Schleher 2010), I focus here on the intensity of production.

Intensity of production addresses the time investment of producers—assuming that increased time investment leads to an increase in the number of goods produced. The identification of the various parameters of specialized production may be more straightforward in complex, state-level societies when craft producers and workshops are obvious in the archaeological record. However, craft specialization is less visible in the archaeological record of middle-range societies, such as the Northern Rio Grande region of the American Southwest. Many specialists in this region were likely part-time, independent producers who worked in their homes, leaving few archaeological traces. This aspect of the archaeological record of middle-range societies requires that proxy indicators of organization of production be used to determine specialization. One proxy indicator that has been used to view the intensity of production is the relative degree of standardization of products (Mills 1996).

Standardization addresses the "relative degree of homogeneity or reduction of variability in the characteristics of pottery" (Rice 1991:268). Standardization is frequently equated with high intensity of production, meaning that the more time producers spend making pots (the higher the intensity of production), the more standardized their products become. Standardization and intensity of production are thought to be related in market-based societies as a result of four variables: (1) crafts made by intensive specialists are mass produced for the sake of economic efficiency; (2) standardization results from quality control; (3) it is a risk aversion tactic based on the conservative nature of pottery production; and (4) standardization and intensity of production are the result of increasing skill developed through repetition and routinization (Rice 1991:268). Similarly, Costin (1991:33) argues that products become more standardized with specialized production because there are fewer producers relative to consumers (basically, fewer hands working on the products), and because producers become more efficient as they intensify production. In nonmarket-based systems, consumer demands for a certain standardized product or social expectations of adherence to standardized canons may also explain why specialized products become more standardized. The relationship between standardization of assemblages and intensity of production may be clearer in complex archaeological societies if workshops or producers are visible archaeologically, and in most middle-range societies in modern settings as well, but the relationship is much less clear in the archaeological record of ancient middle-range societies. These issues are examined to determine which attributes of pottery, if any, may reflect changing levels of standardization of vessels made at San Marcos Pueblo.

The Northern Rio Grande is an ideal place to examine standardization in a middle-range society because we have independent evidence of change in the intensity of specialized production in the wide distribution of glaze ware vessels made at San Marcos Pueblo. The question is not whether specialization occurred, but the extent to which standardization resulted from this specialization. By examining standardization in this known setting, this research will show other researchers which attributes, if any, hold the most promise for examining standardization in other contexts.

USING THE COEFFICIENT OF VARIATION TO QUANTIFY STANDARDIZATION

I employ the coefficient of variation for specific attributes in a class of ceramics to assess the question of standardization. Although based on the standard deviation of a set of measurements, the coefficient of variation is preferable, as it "describes relative variation by expressing the standard deviation as a percentage of the mean. As a result, it removes scale effects" and is comparative across assemblages of different sizes (Longacre, Kvamme, and Kobayashi 1988:103). The larger the coefficient of variation, the more variation is present within the sample. Crown (1995:148–149) notes that most specialist producers documented ethnographically produce wares with coefficients of variation lower than 10 percent while nonspecialists make wares with coefficients of variation above 10 percent. She also notes, however, that specialists do occasionally produce wares with coefficients of variation above 10 percent. Eerkens and

Bettinger (2001:494) argue that the "coefficient of variation is a stable and reliable measure of variation." They develop a range of values that can be used to interpret the relative degree of standardization of assemblages. Their upper baseline is a coefficient of variation of 1.7 percent, although they suggest that coefficients of variation "in the range of 2.5 to 4.5 percent are more typical of the minimum error attainable by individuals in manual production without use of external rulers" (Eerkens and Bettinger 2001:496). Their lower baseline is a coefficient of variation of 57.7 percent, which indicates an unstandardized assemblage (Eerkens and Bettinger 2001:497). This research thus suggests a very wide range for standardized assemblages. The authors conclude that the coefficient of variation "is appropriate for archaeological studies comparing sample variation" (Eerkens and Bettinger 2001:499). The current research was developed with this conclusion in mind.

ETHNOARCHAEOLOGICAL AND ARCHAEOLOGICAL EVIDENCE OF STANDARDIZATION

Some researchers working with modern groups have documented a relationship between level of production intensity and standardization (e.g., Balfet 1965; Bowser 2000; Kvamme, Stark, and Longacre 1996; London 1991; Longacre 1999; Longacre, Kvamme, and Kobayashi 1988). Other researchers have also found evidence to the contrary and have questioned the linkage between standardization and specialization (e.g., Arnold and Nieves 1992; Roux 2003; Stark 1995). For example, Stark (1995) notes variation in standardization by level of production (i.e., specialist or nonspecialist production). Some of the specialist producers she cites do not have more standardized wares than nonspecialists. Arnold and Nieves (1992) suggest that standardization of ceramics is dependent on factors other than degree of specialization, such as potters' perceptions of the allowable variation in particular vessel shapes, the forming technique used, and the intended market. Roux's (2003) research indicates that high-intensity production results in standardized wares in some cases, but other factors including potter skill and vessel size classes impact the degree of standardization with similar rates of production. These ethnoarchaeological studies indicate that the relationship between standardization and intensity of specialization is variable and requires systematic evaluation.

I compared 13 modern groups and eight archaeological data sets available in published literature (Arnold and Nieves 1992; Blackman. Stein, and Vandiver 1993; Crown 1995; Hagstrum 1985; Lindauer 1988; Longacre 1999; Longacre, Kvamme, and Kobayashi 1988; Mills 1995; Powell 2002; Roux 2003; Stark 1995; Toll 1981, 1990). Each of the modern data sets are identified by the researcher as manufacture by specialist or nonspecialist producers. Additional details of these cross-cultural comparisons are presented in my dissertation (Schleher 2010). The variables selected are vessel height and rim or orifice diameter, because they are the variables most commonly examined in ethnographic studies and in archaeological analyses of whole vessels or sherds.

As discussed previously, Crown (1995) suggests that coefficients of variation below 10 percent indicate specialist production, whereas coefficients of variation above 10 percent require additional information to determine if production is specialized or nonspecialized. Table 9.1 shows that this suggestion is empirically supported in the majority of ethnographic cases where specialization is documented; in other words, for the majority of specialists (62–77% of cases) the coefficient of variation is below 10 percent. Even in the cases where the coefficient of variation of one or more ceramic types is above 10 percent, the majority of the ceramic types produced by the specialists are standardized and coefficients of variation are below 10 percent. The only case study for which this is not true is the Amphlett Island specialists (Stark 1995). Amphlett Island producers are specialists even though they produce only 72 pots per year (about 6 pots per month). This low level of intensity may explain why the products made by these specialists are not consistently standardized—these potters may not make vessels frequently enough for standardization to occur. It should also be noted that, of the five ceramic forms made by the Amphlett Island specialists, two forms *do* have coefficients of variation below 10 percent. All the ethnographic nonspecialist cases are between 10 percent and 20 percent.

In contrast, archaeological data from sites in the American Southwest, presented in Table 9.2, show very few coefficients of variation below 10 percent (Crown 1995; Hagstrum 1985; Lindauer 1988; Longacre, Kvamme, and Kobayashi 1988; Mills 1995; Powell 2002; Toll 1981, 1990). The majority of cases (69–76%) are between 10 percent and 30 percent, but a number are even above 30 percent (14–19% of cases). These data suggest two possibilities: (1) the 10 percent coefficient of variation is not the upper limit for specialized production in the prehistoric Southwest or (2) specialized pottery production occurred in only a few cases. Option 2 may be the case, but evidence for specialization in other production parameters suggests otherwise (Costin 1991). For example, Chacoan pottery, for

Table 9.1. Distributions of the Coefficient of Variation in Ethnographically Documented Specialist and Nonspecialist Data Sets

Specialists	*CV for Height*		*CV for Orifice/Aperture*	
	N	%	*N*	%
less than 10% CV	10	76.9	18	62.1
Between 10 and 30% CV	3	23.1	11	37.9
Above 30% CV	0	0	0	0
Total number of data sets	13	100	29	100
Nonspecialists	*CV for Height*		*CV for Orifice/Aperture*	
	N	%	*N*	%
Less than 10% CV	0	0	0	0
Between 10 and 30% CV	1	100	8	100
Above 30% CV	0	0	0	0
Total number of data sets	1	100	8	100

CV = coefficient of variation.

Sources: Arnold and Nieves 1992; Blackman. Stein, and Vandiver 1993; Crown 1995; Hagstrum 1985; Lindauer 1988; Longacre 1999; Longacre, Kvamme, and Kobayashi 1988; Mills 1995; Powell 2002; Roux 2003; Stark 1995; Toll 1981, 1990.

Table 9.2. Distribution of the Coefficient of Variation in US Southwest Archaeological Data Sets

Coefficient of Variation	*CV for Height*		*CV for Orifice/Aperture*	
	N	%	*N*	%
Less than 10%	4	10.8	4	11.1
Between 10 and 30%	28	75.7	25	69.4
Above 30%	5	13.5	7	19.4
Total number of data sets	37	100	36	100

CV = coefficient of variation.

Sources: Crown 1995; Hagstrum 1985; Lindauer 1988; Longacre, Kvamme, and Kobayashi 1988; Mills 1995; Powell 2002; Toll 1981, 1990.

which there is evidence for specialized production through compositional studies, generally has coefficients of variation above 10 percent (Toll 1981, 1990). The significantly greater range of coefficients of variation for archaeological samples compared to ethnographic samples suggests that issues other than a direct link between standardization and specialization are at work.

To sum up, the standardization hypothesis, that specialists produce more standardized products than nonspecialists due to increased skill and efficiency (Rice 1991), is supported, for the most part, by ethnographic data where assemblages have coefficients of variation of less than 10 percent. Archaeological assemblages in the US Southwest, however, have coefficients of variation greater than 10 percent. I suggest that the differences between ethnographic and archaeological studies are the result of one or more other variables that are due to the differences between the archaeological and ethnographic records, including time scale, numbers of production episodes, number of producers, and numbers of vessels examined.

Time Scale

All ethnographic studies are based on pottery made within a short period of time, most often less than one year. Archaeological studies, by contrast, typically include samples made over hundreds of years, making the assemblages a temporal palimpsest. Because this long time-scale means that archaeological samples are produced over a number of generations it also means that the data incorporate the learning cycles of all those producers. Skilled potters did not start out that way and their early periods of learning are included in this time scale variable.

Number of Production Episodes

There are also differences between the number of production episodes in ethnographic and archaeological samples that are due the palimpsest nature of the archaeological record. The assemblage of pottery that the archaeologist recovers is a collective record of a large number of production episodes that occurred over the entire time any ceramic type was being produced. Most archaeological samples are the result of hundreds of production episodes, all of which may contribute to the coefficient of variation for that assemblage.

Number of Producers

Longacre (1999) has documented that the number of producers in a group affects product standardization. For example, he describes variation among four specialists in San Nicolas, whose products range from 3 to 7.5 percent coefficient of variation for the same vessel type. This effect would be magnified when examining archaeological samples because tens to hundreds of producers—whether specialists or not—could have made the vessels over a 200-year period. In addition, this variable also can be affected by multiple producers working on a single pot. The incidence of "multiple hands," or more than one producer working individual pots, has been documented archaeologically by Crown (2007) in the Southwest. A number of different producers, possibly of different skill levels, working on vessels together can increase the variation of the assemblage produced.

Numbers of Vessels Examined or Sample Size

Another variable that contributes to the archaeological analysis of coefficients of variation is the number of vessels examined. A slight increase in coefficient of variation is seen as the number of vessels examined increases. For example, the lowest coefficient of variation (3.4 percent) in the Southwestern archaeological data are for Chaco redware cylinder jars, but only four vessels were examined (Toll 1990).

These variables, in addition to others such as overlapping ceramic classes, likely work in combination to contribute to the large coefficients of variation seen in archaeological samples (Longacre, Kvamme, and Kobayashi 1988). The low coefficient of variation for the four Chaco red ware cylinder jars (3.4 percent) is a function of the small sample size, but it also may be that these four pots were made by one potter during one short production episode. Thus, all the factors are interrelated. The opposite effect can also occur. For instance, the Hohokam samples, with the largest coefficients of variation, were made over a long period of time, probably during a large number of production episodes by a large number of potters (Lindauer 1988).

The current analysis demonstrates that the general patterns found in ethnoarchaeological data are useful for archaeological research. With care, constant comparison between ethnoarchaeological data and the archaeological record yields valuable information on a different scale. When these variables are carefully controlled for in the archaeological sample, ethnographic comparison can yield a greater understanding of the organization of production in the past. Pottery production at San Marcos Pueblo, where we have independent evidence suggesting that production was specialized, is an informative case study with which to test the relationship between standardization and specialization.

SAN MARCOS PUEBLO AND THE CERAMIC SAMPLE

San Marcos was first occupied in the thirteenth century and was abandoned during the Pueblo Revolt of 1680. Direct Spanish contact occurred at San Marcos in 1581 during the Chamuscado and Rodriguez expedition. This site is large, with 43 room blocks and a complex history of use. The extensive archaeological research at the site has yielded large samples of ceramics, some of which were utilized in this study. All six Rio Grande Glaze Ware types, from Glaze A to Glaze F, were recovered from the site during recent University of New Mexico (UNM) fieldwork. A seriation of the glaze ware series shows frequency peaks of glaze ware rim types and a clearly sequential history of use of the individual types at San Marcos Pueblo. The glaze ware series used here is a chronological tool with which to categorize the sample of sherds in this research (Ramenofsky and Schleher 2017; Ramenofsky, Neiman, and Pierce 2009; Larson and others 2017).

There are approximately 60,000 sherds in the UNM collections from San Marcos Pueblo; approximately 3,500 of these are decorated rim sherds that were used in the

Table 9.3. Counts and Percentages of the Sample Tempered with Augite Monzonite

Glaze Type	*Sample Size for Current Analysis*	*Sample with Augite Monzonite Temper*	*Percent Tempered with Augite Monzonite*
A Yellow	79	76	96.20%
B	80	78	97.50%
C	78	68	87.18%
D	78	47	60.26%
E	68	42	61.76%
F	76	61	80.26%
Totals	459	372	81.05%

creation of a pottery seriation (Ramenofsky, Neiman, and Pierce 2009; Ramenofsky and Schleher 2017). The sample selected for this study is outlined in Table 9.3. The first stage of data collection required determining which of the samples selected were tempered with the specific weathered augite monzonite that indicated production at San Marcos (see Dyer 2010; Schleher 2010). Of the 459 sherds, 372 are tempered with weathered augite monzonite (Table 9.3). The remaining sherds are tempered almost exclusively with other Galisteo Basin materials, primarily hornblende latites (Schleher 2010). Only sherds indicating production at San Marcos are included in the remainder of the study.

The overwhelming dominance of local production throughout the glaze ware sequence further supports the assumption, following Warren's (1979) and Shepard's (1942) research, that potters at San Marcos Pueblo produced more vessels than were consumed in their community. This suggests that San Marcos Pueblo was one of the concentrated areas of production in the Northern Rio Grande for Glaze Ware. This is especially suggested for Glaze A, B, and C production, with the assemblage being predominantly manufactured at the site, and with little evidence of any import of wares made elsewhere.

STANDARDIZATION IN VESSEL MORPHOLOGY AT SAN MARCOS PUEBLO

The morphological attributes used for this part of the study were rim diameter, average wall thickness, and maximum rim thickness. Rim diameter was measured in centimeters at the thickest part of the rim using rim diameter templates to obtain orifice diameter. Average wall thickness for each sherd represents an average of three to five measurements of thickness taken the end of the sherd that is opposite from the rim. Maximum rim thickness is an average of three measurements along the thickest point of the rim (Schleher 2010).

To account for the variables that result in differences in standardization of archaeological assemblages discussed previously, I attempted to control for as many of these variables as possible. Time was controlled for by use of the periods of glaze type production, following dendrochronological estimates from Vint (2000). Number of vessels is controlled for by having a similar sample size for each glaze type, although all attributes could not be recorded on every sherd.

Controlling the number of production episodes is not possible for an archaeological assemblage, but the number of producers can be accounted for by a general consideration of the site population. In previous research on pottery production at San Marcos (Schleher 2010, 2017; Schleher, Huntley, and Herhahn 2012), I was not able to account for changes in population throughout each production period, but recent research by Ortman (2017) allows for greater control over population and, thus, the number of possible producers at San Marcos during each production period. Ortman developed estimates of population at San Marcos for 17 time periods (Table 9.4). I used the date ranges for each glaze type to determine an average site population during each of the six glaze type production periods (Table 9.5). To estimate the number of potters, the average population for each glaze type production period is multiplied by the fraction of locally made pots to nonlocal pots presented in Table 9.3 to produce a possible number of potters in the village at any one time. Although this estimate likely overestimates the number of potters per period, it is a way to develop a relative number of potters for each period based on the estimated overall population. This hypothetical number of potters is tied to the proportion of pottery that was made at San Marcos

Table 9.4. Estimated Population of San Marcos Pueblo by Period

Period	*Dates*	*Population Estimate*	*Glaze Period*
1	1050–1175	0	—
2	1175–1200	0	—
3	1200–1250	0	—
4	1250–1275	0	—
5	1275–1315	412	—
6	1315–1350	864	A
7	1350–1400	603	A
8	1400–1425	2,217	A/B
9	1425–1450	2,636	B/C
10	1450–1490	1,014	B/C
11	1490–1515	1,737	D
12	1515–1550	509	E
13	1550–1600	539	E
14	1600–1625	464	E
15	1625–1650	688	E/F
16	1650–1700	629	E/F
17	1700–1760	0	—

Source: Ortman 2017.

Table 9.5. Population Average and Estimated Number of Potters by Glaze Period

Glaze Period	*Date Range*	*Average Population*	*Fraction*	*Potters*
A	1315–1425	1,228	0.96	1,181.3
B	1400–1450	1,580	0.98	1,540.5
C	1425–1490	1,825	0.87	1,591.0
D	1490–1515	1,737	0.60	1,046.7
E	1515–1700	566	0.62	349.4
F	1625–1700	659	0.80	528.5

Note: Date Ranges are dendrochronological cross-dates reported by Vint (2000); all dates CE.

Fraction refers to the fraction of the overall population making pottery based on the ratio of locally made pots to nonlocal pots presented in Table 9.3.

Pueblo by local potters. I present the coefficient of variation from San Marcos in two ways: (1) assemblage level percent coefficient of variation and (2) percent coefficient of variation divided by the estimated number of potters for each glaze ware type, which I call percent coefficient of variation per potter.

Morphological Standardization Results from San Marcos

Average sherd wall thickness and the assemblage coefficient of variation for wall thickness are stable throughout the glaze sequence, with no statistically significant differences among the glaze types (Table 9.6; Figure 9.3). Overall, the assemblage level coefficient of variation is similar throughout the glaze ware sequence, with no indication of increase in the amount of standardization during the intermediate glaze ware production period. The percent coefficient of variation per potter is very low throughout the glaze ware sequence, with the lowest variation from Glaze A through Glaze D. The percent coefficient of variation per potter goes up with Glaze E and F (Table 9.6 and Figure 9.4). Note that although there is a change and an increase in the percent coefficient of variation by potter for the Glaze E and F production periods, the overall percent coefficient of variation is very low—less than 0.08 percent for the entire sequence.

Maximum rim thickness changes throughout the sequence with modifications in the way the rim was formed, but the assemblage range of variation is just as stable for rims as for wall thickness (Table 9.6; Figure 9.3). This is a significant finding for the question of standardization, perhaps even more than the results for wall thickness. The average wall thickness itself did not change significantly throughout the sequence. However, the maximum rim thickness value *does* change significantly over time, yet the degree of assemblage standardization *does not* change significantly. Similar to the wall thickness attribute, the coefficient of variation per potter is very stable from Glaze A through Glaze D, with a slight increase in Glaze E and F (Table 9.6; Figure 9.4). This finding suggests that while potters may have been innovative in developing new rim forms, once a new type of rim was accepted by potters, everyone began making rims the same way. The data suggest that the intentional nature of a change in the rim form does not modify how standardized the attribute is on the vessels (Schleher 2010).

Rim diameter was difficult to measure on some of the sherds because of their small size (the majority of the sherds sampled from San Marcos are from surface contexts). Thus, the results should be taken with this caution in mind. In the future, instead of including all sherds, I would use a minimum of 10 degrees of arc as a cut-off for inclusion, although in the current sample only a few sherds would have been left in the sample.

Table 9.6. Summary Statistics for Sherd Thickness, Rim Thickness, and Rim Diameter by Glaze Type

Glaze Type	**SHERD THICKNESS STATISTICS**				
	No.	*Mean (mm)*	*Std. Dev.*	*% CV*	*% CV /potter*
A	76	5.33	0.72	13.54	0.011
B	78	5.04	0.94	18.56	0.012
C	68	5.28	0.82	15.56	0.010
D	46	5.03	0.91	18.14	0.017
E	42	5.05	0.65	12.89	0.037
F	47	4.91	0.90	18.40	0.035
	Levene's Test P-Value = 0.051				
	MAXIMUM RIM THICKNESS STATISTICS				
	No.	*Mean (mm)*	*Std. Dev.*	*% CV*	*% CV/ potter*
A	14	5.84	0.78	13.38	0.011
B	78	8.04	1.06	13.25	0.009
C	66	7.43	1.11	15.00	0.009
D	47	7.73	1.05	13.54	0.013
E	38	8.66	1.04	12.02	0.034
F	18	6.70	1.02	15.29	0.029
	Levene's Test P-Value = 0.633				
	RIM DIAMETER STATISTICS				
	No.	*Mean (cm)*	*Std. Dev.*	*% CV*	*% CV/ potter*
A	74	29.41	8.55	29.07	0.025
B	76	30.79	7.14	23.19	0.015
C	64	30.05	8.33	27.73	0.017
D	47	30.94	7.36	23.81	0.023
E	40	33.85	8.56	25.29	0.072
F	53	33.26	9.94	29.87	0.057
	Levene's Test P-value = 0.482				

Note: CV = coefficient of variation.

It is also significant to note that I did not find clear size classes in my sample (see Schleher 2010:140 for a discussion of size class determination and a histogram of rim diameters). This is significant because grouping multiple size classes can distort measures of standardization (Crown 1995; Longacre, Kvamme, and Kobayashi 1988). Other researchers *have* found size classes in Rio Grande Glaze Ware samples. At Pecos, Kidder (1936:4–5) noted small (18–21 cm) and large (30 cm) bowl classes. Graves and Eckert (1998:267) found a bimodal size distribution, with small vessels having diameters of 25 cm or less and large vessels having diameters of more than 25 cm. I present the data for all the sherds in the sample, with no size class separation.

The data suggest a pattern of average rim diameter increasing through time (Table 9.6). These average measurements are not significantly different than average rim diameter measurements from other glaze ware–producing sites. For example, glaze ware rim sherds from Tunque Pueblo range from 8 to 50 cm, with most rim diameters between 26 and 34 cm (Morales 1997:780). The San Marcos rim diameters fall within this range.

There is a large amount of variation for this attribute, as seen in high assemblage coefficients of variation for

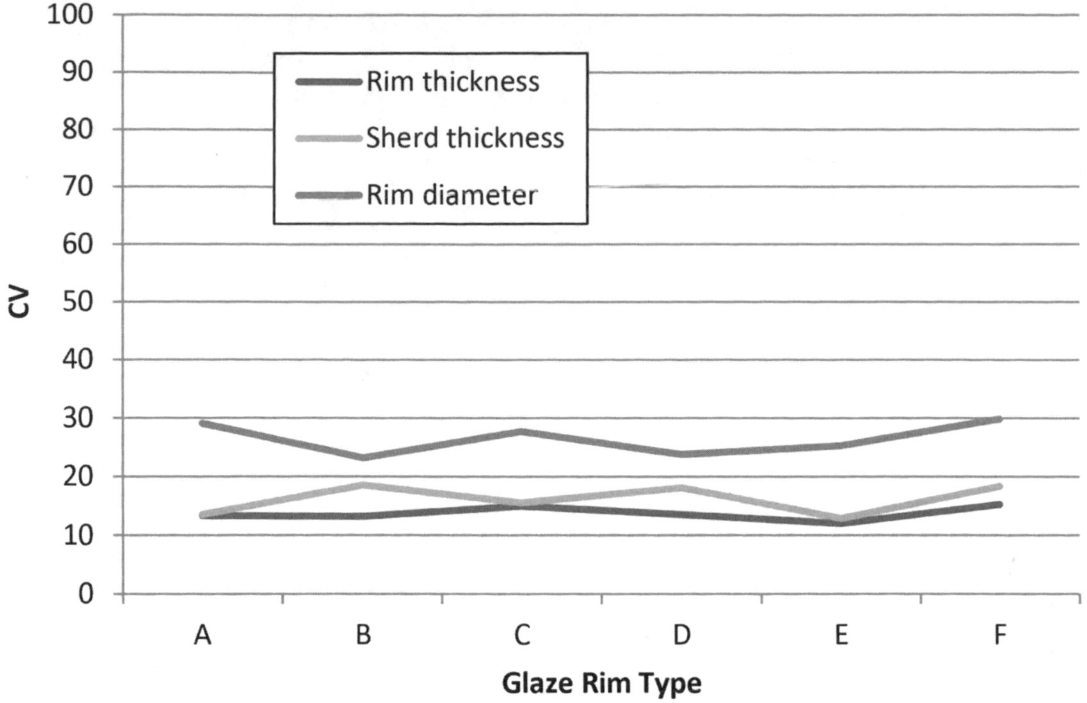

Figure 9.3. Percent coefficient of variation by glaze type.

all types, although there are no dramatic changes in the amount of variation throughout the glaze ware sequence (Table 9.6; Figure 9.3). Percent coefficient of variation for the assemblage level data range from 23 to 30 and Levene's Test P-value indicates no significant differences throughout the sequence. Although this range of variation is not nearly as standardized as those for wall thickness and maximum rim thickness, it may be that separating out different size classes would make this attribute appear more standardized (if size classes could have been identified in the data set). The percent coefficient of variation per potter is similar to the pattern seen for the other two morphological attributes examined, with a low and stable percent coefficient of variation from Glaze A to Glaze D and an increase in variation for Glaze E and F.

The results for these three morphological attributes, wall thickness, maximum rim thickness, and rim diameter, clearly reflect mechanical standardization and the highly stable nature of morphological features of pottery production at San Marcos. No significant differences in assemblage standardization are seen among the glaze ware types through time. Some change is apparent in the percent coefficient of variation per potter, with stable coefficient of variation per potter from Glaze A to Glaze D and a slight increase in variation for Glaze E and F.

In general, the data from San Marcos Pueblo suggest stability in the organization of production. The data show little or no change in the range of assemblage variation throughout the glaze ware sequence and indicate that, at least at San Marcos Pueblo, standardization is not a direct indicator of intensity of pottery production. Comparisons of variation with a consideration of number of producers does produce a slightly different result. Although there is a slight increase in the range of variation per potter for the late glaze ware types, the overall range of coefficient of variation is still extremely low throughout the glaze sequence.

Summary

The expectation of the standardization hypothesis is that standardization would change with changing intensity of production, especially if the number of potters was held constant. Increased intensity of pottery production was documented previously for San Marcos during the periods of production of Glaze A, C, and D types (Shepard 1942; Warren 1979). The overall assemblage results indicate no significant temporal trends in the data to suggest increasing or decreasing levels of standardization for pots produced during these periods. The results of variation *per potter* do, however, show slightly more standardization during these higher intensity periods of production.

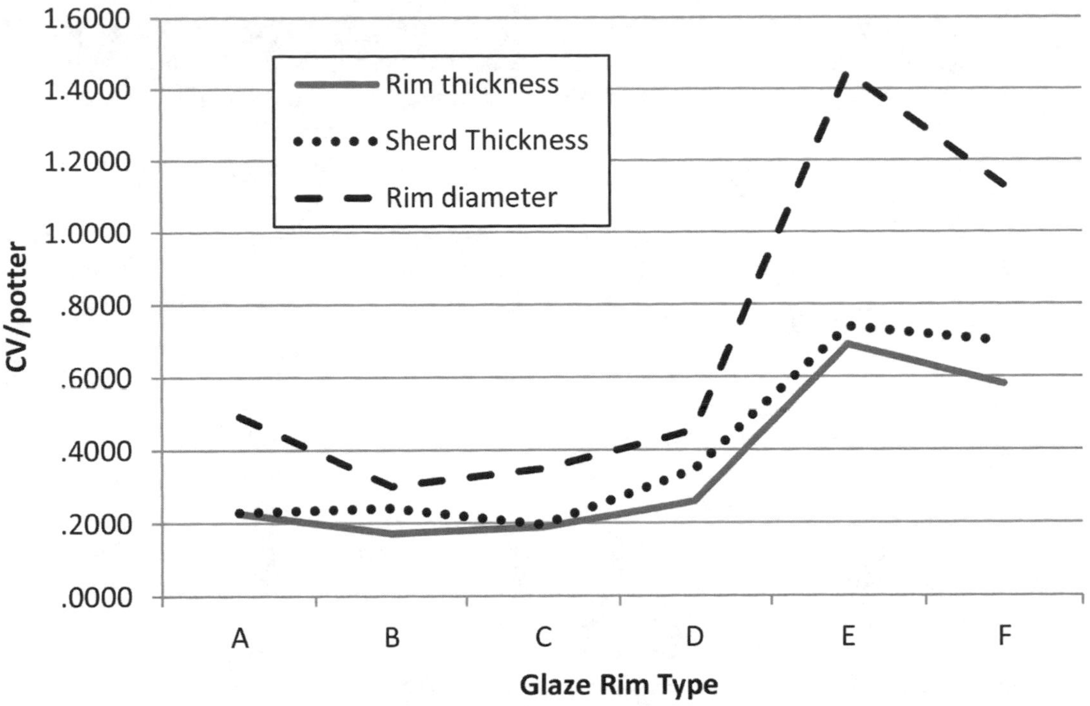

Figure 9.4. Percent coefficient of variation by potter and by glaze type

DISCUSSION

If we look at the overall assemblage data, standardization is not a direct indicator of changes in intensity of production at San Marcos Pueblo. There is no significant increase or decrease in the level of standardization for any morphological attribute examined. Confounding variables including the difficulty of knowing the actual number of producers, conflation of a long time-scale, and other factors, are still a concern in the interpretation of these data. Although this project was developed with the idea that we held many of these factors constant, some factors were not possible to control. When population is used to estimate the number of potters, however, there is a more direct link between standardization and intensity of pottery production for the community.

The notion that standardization does not reflect intensity of production has been discussed by Eric Blinman (1988) who suggests that Prehispanic potters in the Southwest never reached levels of craft specialization that would be reflected in increased standardization in the pottery assemblages produced. This is certainly a possibility. The relatively low levels of production, always at the household level, may not have required potters to produce pots at a high enough rate to modify the level of standardization. The level of production may have been too infrequent to achieve a standardized product. There does, however, seem to be some evidence of increased standardization in certain assemblages documented by others, such as large vessel size (Crown 1995). So many potters may have contributed to assemblages that it may not be possible to recognize true standardization. It seems likely that if there were ever high enough levels of production going on in the Prehispanic American Southwest, they would be in the large, aggregated Classic period towns such as San Marcos with extensive evidence for export of goods to other villages.

A second possible interpretation of these results may be that the confounding factors discussed here blur the record, making it more difficult to sort out these factors due to the sherd sample deriving primarily from surface collection. The relationship of standardization to increased intensity of production is a complex one. Most ethnographic research suggests that, as potters spend more time making vessels, the standardization of their products increases. In archaeological cases, it is often difficult to see this relationship between intensity and standardization. What the results from San Marcos suggest is that, although standardization may be dependent on changes in intensity of production on an individual level, as suggested by many ethnographic examples, standardization of an assemblage produced by a group of potters is blurred by other factors. These factors, including the number of producers, production episodes, vessel size classes, and time, are challenging and sometimes impossible to control in the archaeological record.

When we do account for changing population size, and thus changing numbers of potters and consumers, the relationship between intensity and standardization appears more closely tied. It is significant especially because the lowest percent coefficient of variation per potter at San Marcos occurs during the periods of Glaze A to Glaze D production, which are also the temporal periods with the *highest* population at the site (Tables 9.5 and 9.6). This correlates with the periods of the most intensive production of pottery at San Marcos (as seen in the proportions of locally made pottery; see Schleher 2010). Thus, we have further support for specialization in pottery production in the coefficient of variation per potter that supports the earlier work arguing for specialization at San Marcos (e.g., Shepard 1936, 1942; Warren 1979). Comparisons with earlier sites near San Marcos also support the evidence for specialization and increased intensity of production through time. For example, coefficient of variation for rim diameters on a sample of 251 Santa Fe black-on-white bowls from Agua Fria Pueblo, a Coalition period (CE 1150–1425) period village located less than 15 kilometers from San Marcos is 31.5 percent (Schleher and Eckert 2012), which is higher than the coefficient of variation for bowls of any Glaze Ware type at San Marcos Pueblo (which range from 23 to 29 percent coefficient of variation, as shown in Table 9.6). These data suggest that production of pottery at San Marcos is more standardized overall and, thus, more specialized, than earlier pottery produced in earlier villages in the north-central Rio Grande.

The stability in ceramic production from the 1300s to the late 1600s at San Marcos is surprising, considering the number of obvious social and economic changes that occurred during this period. Spanish contact and eventual Spanish presence, as well as aggregation and pulses in population size surely had social and economic effects on the pueblo's residents. Nonetheless, these perturbations are not reflected in any great change in the measured amount of variation seen in the ceramics produced. Changes occurred with Spanish contact in the introduction of new native-made vessel forms (colono wares), agricultural processing, room size, household composition, the introduction of draft animals, metallurgical production, and dwelling construction in the broader Pueblo region (Dyer 2010; James 1997; Jones 2016; Vaughan 2017). Some of these changes also occurred at San Marcos, yet we do not see drastic changes in the ceramic production system. When we examine the coefficient of variation by potter, we do see a slight increase in the amount of variation, indicating that even when these changes are not visible in assemblage level data, they are reflected by taking population into account and, thus, support more intensive economic specialization in pottery production, especially during the early and intermediate glaze ware periods of production at San Marcos Pueblo.

The results of this study have important implications for interpretations of pueblo economy during the Protohistoric period. The data from one of the largest towns in the Galisteo Basin indicate that the specialized production first suggested by Anna Shepard in the early 1900s occurred and can be identified by close examination of not only the trade and distribution of pottery across the region, but by careful analysis of the products themselves. It is necessary to examine both assemblage level data and data that controls for population in some way to better account for the relationship between producers and consumers. The evidence of specialization in pottery production suggests that the potters at San Marcos were part of the development of regional division of labor that allowed them to focus more intensely on making pottery than others in the region. This in turn suggests that economic growth, and especially an expansion in the regional division of labor, occurred in the Northern Rio Grande from the 1300s through the 1500s, even without formal market mechanisms.

Acknowledgments. Thank you to Scott Ortman for asking me to be a part of this volume and for his help in developing methods to evaluate the relationship of specialization and standardization that accounts for population. This chapter is based on my dissertation and could not have been completed without the support of my dissertation committee, especially my dissertation chair, Patty Crown. Committee members Ann Ramenofsky and Judith Habicht-Mauche also contributed to the final product. Funding for this research was provided by a National Science Foundation Dissertation Improvement Grant (BCS Proposal 0525200) and a number of graduate research and development grants (University of New Mexico). Thanks also to Grant Coffey, who made the map in this chapter. Thanks to Dave Thomas and Anibal Rodriguez (American Museum of Natural History) and Dave Phillips and Catherine Baudoin (Maxwell Museum of Anthropology) to for access to collections from San Marcos Pueblo.

CHAPTER TEN

Martial Rock Art in the Northern Rio Grande: Reconciling the Disjunction between Actual Violence and Its Expressions

Anna E. Schneider

During the thirteenth and fourteenth centuries, Pueblo societies of the Northern Rio Grande Region were transformed in the wake of significant turmoil. During the twelfth and thirteenth centuries the San Juan drainage, and especially the Mesa Verde Region of southwestern Colorado and southeastern Utah, was characterized by considerable violence. This turmoil was a precursor to collapse and abandonment and, by approximately 1280 CE the region was empty. At the same time, villages began to aggregate in the Northern Rio Grande Region of New Mexico. This florescence is often credited to an influx of immigrants from the north (Lipe 2010; Ortman 2010, 2012). In the Northern Rio Grande Region, resulting patterns of violence stood in stark contrast to those previously seen in the Mesa Verde Region. Based on the frequency of trauma on skeletal remains, violence appears to have declined over time, and the nature of this violence was fundamentally different than that of previous centuries. A transformation of social norms and values likely played a role in these changes (Kohler and others 2014:459).

Skeletal evidence suggests that levels of violence declined as San Juan populations joined those of the Northern Rio Grande Region. There is, however, a notable disjunction between the skeletal evidence of violence and depictions of violence in rock art. Although one might expect the frequency of martial imagery to covary with the frequency of skeletal evidence for interpersonal violence, this is not what occurs. In the Mesa Verde Region, where violence was prevalent, martial rock art and war iconography is generally rare (Kuckelman 2000, Kohler and others 2014). And in the Rio Grande Region, martial rock art became increasingly common in the thirteenth and fourteenth centuries, even as skeletal evidence of violence declined (Schaafsma 1992, 2000). In this chapter, I address this disjunction between violence and its expressions and delve into spatial patterns in the prevalence of martial imagery. If patterns in the skeletal data show a decline in overall violence in the Northern Rio Grande Region, why is there more martial imagery in the rock art? How was this imagery distributed across the landscape and what did it signify?

I begin with an overview of patterns of violence in the Mesa Verde and Northern Rio Grande regions. Then, I explore the distribution of martial rock art by comparing rock art tabulations for six previously recorded localities from the two regions: Lower Butler Wash, Petroglyph Point, Petroglyph National Monument, Comanche Gap, the Pajarito Plateau, and Mesa Prieta (Figure 10.1). A seventh locality from the Fremont area, Warrior Ridge, is included in order to provide a comparative data point which shows that martial rock art was common in some areas prior to 1300 CE. Finally, I discuss possible explanations for the patterns observed and present a framework for thinking about the relationship between actual violence and its expressions in the Northern Rio Grande Region. I also discuss the role that this imagery may have played in maintaining internal peace and projecting social unity, arguing that control over internal violence is a key prerequisite for economic development. Ultimately, I argue that patterns observed in martial rock art in the Northern Rio Grande Region reflect broader changes in agglomeration, social organization, and group interaction that supported the episode of economic development discussed elsewhere in this volume.

Figure 10.1. Locations of sites included in the sample. Prepared by the author

VIOLENCE IN THE NORTHERN SOUTHWEST

Existing data indicate that interpersonal violence was pervasive in the San Juan during the Pueblo III (1140–1280 CE) period (Leblanc 1999). In the Mesa Verde Region in particular, this period was characterized by a preference for defensible locations with readily available water, access-restrictive features, towers, and aggregated villages. Intentionally burned buildings, weaponry, and human remains with peri-mortem injuries offer additional testaments to violence at this time (Kuckelman 2006). Kuckelman (2015) argues that this violence resulted from an environmental downturn, triggering resource stress and social instability. At sites like Castle Rock Pueblo, defensive architecture and a defensible location are indicators of a need for protection. These features did not prove to be adequate. Human remains at Castle Rock show evidence of trauma and post-mortem neglect resulting from the violent attack that ended occupation of the village in the 1280s CE (Lightfoot and Kuckelman 2001). The extreme violence at this site was not an isolated incident. Region-wide violence, in combination with environmental stress, social instability, and other factors, stimulated people to emigrate, leaving the Mesa Verde region largely empty by the end of the thirteenth century (Kuckelman 2000, 2006, 2015; LeBlanc 1999).

As the Mesa Verde Region emptied, the Northern Rio Grande Region experienced a steady rise in population and increased settlement aggregation. This concurrent rise and fall of populations is often taken to indicate that people fleeing the Mesa Verde Region resettled in the Northern Rio Grande Region and integrated with indigenous residents (Ford, Schroeder, and Peckham 1972;

Lipe 2010; Ortman 2010; but see Boyer and others 2010 for a dissenting opinion). Unprecedentedly large multi-storied pueblos appeared, and, as people coalesced, village populations increased, and the number of large villages decreased (Anschuetz 2007; Duwe and Anschuetz 2013). New architectural forms suggest decreased household autonomy and greater social investment in the village as a unit as social organization shifted from a kin-based to a sodality-based system (Lipe 2010:279). Vitally, economic development accelerated during this time. The increased agglomeration of populations resulted in the expansion of human connectivity and a transformation of the economy (Chapter 1). In addition to major social and economic changes, war iconography in rock art reached its most highly developed form as quantities increased and motifs diversified (Schaafsma 2000:30). The majority of martial imagery dates to between 1300 and 1600 CE. This increase in martial imagery begs the question of whether it reflects an escalation of actual warfare and violence (Schaafsma 2000:5; Kohler and others 2014:464).

In order to compare levels of violence in these two regions, Kohler and his colleagues (2014) plotted incidences of human skeletal trauma and found that violence (along with population) began to increase dramatically in the late 1000s and peaked in the mid-1100s in the Mesa Verde Region. Levels of conflict spiked following the breakup of the Chacoan system around 1140 CE, and then declined briefly before spiking again between 1260 and 1280 as the final Mesa Verde depopulation took place (Kohler and others 2014). The most common type of trauma in the region was what LeBlanc (1999) describes as "extreme processing." This behavior included mutilation and cannibalism (Kohler and others 2014:449).

Meanwhile, in the Northern Rio Grande Region, levels of conflict remained low to the end of the Prehispanic period, even as the population increased with the influx of migrants from the Mesa Verde Region. Although rates of violence were comparatively lower in the Northern Rio Grande Region, it is important to emphasize that it was never completely absent. There is physical evidence of violence at the Tewa pueblo of Te'ewi in which a massacre of young people, primarily men, took place within a kiva in the 1400s (Kohler and others 2014:458). The Tewa, with their war and scalp societies, maintained a warlike reputation, and Bandelier (1892:165–166) describes a Tewa attack on a Keres village in the Historic period (Schaafsma 1992). War societies, war rituals, and war chiefs who lead war parties and organized the pueblo for defense are well documented ethnographically (Ellis 1951). Fortified villages and defensive architecture have been documented throughout the Northern Rio Grande Region, suggesting a need for protection (Bernardini 1998).

Why were conditions in the Northern Rio Grande region comparatively peaceful even as population increased? Kohler and his co-authors (2014) posit that effective water management, more inclusive social organization, and religious innovations led to decreased violence. Water management included gravel mulching, irrigation, and other techniques that protected farmers from fluctuations in precipitation. Community integration and participation is evidenced by the building of plazas and the emergence of new religious and ceremonial innovations such as sodalities and moieties. The economic system shifted from kin-based production to community-based systems with village level specialization and intercommunity exchange (see Chapter 9), which likely created dependencies that crosscut different groups. Pueblos formed settlement clusters (Chapter 5); warfare may have been confined to struggles between these clusters, meaning that most people living within them were largely insulated from internal violence. Conflict expanded beyond the village-on-village violence of earlier centuries and was transformed into a larger, group-on-group scale (Kohler and others 2014:456).

METHODOLOGY

As observed by Kohler, Schaafsma, and others, there is a disjunction between warfare imagery and skeletal evidence of violence in the Northern Rio Grande Region. In order to explore this disjunction, I examine the distribution of martial imagery across the landscape and, using spatial patterns in the prevalence of martial imagery, I develop a framework for thinking about the relationship between actual violence and its expressions. The question of how martial imagery and skeletal evidence of violence relate is then expanded to explore the idea that this imagery contributed to the maintenance of internal peace and projection of social unity to outsiders. I suggest these factors, in turn, helped to facilitate the economic development described throughout this volume.

It is important to note that violence had many forms prehistorically, including ritual brutality and conflict that could have left few skeletal traces in the archaeological record. Furthermore, skeletal evidence of trauma and rock art depictions of conflict might relate to fundamentally different types of violence. The nuances of how different types of violence manifest themselves in the archaeological record are fertile ground for future research. Here I use evidence of perimortem skeletal trauma because that is what is most visible and unambiguous in the archaeological record. I have focused on the Mesa Verde and Northern Rio Grande regions because of the availability of data on evidence of skeletal trauma as well as the evidence for an ancestor-descendant relationship between these two regions (Kohler and others 2014; Lipe 2010; Ortman 2010, 2012).

Rock art images of conflict provide insight into how violence was conceptualized and communicated symbolically and artistically. Pueblo rock art was created from Basketmaker II through Pueblo IV times (Slifer 1998:40), but for the purposes of this study I focus on the Pueblo III and Pueblo IV periods. The dominant style of Northern Rio Grande Region rock art is a culmination of early Pueblo rock art styles combined with ideas borrowed from the Jornada region to the south. Pueblo III and Pueblo IV rock art reflects the emergence of this characteristic style around 1300 CE (Slifer 1998:41). The Rio Grande style is characterized by petroglyphs and large outlined designs that are often highly stylized and decorative (Schaafsma 1975:129). To identify patterns in the distribution of martial rock art, I compared previously compiled rock art tabulations from six localities (Figure 10.1). This sample was determined primarily by the availability of numerical tabulations of rock art motifs. Although the number of sites is small, the compared data includes complete sampling of specific sites and represents a starting point that can be expanded upon in the future.

For the Mesa Verde Region, I included two panels from Lower Butler Wash in southeastern Utah. These panels were recorded by the San Juan River Rock Art Project and date to the Pueblo III period (1150 –1350 CE). In addition, I included data from Petroglyph Point, a panel located within Mesa Verde National Park and documented in the *Petroglyph Trail Guide*. The trail guide illustrates the petroglyphs at Petroglyph Point and features interpretations of the elements by four Hopi men who visited the park in 1942 (Mesa Verde Museum Association 1986).

I also included Warrior Ridge, a Fremont site located in Nine Mile Canyon in Duchesne County, Utah, that was documented by the Colorado Plateau Archaeological Alliance (Spangler 2011). Based on the ceramic sequence, Warrior Ridge dates to between 900 and 1300 CE. Although this site lies to the north of the ancestral Pueblo area, I chose to include it as an additional comparative data point, due in part to the rarity of martial imagery in Mesa Verde Region rock art and the fact that this is one of the few sites on the greater Colorado Plateau for which rock art motifs have actually been quantified.

Within the Northern Rio Grande Region, rock art from Mesa Prieta is currently being documented as part of the Mesa Prieta Petroglyph Project. Tabulations for 23 different proveniences were included in this analysis (Janet MacKenzie, personal communication 2015). Tabulations from Comanche Gap and Petroglyph National Monument, both compiled by the Rock Art Recording Field School of the Archaeological Society of New Mexico, are also included (Fletcher and Merkt 2006). Finally, the Pajarito Plateau is represented by a tabulation of motifs from 32 sites dating from the mid-twelfth to the late sixteenth century (Munson 2002).

Within each data set, tabulations of motif types were sorted into three categories: martial elements, weapons and weapon bearers, and nonmartial elements. Martial elements are defined here as motifs explicitly related to conflict and warfare: shields, shield bearers, and anthropomorphs depicted in scenes of combat. Motifs that may have symbolic associations with warfare, such as mountain lions and stars, are also included in this category. Mountain lions were symbolic patrons of war and are often important figures in Pueblo war societies (Schaafsma 1992, 2000:62). Among Zuni Bow Priests, who function as earthy representatives of the twin war gods, mountain lion fetishes held special status (Ellis 1951:194). In rock art, images of mountain lions are often associated with other war-related figures (Schaafsma 1992). Similarly, stars—including morning star, falling stars, and comets—are considered a major component of Pueblo warfare iconography (Schaafsma 1992:167, 2000:62). In Tewa ideology, the morning star is often associated with the War God. At Isleta, stars were perceived as "mean" (Parsons 1932:342, 1939:205). Stars are also sometimes associated with scalping. Among the Hopi-Tewa at Hano, scalps are referred to as "Morning Star," and Scalp Women are known as "Dark Star Man" (Parsons 1939; Schaafsma 1992). Furthermore, warrior figures are often star-faced, or carry shields with stars (Schaafsma 1992).

A second category of motifs includes weapons and weapon bearers. Bows and arrows, which suggest either warfare or hunting, were placed in an indeterminate category of their own because, while they do not necessarily refer to warfare or interpersonal violence, the possibility of that association cannot be ruled out. Finally, the nonmartial category includes all elements with no known connotations of warfare or violence.

Using this classification scheme, the relative frequency of martial rock art at each locality is summarized in Table 10.1. Assuming that these proportions derive from roughly

Table 10.1 Rock Art Frequencies at the Sample Sites

Locality	*Elements*	*Number of Elements*	*Percentage of Total*
Warrior Ridge	Martial Elements	94	8.79%
	Suspected Combat Scenes	18	1.68%
	Anthropomorphs in 1-on-1 Combat	52	4.86%
	2 Figured Attacking a 3rd	6	0.54%
	Shields	18	1.68%
	Nonmartial Elements	976	91.21%
	Total Elements	*1,070*	
	Standard Error of the Proportion	*0.87%*	
	95% Confidence Interval	*7.07% to 10.50%*	
Lower Butler Wash	Martial Elements	1	0.95%
	Mountain Lion	1	0.95%
	Nonmartial Elements	104	99.05%
	Total Rock Art Images	*105*	
	Standard Error of the Proportion	*0.95%*	
	95% Confidence Interval	*−0.92% to 2.83%*	
Petroglyph Point	Martial Elements	0	0%
	Nonmartial Elements	14	100%
	Total Rock Art Images	*14*	
	Standard Error of the Proportion	*0%*	
	95% Confidence Interval	*0%*	
Mesa Prieta	Martial Elements	49	1.47%
	Shield Bearers	19	0.57%
	Shields	15	0.45%
	Stars	15	0.45%
	Weapons & Weapon Bearers	48	1.44%
	Nonmartial Elements	3,228	97.08%
	Total Rock Art Images	*3,325*	
	Standard Error of the Proportion	*0.21%*	
	95% Confidence Interval	*1.06% to 1.89%*	
Pajarito Plateau	Martial Elements	145	7.19%
	Shields	30	1.49%
	Shield Bearers	22	1.09%
	Arrow Swallower	7	0.35%
	Banoliers (Torso X)	5	0.25%
	Mountain Lion	9	0.45%
	Stars	72	3.57%

continued

Table 10.1 (continued)

Locality	*Elements*	*Number of Elements*	*Percentage of Total*
Parajito Plateau (continued)	Weapons & Weapon Bearers	22	1.09%
	Nonmartial Elements	1,851	91.72%
	Total Rock Art Images	*2,018*	
	Standard Error of the Proportion	*0.57%*	
	95% Confidence Interval	*6.05% to 8.32%*	
Petroglyph National Monument	Martial Elements	180	0.93%
	Shield	38	0.20%
	Shield Bearer	27	0.14%
	Mountain Lion	11	0.06%
	Star	104	0.54%
	Weapons & Weapon Bearers	116	0.41%
	Nonmartial Elements	19,055	98.47%
	Total Rock Art Images	*19,351*	
	Standard Error of the Proportion	*0.07%*	
	95% Confidence Interval	*0.79% to 1.07%*	
Comanche Gap	Martial Elements	145	3.28%
	Mountain Lion	14	0.32%
	Shield	31	0.70%
	Shield Bearer	26	0.59%
	Star	74	1.67%
	Weapons & Weapon Bearers	32	0.72%
	Nonmartial Elements	4,250	96.0%
	Total Rock Art Images	*4,427*	
	Standard Error of the Proportion	*0.27%*	
	95% Confidence Interval	*2.75% to 3.81%*	

random samples of the rock art at each site, I also calculated standard errors and 95 percent confidence intervals for these proportions.

DISCUSSION

Rock art documentation and interpretation present numerous challenges that must be acknowledged. The proportions presented in Table 10.1 have likely been affected by variation in recording techniques and tabulation methodology across the studies used for this sample. Chronological control is also difficult. Rock art dating typically relies on the identification of temporally significant styles defined through relative dating (Francis 2001; Keyser 2001; Munson 2002; Schaafsma 1985). In the regions discussed in this chapter, rock art has been relatively securely dated through temporally significant styles as well as association with independently dated sites. In addition, interpretations of rock art are often tenuous, and some motifs may be subject to multiple interpretations. For example, while shields are an object directly related to conflict, images of shields have also been interpreted as symbols of family, religious, and social organizations (Cole 1990).

Despite of these caveats, the results strongly suggest that the relative frequency of martial rock art varies across the landscape in a patterned way (Figure 10.2). Furthermore, the calculation of standard error illustrates that, even at a 95 percent confidence interval, Warrior Ridge and Pajarito

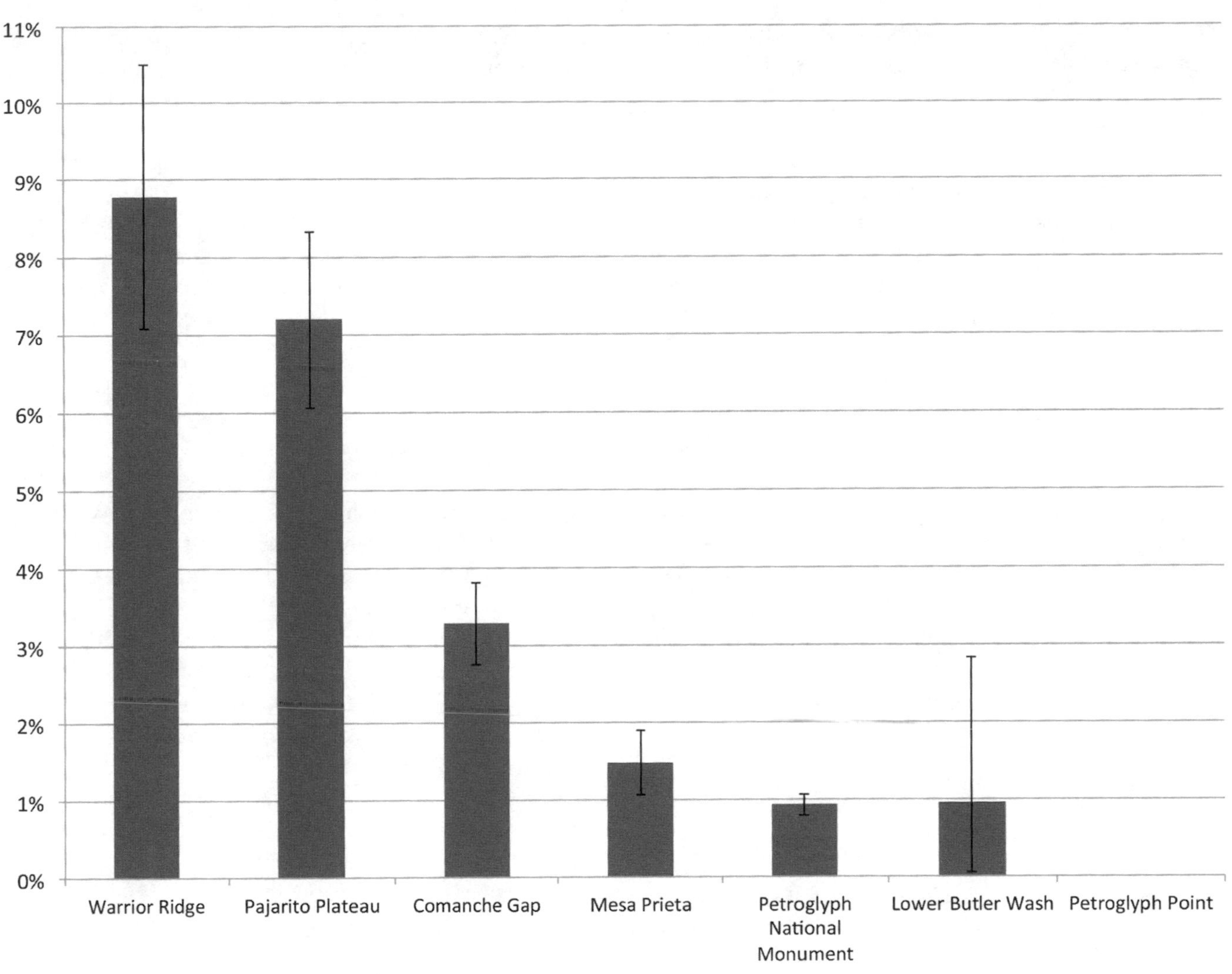

Figure 10.2. Frequency of martial elements with error bars illustrating the 95 percent confidence interval. Prepared by the author.

Plateau exhibit a different pattern than Mesa Prieta, Petroglyph National Monument, Lower Butler Wash, and Petroglyph Point, while Comanche Gap lies somewhere in the middle. It appears that the ratios of martial imagery are truly different and are not the result of sampling bias. What does this nonrandom distribution mean?

Warrior Ridge and the Pajarito Plateau stand out within the sample, each with a martial rock art frequency upwards of seven percent. Located in the Fremont Area, Warrior Ridge provides insight into a region outside the ancestral Pueblo area where violence may not have declined. At Warrior Ridge, 36 percent of the anthropomorphs occur in scenes of combat (Spangler 2011:42). The high rate of martial imagery is consistent with patterns observed across the Colorado Plateau, where shields and shield bearers are significantly more numerous along the Pueblo-Fremont frontier, an area where hostilities may have been intense (Schaafsma 2000:10). The data from the Pajarito Plateau were collected from five locales, including Garcia, Otowi-Tsankawi, Tsirege, Frijoles, and San Miguel. Ethnographically, the plateau is the location of a well-documented boundary between Keres-speaking pueblos to the south and Tewa-speaking pueblos to the north (Munson 2002:2). During Prehispanic times, competition accelerated on the plateau during the thirteenth and fourteenth centuries as population increased and residents of growing settlements vied for limited resources (Munson 2002:3). Arakawa and others (Chapter 7) illustrate the historical development of this boundary using chipped-stone debris. In this area of culture contact, boundary negotiation, and competition, the high frequency of martial rock art is not all that surprising.

On the opposite end of the spectrum, Lower Butler Wash, Petroglyph Point, Petroglyph National Monument, and Mesa Prieta each have relatively low frequencies of martial rock art. Lower Butler Wash and Petroglyph Point—both located in the Mesa Verde Region—were made during a relatively violent time before the exodus to the Northern Rio Grande region. Yet, these two locales have very little or no martial rock art, supporting prior observations of low frequencies of violent imagery in the Pueblo III San Juan Region. Notably, it is possible that the single martial motif observed at Lower Butler Wash—a probable mountain lion—may represent a literal mountain lion rather than symbolic connotations of war. If that is the case, then the rate of martial rock art at this location would be even lower. The other two locales with low frequencies of martial rock art—Petroglyph National Monument and Mesa Prieta—are located within the Northern Rio Grande Region, but are located away from major ethnic boundary areas.

Finally, Comanche Gap occupies a midpoint with a martial rock art frequency of around three percent. Significantly, Comanche Gap is a natural pass in a highly visible volcanic dike that lies at the boundary of the Pueblo and Plains regions on the southern edge of the Galisteo Basin. In this boundary area, the Pueblo people were in contact with Apache and Comanche groups to the east (Schaafsma 1992; Slifer 1998:105). Although the frequency of martial rock art is lower than that found at Warrior Ridge and the Pajarito Plateau, it is nevertheless higher than areas that are located on the interior of a group's territory. Pueblos near this boundary may have been targets of Apache raids, but the Apache may have also been trading partners, and this midrange frequency of martial rock art may be related to the dynamics of exchange.

It is possible that the nature of Plains-Pueblo trade required caution as well as cooperation for successful exchange to take place (see Chapter 11). Ethnographic evidence describes Plains-Pueblo relationships as largely interdependent and cooperative, but also unstable and periodically tense (Schaafsma 1992; Gallegos 1927:30; Schroeder and Matson 1965:129). As described by Habicht-Mauche (1988:169–170), the Plains-Pueblo relationship required "a certain amount of intimidation." With large images of shield-bearing warriors up to five feet across placed prominently at the top of the dike (Figures 10.3 and 10.4), the rock art of Comanche Gap would have accomplished this, making a strong impression on both potential enemies and potential trading partners entering the Galisteo Basin (Schaafsma 1992; Slifer 1998:106). Schaafsma (1992:171) interprets the content, size, and prominent location of the Comanche Gap imagery as "a strong statement of Pueblo strength and social cohesiveness, validating Pueblo presence on the eastern fringe of the Pueblo world." This imagery was intended for a specific audience and served a specific social purpose: the projection of social unity and strength to outsiders.

Two patterns emerge from these data. First, they provide quantitative support for observations previously noted on a more qualitative level, namely, that images of violence do in fact appear in rock art more frequently in the Northern Rio Grande Region than in the Mesa Verde Region. Second, in this sample, martial images appear in higher frequencies in areas of cultural contact and boundary maintenance between disparate groups. If as the skeletal evidence suggests, however, violence declined over time in the Northern Rio Grande Region, then what function did this imagery serve if it was not a literal representation of violence? Here, I discuss several possible explanations for this pattern and connect those explanations to broader trends of economic development discussed elsewhere in this volume.

As is evident in the patterns just described, martial rock art occurs more frequently along social boundaries. Such imagery may have played several roles in Northern Rio Grande society. For example, it may have functioned to glorify warriors and signify militarization. Even if levels of actual violence were comparatively low, warfare was institutionalized in ethnographic Pueblo social organization, ideology, and symbolism (Webster 1976). In this context, martial imagery may have helped to suppress violence by conveying a promise of retaliation should norms of peace and cooperation be breached. Regardless of whether actual violence ever took place, the allusion to it was a tool of social control. In addition, martial rock art may have supported territorial boundary maintenance. Images of violence announced the presence of warriors, helping to delineate and reinforce boundaries on the landscape by communicating a clear message to enemies, friends, and trading partners alike. Paradoxically, boundary maintenance, which may have led to increased conflict *between* groups, could have facilitated peace *within* groups as solidarity increased in the face of a common enemy.

Some scholars (Ember and Ember 1992; Lekson 2002) have argued that violence is predicated by socialization for fear or mistrust. If this socialization was directed outwardly towards rival groups, the positive internal result would

Figure 10.3. A shield bearer at Comanche Gap. Photo by Scott G. Ortman.

Figure 10.4. Highly visible martial imagery at Comanche Gap. Photo by Scott G. Ortman.

be an increased sense of solidarity (against those real or perceived enemies). Martial rock art in the Northern Rio Grande Region may have functioned to reflect and reinforce this outwardly directed fear and associated internal cohesion.

Given these possibilities, how can we explain the absence of martial rock art in the Mesa Verde Region, where skeletal evidence of violence is relatively abundant? If, in the Northern Rio Grande region, the concentration of martial images at ethnic boundary zones is related to the maintenance of internal peace and a push of violence out to the ethnic group level, then perhaps the absence of martial rock art in the Mesa Verde Region is related to the endemic and unstructured nature of violence in the thirteenth century. If violence was ubiquitous and internecine, there would not have been a clear audience for images of martial rock art. During an era in which the organization of society was kin-based, warfare would have also been kin-based and enemies may have changed situationally as alliances and rivalries shifted. With no persistent boundaries, military frontiers would not have existed. With violence occurring among groups and individuals on multiple scales and in different combinations, the need to delineate social and ethnic boundaries was perhaps not as relevant as it would later become in the Northern Rio Grande region, where social organization shifted to the larger scale of community-wide sodalities. Notably, while much Northern Rio Grande Region rock art appears to have been intended to communicate a message to outsiders along an ethnic boundary—for example, the highly visible and outward facing warrior motifs at Comanche Gap—the few instances of martial rock art in the Mesa Verde Region are not highly visible. For example, a panel depicting anthropomorphs in battle at Castle Rock Pueblo would only have only been seen by individuals within the pueblo itself. Perhaps, rather than marking a boundary or sending a message to outsiders, this panel may simply have commemorated an actual event after the fact.

Finally, we must consider the significance of martial rock art to Mesa Verde migrants and their descendants. Given the likelihood that Mesa Verde people did relocate to the Northern Rio Grande, what did such images mean to them as people with a legacy of violence? The Pueblo societies that emerged in the Northern Rio Grande incorporated the experiences of the migrants, and it can be speculated that, as migrants and their descendants contributed to the formation of new social and religious institutions, they may have wished to avoid further violence. This desire would have helped to shape the character of Pueblo societies in the following centuries (Kohler and others 2014:459). Martial rock art may have served as a deterrent against additional violence, as well as a remembrance of past violence.

The possible explanations for higher rates of martial rock art in the Northern Rio Grande Region all share one common theme. They provide insight into how peace was maintained and increasing cohesion and aggregation was facilitated. This, in turn, has important implications for how groups interacted with one another during a period of sustained economic development. In the next section, I discuss the relationships between internal peace, the management of boundaries, and economic development.

ECONOMIC IMPLICATIONS OF MARTIAL ROCK ART

Although this study is preliminary, it strongly suggests that martial rock art in the Northern Rio Grande region is concentrated along boundaries where different ethnic groups came into contact. This pattern has important implications both for how groups interacted with one another and how they functioned internally. During this period, rock art evidence suggests that violence occurred between ethnic groups, rather than between villages or individuals. Martial imagery along boundaries between these groups may have served a dual purpose of reinforcing divisions between rival groups on the landscape and facilitating increased internal peace and solidarity as social unity was projected outward.

The maintenance of boundaries and reinforcement of internal peace and cohesion has important social and economic implications. In the Northern Rio Grande Region during the thirteenth and fourteenth centuries, significant socioeconomic shifts were underway. Public architecture reflected changes in social and political organization, and material culture underwent significant development as an influx of new styles and ideas arrived from elsewhere (Chamberlin 2011; Lipe 2010; Ruscavage-Barz and Bagwell 2006; Wendorf and Reed 1955). The economic system transitioned from a kin-based system to a "community-based system with significant village-level specialization and regularized intercommunity exchange" (Kohler and others 2014:456) Exchange increased and Pueblo-Plains trade became a major source of goods (see Chapter 11). These economic trends reinforced interdependencies that united groups beyond the household level, with larger and more diverse groups operating at new scales of social integration.

Architecture also changed dramatically. Before the depopulation of the Mesa Verde Region, unit pueblos were a standardized and widely shared architectural form (Lipe 2010). After the depopulation, unit pueblos disappeared and Classic period pueblos were organized into clusters, suggesting cooperation among the pueblos that were grouped together (Chapter 5; Kohler and others 2014:456). Spielmann (1994) argues that these clusters can be understood as confederacies.

Confederacies would have maintained internal peace made it possible for people to safely build more extensive social and economic networks. As the scale of social identification increased during this period of agglomeration, larger social networks meant more economic opportunities. As discussed by Ortman and Davis (Chapter 1), the key factors that promoted economic growth during this period were innovations that promoted intercommunity mobility and made it possible for Pueblo people to live in, and interact with, larger communities. Perhaps, as martial rock art served to delineate boundaries between ethnic groups, the corresponding increase in internal social cohesion resulted in increased interaction, exchange of knowledge, new divisions of labor, increased flows of goods and services, and decreases in transport costs within those boundaries. As Ortman and Davis, observe, the size of the social network depends on the size and density within which human groups can peacefully interact.

CONCLUSIONS

As Ortman and Davis (Chapter 1) observe, many economists have argued that economic growth stems from technological change. However, this study hints at ways social change can also facilitate this process. The social networks delineated and reinforced by the distribution of martial rock art may have been the same networks that enabled increased flows of goods and services. The rock art patterns described here reflect the community and intercommunity organization that helped to facilitate sustained economic development in a nonindustrial and relatively egalitarian society.

This chapter is exploratory in nature and there are numerous avenues for further research. First, more tabulation should be done during survey and rock art documentation, especially in the Mesa Verde Region, to expand the database for studies of this nature. This chapter focused on the patterning of martial rock art in the Northern Rio Grande Region but integrating additional sites from the Mesa Verde Region would enable more in-depth comparison between the two areas. An expanded data set would likely shed additional light on the changing nature of violence and social life during the demographic transitions of the thirteenth century. Second, future studies could be expanded to include other types of imagery such as kiva murals or other types of motifs that could provide insight into other questions of iconography and social dynamics. Third, geology and landscape should be examined as a possible alternative explanation for the patterns seen here. While ancient artists may have selected locations for rock art based on sociopolitical dynamics of their time, their choices were likely also influenced by the availability of appropriate surfaces for rock art. If it can be proven that the patterns demonstrated here hold even when ideal locations for rock art, and for social boundaries, are taken into account, the argument will be strengthened significantly. Finally, preservation should be considered, as it is possible that some areas were more favorable for preservation of rock art than others, therefore affecting the areas represented within the sample.

Although preliminary, this study demonstrates that the relative frequency of martial rock art increased through time and is patterned across the Northern Rio Grande landscape. Although the simplest explanation for images of violence and warfare would be to equate them with actual violence and warfare, Kohler and his co-authors (2014) argue for declining violence over time, and this prompts us to consider other possibilities. It is apparent that an increase in war iconography following the depopulation of the Mesa Verde Region does not coincide with an increase in actual violence. Instead of documenting warfare, the rock art included in this study likely reflects "the formation of social institutions whose identity and beliefs were stated in and reinforced by . . . rock art" (Schaafsma 2000:162). As radical social and economic transformations took place in the Northern Rio Grande region, violence was suppressed, new social institutions emerged, and new levels of economic activity were facilitated. During this period, rock art images of warfare and violence may have, paradoxically, played an important role in the formation and maintenance of a more peaceful Pueblo society.

Acknowledgments. Many thanks to Janet MacKenzie, Ann Phillips, and Jerry Spangler, who generously shared their data for this project.

CHAPTER ELEVEN

"The Ambassador's Herb": Tobacco Pipes as Evidence for Village Specialization and Interethnic Exchange in the Northern Rio Grande

Kaitlyn E. Davis

SOCIAL TECHNOLOGIES OF ECONOMIC EXPANSION IN PLAINS-PUEBLO EXCHANGE

The research presented in this volume provides strong evidence for economic change and expansion in the Rio Grande pueblos. This expansion, as well as shifts in movement and aggregation among and within communities, is correlated with shifts and growth in intercommunity interaction and economic integration (see Chapter 1). This chapter identifies some of the challenges involved in expanding the scope of economic integration in a changing inter-regional tribal landscape and explores some of the social technologies and ritual systems Pueblo people developed and used to help overcome those challenges. Specifically, I focus on increased interaction with Plains communities, the development of a network of villages along particular corridors of travel, and the emergence of specific Pueblo settlements as trade centers.

Evidence for a ritualized dimension of Plains-Pueblo interaction that helped to alleviate some of the barriers to this expanding economic system is the subject of this chapter. This discussion connects to other ideas presented in this volume, including ways to mediate or monitor intergroup contact in frontier or border spaces (Chapter 10), shifts in patterns of production and specialization (Chapter 4), and how to create a shared sense of justice across tribal and ethnic boundaries as the scale of economic integration increases (Chapter 1).

Plains-Pueblo interaction was a subject of interest for chroniclers of Spanish expeditions and is of longstanding interest among scholars as well. Trade between Pueblo and Plains groups was directly observed by the first Spanish explorers and is evident in the archaeological record as well. Many studies have focused on the economics of Plains-Pueblo trade, but relatively little is known about the social processes, negotiations, and rituals that accompanied the interactions between individuals from these two very different cultures (Baugh 1991; Boyd 1997; Habicht-Mauche 2008; Hamalainen 2008; Lintz 1991; Speth 2005; Speth and Newlander 2012; Spielmann 1991; Wilcox 1991). For example, where did Plains traders meet their Pueblo customers? How did they navigate differences in culture, language barriers, or dissimilar social customs? In this chapter, I argue that smoking pipes offer an important line of evidence regarding this critical social component of the Plains-Pueblo macroeconomy. More specifically, I suggest the archaeological record of smoking pipes provides a useful proxy for interregional interaction and provides evidence that certain villages specialized in this activity.

Native North American pipes are found in a variety of distinctive regional styles. In the ethnohistoric literature, pipes are mentioned as one of the types of objects that helped cement trade partnerships (Ford 1972a; Sahlins 1972). Pipes also played a role in religious ceremonies and functioned as status and identity symbols (Carmody 2015; Graham et al 2007; Parsons 1936). "The ritual of the Sacred Pipe is particularly available to outsiders, because it is a ritual of sharing, of communion; it is central to the rituals of adoption and friendship" (Paper 1988:43). In the calumet ceremony on the Plains and in Eastern North America, for example, dances involving pipes and pipe smoking occurred as part of welcoming ceremonies, which also helped establish trade relationships and provide occasions for trades to occur (Blakeslee 1975:150; Hall 1997:1). "A leading member of a band or village was expected to have a number of Calumet relationships with the leading members of other tribes, bands, villages, and clans. It was this set of relationships that allowed peaceful visiting and trade between alien groups" (Blakeslee 1975:149).

If pipes, as ethnohistoric and ethnographic records indicate, were used in ceremonies to mediate trade interactions and ceremonies associated with welcoming visitors, then analyzing the materials, forms, designs, and locations of these objects should provide useful information about Protohistoric interaction networks. Determining the locations where these objects were used and discarded can also contribute to a better understanding of the mechanisms of trade and interaction.

Archaeological evidence suggests that Plains-Pueblo interaction increased in frequency and scale around 1450 CE and the ethnohistoric literature mentions ceremonies as a key means of negotiating trade relationships at the time of Spanish contact in the late 1500s (Bamforth n.d.; Baugh 1991; Boyd 1997; Habicht-Mauche 2008; Lintz 1991; Spielmann 1991 Hammond and Rey 1966; Seymour 2015). For example, Spanish chronicles from the 1500s discuss visitors at the pueblos along the border of the Pueblo and Plains regions, such as Pecos, going into the kivas (Hammond and Rey 1966). If pipes were involved in welcome and trade and alliance ceremonies, and visitors at these pueblos were brought into the kivas (where some of these ceremonies likely took place), then finding a higher concentration of pipes in these locations would support the connection of pipes to trade negotiations and inter-group meetings.

In this chapter, I explore questions of trade center specialization, interethnic exchange, and the ritual component of economic expansion during this time of increased Plains-Pueblo trade. I focus on the archaeological record of smoking pipes as a proxy for all these activities. The three primary lines of evidence I consider are (1) the density of pipes in deposits at various sites in the Northern Rio Grande, (2) proportions of pipe raw materials across time and space, and (3) elaboration of pipe design styles at potential trade center sites. If, as hypothesized, smoking pipes played a key role in rituals that facilitated these Plains-Pueblo exchanges, the archaeological record should reflect an increased concentration of pipes at trade centers, an increase in Plains-style pipes and materials after 1450, and an increase in elaboration of pipes at trade centers.

BACKGROUND

In this section, I provide an overview of what is already known about the need for mechanisms to promote trust and fairness when different groups come together, what existing literature says about the role of pipes as such a mechanism, and previous research on Plains-Pueblo trade and village specialization.

Negotiation and Ritual Component of Economic Expansion

A wide range of evidence suggests that humans generally benefit from larger-scale social networks, but people do not seem to be innately predisposed to trust strangers from other groups to the point that social networking is productive (Morris 2004, 2013; Ortman, Davis, Lobo, Smith, Bettencourt, and Trumbo. 2016; Kelly 2013; Sahlins 1972). As a result, people must develop cultural means of extending trust, especially in cases where there is no central government to monitor exchanges. Many have pointed to ritual as a key social technology for solving these kinds of problems within middle-range societies and I believe it has played an important role in *interethnic* social integration as well (Lipe and Hegmon 1989; Spielmann 1998a, 2002). The case of Plains-Pueblo interaction provides a situation where one can test this idea. Several lines of evidence suggest that smoking pipes were part of the set of token value objects that cemented trade partnerships. Hopi ethnohistoric accounts also point to the importance of pipes in ceremony (Parsons 1936). Beyond the Southwest, the form and role of pipes has been studied across North America, highlighting the pipe as a symbol of status, an important part of religious ceremonies, and an important element of interband trade (Graham and others 2007:486; Carmody 2015; Blakeslee 1981). The importance of the pipe in life transition events and the connection of pipe designs to social or political identity has also been studied elsewhere, notably in Ireland (Hartnett 2004:133).

Much of the more detailed literature on the role of pipes in ritual and trade comes from ethnohistoric and ethnographic accounts. Parsons (1936:775–779) described different ceremonies in which pipes were used in the Southwest, such as the Hopi flute ceremony. Other scholars have discussed the role of pipes in ceremonies on the Plains and have gathered previously recorded ethnographic accounts of the use of pipes in ceremonies of welcome and adoption between different groups in North America (Blakeslee 1975; Hall 1997; Paper 1988; Seymour 2015). McGuire's (1899:361) compilation of early ethnographic accounts of pipe smoking in North America noted that "early voyagers refer to the employment of tobacco in all treaties, councils, and functions of every kind, including social intercourse, in divination, and in curing of disease." More recently, scholars have pointed to "token value objects," or particular types of items that gain additional value because of the relationships or events they indicate or represent, as being important for fostering reciprocity and exchange relationships and as the key of ritual and specialization (Sahlins 1972; Snow 1981). Such studies suggest that specialized trade centers should exhibit evidence of ritualized trade activity as evidenced by pipes. Evans (2013) noted that the materials from which pipes recovered in the Arkansas River Basin were made indicate long distance exchange, but Hill (1998a:218) noted that the ritual consumption aspects of the implied trade interactions still need more attention. Hill's sentiments echoed Harrison's (1984:15–17) views about ritual aspects of trade. Harrison noted specifically that further study of designs on pipes of Plains and Pueblo origin found in Texas could provide clues about the religious understanding of the people exchanging and using them. Among the Pueblos, ethnographic observations at Santa Clara and Picuris revealed the importance of smoking pipes in ceremonies of initiation and medicine (Switzer 1969:34): "Ritual pipe smoking is an integral part of Pueblo ceremonialism, and I believe that the number of pipes in use in pre-[Hispanic] times indicates that they were of some importance."

Plains-Pueblo Macroeconomy

When examining Plains-Pueblo interaction, one line of research aims to study how Pueblo and Plains people complemented each other with the different resources they could provide. Ford (1972a:38) believed both ceremonial and utilitarian goods were traded, in addition to people moving between the two regions as part of alliance-forming marriages. Items that were traded include livestock, meat products, woven goods, pottery, salt, shells, turquoise, and silver. Ceremonial items and knowledge that was traded within and between regions included the pipe dance. Spielmann (1991) used the evidence of Plains shell and lithics found in Pueblo middens and Pueblo glaze ware found in Plains middens to claim a mutualistic or symbiotic model of Plains-Pueblo exchange These exchanges of complementary resources sometimes occurred through willing trade between both groups. At other times Plains people raided New Mexico villages for Pueblo goods.

Other scholars have studied conflict and prestige as motivators for interaction. For example, Wilcox (1981) noted that competition for trade partners occurred, with Plains groups vying for relationships with specific Pueblos. Baugh (2008) used a conflict and prestige model to examine Protohistoric period trade interactions. His case study was Kirikiris-Pueblo trade, since Kirikiris (ancestral Wichita) artifacts have been found at Pecos and other eastern frontier pueblos. In his model, conflict leads to leadership, which leads to a circuit of trade, wealth, prestige, and power. The geopolitical landscape helped explain different outcomes of negotiations (Baugh 2008:416). Baugh acknowledges that diplomacy was an important part of conflict resolution, especially what he calls the "sacred canopy of trade"— religious objects (such as eagle feathers, turquoise, and tobacco) that were exchanged while more mundane goods were bartered in the background. These transactions were further reinforced by various social relationships such as trade partnerships, fictive kin ties, and intermarriage within the macroeconomy (Baugh 1991, 2008:417). Smoking pipes were clearly involved in this sacred canopy of trade.

In addition to variation in motivation, trade also varied in scale. Ford (1972a) outlined three systems of trade in the Southwest: individual itinerant traders, trading periods at saint's day fiestas, and exchange of ceremonial goods that accompanied the lending of ceremonial services by ritual personnel. According to historical accounts, certain pueblos engaged in trade on larger scales than others. They facilitated trade between regions by acting as Plains-Pueblo pathways. These pueblos include Pecos, San Cristobal, and Gran Quivira (Hammond and Rey 1966:37–39).

Trade and interaction between Plains and Pueblo groups occurred both before and after Spanish contact, but it clearly intensified and became more formalized during the fifteenth century (Lintz 1991:93). This shift in interaction around 1450 CE was driven in part by changes in social organization and environmental stresses on the Plains (Bamforth n.d.). Drought on the Plains along with a population replacement and changes in lifestyles (from pit house farmers to more mobile groups) increased opportunities for interaction with Pueblo communities, which is reflected in an increase in Plains materials in middens dating from the late fifteenth century at frontier pueblos such as Pecos (Bamforth, personal communication April 7, 2015). Lintz (1991:93–94) noted that there was a marked increase in the quantity and variety of Pueblo goods on the Plains after 1350 CE, but there is evidence of interaction in the archaeological record dating as far back as 1200 CE. An increase in nonlocal ceramics in eastern border pueblos around that time provides support for this shift (Speth 2005:130–131). Wilcox (1991) and others have used raw materials to track trade networks, and my study of pipe raw materials presented here builds on this. The Plains groups that visited the eastern pueblo trade centers such as Pecos were recorded in Spanish chronicles in the 1500s as Querechos and Teyas, who are believed to be Apachean and Caddoan groups, respectively (Bamforth n.d.). The area occupied by these groups roughly equates to present-day western Kansas, Oklahoma, and northern Texas.

Village Specialization

In studies of Pueblo exchange systems, Ford (1972a:37) noted that, "sedentary villages specialized to facilitate trade." He studied ethnohistoric and ethnographic records, along with archaeological evidence, from six Tewa Pueblo villages (San Ildefonso, San Juan, Ohkay Owingeh, Nambe, Tesuque, and Santa Clara), and charted which goods particular pueblos contributed to the exchange system (Ford 1972a:38–39). Artifact tabulations for sites in the Northern Rio Grande also support the idea of village economic specialization. For example, Tsama pueblo had a significantly higher concentration of pendants in a localized area of the site than contemporaneous pueblos, San Marcos Pueblo appears to have specialized in the production of glaze-painted pottery (Schleher, this volume), and certain villages in the Rio Chama drainage may have specialized in cotton textile production (Chapters 2, 3, and 9; Davis and Ortman 2015). The concentration of smoking pipes in specific communities may provide evidence of village-level specialization in inter-ethnic trade. Specialization, in this context, involves a village or community developing and giving greater focus to specific architecture, technologies, and techniques to facilitate production of a particular good or service at a greater rate than other villages or communities. Given this definition, villages such as Pecos—which had excess kiva space, concentrations of trade items, and concentrations of pipes that were likely used to facilitate exchange and interaction—appear to have specialized as trade centers (Davis 2017).

Case Study Region and Sites

For this study I examined information from 17 pueblos (Table 11.1) which were selected on the basis of location (distance the Plains), temporal range (occupation before and/or after 1450), availability of site reports, and tabulation of smoking pipes. I also examined reports for a selection of Plains sites to use as a comparison. The Pueblo sites whose occupation ceased before or around 1450 were Arroyo Hondo, Te'ewi, Leaf Water (Kapo'ouingeh), Pindi, Pot Creek, and Tsama West. The sites occupied after 1450 were: Pecos, Gran Quivira, Howiri, Unshagi, San Cristobal, Tsama Middle/East, Cuyamungue, Tonque, Pueblo del Encierro, Poshu'ouingeh, and Ponsipa'akeri. Based on oral tradition, ethnohistorical evidence, or the presence of Plains artifacts, the sites explicitly cited as Plains-Pueblo trade centers include Pecos, Gran Quivira, and Pot Creek (Wilcox 1981:380). These pueblos range in occupation from 1200 to 1838 CE and vary in size and degree of site specialization. They also belong to different Northern Rio Grande settlement clusters (Adams and Duff 2004). Archaeological research on other pueblos in the region, such as Picuris, do not list smoking pipes in their site reports, but evidence of "tobacco exchange" was noted in that particular case (Adler and Dick 1999:35).

METHODS AND ANALYSES

The evidence discussed in the following section stems primarily from accessible Northern Rio Grande site reports with smoking pipe tabulations and photographs (Table 11.1). The Pecos Pueblo pipe collection (housed at Pecos National Historical Park) and the Gran Quivira pipe collection (housed at the National Park Service Western Archeological and Conservation Center in Tucson) were analyzed for material, form, and surface design by the author. The three main analyses presented here include (1) the relative density of pipes across sites, (2) the variety of raw materials used in sites occupied before and after 1450 CE, and (3) the degree of elaboration of pipes at trade centers in comparison to other sites.

Regional Pipe Density

To assess whether Pecos and Gran Quivira (the two largest Plains-Pueblo trade centers in the study sample) actually have greater concentrations of pipes than other sites, it is necessary to account for differential amounts of excavation across pueblos. Ordinarily, this is accounted for by comparing the artifact class of interest (in this case pipes) to the amount of a low income-elasticity, or utilitarian, artifact class with a fairly regular accumulation rate, such as cooking pottery (see Chapter 1). Unfortunately, due to variation in quantification across reports, there were no artifact-based measures I could use to standardize pipe recovery by overall assemblage size. In addition, some of the sites had specific provenience information recorded for the pipes (such as whether they were recovered from a room floor, or a kiva niche, or a burial for example), but others did not, so I was unable to determine how many pipes were from different types of contexts across sites. Thus, the only feasible option was to divide the raw count of pipes and fragments overall at each site by the number of excavated rooms at each site. The room count information was the only quantity, besides pipes, that was tabulated for all sites in my sample. I acknowledge that this limitation may lead to a biased sample and skew the results somewhat, but, even factoring in this limitation, some compelling patterns are present. The excavated room

Table 11.1. Smoking-Pipe Data for 17 Northern Rio Grande Sites

Site No.	*Site Name*	*Time Period*	*Pipe Numbers and Materials*				*Number of Rooms Excavated*	*Sources*
			Total	*Stone*	*Clay*	*Bone*		
625	Pecos	PIII–PV (1250–1838 CE, specifically)	866	27	839	0	153	Kidder 1979; Davis 2017
123	Unshagi	1375–1605/1628 CE	52	0	52	0	100	Reiter 1939
12	Arroyo Hondo	Early 1300s–1425 CE, intermittent	48	0	48	0	150	Habicht-Mauche 1993
80	San Cristobal	ca. 1400 CE–Spanish contact	40	4	35	1	72	AMNH 2013
120	Gran Quivira	PIV (ca. 1300–1675 CE, specifically)	37	24	13	0	37	Hayes, Young, and Warren 1981; independent analysis
260	Pot Creek	1000–1350 CE	27	0	27	0	62	Wetherington 1968
70	Pueblo del Encierro	late 1200s–late 1700s CE, intermittent	25	7	18	0	91	Snow 1976; Warren 1976a
38	Cuyamungue	1300s–1680 CE	16	0	16	0	64	Wendorf and Wilmeth 1952
252	Te'ewi	Mid-1200s–1500 CE	15	5	10	0	27	Wendorf 1953
297	Ponsipa'akeri	Coalition and Classic (PIII–PIV)	11	0	11	0	24	CCAC 2014
1	Pindi	PII–PIII (pre-1450 CE)	10	0	10	0	191	Stubbs and Stallings 1953
274	Poshu'ouingeh	Classic (PIV)	9	?	?	?	109	Jeancon 1923
909	Tsama West	Coalition	7	0	7	0	18	CCAC 2014
908	Tsama Middle & East	Classic (PIV)	6	0	6	0	18	CCAC 2014
71	Howiri	PIV (1400s CE, specifically)	4	4	0	0	15	Fallon 1987; Mick-O'Hara 1987
300	Leaf Water (Kapo'ouingeh)	1300–1350 CE	2	0	2	0	18	Luebben 1953
240	Tonque	PIV (1428–1496 CE, specifically)	2	0	2	0	82	Barnett 1969

Note: Site numbers are Laboratory of Anthropology (LA) designations.
AMNH = American Museum of Natural History.
CCAC = Crow Canyon Archaeological Center.

counts were obtained either from direct reporting in site reports, or from counting the rooms labeled "excavated" on a site map.

Raw Material Comparison

For the material tabulations, I distinguished stone and bone from clay pipes (and made notes of more detail if provided) based on how the pipes were recorded in the site reports. The Pecos pipes were also examined by Kate Zeigler (of Zeigler Geologic Consulting, LLC), a geologist with expertise in stones and minerals of the New Mexico and environs to check the material type classifications made over the years by curators. I then depicted the ratio of pipe materials at each site visually in ArcGIS to better assess spatial and temporal patterns in smoking pipe material type in the region. Clay was the most common material used to form pipes at the period of interest in the Southwest, whereas stone was the most common material used on the Plains (Kidder 1979; Paper 1988).

Degree of Elaboration

Specialization can also be traced through stylistic attributes, which can connect specific objects to the communities in which they were manufactured. Although I acknowledge that it is potentially problematic to link a particular style of object to a specific community of people, comparing differences in stylistic attributes has been shown to be useful in tracing the movement of people or their ideas and influence. Janusek (2002) discusses the merits of (and issues with) using material culture to study identity. For this to work, one needs multiple categories of material culture that can be studied using multiple lines of evidence. Even then, there is seldom a straightforward association between style and identity. In light of these problems, some have argued that style is no longer a useful concept. "Style has little conceptual use beyond a vernacular distinction between social forms distinguished within a consumerist society" (Boast 1997:191). Others, particularly in prehistoric migration studies, have pointed out that stylistic differences sometimes are the only, or one of the few, ways of tracking ancient movements of people (Cameron 1998). Regardless of whether scholars use the term "style" or not, style is still inferred, not only from the traits of the objects of study, but also in the methods and writings of the archaeologists themselves (Conkey and Hastorf 1990:2). Differences in form, design, and use of material culture do have meaning, so in my view style remains a useful concept. The problems with how to link materials and people are best addressed by acknowledging the limitations of this link, clearly explaining how one is defining style, and keeping in mind the context of the materials one is examining (both the context of other materials and the social context).

Not all site reports tabulated pipe forms and, for some sites, only a portion of the total pipes were tabulated by form. Nevertheless, when formal descriptions were given, I tabulated the recovered pipes using the system A.V. Kidder (1979) developed for the Pecos pipe collection, which he excavated between 1915 and 1927. Switzer (1969) completed the most recent pan-southwestern report on pipe forms, and Paper (1988) published the most recent pan-North American report on form classifications. I added their categories to Kidder's for classifying forms that were not local to the Rio Grande (Figure 11.1). For site reports where there was not enough information on each pipe to determine which of the established categories an object belonged to, I tabulated them according to how they were categorized in the site report. Style includes not only form, but also surface design. Analyzing form and surface design provides useful information not only on the identity or cultural influence of the person creating the object, but also the level of skill and time invested in producing it.

Simple tubular pipes were considered representative of Northern Rio Grande technology, and elbow and "elaborate: effigy" pipes were considered representative of Plains technology (Wendorf 1953:94–98). The elaborate pipes with flattened mouthpieces, called "elaborate: Pecos-style," are considered to be reflective of Plains flattened pipe stems (Wendorf 1953). It is also possible that these mouthpieces, which have the shape of a fish tail, are suggestive of an association between smoke and a watery spirit world in addition to being a common stylistic attribute of Plains pipes. I suggest that the Pecos-style pipe form reflects a blend of Plains and Southwest styles. If so, it implies a larger level of sustained interaction than if the two regional styles had remained distinct. Many of these sites I examined were excavated in the early 1900s, and thus the resolution of provenience is not fine enough to determine if there are temporal trends in the prevalence of manufacture of these different forms.

RESULTS

The results presented below demonstrate that pipes were differentially produced, distributed, and consumed in the protohistoric Northern Rio Grande. This adds to the lines of evidence for economic specialization at the village level and provides more information on inter-ethnic trading activities.

Simple Tubular: roughly conical or cylindrical, with no "fishtail" or diamond-shaped mouthpiece or relief or bends in the form.

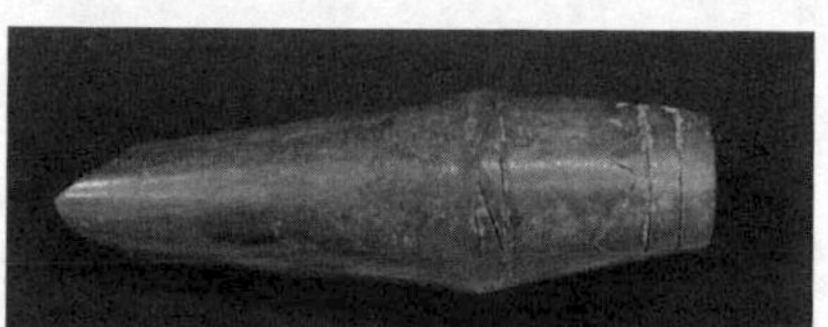

Elaborate: has fishtail or diamond-shaped mouthpiece and often has 3-D relief on sides of bowl body.

Eleaborate: (Effigy): in the shape of an animal or human.

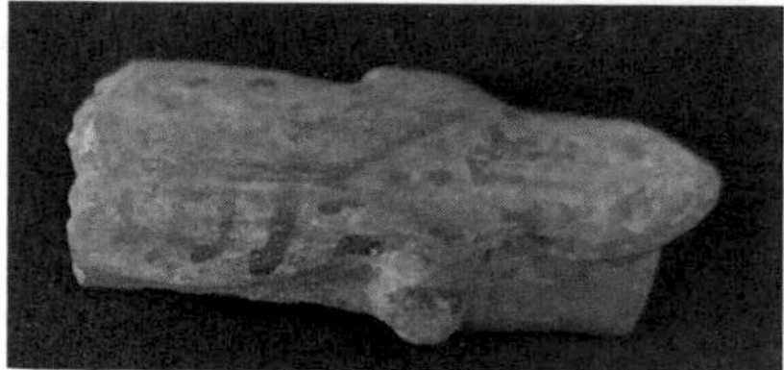

Elbow: approximately ninety-degree angle between the stem/mouth end of the pipe and the bowl end.

Pipe Plug: solid piece of material placed inside the pipe.

Figure 11.1. The most common pipe form categories found at Pecos, based on identifications by Kidder (1979). Kidder listed the pipe plug as a form, so it is included in this figure. Although a "pipe plug" is not a pipe itself, the shape and size of the plug provide useful clues as to the forms of the pipes in which they were placed. The "Elaborate" category and "Elaborate-Pecos-Style" category are synonymous. From top to bottom: *clay pipe* from Pecos Pueblo: Peabody Catalog No. 73199, NPS catalog No. PECO10129; *clay pipe* from Pecos Pueblo: NPS catalog No. PECO261; *clay pipe* from Pecos Pueblo: Peabody Catalog No. 67365, NPS Catalog No. PECO9927; *stone pipe* from Pecos Pueblo: Peabody Catalog No. 72024, NPS Catalog No. PECO10365; and *clay pipe* plug from Pecos Pueblo: Peabody Catalog No. 66380, NPS Catalog No. 10223. Objects with Peabody catalog numbers are curated through the Robert S. Peabody Institute of Archaeology and housed at Pecos National Historical Park. PECO261 is curated and housed by Pecos National Historical Park. Photos by the author.

Regional Pipe Density

After reviewing the site reports and completing visual analysis of the pipes from two major trade centers (Pecos and Gran Quivira), it was apparent that pipes and pipe-related objects were more frequently deposited (per excavated room) at sites reported to be trade centers than at sites that were not. There was also a greater variety of raw materials used to make pipes in sites occupied after 1450 CE, coincident with the expansion in Plains-Pueblo trade. Finally, not only were pipes more frequently used at trade centers, but their forms and surface designs were more elaborate as well.

Figure 11.2 shows that only Pecos and Gran Quivira have pipe-to-excavated-room ratios greater than or equal to 1. Pecos in particular has a pipe density that is about five times greater than other sites in the study region. Pecos also has a higher proportion of unfinished and partially finished pipes than sites with lower pipe densities (for example, the form is complete, but the bore hole is not completely drilled). This supports the village specialization concept because it demonstrates that pipes were actively being produced at this site in addition to being used more frequently. The higher concentration of pipes at Gran Quivira, Pecos, and other frontier pueblos points not only to specialization at the village level, but also provides insight into the particular objects that played special roles in interethnic trade.

Raw Material Comparison

The seventeen sites in this study contained mostly clay pipes, followed by stone, and one bone pipe, which was found at San Cristobal (Figure 11.3). One pipe found at Gran Quivira also contained some metal. The pueblos at which stone pipes have been found include Pecos, Te'ewi, Gran Quivira, Howiri, San Cristobal, and Pueblo del Encierro. Of these, all but Te'ewi were occupied primarily after 1450 CE, and Te'ewi was occupied until at least 1500. In

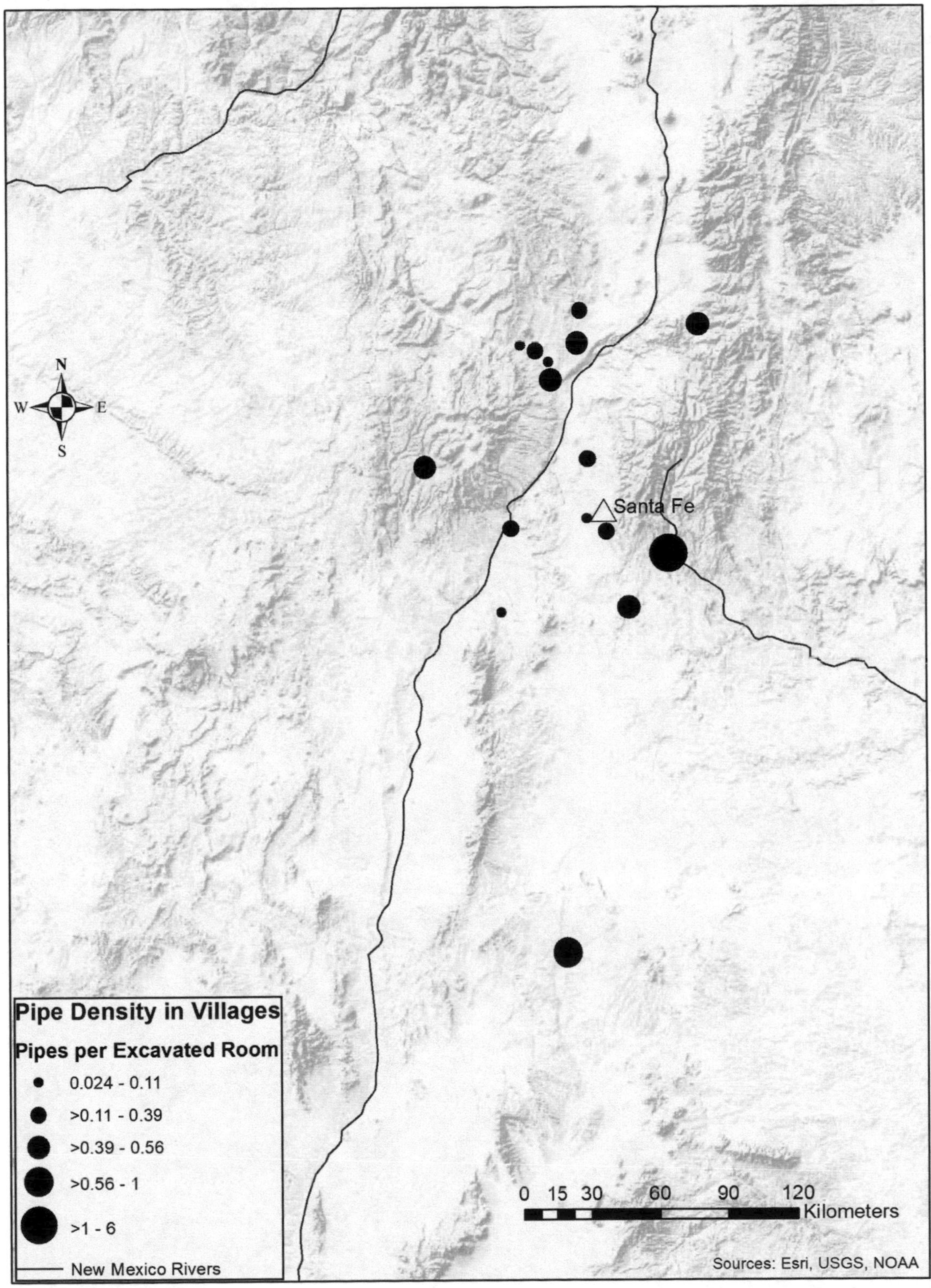

Figure 11.2. Spatial analysis of pipe density in the Rio Grande. Data are the number of pipes divided by the number of excavated rooms for each of the Rio Grande pueblos with available site reports with pipe tabulations. Pecos had the densest concentration of pipes (5.7 pipes/room), followed by Gran Quivira (1 pipe/room). Both were documented as trade centers in ethnohistorical accounts. Prepared by author.

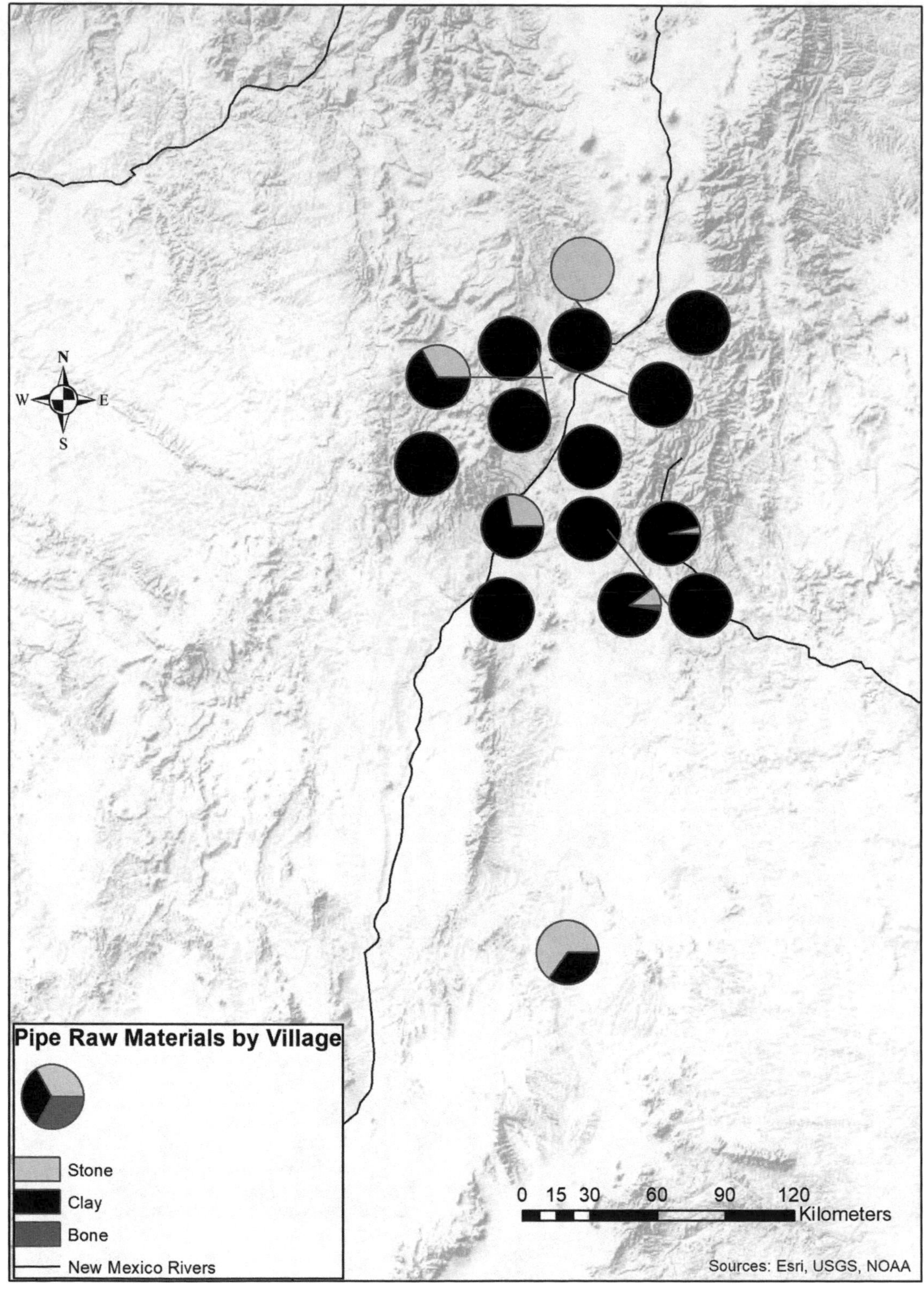

Figure 11.3. Proportion of pipe materials found at each pueblo. Most sites had a majority of clay pipes, with the exception of Howiri (only stone pipes reported) and Gran Quivira (24 stone pipes and 13 clay pipes reported). Only one bone pipe was found, at San Cristobal. Prepared by author.

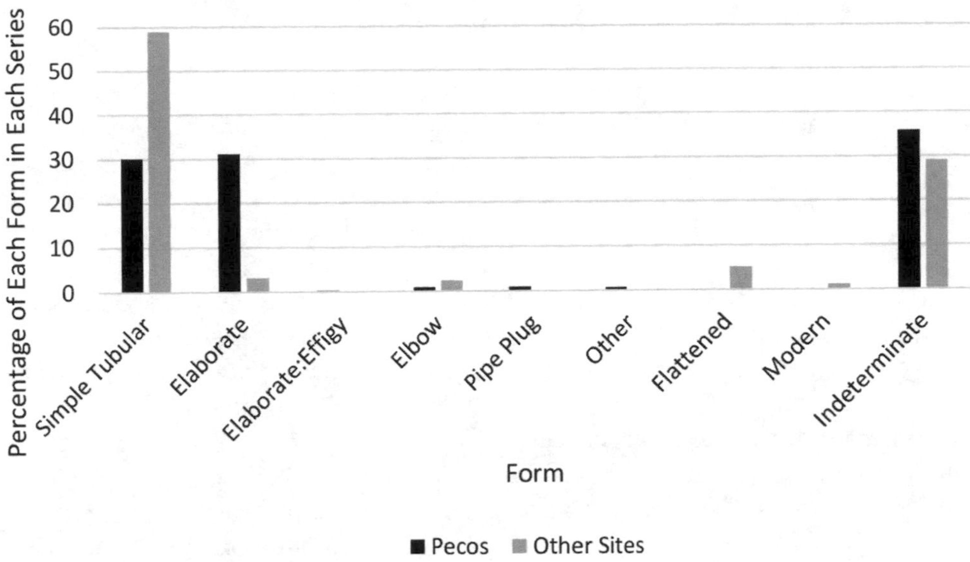

Figure 11.4. Comparison of pipe form tabulations at Pecos versus other Rio Grande sites. The "elaborate" category in this bar graph refers to "elaborate: Pecos-style." Elaborate: effigy pipes were present at Pecos, but they comprised less than 1 percent of the assemblage (0.7%) and thus are not visible on the graph. "Flattened" and "modern" are two categories from site reports where the objects were not described in enough detail for me to reclassify them according to the classification system outlined in Figure 11.1. Although a "pipe plug" is not a pipe form, the shape and size of the plug do provide some useful clues as to the form of the pipes in which they were placed. The data presented here are from the 17 sites listed in Table 11.1. Prepared by author.

addition, both Pecos and Gran Quivira were interregional trade hubs. Given that pipes made of stone are considered to be characteristic of Plains pipe technology, the concentration of stone pipes in post-1450 CE sites corroborates other lines of evidence that indicate an intensification of Plains-Pueblo interaction at this time. Metal pipes, such as the one found at Gran Quivira, have been associated with the Sioux and other Plains tribes, but are otherwise unknown among the Pueblos. Howiri is the only site from which stone pipes but no clay pipes indicative of southwestern pipe technology have been reported.

Degree of Elaboration

The simple tubular pipe was the most common form across sites (Figure 11.4). This is consistent with the findings of previous studies (Ariss 1939; Paper 1988; Switzer 1969). In this sample, elaborate: Pecos-style pipes were largely unique to Pecos. Most of the elaborate: Pecos-style and elaborate: effigy pipes (with some sort of 3-D relief) were found at Pecos, although multiple examples were also found at Sapawe and Cuyamungue. Elbow pipes were found at a few other sites including Gran Quivira and Arroyo Hondo.

The designs found on the Pueblo pipes examined here were primarily geometric. Multiple *clay* pipes from the study area also had characteristic *Plains* forms, suggesting a blend of Plains and Pueblo pipe-making traditions. For example, Te'ewi had seven tubular clay pipes (Pueblo material and form) with flattened mouthpieces, an Eastern or Plains style (Wendorf 1953:65). Other pipes were of Plains forms, but were made from *local* Pueblo stone, including several from Pecos (Kidder 1979:85).

Overall, the pipes from Gran Quivira reflect more elaboration with regard to material, and the pipes from Pecos reflect more elaboration with regard to form and surface design. This suggests that pipes not only occur in higher frequency at trade centers, but the pipes made in these particular villages were actually distinctive. This is an indication of village-level craft specialization in pipe manufacture. The more elaborate and intricately designed pipes likely required greater skill and time to produce, thus suggesting more investment in pipe-related activity, especially at Pecos, compared to the other sites examined.

CONCLUSIONS

Tabulation and detailed recording of pipes at a number of sites in the Northern Rio Grande Region support the hypothesis that pipes were an important accoutrement of interregional interaction and trade. Used pipes, and pipes in various stages of manufacture, were deposited more frequently at sites noted as trade centers in Spanish chronicles, and most of the Plains-associated stone pipes were found in pueblos occupied after 1450 CE, the period of most intensive Plains-Pueblo exchange. The fact that Pecos was such an outlier in pipe form and quantity reinforces the idea that Pecos was a specialized trade center involved in interregional exchange. Besides providing more artifact-based evidence to support ethnohistoric accounts, this study also offers new information regarding the likely social and ritual mechanisms that supported interregional exchange. Specifically, the higher density of pipes at trade centers overall supports the hypothesis that pipe smoking rituals helped facilitate the uptick in trade between Plains and Pueblo people after 1450 CE.

Although smoking pipes have often been discussed in excavation reports, site-to-site comparisons of these objects have been rare. Regional comparisons and individual site typologies have been established (Switzer 1969; Kidder 1979; and Brown 1996), but with the exception of Thibodeau's (1993:186) tabulations of data from about six sites for the Arroyo Hondo Pottery volume, few inter-site investigations have occurred. This particular class of artifact deepens understandings of Plains-Pueblo interaction by bringing to light the ritual dimension of inter-ethnic trade activity. In Native America, tobacco was often considered to be the "ambassador's herb" (McGuire 1899). Examining pipes and smoking customs thus provides a glimpse into the ceremonial aspects of trade negotiations.

At a regional level, the varying density, material composition, and stylistic elaboration of pipes provides an additional line of evidence to support the concept of village-level specialization in Prehispanic times. Evidence that pipes were produced at trade centers, had the most elaborate and varied forms, and were used most frequently at these sites, provides evidence of a connection between pipe production and consumption and specialization in interregional trade. Based on ethnographic and ethnohistorical accounts, this correlation is due at least in part to the role of smoking practices as part of customs of negotiation and mediation among individuals and groups.

This study adds an additional line of evidence for understanding Plains-Pueblo exchange, village specialization, and the Northern Rio Grande Pueblo economy overall. There is a wealth of evidence for the increase in Plains-Pueblo trade around 1450 CE, in which some Pueblo villages acted as trade centers. This study adds evidence that pipe-smoking rituals were a critical component of these developments. I have argued that, if the individuals involved in this trade used pipe-smoking rituals to promote trust and to provide supernatural sanction for trade partnerships, initiation, and agreements, the archaeological record should show the following patterns: (1) pipes should be denser in deposits at trade centers; (2) evidence of pipe manufacture should be most prevalent at those same centers; (3) the incidence of Plains-associated stone pipes should increase in Pueblo sites after 1450 CE; and (4) more symbolic elaboration should be apparent on pipes found at trade centers. The data presented here are consistent with all these expectations.

These results suggest that finding ways to mediate interactions and establish shared customs to facilitate exchange were important aspects of expanding economic integration in the Northern Rio Grande. Shared smoking customs and exchanges of pipes with trade partners appears to have been one means of achieving this. Thus, artifact-based evidence suggesting the importance of pipes in Plains-Pueblo interaction and exchange adds an important cultural dimension to efforts to explain Northern Rio Grande economic development.

CHAPTER TWELVE

Economic Growth in the Past: Empirics, not Ontology

José Lobo

Did economic growth, in the general sense of increasing material and cultural output, occur prior to the Industrial Revolution? This is a straightforward question that, at a quick glance, seems as though it ought to be answerable in a similarly straightforward manner. Yet, the dominant traditions in archaeological and anthropological research either have not answered it, have answered it in the negative, or exiled the question beyond the reach of legitimate scholarly pursuit. There are many reasons for this peculiar, and long-lasting, insistence that the past was drastically unlike the present, at least from the perspective of "economic growth." Such a supposition became an almost default analytical stance after the influential work of Polanyi and Finley, which highlighted the many differences between ancient economies and those characteristic of the modern world (Finley 1973; Polanyi 1944, 1977). And if the way production and exchange occurred in ancient societies was incommensurably different from economic activity in the present or even the recent past, then ancient societies were axiomatically a "foreign country" in regard to the production of material and cultural output. What should be, by all rights, an empirical question (did economic growth occur in ancient societies?) became a matter of ontological certainty (economic growth could not occur prior to modernity).

The apparent stranglehold that economics, as a field and as a community of inquiry, has had on the phenomenon of economic growth—how it is defined, measured, modeled, and explained—has unnecessarily hindered examination of whether economic growth occurred in the past; and if it did, what the drivers of change in the material and cultural output of a society were. A major culprit in the decoupling of economic growth as a phenomenon from the practice of archaeology and anthropology as investigations into human history over the *longue durée* is the explanatory framework that economists privileged during the latter half of the twentieth century. The manner in which economic growth came to be explained—from Solow (1956) to Romer (1986)—emphasized "technological change," "knowledge spillovers," "human capital accumulation," and "R&D investments" that seem to render growth an exclusively modern process. But there is a prior explanatory framework—Smithian growth—that has remained salient for explaining how the material outputs of past societies changed over time. Recent work has recaptured this tradition, which together with recent developments in *institutional economics*, makes it compelling to ask whether economic growth occurred in ancestral Puebloan society and should make us confident that answering in the affirmative does not imply a crude analogy between Puebloan society and modern capitalism.

My intention here is to show that key concepts in the study of contemporary growth are not necessarily associated with modernity (that is, the period since the Industrial Revolution), that there are a variety of processes and mechanisms that can generate growth, and that culture (not markets) is nowadays central to the study of growth. The vocabulary of economics can be delinked from the study of modern capitalist economies. *The problem of economics is the economic problem*, which every human agglomeration from hunter-gatherer bands to today's economies must solve, and its resolution involves conventions, rules, incentives, evaluations of worth, cooperation, exchange, and coordination of labor; in short, culture and institutions. To argue that every society has faced an economic problem does not address the separate question of how important, embedded, clearly conceived or even linguistically recognized economic activity as a separate realm of social action was in premodern societies. The contributions to this volume demonstrate that studying economic growth in the past is primarily a matter of empirical research, not mainly of *a priori* theorizing. The importance of the results (conceptual and empirical) assembled in the present collection is that they represent an inquiry about the presence of growth in a context that is even more socially distant from modernity than Medieval Europe, the Roman Empire, or the Mediterranean during the classical Greek era. The inquiry sits squarely in the practice of economic history or economic archaeology (if the distinction matters).

Before proceeding I want to remark on something obvious yet very often glossed over when the presence of economic growth is used to draw a sharp demarcation between the "past" and the "present." Even if one were to insist on making high rates of economic growth a hallmark of modernity, they are not synonymous. Economic growth has not been the experience of every society since the mid-nineteenth century nor is it a condition that, once experienced, becomes part of the "national character." Argentina was an economic powerhouse in 1850 but has not been so during the past few decades. China's vertiginous growth rates over the past 40 years followed decades (and even centuries) of impoverishment. Indeed, many economies today are not growing and some are getting poorer. Economic growth, as a phenomenon, a historical episode, a dynamical process with ups and downs, needs to be identified, dated and explained (Lucas 1988). It is never inevitable, and by no means should it be taken for granted, whether in the present or in the past.

PROBLEMS, PROBLEMS

What is an economy? An economy consists of all activities aimed at the production of goods (material and cultural), their distribution, and their consumption (Blau 1964). An economy reflects the specific ways in which members of a society make their living and survive, what technologies they employ, what social relations they enter into, how they coordinate labor, and what the specific behaviors (individual and collective) they engage in in association with various productive activities (Pryor 1977). An economic system comprises the totality of institutions, organizations, rules, and norms that specify who does what in an economy, and that channel and influence the production and distribution of tangible and intangible goods (Pryor 2005).

What is the *economic problem*? As a field of inquiry, economics studies how individuals, groups, and organizations manage scarce resources (which have alternative uses) to achieve desired ends including obtaining and producing goods (Earle 2002; Samuelson 1947; Sahlins 1972). The economic problem can be divided into three distinct subproblems: resource allocation, coordination, and exchange or distribution. *The resource allocation problem* occurs whenever there is a situation of scarcity of resources (including human effort) that have alternative uses. These resources need to be secured and allocated, and decisions (choices) made as to their use by one or more resource-controlling players to attain a desired outcome (Hurwicz 1973). The *coordination problem* refers to why and how individuals interact to achieve economic outcomes (O'Driscoll 1977). The *exchange* (or *distribution*) *problem* is the problem of how to exchange (i.e., transfer control over) goods and resources for mutual benefit (Samuelson and Nordhaus 2004). These three problems can be solved in a variety of ways, with any particular set of solutions involving rules, norms, valuations, and institutions (i.e., culture). The market mechanism emblematic of capitalism is just one way of addressing these problems. To recognize that there was an Aztec economy and a market through which goods flowed among locations, communities, and individuals in the Aztec world does not in any way wash away the distinctiveness of Aztec society (Hirth 2016). Essentially, the solutions to these three problems require a social system by which individuals seek, make, sustain, repair, adjust, construct, sanction, and benefit from social relationships and interactions (Fiske 1992). Framed in this manner, the problem of economics and its constituent subproblems are faced by every human agglomeration.

What is the problem of economic growth? Economic growth is an increase in the material and cultural output of a society requiring the use of energy and resources, or, equivalently, the manipulation of matter, energy, and information. To avoid Malthusian immiseration, a social group that increases in (population) size must also increase its material output or secure access to more output. No presumption is made that increasing output is necessarily rarefied to be normatively more important than other social outcomes or goals. The problem of economic growth can be formulated more generally as the *problem of social development*:

> As I see it, the real question at issue is about what I would call social development, by which I mean social

groups' abilities to master their physical and intellectual environments and get things done in the world. . . . Putting matters more formally, social development is the bundle of technological, subsistence, organizational, and cultural accomplishments through which people feed, clothe, house, and reproduce themselves, explain the world around them, resolve disputes within their communities, extend their power at the expense of other communities, and defend themselves against others' attempts to extend power [Morris 2013:3–5].

So stated, the problem of economic growth can be posed and investigated for any human society.

Turning the presence or absence of economic growth in any society into an empirical question before engaging in debates as to what drove or hindered such growth presupposes that growth can be documented. This, in turn, assumes agreement on a measure of economic output that presumes agreement on the method of quantification and the manner of verification. And lest we forget, data must be available, directly or indirectly, that correspond to the variable of interest. For contemporary societies the *problem of measuring economic output* is solved by using gross domestic product (GDP) as a *monetary* measure of an economy's tangible and intangible goods (i.e., goods and services). Want to know by how much the economy of China grew between 1980 and 2015? Go to the website of the World Bank's Development Indicators, choose from among several ways of measuring GDP, and download the file containing the data for China.[1] But there is nothing obvious about using GDP as the measure of an economy's size, nor is it a trivial exercise, as attested by dedicated staff and sophisticated statistical techniques by which the GDP of the United States is measured (Lepenies 2016; Bureau of Economic Analysis 2015). Bypassing the discussion of whether GDP is a useful measure, nothing precludes measuring the equivalent of GDP for ancient societies. Nothing, that is, except for the availability of suitable data (e.g., Bowman and Wilson 2009; Goldsmith 1984; Lo Cascio and Malanima 2009). But more importantly, nothing precludes using other measures—per capita caloric intake, material used in the construction of roads or temples, house size and household possessions, the quantity of goods exchanged through trade, acreage of land devoted to farming, and so on—as indicators of output and, assuming such indicators can be constructed for different points in time, as measures of economic growth. Theoretical coherence, data availability, reliability judgments, and a mechanism for reaching (temporary) consensus on a variable's usefulness are the limits on proposing and using measures of economic growth.

A PECULIAR ACCOUNTING EXERCISE

Explaining why some economies grow while others do not—identifying and quantifying the drivers of economic growth—has been a preoccupation of economists for a long time. The way economic growth has been quantified and attempts at explaining its drivers over the past six decades or so has unwittingly resulted in economic growth becoming an irrelevant topic for students of ancient human societies. The dominant explanatory narrative (and its associated set of concepts and methods) obscured an earlier, and complementary, explanatory framework that more easily lends itself to the study of economic growth in preindustrial societies. But first, a bit of accounting.

One of the workhorse concepts in economics is that of a *production function*: a mathematical abstraction that relates quantities of physical output of any production process to quantities of physical inputs. A production function is an expression of the technological relation between inputs (factors of production) and outputs (Robinson 1953).[2] The most common inputs are human labor, capital (artifacts or physical assets that enhance human labor), and natural resources. The production function framework facilitates distinguishing between two types of economic growth. An increase in economic output caused by increases in the amount of inputs available for use (more people, additions to land used for agriculture) is called *extensive growth* whereas output growth caused by a more efficient use of inputs (i.e., increases in productivity) is referred to as *intensive growth* (Senhadji 1999; Acemoglu and Robinson 2012).[3] Extensive growth could occur through increased exploitation of the labor force, and the increase in labor force could come about through slave labor. Intensive growth, in contrast, implies an increase in the efficiency of production such that each worker creates more goods or provides more services, leading to an increase in the total

[1] https://data.worldbank.org/indicator?tab=all

[2] More than a function in the strict mathematical sense, a production function is more like an accounting device to keep track of inputs (what goes in) and outputs (what goes out).

[3] A productivity measure is expressed as the ratio of output to inputs used in a production process, that is, output per unit of input.

amount of output generated per capita (Jones and Vollrath 2013). Extensive growth is generally seen as unsustainable over the long run due to resource depletion, stabilization in population growth rates, or lack of new territory to conquer.

Note that the concept of a production function is not inherently restricted to a modern setting. A production function is a model that serves to focus thinking about how output is produced by any collection of interacting humans. Recognizing the important role of energy for any production process, regardless of era or culture, a societal process of production can be more generally represented as $Y = A{*}f(L,T,R)$, with Y denoting output, labor (L) and tools (T) are the standard factors of production and R refers to natural resources (for example, coal or lithium). This notation indicates that the total output of a social group is given by some function of labor, tools, and natural resources multiplied by the additional factor A. Following Malanima (2014), the factors of production can be conceptualized, from the viewpoint of energy, as "converters" able to extract energy from resources (from foodstuffs, firewood, coal, oil, or natural gas) to transform materials into goods and services. The A term incorporates knowledge about how to generate energy and use it to transform matter into mechanical work, heat and light. Changes in how human agglomerations have used energy is after all a prominent theme in several grand historical narratives seeking to explain human socioeconomic and cultural development (e.g., Diamond 1997; Morris 2013; Perez 2002; Smil 2017; White 1959).

To the extent that a production function—which was originally conceived as $Y = f(L,K,R)$ with Y denoting output and K denoting capital—is an accurate description of how output is generated, increases in output must result from increases in the quantity of inputs used. When Robert Solow (1956, 1957) examined this assumption in two very influential papers published in the late 1950s, it was realized that increases in labor and capital were insufficient to account for recorded increases in GDP. The data used by Solow came from national income accounts produced by the Bureau of Economic Analysis in the US Department of Commerce. Faced with this failure of an accounting exercise, a new term (or variable) was inserted into the production function to account for the "residual" amount of growth: $Y = A{*}f(L,K,R)$. Strictly speaking the "A term" (often referred to as "total factor productivity") adjusts for the portion, or residual amount, of output not explained by traditionally measured inputs of labor and capital used in production. The unaccounted part of growth in GDP is taken to represent increases in productivity, that is, getting more output with the same inputs (Hulten 2009). The source of heightened productivity came to be attributed the effects of technology or knowledge in economic production (Comin 2008).

Growth accounting became one of the most important empirical exercises in modern economics and as a standardized procedure it is used to measure the contribution of different production factors to economic growth. The framework of growth accounting made it possible to highlight the roles of other factors besides technology in explaining the absence of productivity growth. When Weitzman (1970) implemented the Solow approach for the Soviet Union he found that increases in the use of factor inputs explained most of the USSR's economic growth. Assuming correctly that there were many research and development efforts in the former Soviet Union and that the quality of technical research in the former country was high, Weitzman concluded that the deficiency in Soviet economic performance was institutional in nature.

TECHNOLOGY, THE DIVISION OF LABOR, AND AGGLOMERATION

Following these growth accounting exercises, efforts to understand the sources of and impediments to economic growth came to revolve around explaining the residual that was left over after accounting for labor, capital, and resources (or, more glamorously, explaining the determinants of technological progress). The various approaches that economic growth theory has taken since the mid-1950s have had as a common thread an emphasis on developments in science and technology (invention and innovation) as the main drivers of growth in economic productivity (see Acemoglu 2009; Aghion and Howitt 2008; Jones and Vollrath 2013 for a detailed treatment of the various approaches to explaining economic growth). These explanations have had an overwhelming whiff of modernity to them, although invention and technological change have occurred throughout the history of the human species (Boyd, Richerson, and Henrich 2013; Couch 1989; Derry 1961; Greene 2000; Hodges 1970; Landels 1978; Mokyr 2005; Pacey 1991; Usher 1954; Wilson 2002). One need not deny that the pace of technological change has accelerated since the late eighteenth century or engage in facile comparisons of technological change across eras to inquire—pending hard detective work—as to the role of technological change in economic growth (broadly understood) in ancient societies.

Regardless of the relative importance of technological change as a cause of economic growth in the preindustrial past (a matter to be settled empirically) there is another analytical framework with which to assess the extent and rate of growth in the past, one with a long pedigree that is animated by underlying social processes (agglomeration, specialization, exchange) of broad relevance and ought to be familiar: Smithian growth. Although there is no specific section of Adam Smith's (1776) *The Wealth of Nations* that presents a fully developed model of economic growth, interspersed throughout the book are observations and arguments as to conditions that can facilitate increases in labor productivity (Stull 1986).

Smith observed that specialization made possible through the division and coordination of labor can generate significant increases in the productivity of individual labor. Specialization can also be facilitated by market growth brought about by either increases in the size of domestic markets (almost synonymous with increases in population size) or increases in the amount of trade.[4] These insights came to constitute the foundations for a theory of economic growth that is not reliant on technological change for driving productivity increases (Barcai 1969; Eltis 2000; Lucas 1988; Malerba 1992; Rosen 1978; Rosenberg 1968; Samuelson 1977; Stigler 1951; Yang and Borland 1991; Young 1928).

The standard interpretation of Smith's famous statement regarding the extent of the market is that larger markets support larger levels of production that, in turn, demand increasing separation of this production into discrete components and increasing concentration of individuals on specific tasks. A richer interpretation of this statement, which is not restricted to market economies, is that the extent of the division of labor is related to the number of individuals who interact with each other in pursuit of their livelihoods. From this perspective, Smithian growth is a manifestation of the effects of increased population size and interaction for social organization, the diversity of tasks and tools, and productivity (individual and group-level), phenomena of long-standing interest to anthropologists, archaeologists, sociologists, and economists (Blau 1970; Boserup 1981; Carneiro 2000; Dumond 1965; Durkheim 1984; Ember 1963; Henrich 2015; Johnson 1982; Johnson and Earle 2000; Kline and Boyd 2010; Kremer 1993; Lee 1988; Naroll 1956; Simon 1986; Shennan 2002).[5] There is another way in which increased productivity could have occurred: if individuals worked harder (more effort per unit of time) in response to a religious or social obligation, or, as one reviewer of this chapter put it, in order to be part of "the emotionally rewarding tapestry" of community life. But aside from the empirical difficulties of recognizing increases in productivity resulting from increasing individual effort (while keeping the number of producers the same), it is very difficult to imagine such a situation being long-lasting, whether in the ancient pueblos or the Stalinist Soviet Union.

BACK TO THE PUEBLOS

Among historians, economists, and archaeologists there is growing awareness that ancient economies were not stagnant, but experienced change, including extended periods of (relative) growth and decline. This has led to an increasing awareness of economic efflorescences in specific times and places in the preindustrial past (Goldstone 2002). The study of economic growth in the past is not reduced to looking for evidence of technological change, nor is it even a matter of choosing between the relevance of intensive growth and the greater likelihood of Smithian growth, but rather of creatively deploying the repertoire of concepts and tools now available to investigate the nature and magnitude of growth, how broadly its benefits were felt, what caused it, and how it compared to that of different or later eras. Were there extensive, long-distance trade networks in antiquity (Hull and others 2014; Huster 2018; Stark and Ossa 2010; Temin 2012)? Were several of the ingredients for Smithian growth recognizably present in ancient societies for some specific periods (Algaze 2008; Harper 2017; Jongman 2014b; Kelly 1997; Maddison 1998; Manning 2018; Ober 2015; Silver 2007)? Was there an

[4] Both phenomena are captured in the celebrated dictum that is the title of chapter three of Book I of *Wealth of Nations*—"That the Division of Labour is Limited by the Extent of the Market." The productivity gains generated from an enhanced division of labor are attributed to the energy saved by increasing the intellectual and manual deftness of each worker, through learning by doing, reducing the number of times individuals switch between tasks, and the accumulation of minor innovations resulting from attempts to improve standard procedures (Arrow 1962; Auerswald and others 2000; Bettencourt 2014; Solow 1997; von Hippel and Tyre 1995).

[5] The effect of population size can in turn be approached more generally as the effect of scale on the behavior and dynamics of a system, as discussed by Phil Anderson (1972) in one of the foundational papers of complexity science "more is different." "The whole is greater than the sum of its parts" is the Aristotelian version of the insight, or if the reader prefers her philosophy served with a Hegelian flavor, "qualitative changes induced by quantitative changes." For a nonphilosophical treatment of the effects of scale on system behavior, see Miller (2016).

increase in the number of occupations with increasing urban population (Hanson, Ortman, and Lobo 2017)? Was the phenomenon of "increasing returns to scale"—whereby output increases more rapidly than population size—operative in a premodern society (Ortman et al. 2015)? These are all answerable questions, even if tentative in tone and cautiously framed, and are the result of empirical scientific work, not ontological debates.

The essays collected in the present volume represent a contribution to the study of economic growth in the past, not merely by bringing another geographic area and culture into the set of societies that have been investigated but, more importantly, by posing questions about growth in the context of relatively small-scale societies. The empirical challenges are severe but not insurmountable. Ortman and Davis forcefully argue (Chapter 1) for the uniquely important role of the archaeological record for informing and validating theories of economic development as a general process and demonstrate the possibility of constructing output measures on the basis of archaeological data. In the case of Pueblo society in the Northern Rio Grande, Ortman and Davis show that output and demographic data can be assembled indicating change and growth, and they show the empirical relevance of the phenomenon of agglomeration (the effect on individual-level productivity of individuals residing in close proximity and engaging in productive activities) as a process capable of explaining the recorded changes in material output and quality of life.

The resurgence of interest in the role of "institutions" (what anthropologists would broadly denote by "culture") in promoting or hindering actions by individuals—risk-taking, learning, investing, inventing, modifying standard practices, sharing information—that would be conducive to economic development has highlighted the role of changes in institutional settings and cultural frameworks for economic growth (Acemoglu and Robinson 2012; North 1994). Did the ancient Pueblos of the Southwest exhibit the institutional arrangements, norms, and incentives that would have encouraged specialization, invention (technical or organizational), and innovation? Did these institutional arrangements change? How can one document such changes in the absence of written records? In Chapter 10 Schneider ingeniously weaves together skeletal evidence and rock art (a canonical instance of cultural expression) to argue that the temporal disjunction between episodes of violence and the formation of the rock art representing such violence can be interpreted as evidence for a society very much aware of the benefits of peace and the need to dampen violence. In effect Schneider uses rock art as evidence for the presence of and change in institutional setting.

That cultural infrastructure (who can do what with whom, how trust is earned and maintained, how cooperation is achieved and its benefits distributed) matters greatly in a society's material life is not, of course, a novel insight.[6] But Eiselt in Chapter 2 and Camilli and her colleagues in Chapter 3 show how the Tewa economy, an archetypal nonindustrial economy, involved the novel integration of social practices (trade networks, mobile workforces) and technologies (cobble-bordered and gravel-mulched fields) to extract an adequate agricultural output so that Tewa people could "get things done in the world." And how else but through culture (institutions) could such an integration be done? It is very hard not to give in to the temptation to reformulate Chapters 2 and 3 as a classic instance of Smithian growth (well, hard for an economist at least).

The various social processes by which individuals can learn from and copy one other, share and transmit information, and jointly invent are facilitated by physical proximity (as well as by social proximity). Obviously Puebloan society nucleated in settlements and although the distinction often made in economic geography between residential community and workplace community is not as relevant here, the question of how and why Pueblo people clustered together obviously is. This investigation raises the challenge that is all too familiar in archaeology of deducing social interactions based on physical remains. Was the way in which Puebloan settlement clusters formed conducive to productivity gains? In Chapter 5 Cruz and Ortman evaluate different models of spatial social organization against what is known about settlement clusters in the Rio Chama Valley. What could be regarded as a frustrating research outcome—namely that the available evidence does not clearly declare any of the extant models a winner—raises an exciting scientific possibility: that Pueblo people developed a form of spatial social integration that achieved the benefits generally common to such integration in the absence of clear and consistent settlement hierarchies. This insight is reinforced by Ortman and Coffey's (Chapter 6) treatment of that emblematic feature of Pueblo social life—public dances—as the mechanism through which putative advantages of agglomeration were achieved. Ortman and Coffey's approach takes a formal theoretical framework

---

[6] Nor would it have been to the author of *The Theory of Moral Sentiments* (Smith 1759), an exploration into the ethical, psychological, and institutional underpinnings (besides the technological and scale considerations) that make trade and a division of labor possible.

that has found applicability across varied socioeconomic settings (see the references in their chapter) and matches it with new data to make inferences about the social networks that characterized Pueblo life.

To claim that the central economic facts underpinning economic analysis are those of finite resources (and inputs) and boundedness (of effort) is not to claim that economic life is synonymous with social life. Economic goods need not be valued only for their role in a system of production. This is shown very clearly by Meehan in Chapter 4 with regard to cotton textile production. The conclusion that cotton "entangled" Pueblo communities in "complex webs of interactions" is a statement of general analytical applicability ranging from the Bronze age to today's mining of tantalum (an important component in cell phones). Principal channels of entanglement in the Puebloan space were (as has been the case throughout economic history) trade networks and tool-procurement channels. Accordingly, in Chapter 7, Arakawa and colleagues seek to show a strong linkage between population density and tool usage and distribution, the sort of linkage Boserup argued had great explanatory power: population change inducing changes in technology and agricultural production.

Specialization is almost an indispensable ingredient for any process of development driven by productivity improvements and has long been viewed as a defining consequence of urbanization and the transition to sedentism (Bairoch 1988). Was settlement specialization a feature of Puebloan society? Although few communities in the Prehispanic Southwest exhibit direct and clear-cut evidence of specialized production, Schleher argues in Chapter 9 that there is evidence that San Marcos Pueblo, one of the largest communities, did specialize in the production of one type of pottery. Duwe (Chapter 8) also argues that the flow and distribution of distinctive pottery produced in specific regions changed with the populations of those regions. These changes may reflect the relationship between density and specialization (and thus export of finished products) or they may reflect a tendency for manufactured goods to flow from high-density to low-density areas, with countervailing flows of agricultural produce. Davis (Chapter 11) provides further evidence for settlement-based specialization in the production of tobacco pipes and, more importantly, their use in ritualized interethnic trade diplomacy. Specialization, defined as production over the needs of the household, and detected via the production of goods in specific locations, was clearly a feature of Puebloan society in the Northern Rio Grande area. Which is to say, specialization was a salient feature of this settlement system.

What is one to make of the various results, insights, and stories collected in this volume? First, and foremost, Pueblo people had an economic history (which archaeological practice renders detectable and measurable), and found ways, unique but recognizable, to solve the economic problems presented in this volume. No doubt the quality and the details of the evidence presented in the assembled chapters will be critically evaluated by experts, but for now, let's tentatively accept the following conclusions regarding the Northern Rio Grande Pueblo economy: (1) there was demographic change (population increases associated with the formation and growth of settlements, and spatial adjustments in population density over time); (2) there were trade networks linking settlements and regions, as well as movement of individuals performing labor at different locations; (3) specialization in the production of everyday and craft goods occurred; (4) there were increases in agricultural output from which increases in productivity can be inferred to have also taken place; and (5) there were increases in per capita utilization of housing space. Given these results, let us be bold and claim that there was at least one episode of economic efflorescence in Puebloan history.[7]

Puebloan economic history represents an important addition to the historiographic work documenting occurrences of growth and material improvement before the Industrial Revolution, and in this case in a non-Western and nonstate setting (Jones 1988). Most of the essential ingredients for Smithian growth were in place in the Northern Rio Grande Region but they were expressed and integrated in a recognizably Puebloan way. There is an aspect to this possible instance of Smithian growth that is particularly notable and makes the investigation into Puebloan economics truly a contribution to the comparative study of socioeconomic development. Smithian growth stands in stark contrast to growth dynamics driven by technological change (and especially technological change involving the use of energy sources), but historical experience most likely involves the interplay between productivity gains generated by technological change *and* productivity gains from the division of labor, specialization, and trade. This makes for a greater range of pathways for social development but does present a bothersome example of confounding effects that are difficult to disentangle in a modern context. This is why the results presented in this volume are so important. The growth and development story provided by these

[7] Goldstone (2002) proposed the concept of efflorescence as a more informative intermediate between stagnation and growth with an efflorescence denoting a period of demographic and material improvement.

studies occurred in a setting in which disruptive or radical technological change did not occur. This is not to say that ingenuity, innovation, and adaptive intelligence were not amply present, but the technologies for energy capture available to farmers, potters, and house builders did not fundamentally differ throughout the period covered by the investigations reported here. Pueblo economic history thus provides a useful context for investigating the drivers of Smithian growth. In this way, it may contribute to a general theory of economic growth that is relevant for all of us.

Economists Deirdre McCloskey (1976) and Paul Romer (1996) have made eloquent pleas for theory construction in economics to be informed by history (which under their broad interpretation of the subject surely includes archaeology). A rich theory of economic development has to acknowledge that a sharp boundary between stagnation and development is inadequate to describe economic life before the Industrial Revolution. In a similar vein, the Northern Rio Grande Pueblos provide evidence that small-scale, nonindustrial, nonmonetized, and relatively egalitarian societies could generate social development. This realization should compel economic historians, economic archaeologists, economic growth theorists, and practitioners of other disciplines to talk with each, intensely, so that a truly deep and insightful theory of socioeconomic development can be built.

References Cited

Abbott, David R., Alexa M. Smith, and Emiliano Gallaga
2007 Ballcourts and Ceramics: The Case for Hohokam Marketplaces in the Arizona Desert. *American Antiquity* 72(3):461–484.

Abul-Megd, A. Y.
2002 Wealth Distribution in an Ancient Egyptian Society. *Physical Review E* 66(057104):1–3.

Acemoglu, Daron
2009 *Introduction to Modern Economic Growth.* Princeton University Press, Princeton.

Acemoglu, Daron, and James A. Robinson
2012 *Why Nations Fail: The Origins of Power, Prosperity and Poverty*. Crown, New York.

Adams, E. Charles, and Andrew I. Duff
2004 Settlement Clusters and the Pueblo IV period. In *The Protohistoric Pueblo World, A.D. 1275–1600*, edited by E. Charles Adams and Andrew I. Duff, pp. 3–16. University of Arizona Press, Tucson.

Adams, E. Charles and Andrew I. Duff (editors)
2004 *The Protohistoric Pueblo World, A.D. 1275–1600.* University of Arizona Press, Tucson.

Adler, Michael A.
1989 Ritual Facilities and Social Integration in Nonranked Societies. In *The Architecture of Social Integration in Prehistoric Pueblos*, edited by William D. Lipe and Michelle Hegmon, pp. 35–52. Occasional Papers No. 1. Crow Canyon Archaeological Center, Cortez, Colorado.
1996 Land Tenure, Archaeology, and the Ancestral Pueblo Social Landscape. *Journal of Anthropological Archaeology* 15:337–371.

Adler, Michael A., and Herbert W. Dick
1999 *Picuris Pueblo through Time: Eight Centuries of Change at a Northern Rio Grande Pueblo.* Southern Methodist University, Dallas.

Aghion, Philippe, and Peter Howitt
2008 *The Economics of Growth*. The MIT Press, Cambridge, Massachusetts.

Ahlstrom, Richard V. N., Carla R. Van West, and Jeffrey S. Dean
1995 Environmental and Chronological Factors in the Mesa Verde-Northern Rio Grande Migration. *Journal of Anthropological Archaeology* 14(2):125–142.

Algaze, Guillermo
2008 *Ancient Mesopotamia at the Dawn of Civilization: The Evolution of an Urban Landscape.* University of Chicago Press, Chicago.

Allen, Robert C.
2009 *The British Industrial Revolution in Global Perspective*. Cambridge University Press, Cambridge, United Kingdom.

Altschul, Jeffrey H., Keith W. Kintigh, Terry H. Klein, William H. Doelle, Kelley A. Hays-Gilpin, Sarah A. Herr, Timothy A. Kohler, Barbara J. Mills, Lindsay M. Montgomery, Margaret C. Nelson, Scott G. Ortman, John N. Parker, Matthew A. Peeples, and Jeremy A. Sabloff
2017 Fostering Synthesis in Archaeology to Advance Science and Benefit Society. *Proceedings of the National Academy of Science of the U.S.A.* 114(42):10999–11002.

American Museum of Natural History (AMNH)
2013 Nels Nelson Galisteo Basin Collections at AMNH. Inventory available from the American Museum of Natural History, New York.

Anderson, David G.
1994 *The Savannah River Chiefdoms: Political Change in the Late Prehistoric Southeast.* University of Alabama Press, Tuscaloosa.

Anderson, Phil
1972 More Is Different. *Science*, 177: 393–396.

Anschuetz, Kurt F.
1993 Preliminary Report for the 1992 Field Season: The University of Michigan Rio del Oso Archaeological Survey, Española Ranger District, Santa Fe National Forest. Submitted to Española Ranger District, Santa Fe National Forest, Española. Ms. on file, USDA, US Forest Service, Southwest Region, Santa Fe National Forest, Santa Fe.

1995 Saving a Rainy Day: The Integration of Diverse Agricultural Technologies to Harvest and Conserve Water in the Lower Rio Chama Valley New Mexico. In *Soil, Water, Biology, and Belief in Prehistoric and Traditional Southwestern Agriculture*, edited by H. Wolcott Toll, pp. 25–39. Special Publication 2. New Mexico Archaeological Council, Albuquerque.

1998 *Not Waiting for the Rain: Integrated Systems of Water Management by Pre-Columbian Pueblo Farmers in North-Central New Mexico*. Unpublished PhD dissertation, Department of Anthropology. University of Michigan, Ann Arbor.

2001 Soaking It All In: Northern New Mexican Pueblo Lessons of Water Management and Landscape Ecology. In *Native Peoples of the Southwest: Negotiating Land, Water, and Ethnicities*, edited by Laurie Weinstein, pp. 49–78. Greenwood, Westport, Connecticut.

2005 Landscapes as Memory: Archaeological History to Learn From and to Live By. In *Engaged Anthropology: Essays in Honor of Richard I. Ford*, edited by Michelle Hegmon and Sanday Eiselt, pp. 52–72. Museum of Anthropology, University of Michigan, Ann Arbor.

2006 Tewa Fields, Tewa Traditions. In *Canyon Gardens: The Ancient Pueblo Landscapes of the American Southwest*, edited by V.B. Price and B.H. Morrow, pp. 57–74. University of New Mexico Press, Albuquerque.

2007 Room to Grow with Rooms to Spare: Agriculture and Big-Site Settlements in the Late Pre-Columbian Tewa Basin Pueblo Landscape. *Kiva* 73(2):173–194.

2014 *Final Report: Perspectives on Managing Multi-Cultural Landscapes: Use, Access, and Fire-Fuels Management Attitudes and Preferences of User Groups Concerning the Valles Caldera National Preserve (VCNP) and Adjacent Areas.* USDA Forest Service Joint Venture Agreement Number: 07-JV-11221602. Prepared for USDA, Forest Service, Rocky Mountain Research Station, Fort Collins, Colorado, and Valles Caldera Trust, Valles Caldera National Preserve, Jemez Springs, New Mexico. On file, USDA, Forest Service, Rocky Mountain Research Station, Fort Collins, Colorado.

Anschuetz, Kurt F., and Christopher Banet
2012 Yunge Hills Survey Objectives, Methods, and Field Observations. In *Late-Pre-Columbian and Early Historic Period Pueblo Farming in the Yunge Hills Area of the San Juan Pueblo Grant*, by Eileen L. Camilli, Kurt F. Anschuetz, Susan J. Smith, and Christopher D. Banet, pp. 4.1–102. Report prepared for USDI,, Bureau of Indian Affairs, Southwest Regional Office, Albuquerque, and US Department of Justice, Indian Resources Section, Denver. Ebert and Associates, Albuquerque.

Anschuetz, Kurt F., Steven R. Dominguez, and Eileen L. Camilli
1999 *An Archaeological Study of Pre-Columbian Agricultural Features at LA 125767, Taos Resource Area, Albuquerque District, Bureau of Land Management and New Mexico State Lands in Rio Arriba County, New Mexico.* Prepared for US Department of Justice, Denver, and USDI, Bureau of Indian Affairs, Regional Water Rights, Albuquerque Area Office, Albuquerque. Ebert and Associates, Albuquerque.

Anschuetz, Kurt F., and Louie Hena
1999 A Tradition of Farming Northern Rio Grande Pueblo Lessons of Land Stewardship and Sustainability Agriculture. Manuscript No. 3734. On file, Laboratory of Anthropology Library, Museum of New Mexico, Santa Fe.

Anschuetz, Kurt F., and Cherie L. Scheick
2006 The Española Basin Geographic Subdivision. In *A Study of Pre-Columbian and Historic Uses of the Santa Fe National Forest: Competition and Alliance in the Northern Middle Rio Grande,* edited by Cherie L. Scheick, pp. 169–234. Southwest Region Report No. 18. USDA, US Forest Service, Southwest Region, Santa Fe National Forest, Santa Fe.

Anschuetz, Kurt, F., Eileen L. Camilli, and Christopher D. Banet
2006 *Documentation of Pre-Columbian Pueblo Farmland Irrigation on the San Juan Pueblo*

Grant near the San Juan Airport within the Geographic Scope of New Mexico v. Abbott. Prepared for and on file at US Department of Justice, Denver, and USDI Bureau of Indian Affairs, Regional Water Rights, Albuquerque Area Office, Albuquerque.

2016 The Stuff of History, Landscapes, Section 36, Agricultural Landscapes. In *Oxford Handbook of Southwest Archaeology*, Part 3, edited by Barbara J. Mills and Severin M. Fowles, pp. 697–714. Oxford University Press, Oxford.

Anschuetz, Kurt F., Steven R. Dominguez, and Eileen L. Camilli

2000 *An Archaeological Study of Pre-Columbian Agricultural Features at LA 125767, Taos Resource Area, Albuquerque District, Bureau of Land Management and New Mexico State Lands in Rio Arriba County, New Mexico*. Prepared for US Department of Justice, Denver, and USDI, Bureau of Indian Affairs, Regional Water Rights, Albuquerque Area Office, Albuquerque. Ebert and Associates, Albuquerque.

Anschuetz, Kurt F., Esperanza Gonzales, Tessie Naranjo, and Susan J. Smith

2001 *AR-03-02-02-0296/0543 (LA 89391/LA 118494) within the proposed El Rito Cemetery Association Special-Use Permit Parcel, El Rito Ranger District, Carson National Forest, Río Arriba County, New Mexico*. Community and Cultural Landscape Contribution X. Challenge Cost-Share Grant No. R3F2-99-CCS-003 9 among the El Rito Cemetery Association, the Carson National Forest, and the Río Grande Foundation for Communities and Cultural Landscapes. Rio Grande Foundation for Communities and Cultural Landscapes, Santa Fe.

Arakawa, Fumiyasu

2006 *Lithic Raw Material Procurement and the Social Landscape in the Central Mesa Verde Region, A.D. 600–1300*. Unpublished PhD dissertation, Department of Anthropology, Washington State University, Pullman, Washington.

2012 Cyclical Cultural Trajectories: A Case Study from the Mesa Verde Region. *Journal of Anthropological Research*. 68:35–69.

Arakawa, Fumiyasu, Scott G. Ortman, M. Steve Shackley, and Andrew Duff

2011 Obsidian Evidence of Interaction and Migration from the Mesa Verde Region, Southwest Colorado. *American Antiquity* 76:773–795.

Ariss, Robert

1939 Distribution of Smoking Pipes in the Pueblo Area." *New Mexico Anthropologist* 3(3–4):53–57.

Arnold, Dean E.

1985 *Ceramic Theory and Cultural Process*. Cambridge University Press, Cambridge.

Arnold, Dean E., and Alvaro L. Nieves

1992 Factors Affecting Ceramic Standardization. In *Ceramic Production and Distribution: An Integrated Approach*, edited by George J. Bey III, pp. 93–113. Westview Press, Boulder.

Arnold, Jean E.

1992 Complex Hunter-Gatherer-Fishers of Prehistoric California: Chiefs, Specialists, and Maritime Adaptations of the Channel Islands. *American Antiquity* 57(1):60–84.

Arrow, Kenneth J.

1962 The Economic Implications of Learning by Doing. *Review of Economics and Statistics* 29(3):155–173.

1994 The Division of Labor in the Economy, the Polity, and Society. In *The Return to Increasing Returns*, edited by James M. Buchanan and Yong J. Yoon, pp. 69–84. University of Michigan Press, Ann Arbor.

Auerswald, Philip, Stuart Kauffman, José Lobo, and Karl Shell

2000 The Production Recipes Approach to Modeling Technological Innovation: An Application to Learning by Doing. *Journal of Economic Dynamics & Control* 24(3):389–450.

Bairoch, Paul

1988 *Cities and Economic Development: from the Dawn of History to the Present*. University of Chicago Press, Chicago.

Balfet, Helene

1965 Ethnological Observations in North Africa and Archaeological Interpretation. In *Ceramics and Man*, edited by F. R. Matson, pp. 161–177. Viking Fund Publications in Anthropology No. 41. Aldine, Chicago.

Bamforth, Douglas

n.d. Settled Farmers and Their Neighbors, Part 2: The Later Plains Village Period, AD 1250 to 1500. Draft chapter, in process.

Bandelier, Adolph F.

1892 *Final Report of Investigations among the Indians of the Southwestern United States, Carried on in the Years from 1880 to 1885, vol. 2*. Papers of the Archaeological Institute of America, American

Bandelier, Adolph F. (continued)
Series, Vol. 3 and 4. John Wilson and Son, Cambridge, Massachusetts.

Barcai, Haim
1969 A Formal Outline of a Smithian Growth Model. *The Quarterly Journal of Economics*, 83(3):396–414.

Barnett, Franklin
1969 *Tonque Pueblo: a Report of Partial Excavation of an Ancient Pueblo IV Indian Ruin in New Mexico*. Albuquerque Archaeological Society, Albuquerque.

Baugh, Timothy G.
1991 Ecology and Exchange: The Dynamics of Plains-Pueblo Interaction." In *Farmers, Hunters, and Colonists: Interaction between the Southwest and the Southern Plains*, edited by Katherine A. Spielmann, pp. 107–127. University of Arizona Press, Tucson.
2008 The Anthropologies of Trade and Exchange: An Essay on Kirikir'i.s and Southern Plains Political Economy. *Plains Anthropologist* 53(208):415–430.

Beaglehole, Ernest
1937 *Notes on Hopi Economic Life*. Publications in Anthropology No. 15. Yale University Press, New Haven.

Beal, John D.
1987 *Foundation of the Rio Grande Classic: the Lower Chama River, A.D. 1300–1500*. Report submitted to the New Mexico Office of Cultural Affairs. Historic Preservation Division, Santa Fe. Southwest Archaeological Consultants, Inc., Albuquerque.

Bennet, Hugh Hammond
1939 *Soil Conservation*, first edition. McGraw-Hill, New York.

Benson, Larry, Kenneth L. Petersen, and John R. Stein
2007 Anasazi (Pre-Columbian Native American) Migrations During the Middle-12th and Late-Thirteenth Centuries—Were They Drought Induced? *Climate Change* 83:187–213.

Bernardini, Wesley
1998 Conflict, Migration, and the Social Environment: Interpreting Architectural Change in Early and Late Pueblo IV Aggregations. In *Migration and Reorganization: The Pueblo IV Period in the American Southwest*, edited by Katherine A. Spielmann, pp. 91–114. Research Paper No. 51. Arizona State University, Tempe.

Bettencourt, Luis M. A.
2013 The Origins of Scaling in Cities. *Science* 340:1438–1441.
2014 Impact of Changing Technology on the Evolution of Complex Informational Networks. *Proceedings of the IEEE* 102(12):1878–1891.

Biddiscombe, J.
2003 *Sinagua Subsistence Strategies at Elden Pueblo: A Macrobotanical Study*. Unpublished Master's thesis, Department of Anthropology, Northern Arizona University, Flagstaff.

Blackman, M. James, Gil J. Stein, and Pamela B. Vandiver
1993 The Standardization Hypothesis and Ceramic Mass Production: Technological, Compositional, and Metric Indexes of Craft Specialization at Tell Leilan, Syria. *American Antiquity* 58(1):60–80.

Blakeslee, Don
1975 *The Plains Interband Trade System*. Unpublished PhD dissertation, Department of Anthropology, University of Wisconsin, Milwaukee.
1981 The Origin and Spread of the Calumet Ceremony. *American Antiquity* 46(4):759–768.

Blanton, Richard E., and Lane Fargher
2008 *Collective Action in the Formation of Pre-Modern States*. Springer, New York.

Blanton, Richard E., Stephan A. Kowalewski, Gary Feinman, and Jill Appel
1993 *Ancient Mesoamerica: A Comparison of Change in Three Regions*, second edition. Cambridge University Press, Cambridge, United Kingdom.

Blau, Peter M.
1964 *Exchange and Power in Social Life*. John Wiley, New York.
1970 A Formal Theory of Differentiation in Organization. *American Sociological Review*, 35:201–281.

Blinman, Eric
1988 *The Interpretation of Ceramic Variability: A Case Study from the Dolores Anasazi*. Unpublished PhD dissertation, Washington State University, Pullman.

Boast, Robin
1997 A Small Company of Actors: A Critique of Style." *Journal of Material Culture* 2(2):173–198.

Bocinsky, R. Kyle, and Timothy A. Kohler
2014 A 2,000-year Reconstruction of the Rain-fed Agricultural Niche in the US Southwest. *Nature Communications* 5:5618. doi: 5610.1038/ncomms6618.

Bodley, John H.
2003 *The Power of Scale* M.S. Sharp, Armonk, New York.

Bohrer, Vorsila L.
1962 Ethnobotanical Materials from Tonto National Monument. In *Archaeological Studies at Tonto National Monument, Arizona*, by Charlie Steen, Lloyd M. Pierson, Vorsila L. Bohrer, and Kate Peck Kent, pp. 75–114. Technical Series No. 2. Southwest Monuments Association, Globe, Arizona.

Boland, Richard J., and Ram V. Tenkasi
1995 Perspective Making and Perspective Taking in Communities of Practice. *Organization Science* 6(4):350–372.

Boserup, Ester
1965 *The Conditions of Agricultural Growth: The Economics of Agrarian Change Under Population Pressure*. Aldine, Chicago.
1981 *Population and Technological Change: A Study of Long-Term Trends*. University of Chicago Press, Chicago.

Bosker, Maarten, Steven Brakman, Harry Garretsen, Herman De Jong, and Marc Schramm
2008 Ports, Plagues and Politics: Explaining Italian City Growth 1300–1861. *European Review of Economic History* 12(1):97–131.

Bourdieu, Pierre
1977 *Outline of a Theory of Practice*. Cambridge University Press, Cambridge.

Bower, Nathan W., Steve Faciszewski, Stephen Renwick, and Stewart Peckham
1986 A Preliminary Analysis of Rio Grande Glazes of the Classic Period Using Scanning Electron Microscopy with X-ray Fluorescence. *Journal of Field Archaeology* 13(2):307–315.

Bowman, Alan, and Andrew Wilson
2009 *Quantifying the Roman Economy: Methods and Problems*. Oxford University Press, New York.

Bowman, Alan and Andrew Wilson (editors)
2011 *Settlement, Urbanization and Population*. Oxford University Press, Oxford.

Bowser, Brenda J.
2000 From Pottery to Politics: An Ethnoarchaeological Case Study of Political Factionalism, Ethnicity, and Domestic Pottery Style in the Ecuadorian Amazon. *Journal of Archaeological Method and Theory* 7(3):219–248.

Boyd, Douglas K.
1997 Late Prehistoric II (AD 1100/1200–1541) and Protohistoric (AD 1541–1750) Periods. In *Caprock Canyonlands Archaeology: A Synthesis of the Late Prehistory and History of Lake Alan Henry and the Texas Panhandle-Plains*, Vol. II. Reports of Investigations No. 110. Prewitt and Associates, Austin.

Boyd, Robert, Peter J. Richerson, and Joseph Henrich
2013 The Cultural Evolution of Technology: Facts and Theories. In *Cultural Evolution: Society, Technology, Language, and Religion*, edited by Peter Richerson and Morten H. Christiansen, pp. 119–142. MIT Press, Cambridge, Massachusetts.

Boyer, Jeffrey, James Moore, Steven Lakatos, Nancy Akins, C. Dean Wilson, and Eric Blinman
2010 Remodeling Immigration: A Northern Rio Grande Perspective on Depopulation, Migration, and Donation-Side Models. In *Leaving Mesa Verde: Peril and Change in the Thirteenth-Century Southwest*, edited by Timothy A. Kohler, Mark D. Varien, and Aaron M. Wright, pp. 285–323. University of Arizona Press, Tucson.

Bradfield, R. Maitland
1971 *The Changing Pattern of Hopi Agriculture*. Royal Anthropological Institute of Great Britain and Ireland, London.

Bremer, J. Michael
1995a AR-03-10-06-1230. Site form on file, Archaeological Records Management System, Historic Preservation Division and Museum of New Mexico, Santa Fe.
1995b AR-03-10-06-1231. Site form on file, Archaeological Records Management System, Historic Preservation Division and Museum of New Mexico, Santa Fe.

Breternitz, David A.
1966 *An Appraisal of Tree-Ring Dated Pottery in the Southwest*. Anthropological Papers No. 10. University of Arizona Press, Tucson.

Brown, Barton McCaul
1987 Population Estimation from Floor Area: A Restudy of "Naroll's Constant.". *Behavior Science Research* 22(1–4):1–49.

Brown, Peter, and Aaron Podolefsky
1976 Population Density, Agricultural Intensity, Land Tenure, and Group Size in New Guinea Highlands. *Ethnology* 15:211–238.

Broxton, David E., Frazer Goff, and Kenneth Wohletz
2008 The Geology of Los Alamos National Laboratory as a Backdrop for Archaeological Studies on the Pajarito Plateau. In *The Land Conveyance and Transfer Project: 7000 Years of Land Use on the Pajarito Plateau*, Vol. 1, Baseline Studies, edited by Bradley J. Vierra and Kari M. Schmidt,

Broxton, David E., Frazer Goff, and Kenneth Wohletz (continued)

pp. 7–30. LAUR-07-6205. US Department of Energy, National Nuclear Security Administration, Los Alamos National Laboratory, Ecology and Air Quality Group, Los Alamos.

Bugé, David E.

1984 Prehistoric Subsistence Strategies in the Ojo Caliente Valley, New Mexico. In *Prehistoric Agricultural Strategies in the Southwest*, edited by Suzanne K. Fish and Paul R. Fish, pp. 27–34. Anthropological Research Papers No. 33. Arizona State University, Tempe.

Brumfiel, Elizabeth M., and Timothy K. Earle

1987 Specialization, Exchange, and Complex Societies: An Introduction. In *Specialization, Exchange, and Complex Societies*, edited by Elizabeth M. Brumfiel and Timothy K. Earle, pp. 1–9. Cambridge University Press, Cambridge.

Bureau of Economic Analysis

2015 *Measuring the Economy: A Primer on GDP and the National Income and Product Accounts.* US Department of Commerce, Washington, DC.

Cameron, Catherine M.

1998 Coursed Adobe Architecture, Style, and Social Boundaries in the American Southwest. In *The Archaeology of Social Boundaries*, edited by Miriam Stark, pp. 193–217. Smithsonian Institution Press, Washington, DC.

Camilli, Eileen L.

2012a Gravel Mulch Excavations. In *Late Pre-Columbian and Early Historic Period Pueblo Farming in the Yunge Hills Area of the San Juan Pueblo Grant*, by Eileen L. Camilli, Kurt F. Anschuetz, Susan J. Smith, and Christopher D. Banet, pp. 5.1–5.50. Report prepared for USDI, Bureau of Indian Affairs, Southwest Regional Office, Albuquerque, and US Department of Justice, Indian Resources Section, Denver. Ebert and Associates, Albuquerque.

2012b Pre-Columbian Pueblo Occupation and Agricultural Field Features in the Lower Rio Chama Basin. In *Late-Pre-Columbian and Early Historic Period Pueblo Farming in the Yunge Hills Area of the San Juan Pueblo Grant*, by Eileen L. Camilli, Kurt F. Anschuetz, Susan J. Smith, and Christopher D. Banet, pp. 3.1–3.56. Report prepared for USDI, Bureau of Indian Affairs, Southwest Regional Office, Albuquerque, and US Department of Justice, Indian Resources Section, Denver. Ebert and Associates, Albuquerque.

Camilli, L. Eileen, Christopher D. Banet, and Susan J. Smith

2010 Adapting Agricultural Landscapes for Cotton Production: Archaeological, Palynological, and Pedological Investigation of Classic Period Field Technologies at San Ildefonso Pueblo. Presented at the Archeological Society of New Mexico Annual Meeting: Tradition and Continuity, Honoring Glenna Dean. Santa Fe, April 30–May 2, 2010.

Camilli, L. Eileen, Kurt F. Anschuetz, Susan J. Smith, and Christopher D. Banet

2012 *Late-Pre-Columbian and Early Historic Period Pueblo Farming in the Yunge Hills Area of the San Juan Pueblo Grant*. Prepared for USDI, Bureau of Indian Affairs, Southwest Regional Office, Albuquerque, and US Department of Justice, Indian Resources Section, Denver. Ebert and Associates, Albuquerque.

Camilli, Eileen L., Christopher Banet, Amy Hoeptner, and Kurt F. Anschuetz, with contributions by Susan J. Smith

2004a El Potrero Site 1 (LA 138467). Recorded for the US Department of Justice Denver, Colorado, and the USDI Bureau of Indian Affairs, Regional Water Rights, Southwest Regional Office, Albuquerque, New Mexico. Site form on file, Archaeological Records Management Section, Historic Preservation Division, Office of Cultural Affairs, and Laboratory of Anthropology, Museum of New Mexico, Santa Fe.

2004b Quarteles Site 1 (LA 138468). Recorded for the US Department of Justice Denver, Colorado, and the USDI Bureau of Indian Affairs, Regional Water Rights, Southwest Regional Office, Albuquerque, New Mexico. Site form on file, Archaeological Records Management Section, Historic Preservation Division, Office of Cultural Affairs, and Laboratory of Anthropology, Museum of New Mexico, Santa Fe.

2004c Tsimajo Site 1 (LA 138469). Recorded for the U.S. Department of Justice Denver, Colorado, and the USDI Bureau of Indian Affairs, Regional Water Rights, Southwest Regional Office, Albuquerque, New Mexico. Site form on file, Archaeological Records Management Section, Historic Preservation Division, Office of Cultural Affairs, and Laboratory of Anthropology, Museum of New Mexico, Santa Fe.

2004d Tsimajo Site 2 (LA 138479). Recorded for the U.S. Department of Justice Denver, Colorado, and the USDI Bureau of Indian Affairs, Regional Water Rights, Southwest Regional Office,

Albuquerque, New Mexico. Site form on file, Archaeological Records Management Section, Historic Preservation Division, Office of Cultural Affairs, and Laboratory of Anthropology, Museum of New Mexico, Santa Fe.

Carlin, A. Roberta, Barbara DeMarco, Jerry R. Craddock, and John H. R. Polt

2013 Archivo General de Indias, Sevilla, Audiencia de Mexico, Legajo 26, 48-E, Fols. 40r-54v. In *Desertion of the Colonists of New Mexico 1601*, Part 3, pp. 1–40, English translation section. Research Center for Romance Studies, University of California at Berkeley. Available online: https://escholarship.org/uc/item/452289m6.

Carmody, Stephen

2015 *Secrets in the Smoke: Prehistoric Tobacco Use in Tennessee*. Tennessee Council for Professional Archaeology. https://tennesseearchaeologycouncil.wordpress.com/ 2015/09/23/30-days-of-tennessee-archaeology-2015-day-23/.

Carneiro, Robert L.

1962 Scale Analysis as an Instrument for the Study of Cultural Evolution. *Southwestern Journal of Anthropology* 18:149–169.

1967 On the Relationship Between Size of Population and Complexity of Social Organization. *Southwestern Journal of Anthropology* 23:234–243.

2000 The Transition from Quantity to Quality: A Neglected Causal Mechanism in Accounting for Social Evolution. *Proceedings of the National Academy of Science of the U.S.A.* 97(23):12926–12931.

Casselberry, Samuel E.

1974 Further Refinement of Formulae for Determining Population from Floor Area. *World Archaeology* 6:118–122.

Cesaretti, Rudolph, Jose Lobo, Luis M. A. Bettencourt, Scott G. Ortman, and Michael E. Smith

2016 Population-Area Relationship for Medieval European Cities. *PLOS ONE* 11(10):e0162678.

Chamberlin, Matthew A.

2011 Plazas, Performance, and Symbolic Power in Ancestral Pueblo Religion. In *Religious Transformation in the Late Pre-Hispanic Pueblo World*, edited by Donna M. Glowacki and Scott Van Keuren, pp. 130–152. University of Arizona Press, Tucson.

Chavez, K. L.

1992 The Organization of Production and Distribution of Traditional Pottery in South Highland Peru. In *Ceramic Production and Distribution: An Integrated Approach*, edited by George J. Bey III and Christopher A. Pool, pp. 49–92. Westview Press, Boulder.

Chick, Garry

1997 Cultural Complexity: The Concept and Its Measurement. *Cross-Cultural Research* 31(4):275–307.

Chisholm, Michael

1970 *Rural Settlement and Land Use*. Aldine, Chicago.

Clark, John E., and Kenneth G. Hirth

2003 A Review of Twentieth-Century Mesoamerican Obsidian Studies. In *Mesoamerican Lithic Technology: Experimentation and Interpretation*, edited by John Clark, Peter Kelterborn, and Kenneth G. Hirth, pp. 15–54. University of Utah Press, Salt Lake City.

Clark, John E., and William J. Parry

1990 Craft Specialization and Cultural Complexity. In *Research in Economic Anthropology*, vol. 12, edited by Barry Isaac, pp. 289–346. Emerald Publishing, Bingley, United Kingdom.

Clarke, Steven K.

1971 *A Method for the Determination of Prehistoric Pueblo Population Estimates*. Center for Man and Environment, Prescott College, Prescott, Arizona.

Clary, Karen

1987 *Pollen Evidence for the Agricultural Utilization of Late Classic Period (A.D. 1300–1500) Puebloan Gravel Mulch Terrace Gardens in the Rio Chama, in the Vicinity of Medanales, New Mexico*. Castetter Laboratory for Ethnobotanical Studies Technical Report No. 198. University of New Mexico, Albuquerque.

Cole, Sally L.

1990 *Legacy on Stone: Rock Art of the Colorado Plateau and Four Corners Region*. Johnson Publishing, Boulder, Colorado.

Comin, Diego

2008 *Total Factor Productivity*. Available: http://www.people.hbs.edu/dcomin/def.pdf. .

Conkey, Margaret W, and Christine A. Hastorf.

1990 Introduction. In *The Uses of Style in Archaeology*, edited by Margaret W. Conkey and Christine A. Hastorf, pp. 1–4. Cambridge University Press, Cambridge.

Cordell, Linda S.

1991 Anna O Shepard and Southwestern Archaeology: Ignoring a Cautious Heretic. In *The Ceramics Legacy of Anna O. Shepard*, edited by Ronald L. Bishop and Frederick W. Lange, pp. 132–153. University Press of Colorado, Boulder.

Cordell, Linda S. (continued)
1998 *Before Pecos: Settlement Aggregation at Rowe, New Mexico*. Anthropological Papers No. 6. Maxwell Museum of Anthropology, Albuquerque.

Cordell, Linda S., and Judith A. Habicht-Mauchc
2012 Practice Theory and Social Dynamics among Prehistoric and Colonial Communities in the American Southwest. In *Potters and Communities of Practice: Glaze Paint and Polychrome Pottery in the American Southwest, A.D. 1250–1700*, edited by Linda S. Cordell and Judith A. Habicht-Mauche, pp.1–7. Anthropological Papers No. 75. University of Arizona Press, Tucson.

Cordell, Linda S., and Judith A. Habicht-Mauche (editors)
2012 *Potters and Communities of Practice: Glaze Paint and Polychrome Pottery in the American Southwest, A.D. 1250–1700*. Anthropological Papers No. 75. University of Arizona Press, Tucson.

Cordell, Linda S., Amy C. Earls, and Martha R. Binford
1984 Subsistence Systems in the Mountainous Settings of the Rio Grande Valley. In *Prehistoric Agricultural Strategies in the Southwest*, edited by Susanne K. Fish and Paul R. Fish, pp. 233–241. Anthropological Research Papers No. 33. Arizona State University, Tempe.

Costin, Cathy L.
1991 Craft Specialization: Issues in Defining, Documenting, and Explaining the Organization of Production. In *Archaeological Method and Theory*, Vol., 3, edited by Michael B. Schiffer, pp. 1–56. Academic Press, New York.
2001 Craft Production Systems. In *Archaeology at the Millennium: A Sourcebook*, edited by G. M. Feinman and T. D. Price, pp. 273–327. Kluwer Academic/Plenum, New York.

Costin, Cathy L., and Melissa B. Hagstrum
1995 Standardization, Labor Investment, Skill, and the Organization of Ceramic Production in Late Prehispanic Highland Peru. *American Antiquity* 60:619–639.

Couch, Carl, Jr.
1989 Oral Technologies: A Cornerstone of Ancient Civilizations? *The Sociological Quarterly*, 30: 587–602.

Creamer, Winifred
1993 *The Architecture of Arroyo Hondo Pueblo, New Mexico*. Arroyo Hondo Archaeological Series, Vol. 7. School of American Research Press, Santa Fe.
1996 Developing Complexity in the American Southwest: Constructing a Model for the Rio Grande Valley. In *Emergent Complexity: The Evolution of Intermediate Societies*, edited by Jeanne E. Arnold, pp. 91–106. Archaeological Series No. 9. International Monographs in Prehistory. Ann Arbor, Michigan.

Creamer, Winifred, and Lisa Renken
1994 Testing Conventional Wisdom: Protohistoric Ceramics and Chronology in the Northern Rio Grande. Paper presented at the 59th annual meetings of the Society for American Archaeology, Anaheim.

Crotty, Helen
1995 *Anasazi Mural Art of the Pueblo IV Period, A.D. 1300–1600: Influences, Selective Adaptation, and Cultural Diversity in the Prehistoric Southwest*. Unpublished PhD dissertation, Department of Art History, University of California, Los Angeles.

Crow Canyon Archaeological Center (CCAC)
2014 Research Database. Crow Canyon Archaeological Center, Cortez.

Crown, Patricia L.
1991 Evaluating the Construction Sequence and Population of Pot Creek Pueblo, Northern New Mexico. *American Antiquity* 56(2):291–314.
1995 The Production of the Salado Polychromes in the American Southwest. In *Ceramic Production in the American Southwest*, edited by Barbara J. Mills and Patricia L. Crown, pp. 142–166. University of Arizona Press, Tucson.
2007 Life Histories of Pots and Potters: Situating the Individual in Archaeology. *American Antiquity* 72(4):677–690.

Crown, Patricia L., Janet D. Orcutt, and Timothy A. Kohler
1996 Pueblo Cultures in Transition: The Northern Rio Grande. In *The Prehistoric Pueblo World: CE 1150–1350*, edited by Michael A. Adler, pp. 188–204. University of Arizona Press, Tucson.

Curewitz, Diane C.
2008 *Changes in Northern Rio Grande Ceramic Production and Exchange, Late Coalition Through Classic (CE 1250–1600)*. Unpublished Ph.D. dissertation, Department of Anthropology, Washington State University, Pullman.

Curewitz, Diane C., and Franklin F. Foit, Jr.
2018 Shards in Sherds: Identifying Production Locations and Exchange Patterns using Electron Microprobe Analysis of Volcanic Ash Temper in Northern Rio Grande Biscuit Ware. *Journal of Archaeological Science: Reports* 17:487–498.

Curewitz, Diane, and Sheila Goff
2012 The Right Ingredients: Southern Cerrillos Hills Lead in Paint on Pajarito Plateau-Produced Glaze-Painted Pottery. In *Potters and Communities of Practice: Glaze Paint and Polychrome Pottery in the American Southwest, A.D. 1250–1700*, edited by Linda S. Cordell and Judith A. Habicht-Mauche, pp. 75–84. Anthropological Papers No 75. University of Arizona Press, Tucson.

d'Alpoim Guedes, Jade A., Stefani A. Crabtree, R. Kyle Bocinsky, and Timothy A. Kohler
2016 Twenty-first Century Approaches to Ancient Problems: Climate and Society. *Proceedings of the National Academy of Science of the U.S.A.* DOI: 10.1073/pnas.1616188113.

Davis, John C.
1986 *Statistics and Data Analysis in Geology*, second edition. John Wiley and Sons, New York.

Davis, Kaitlyn
2017 *"The Ambassador's Herb": Tobacco Pipes as Evidence for Plains-Pueblo Interaction, Interethnic Negotiation, and Ceremonial Exchange in the Northern Rio Grande.* Unpublished Master's thesis, Department of Anthropology, University of Colorado, Boulder.

Davis, Kaitlyn, and Scott Ortman
2015 *Transformation in Daily Activity at Tsama Pueblo, New Mexico.* Paper presented at the 80th annual meeting of the Society for American Archaeology, San Francisco.

Dean, Glenna
1989 *Pollen Analysis of Archaeological Samples from Possible Anasazi Agricultural Fields at LA 6599 and LA 59659, Rio Chama Valley, New Mexico.* Castetter Laboratory for Ethnobotanical Studies Technical Report No. 246. Department of Biology, University of New Mexico, Albuquerque.
1991 *Pollen Analysis of Archaeological Samples from Basketmaker and Anasazi Agricultural Features at LA 75287 and LA 75288, Abiquiu West Project, Rio Chama Valley, New Mexico.* Castetter Laboratory for Ethnobotanical Studies, Technical Report No. 302. University of New Mexico, Albuquerque.
1994a *Pollen Analysis of 19 Samples from Anasazi Agricultural Features at LA 71506, Rio Del Oso Project, Rio Arriba County, New Mexico.* Archaeobotanical Services Technical Series Report No. 943. University of New Mexico, Albuquerque.
1994b *Pollen Analysis of 36 Samples from Rock Alignments at Anasazi Sites LA 380, LA 69807, Zuni 1, Z2:99, Tepako I, S2:71, Y2:31, UP 5-1, and El Rito Sites 1, 12, 18, 19, 20, 27, 29, 30, 31, 39, 40, 41, and 42, Zuni-Lower Rio Chama Area, McKinley and Rio Arriba Counties, New Mexico.* Archaeobotanical Technical Services Report No. 949. University of New Mexico, Albuquerque.
1995 In Search of the Rare: Pollen Evidence of Prehistoric Agriculture. In *Soil, Water, Biology, and Belief in Prehistoric and Traditional Southwestern Agriculture*, edited by H. Wolcott Toll, pp. 353–359. Special Publication No. 2. New Mexico Archaeological Council, Albuquerque.
1997a *Pollen Analysis of 10 Samples from Anasazi Agricultural Features at LA 101346 and LA 101348, Rio del Oso Project, Rio Arriba County, New Mexico.* Archaeobotanical Services Technical Series Report No. 971. University of New Mexico, Albuquerque.
1997b Pollen Studies. In *A Survey of Portions of the El Rito and Ojo Caliente Drainages, Rio Arriba County, New Mexico*, by Timothy D. Maxwell, pp. 51–58. Archaeological Notes 160. Museum of New Mexico, Office of Archaeological Studies, Santa Fe.
1997c Would History Be Different if We'd Known about Anasazi Cotton? *SPIN-OFF* Fall:61–62.
1998 Finding a Needle in a Palynological Haystack: A Comparison of Methods. In *New Developments in Palynomorph Sampling, Extraction, and Analysis*, edited by Vaughn M. Bryant, Jr., and John H. Wrenn, pp. 53–59. Contribution Series No. 33. American Association of Stratigraphic Palynologists, Houston.

De Long, J. Bradford, and Andrei Schleifer
1993 Princes and Merchants: European City Growth before the Industrial Revolution. *Journal of Law and Economics* 36(2):671–702.

Derry, Trevor
1961 *A Short History of Technology from the Earliest Times to A.D. 1900.* Oxford University Press, Oxford.

Diamond, Jared
2005 *Guns, Germs, and Steel: The Fates of Human Societies.* W.W. Norton, New York.

Dickson, D. Bruce, Jr.
1975 Settlement Pattern Stability and Change in the Middle Northern Rio Grande Region, New Mexico: A Test of Some Hypotheses. *American Antiquity* 40:159–171.
1979 *Prehistoric Pueblo Settlement Patterns: The Arroyo Hondo, New Mexico, Site Survey.* Arroyo

Dickson, D. Bruce, Jr. (continued)
Hondo Archaeological Series, Vol. 2. School of American Research, Santa Fe, and University of New Mexico Press, Albuquerque.

Dominguez, Steven R.
2000a *Assessing the Hydrologic Functions of Prehistoric Grid Gardens in North Central New Mexico.* Unpublished PhD dissertation, Department of Anthropology, University of New Mexico. Albuquerque. University Microfilms, Ann Arbor.
2000b Assessing the Hydrologic Functions of Pueblo Cobble Border and Gravel Mulch Agricultural Technologies at La Mesita. In *An Archaeological Study of Pre-Columbian Agricultural Features at LA 125767, Taos Resource Area, Albuquerque District, Bureau of Land Management and New Mexico State Lands in Rio Arriba County, New Mexico*, by Kurt F. Anschuetz, Steven R. Dominguez, and Eileen L. Camilli, pp 6.1–6.75. Prepared for US Department of Justice, Denver, and USDI, Bureau of Indian Affairs, Regional Water Rights, Albuquerque Area Office, Albuquerque. Ebert and Associates, Albuquerque.

Doolittle, William E.
2000 *Cultivated Landscapes of Native North America.* Oxford University Press, New York.

Dougherty, Julia D.
1980 *An Archaeological Evaluation of Tsiping Ruin (AR-03-10-01-01).* Santa Fe National Forest, Southwestern Region, USDA Forest Service.

Douglas, William B.
1912 *A World Quarter Shrine of the Tewa Indians.* Records of the Past, Vol 11, part 4. Records of the Past Exploration Society, Washington DC.
1917 *Notes on the Shrines of the Tewas and Other Pueblo Indians.* Proceedings of the Nineteenth International Congress of Americanists, December 1915, edited by Frederick W. Hodge, pp. 344–378. International Congress of Americanists, Washington, DC.

Dozier, Edward P.
1970 *The Pueblo Indians of North America.* Holt, Rinehart and Winston, New York.

Drennan, Robert D., C. Adam Berrey, and Christian E. Peterson
2015 *Regional Settlement Demography in Archaeology.* Eliot Werner Publications, Bristol, Connecticut.

Duff, Andrew I.
2002 *Western Pueblo Identities: Regional Interaction, Migration, and Transformation.* University of Arizona Press, Tucson.

Duff, Andrew I., and Richard H. Wilshusen
2000 Prehistoric Population Dynamics in the Northern San Juan Region, A.D. 950–1300. *Kiva* 66(1):167–190.

Dumond, Don E.
1965 Population Growth and Cultural Change. *Southwestern Journal of Anthropology*, 21(4): 302–324.

Dunbar, Nelia W.
2005 Quaternary Volcanism in New Mexico. In *New Mexico Museum of Natural History and Science Bulletin No. 28*, edited by S. G. Lucas and K. E. Ziegler, pp. 95–106. New Mexico Museum of Natural History and Science, Albuquerque.

Durkheim, Emile
1984 *The Division of Labor in Society.* Free Press, New York.

Duwe, Samuel
2008 How Accurate were H. P. Mera's Maps?: A Comparison with Micro-Topographic Spatial Data from the Northern Rio Grande Region, New Mexico. Paper presented at the 72nd Annual Meeting of the Society for American Archaeology, Vancouver, British Columbia.
2011 *The Prehispanic Tewa World: Space, Time and Becoming in the Pueblo Southwest.* Ph.D. Dissertation, Anthropology, University of Arizona, Tucson.
2013 Appendix 4: Site Descriptions of 10 Ancestral Ohkay Owingeh Sites in the Rio Chama Watershed. In *Population History, Agricultural Land Use and Cultural Continuity in the Ohkay Owingeh Homeland, Rio Chama Watershed*, edited by B. Sunday Eiselt and J. Andrew Darling. Prepared for Ohkay Owingeh Pueblo, *New Mexico v. Aragon*. Southwest Heritage Foundation.
2016 Cupules and the Creation of the Tewa Pueblo World. *Journal of Lithic Studies* 3(3):1–22.

Duwe, Samuel, and Kurt F. Anschuetz
2013 Ecological Uncertainty and Organizational Flexibility on the Prehispanic Tewa Landscape: Notes from the Northern Frontier. In *Mountain and Valley: Understanding Past Land Use in the Northern Rio Grande Valley, New Mexico*, edited by Bradley J. Vierra, pp. 95–112. University of Utah Press, Salt Lake City.

Duwe, Samuel, B. Sunday Eiselt, J. Andrew Darling, Mark D. Willis, and Chester Walker
2016 The Pueblo Decomposition Model: A Method for Quantifying Architectural Rubble to

Estimate Population Size. *Journal of Archaeological Science* 65: 20–31.

Dyer, Jennifer Boyd
2010 *Colono Wares in the Western Spanish Borderlands: A Ceramic Technological Study.* Unpublished PhD dissertation, Department of Anthropology, University of New Mexico, Albuquerque.

Dyson-Hudson, Rada, and Eric A. Smith
1978 Human Territoriality: An Ecological Reassessment. *American Anthropologist* 80(1):21–41.

Earle, Timothy
2002 *Bronze Age Economics.* Westview Press, New York.

Eckert, Suzanne L.
2006 The Production and Distribution of Glaze-Painted Pottery in the Pueblo Southwest: A Synthesis. In *The Social Life of Pots: Glaze Wares and Cultural Dynamics in the Southwest,* AD *1250–1680* edited by Judith A. Habicht-Mauche, Suzanne L. Eckert, and Deborah L. Huntley, pp. 34–59. University of Arizona Press, Tucson.
2007 Understanding the Dynamics of Segregation and Incorporation at Pottery Mound through Analysis of Glaze-Decorated Bowls. In *New Perspectives on Pottery Mound Pueblo,* edited by Polly Schaafsma, pp. 55–73. University of New Mexico Press, Albuquerque.

Eckert, Suzanne L., and Linda S. Cordell
2004 Pueblo IV Community Formation in the Central Rio Grande Valley. In *The Protohistoric Pueblo World,* A.D. *1275–1600,* edited by E. Charles Adams and Andrew I. Duff, pp. 35–42. University of Arizona Press, Tucson.

Eckert, Suzanne L., Kari L. Schleher, and William D. James
2015 Communities of Identity, Communities of Practice: Understanding Santa Fe Black-on-White Pottery in the Española Basin of New Mexico. *Journal of Archaeological Science* 63:1–12.

Eerkens, Jelmer W., and Robert L. Bettinger
2001 Techniques for Assessing Standardization in Artifact Assemblages: Can We Scale Material Variability? *American Antiquity* 66(3):493–504.

Eiselt, B. Sunday, and J. Andrew Darling
2013 *Population History, Agricultural Land Use and Cultural Continuity in the Ohkay Owingeh Homeland, Rio Chama Watershed.* Prepared for Ohkay Owingeh (San Juan) Pueblo for *New Mexico v.* Aragon et al. Report No. 2012-1. Southwest Heritage Research, Dallas.
2017 A Bird's-eye View of Proto-Tewa Subsistence Agriculture: Making the Case of Floodplain Farming in the Ohkay Owingeh Homeland, New Mexico. *American Antiquity* 82:397–413.

Eiselt, B. Sunday, J. Andrew Darling, Samuel Duwe, Mark Willis, Chester Walker, William Hudspeth, and Leslie Reeder-Myers
2017 A Bird's-Eye View of Proto-Tewa Subsistence Agriculture: Making the Case for Floodplain Farming in the Ohlay Owingeh Homeland, New Mexico. *American Antiquity* 82(2): 397–413.

Ellis, Florence Hawley
1951 Patterns of Aggression and the War Cult in Southwestern Pueblos. *Southwestern Journal of Anthropology* 7(2):177–201.
1968 San Juan Pueblo's Water Use. Ms. on file, New Mexico State Engineer Office, Santa Fe.
1987 The Long Lost "City" of San Gabriel del Yungue, Second Oldests European Settlement in the United States. In *When Cultures Meet: Remembering San Gabriel Del Yungue Oweengeh,* pp. 10–39. Sunstone Press, Santa Fe.

Eltis, Walter
2000 *The Classical Theory of Economic Growth.* Palgrave Macmillan, London.

Ember, Carol R., and Melvin Ember
1992 Resource Unpredictability, Mistrust, and War. *Journal of Conflict Resolution* 36:242–262.

Ember, Melvin
1963 The Relationship between Economic and Political Development in Nonindustrial Societies. *Ethnology* 2:228–248.

Emery, Irene
1953 Fabric Material from Te'ewi. In *Salvage Archaeology in the Chama Valley, New Mexico,* assembled by Fred Wendorf, pp. 101–102. Monograph No. 17. School of American Research, Santa Fe.

Evans, Chaz
2013 Put This In Your Pipe and Smoke It: Just Because It's Red Doesn't Mean It's Catlinite. In *From the Pueblos to the Southern Plains: Papers in Honor of Regge N. Wiseman* (Vol. 40), edited by Emily J. Brown, Carol J. Condie, and Heather K. Cotty, pp. 85–96. Paper No. 39. Archaeological Society of New Mexico, Albuquerque.

Fallon, Denise
1987 Archaeological History of the Northern Rio Grande. In *Howiri: Excavation at a Northern Rio Grande Biscuit Ware Site,* edited by Denise Fallon and Karen Welling, pp. 9–12. Note No. 261B. Laboratory of Anthropology, Santa Fe.

Feinman, Gary
2011 Size, Complexity and Organizational Variation: A Comparative Approach. *Cross-Cultural Research* 45(1):37–59.

Finley, Moses I.
1973 *The Ancient Economy*. University of California Press, Berkeley.

Fisher, Christopher T., J. Brett Hill, and Gary M. Feinman (editors)
2009 *The Archaeology of Environmental Change*. University of Arizona Press, Tucson.

Fiske, Alan P.
1992 The Four Elementary Forms of Sociality: Framework for a Unified Theory of Social Relations. *Psychological Review* 99:689–723.

Flannery, Kent V., and Joyce Marcus
2012 *The Creation of Inequality: How Our Prehistoric Ancestors Set the Stage for Monarchy, Slavery, and Empire*. Harvard University Press, Cambridge, Massachusetts.

Fletcher, Milford, and Maynard Merkt
2006 Frequency of Occurrence of Classified Petroglyphs at Two New Mexico Sites. *American Indian Rock Art* 32:31–44.

Ford, Richard I.
1972a Barter, Gift, or Violence: An Analysis of Tewa Intertribal Exchange. In *Social Exchange and Interaction*, edited by Edwin Wilmsen, pp. 21–45. Anthropological Papers No. 46. Museum of Anthropology, University of Michigan, Ann Arbor.
1972b An Ecological Perspective on the Eastern Pueblos. In *New Perspectives on the Pueblos*, edited by Alfonso Ortiz, pp. 1–17. School of American Research, Santa Fe
1980 The Color of Survival. *Discovery* 1980:17–29. School of American Research, Weatherhead Foundation, Santa Fe.
1992 *An Ecological Analysis Involving the Population of San Juan Pueblo, New Mexico*. Garland Publishing, New York.

Ford, Richard I., and Roxanne Swentzell
2015 Pre-Contact Agriculture in Northern New Mexico. In *Traditional Arid Land Agriculture: Understanding the Past for the Future* edited by Scott E. Ingram and Robert C. Hunt, pp. 330–357. University of Arizona Press, Tucson.

Ford, Richard I., Albert H. Schroeder, and Stewart L. Peckham
1972 Three Perspectives on Puebloan Prehistory. In *New Perspectives on the Pueblos*, edited by Alfonso Ortiz, pp. 19–39. University of New Mexico Press, Albuquerque.

Fouquet, Roger, and Stephen Broadberry
2015 Seven Centuries of European Economic Growth and Decline. *Journal of Economic Perspectives* 29(4):227–244.

Fowles, Severin M.
2004 Tewa versus Tiwa: Northern Rio Grande Settlement Patterns and Social History, A.D. 1275 to 1540. In *The Protohistoric Pueblo World, A.D. 1275–1600*, edited by E. Charles Adams and Andrew I. Duff, pp. 17–25. University of Arizona Press, Tucson.

Fowles, Severin M., Leah Minc, Samuel Duwe, and David V. Hill
2007 Clay, Conflict, and Village Aggregation: Compositional Analyses of Pre-Classic Pottery from Taos, New Mexico. *American Antiquity* 72(1):125–152.

Francis, Julie E.
2001 Style and Classification. In *Handbook of Rock Art Research*, edited by D. S. Whitley, pp. 221–244. Altamira Press, New York.

Franklin, Hayward
2009 Montaño Bridge (LA 33223) Ceramic Analysis. In *Report on 1988 Data Recovery at the Montaño Site Complex (LA 33223) and Subsequent Analysis of Collections*, edited by Gerry Raymond. Criterion report submitted to the City of Albuquerque.

Gallegos, Lumero Hernan
1927 *The Gallegos Relation of the Rodriguez Expedition to New Mexico*. Translated and edited by George P. Hammond and Agapito Rey. El Palacio Press, Santa Fe.

Galor, Oded
2005 From Stagnation to Growth: Unified Growth Theory. In *Handbook of Economic Growth*, Vol. 1A, edited by Philippe Aghion and Steven N. Durlauf, pp. 171–293. Elsevier B.V., New York.

Garraty, Christopher P., and Barbara L. Stark (editors)
2010 *Archaeological Approaches to Market Exchange in Ancient Societies*. University Press of Colorado, Boulder.

Gauthier, Rory
1987 Ceramics. In *Howiri: Excavation at a Northern Rio Grande Biscuit Ware Site*, edited by Denise Fallon and Karen Wening, pp. 35–58. Laboratory of Anthropology, Santa Fe.

Gell-Mann, Murray
2011 Regularities in Human Affairs. *Cliodynamics* 2(1):52–70.

Gerow, Peggy, and Alexander Kurota
2004 *Across the Caja del Rio Plateau II: Hunters and Farmers in the Norther Rio Grande.* Office of Contract Archaeology, University of New Mexico, Santa Fe.

Gish, Jannifer, and Jeanne L. DeLanois
1993 Special Studies, Large Fraction Pollen Scanning and Its Application in Archaeology. In *Subsistence and Environment*, edited by Joseph C. Winter, pp. 211–223. *Across the Colorado Plateau: Anthropological Studies for the Transwestern Pipeline Expansion Project,* Vol. 15 (part1–3, book 1 of 2). Office of Contract Archaeology and Maxwell Museum of Anthropology, University of New Mexico, Albuquerque.

Glaeser, Edward L.
2011 *Triumph of the City: How Our Greatest Invention Makes Us Richer, Smarter, Greener, Healthier, and Happier*. Penguin Press, New York.

Glaeser, Edward L., and Joshua D. Gottlieb
2009 The Wealth of Cities: Agglomeration Economics and Spatial Equilibrium in the United States. *Journal of Economic Literature* 47(4):983–1028.

Glaeser, Edward L., Jose A. Scheinkman, and Andrei Shleifer
1995 Economic Growth in a Cross-Section of Cities. *Journal of Monetary Economics* 36(1):117–143.

Glascock, Michael D.
1992 Characterization of Archaeological Ceramics at MURR by Neutron Activation Analysis and Multivariate Statistics. In *Chemical Characterization of Ceramic Pastes in Archaeology*, edited by Hector Neff, pp. 11–26. Prehistory Press, Madison.

Glassow, Michael A.
1980 *Prehistoric Agricultural Development in the Northern Southwest*. Anthropological Papers No. 16. Ballena Press, Socorro, New Mexico.

Glowacki, Donna M., and Scott G. Ortman
2012 Characterizing Community-Center (Village) Formation in the VEP Study Area. In *Emergence and Collapse of Early Villages: Models of Central Mesa Verde Archaeology*, edited by Timothy A. Kohler and Mark D. Varien, pp. 219–246. University of California Press, Berkeley.

Goldsmith, Raymond W.
1984 An Estimate of the Size and Structure of the National Product of the Early Roman Empire. *The Review of Income and Wealth* 30:263–288.

Goldstone, Jack A.
2002 Efflorescences and Economic Growth in World History: Rethinking the "Rise of the West" and the Industrial Revolution. *Journal of World History* 13(2):323–389.

Graham, Willie, Carter L. Hudgins, Carl R. Lounsbury, Fraser D. Neiman, and James P. Whittenburg
2007 Adaptation and Innovation: Archaeological and Architectural Perspectives on the Seventeenth-Century Chesapeake. *The William and Mary Quarterly*, third series, 64(3):451–522.

Graves, William M., and Suzanne L. Eckert
1998 Decorated Ceramic Distributions and Ideological Developments in the Northern and Central Rio Grande Valley, New Mexico. In *Migration and Reorganization: The Pueblo IV Period in the American Southwest*, edited by Katherine A. Spielmann, pp. 263–283. Anthropological Research Papers No. 51. Arizona State University, Tempe.

Graves, William M., and Katherine A. Spielmann
2000 Leadership, Long-Distance Exchange, and Feasting in the Protohistoric Rio Grande. In *Alternative Leadership Strategies in the Prehispanic Southwest*, edited by Barbara J. Mills, pp. 45–59. University of Arizona Press, Tucson.

Greene, Kevin
2000 Technological Innovation and Economic Progress in the Ancient World: M. I. Finley Re-considered. *The Economic History Review* 53(1):29–59.

Habicht-Mauche, Judith A.
1988 *An Analysis of Southwestern-Style Utility Ware Ceramics from the Southern Plains in the Context of Protohistoric Plains-Pueblo Interaction.* Ph.D. dissertation, Department of Anthropology, Harvard University, Cambridge, Massachusetts

1993 *The Pottery from Arroyo Hondo Pueblo, New Mexico: Tribalization and Trade in the Northern Rio Grande.* Arroyo Hondo Archaeological Series No. 8. School of American Research Press, Santa Fe.

1995 Changing Patterns of Pottery Manufacture and Trade in the Northern Rio Grande Region. In *Ceramic Production in the American Southwest*, edited by Barbara J. Mills and Patricia L. Crown, pp. 167–199. University of Arizona Press, Tucson.

2002 Torturing Sherds: Ceramic Petrography and the Development of Rio Grande Archaeology. In *Traditions, Transitions, and Technologies: Themes in Southwestern Archaeology*, edited by

Habicht-Mauche, Judith A. (continued)
Sarah H. Schlanger, pp. 49–58. University Press of Colorado, Boulder.
2008 Captive Wives? The Role and Status of Nonlocal Women on the Protohistoric Southern High Plains. In *Invisible Citizens: Captives and Their Consequences*, edited by Catherine M. Cameron, pp. 181–204. University of Utah Press, Salt Lake City.

Habicht-Mauche, Judith A., Suzanne L. Eckert, and Deborah L. Huntley (editors)
2006 *The Social Life of Pots: Glaze Wares and Cultural Dynamics in the Southwest, AD 1250–1680*. University of Arizona Press, Tucson.

Hagstrum, Melissa B.
1985 Measuring Prehistoric Ceramic Craft Specialization: A Test Case in the American Southwest. *Journal of Field Archaeology* 12(1):65–75.

Hall, Lauren Reynolds.
2007 *Characterization, Analysis and Interpretation of the Surface Finishes of Kiva E, Long House, Mesa Verde National Park*. Unpublished Master's thesis, University of Pennsylvania, Philadelphia.

Hall, Robert L.
1997 *An Archaeology of the Soul: North American Indian Belief and Ritual*. University of Illinois Press, Champaign.

Hamalainen, Pekka
2008 *The Comanche Empire*. Yale University Press, New Haven.

Hammond, George P., and Agapito Rey
1953 *Don Juan de Oñate: Colonizer of New Mexico, 1595–1628*. University of New Mexico Press, Albuquerque.
1966 *The Rediscovery of New Mexico, 1580–1594: The Expeditions of Chamuscado, Espejo, Castaño de Sosa, Morlete, and Leyva de Bonilla and Humaña*. University of New Mexico Press, Albuquerque.

Hanson, John W.
2016 *An Urban Geography of the Roman World, 100 B.C. to A.D. 300*. Archaeopress, Oxford.

Hanson, John W., and Scott G. Ortman
2017 A Systematic Method for Estimating the Populations of Greek and Roman Settlements. *Journal of Roman Archaeology* 30:301–324.

Hanson, John W., Scott G. Ortman, and Jose Lobo
2017 Urbanisation and the Division of Labour in the Roman Empire. *Journal of the Royal Society Interface* 14(136):1–12.

Hanson, John W., Scott G. Ortman, Luis M. A. Bettencourt, and Liam C. Mazur
2019 Urban Form, Infrastructure, and Spatial Organization in the Roman Empire. *Antiquity*, in press.

Harlow, Francis H.
1965 Recent Finds of Pajaritan Pottery. *El Palacio* 72(2):27–33.
1973 *Matte-Paint Pottery of the Tewa, Keres, and Zuni Pueblos*. School of American Research Press, Santa Fe.

Harper, Kyle
2017 *The Fate of Rome: Climate, Disease, and the End of an Empire*. Princeton University Press, Princeton.

Harrington, John P.
1916 *The Ethnogeography of the Tewa Indians*. Twenty-ninth Annual Report of the Bureau of American Ethnology, pp 29–636. US Government Printing Office, Washington, DC.

Harrison, Billy R.
1984 Prehistoric Trade Pipes in the Texas Panhandle. Ms. on file at the Panhandle-Plains Historical Society, Canyon, Texas.

Harro, Douglas R.
1997 *Patterns of Lithic Raw Material Procurement on the Pajarito Plateau, New Mexico*. Unpublished Master's thesis, Department of Anthropology, Washington State University, Pullman.

Hartnett, Alexandra
2004 The Politics of the Pipe: Clay Pipes and Tobacco Consumption in Galway, Ireland. *International Journal of Historical Archaeology* 8(2):133–147.

Hasbargen, Jim
1997 *Identification of Prehistoric Fields through Palynological Evidence*. Unpublished Master's thesis, Department of Anthropology, Northern Arizona University, Flagstaff.

Hayes, Alden C., Jon Nathan Young, and A.H. Warren
1981 *Excavation of Mound 7, Grand Quivira National Monument, New Mexico*. Publications in Archaeology No. 16. National Park Service, US Department of the Interior, Washington, DC.

Head, Genevieve, and Janet D. Orcutt
2002 *From Folsom to Fogelson: The Cultural Resources Inventory Survey of Pecos National Historical Park*. Intermountain Cultural Resources Management Professional Paper No. 66. USDI, National Park Service, Washington, DC.

Henderson, Donald C., and Earl F. Sorensen
1968 *Consumptive Irrigation Requirements of Selected Irrigated Areas in New Mexico*. Agricultural Experiment Station Bulletin No. 531. New Mexico State University, Las Cruces.

Henderson, J. Vernon
2003 Urbanization and Economic Development. *Annals of Economics and Finance* 4:275–341.
2013 *Urban Development: Theory, Fact and Illusion.* Oxford University Press, Oxford.

Henrich, Joseph
2004 Demography and Cultural Evolution: How Adaptive Cultural Processes can Produce Maladaptive Losses: The Tasmanian Case. *American Antiquity* 69(2):197–214.
2015 *The Secret of Our Success: How Culture Is Driving Human Evolution, Domesticating Our Species, and Making Us Smarter.* Princeton University Press, Princeton

Herhahn, Cynthia L.
1995 *An Exploration of Technology Transfer in the Fourteenth-Century Rio Grande Valley, New Mexico: A Compositional Analysis of Glaze Paints.* Unpublished Master's thesis, Department of Anthropology, Arizona State University, Tempe.
2006 Inferring Social Interactions from Pottery Recipes, Rio Grande Glaze Paint Composition and Cultural Transmission. In *The Social Life of Pots: Glaze Wares and Cultural Dynamics in the Southwest A.D. 1250–1680*, edited by Judith A. Habicht-Mauche, Suzanne L. Eckert, and Deborah L. Huntley, pp. 177–196. University of Arizona Press, Tucson.

Herhahn, Cynthia L., and J. Brett Hill
1998 Modeling Agricultural Production Strategies in the Northern Rio Grande Valley, New Mexico. *Human Ecology* 26:469–487.

Herhahn, Cynthia L., and Deborah L. Huntley
2017 Dynamic Knowledgescapes: Rio Grande and Salinas Glaze Ware Production and Exchange. In *Landscapes of Social Transformation in the Salinas Province and the Eastern Pueblo World*, edited by Katherine A. Spielmann, pp. 203–238. University of Arizona Press, Tucson.

Hewett, Edgar L.
1906 *Antiquities of the Jemez Plateau, New Mexico.* Bureau of American Ethnology Bulletin No. 32. Smithsonian Institution, Washington, DC.
1953 *Pajarito Plateau and Its Ancient People*, second edition. University of New Mexico Press, Albuquerque. Originally published 1938 by University of New Mexico Press and School of American Research, Albuquerque and Santa Fe.

Hill, J. Brett
1998a Agricultural Production and Specialization among the Eastern Anasazi during the Pueblo IV Period. In *Migration and Reorganization: The Pueblo IV Period in the American Southwest*, edited by Katherine A. Spielman, pp 209–232. Anthropological Research Papers No. 51. Arizona State University, Tempe.
1998b Ecological Variability and Agricultural Specialization among the Protohistoric Pueblos of Central New Mexico. *Journal of Field Archaeology* 25(3):275–294.

Hill, James N.
1970 *Broken K Pueblo: Prehistoric Social Organization in the American Southwest.* Anthropological Papers No. 18. University of Arizona Press, Tucson.

Hill, James N., and W. Nicholas Trierweiler
1986 Prehistoric Responses to Food Stress on the Pajarito Plateau, New Mexico: Technical Report and Results of the Pajarito Archaeological Research Project, 1977–1985. Final Report to the National Science Foundation. Ms. on file, Department of Anthropology, University of California, Los Angeles.

Hill, James N., William N. Trierweiler, and Robert W. Preucel
1996 The Evolution of Cultural Complexity: A Case from the Pajarito Plateau, New Mexico. In *Emergent Complexity: The Evolution of Intermediate Societies*, edited by Jeanne E. Arnold, pp. 107–127. International Monographs in Prehistory, Madison, Wisconsin.

Hirth, Kenneth
2016 *The Aztec Economic World: Merchants and Markets in Ancient Mesoamerica.* Cambridge University Press, Cambridge.

Hodder, Ian
2012 *Entangled: An Archaeology of the Relationships between Humans and Things.* Wiley-Blackwell, Chichester.

Hodges, Henry
1970 *Technology in the Ancient World.* Random House, New York.

Holloway, Richard G.
1995 *Intensive Systematic Microscopy of Suspected Agricultural Fields from Sites LA 83116, LA 83117,*

Holloway, Richard G. (continued)
and LA 83151, Ojo Caliente Valley, Rio Arriba County, New Mexico. Castetter Laboratory for Ethnobotanical Studies Technical Report No. 410. University of New Mexico, Albuquerque.

2009 Appendix 1. Pollen Analysis of a Sedimentary Column from LA 105710 and Intensive Scan Microscopy Analysis of Five Agricultural Sites. In *Living on the Northern Rio Grande Frontier: Eleven Classic Period Pueblo Sites and an Early Twentieth-Century Spanish Site near Gavilan, New Mexico*, vol. 2, by James L. Moore. Archaeological Notes 315. Office of Archaeological Studies, Museum of New Mexico, Santa Fe.

Huckell, Lisa W.
1993 Plant Remains from the Pinaleño Cotton Cache, Arizona. *Kiva* 59:147–203.

Hudspeth, William
2000 *The Evolutionary Ecology of Behavioral Response to Risk Among Prehistoric Agriculturalists of the Lower Rio Chama, New Mexico*. Unpublished Ph.D. dissertation, Department of Anthropology, University of New Mexico, Albuquerque.

2013 *Agricultural Constraints, Opportunities, and Strategies in the Ohkay Owingeh Homeland*. Prepared for Ohkay Owingeh Pueblo, *New Mexico ex rel. State Engineer v. Aragon*. Rio Abajo Digital Mapping Services, Albuquerque.

Hull, Sharon, Mostafa Fayek, Joan Mathien, and Heidi Roberts
2014 Turquoise Trade of the Ancestral Puebloan: Chaco and Beyond. *Journal of Archaeological Science*, 45: 187–195.

Hulten, Charles R.
2009 *Growth Accounting*. Working Paper No. 15341. National Bureau of Economic Research, Cambridge, Massachusetts.

Hunter, Andrea
2005 *Northern Sinagua Plant Use at Bench Pueblo*. Report submitted to Department of Anthropology, Grinnell College, Grinnell, Iowa. Available from author, Department of Anthropology, Northern Arizona University, Flagstaff.

Huntley, Deborah L., Thomas Fenn, Judith A. Habitch-Mauche, and Barbra J. Mills
2012 Pigments and Long-Distance Procurement Strategies in the Late Prehispanic Southwest. In *Potters and Communities of Practice: Glaze Paint and Polychrome Pottery in the American Southwest, AD 1250–1700*, edited by Linda S. Cordell and Judith A. Habicht-Mauche, pp. 8–18. University of Arizona Press, Tucson.

Huntley, Deborah L., Katherine A. Spielmann, Judith A. Habicht-Mauche, Cynthia L. Herhahn, and A. Russell Flegal
2007 Local Recipes or Distant commodities? Lead Isotope and Chemical Compositional Analysis of Glaze Paints from the Salinas Pueblos, New Mexico. *Journal of Archaeological Science* 34:1135–1147.

Hurwicz, Leonid
1973 The Design of Mechanisms for Resource Allocation. *American Economic Review* 63 (2): 1–30.

Huster, Angela C.
2018 Regional-level Exchange in Postclassic Central Mexico. *Journal of Anthropological Archaeology* 50:40–53.

James, Steven R.
1997 Change and Continuity in Western Pueblo Households during the Historic Period in the American Southwest. *World Archaeology* 28(3):429–456.

Janusek, John W.
2002 Out of Many, One: Style and Social Boundaries in Tiwanaku. *Latin American Antiquity* 13(1):35–61.

Jeançon, Jean A.
1912 Ruins at Pesedeuinge. *Records of the Past* 11:28–37.

1923 *Excavations in the Chama Valley, New Mexico*. Bulletin No. 81. Bureau of American Ethnology, Washington, DC.

Johnson, Allen W., and Timothy K. Earle
2000 *The Evolution of Human Societies: From Foraging Group to Agrarian State*, second edition. Stanford University Press, Palo Alto.

Johnson, Gregory A.
1982 Organizational Structure and Scalar Stress. In *Theory and Explanation in Archaeology: The Southampton Conference*, edited by Colin Renfrew, Michael J. Rowlands and Barbara Abbot Segraves, pp. 389–421. Academic Press, New York.

Jolie, Ruth Burgett
2014 Exploring Textile Traditions, Gender Shifts, and Social Capital in the American Southwest. *North American Archaeologist* 35(4):375–403.

Jones, Charles I.
2013 *Introduction to Economic Growth*. W. W. Norton, London.

Jones, Charles I., and Paul M. Romer
2010 The New Kaldor Facts: Ideas, Institutions, Population, and Human Capital. *American Economic Journal: Macroeconomics* 2(1):224–245.

Jones, Charles I., and Dietrich Vollrath
2013 *Introduction to Economic Growth*. W.W. Norton, New York.

Jones, Deborah L.
1995 *Identifying Production Groups within a Single Community: Rio Grande Glaze-Decorated Ceramics at Quarai Pueblo*. Unpublished Master's thesis, Department of Anthropology, Arizona State University, Tempe.

Jones, Emily Lena
2016 Changing Landscapes of Early Colonial New Mexico: Demography, Rebound, and Zooarchaeology. In *Exploring Cause and Explanation: Historical Ecology, Demography, and Movement in the American Southwest,* edited by Cynthia L. Herhahn and Ann F. Ramenofsky, pp. 73–92. University of Utah Press, Salt Lake City.

Jones, Eric L.
1988 *Growth Recurring: Economic Change in World History*. Clarendon Press, Oxford.

Jones, Volney H.
1936 A Summary of Data on Aboriginal Cotton of the Southwest. In *Symposium on Prehistoric Agriculture*. University of New Mexico Bulletin, Anthropology Series 1(5):51–64. University of New Mexico, Albuquerque.

Jongman, Willem M.
2014a The New Economic History of the Roman Empire. In *Quantifying the Greco-Roman Economy and Beyond*, edited by Francois Callatay, pp. 169–188. Edipuglia, Bari.
2014b Re-constructing the Roman economy. In *Cambridge History of Capitalism,* Vol. 1, From Ancient Origins to 1848, edited by Larry Neal and Jeffrey G. Williamson, pp. 75–100. Cambridge University Press, Cambridge.
2014c Why Modern Economic Theory Applies, Even to the Distant Roman Past. In *Proceedings of the 23rd Annual Theoretical Roman Archaeology Conference*, edited by Hannah Platts, John Barron, Caroline Lundock and Justin Yoo, pp. 27–36. Oxbow Books, Oxford.

Joyce, Rosemary A.
2012 Thinking about Pottery Production as Community Practice. In *Potters and Communities of Practice: Glaze Paint and Polychrome Pottery in the American Southwest,* AD *1250–1700,* edited by Linda S. Cordell and Judith A. Habicht-Mauche, pp. 149–154. University of Arizona Press, Tucson.

Kander, Astrud, Paolo Malanima, and Paul Warde
2014 *Power to the People: Energy in Europe Over the Last Five Centuries*. Princeton University Press, Princeton.

Kelly, Morgan
1997 The Dynamics of Smithian Growth. *The Quarterly Journal of Economics* 112:939–964.

Kelly, Robert L.
2013 *The Lifeways of Hunter-Gatherers: The Foraging Spectrum*. Cambridge University Press, Cambridge, United Kingdom.

Kent, Kate Peck
1983 *Prehistoric Textiles of the Southwest*. University of New Mexico Press, Albuquerque.

Keyser, James D.
2001 Relative Dating Methods. In *Handbook of Rock Art Research*, edited by D.S. Whitley, pp. 116–138. Altamira Press, New York.

Kidder, Alfred Vincent
1915 *Pottery of the Pajarito Plateau and Some Adjacent Regions in New Mexico*. Memoirs of the American Anthropological Association, Vol. 2(6). Lancaster, Pennsylvania.
1936 *The Pottery of Pecos*, Vol. 2, part I. The Glaze-Paint, Culinary, and Other Wares. Yale University Press, New Haven.
1958 *Pecos, New Mexico: Archaeological Notes.* Papers of the Robert S. Peabody Foundation, Phillips Academy, Andover, Massachusetts.
1979 *The Artifacts of Pecos*. Garland, New York. Originally published 1932 as Papers of the Southwestern Expedition No. 6, Yale University Press, New Haven.

Kidder, Alfred V., and Charles A. Amsden
1931 *Pottery of Pecos,* Vol. 1. Yale University Press, New Haven.

Kintigh, Keith
1985 *Settlement, Subsistence, and Society in Late Zuni Prehistory*. Anthropological Papers No. 44. University of Arizona Press, Tucson.

Kintigh, Keith W., Jeffrey H. Altshul, Mary C. Beaudry, Robert D. Drennan, Ann P. Kinzig, Timothy A. Kohler, W. Frederick Limp, Herbert D. G. Maschner, William K. Michener, Timothy R. Pauketat, Peter N. Peregrine, Jeremy A. Sabloff, Tony J. Wilkinson, Henry T. Wright, and Melinda A. Zeder
2014 Grand Challenges for Archaeology. *American Antiquity* 79(1):5–24.

Kline, Michelle A., and Robert Boyd
2010 Population Size Predicts Technological Complexity in Oceania. *Proceedings of the Royal Society B*, 277: 2559–2564.

Kohler, Timothy A.
1990 *Bandelier Archaeological Excavation Project: Summer 1989 Excavations at Burnt Mesa Pueblo*. Report of Investigations No. 62. Department of Anthropology, Washington State University, Pullman.

Kohler, Timothy A. (editor)
2004 *Archaeology of Bandelier National Monument: Village Formation on the Pajarito Plateau, New Mexico*. University of New Mexico Press, Albuquerque.

Kohler, Timothy A., Sarah A. Herr, and Matthew J. Root
2004 The Rise and Fall of Towns on the Pajarito (A.D. 1375–1600). In *Archaeology of Bandelier National Monument: Village Formation on the Pajarito Plateau, New Mexico*, edited by Timothy A. Kohler, pp. 215–264. University of New Mexico Press, Albuquerque.

Kohler, Timothy A., Robert P. Powers, and Janet D. Orcutt
2004 Bandelier from Hamlets to Towns. In *Archaeology of Bandelier National Monument: Village Formation on the Pajarito Plateau*, edited by Timothy A. Kohler, pp. 293–304. University of New Mexico Press, Albuquerque.

Kohler, Timothy A., R. Kyle Bocinsky, Denton Cockburn, Stefani A. Crabtree, Mark D. Varien, Kenneth E. Kolm, Schaun Smith, Scott G. Ortman, and Ziad Kobti
2012 Modeling Prehispanic Pueblo Societies in Their Ecosystems. *Ecological Modeling* http://dx.doi.org/10.1016/j.ecolmodel.2012.01.002.

Kohler, Timothy A., Scott G. Ortman, Katie E. Grundtisch, Carly Fitzpatrick, and Sarah M. Cole
2014 The Better Angels of Their Nature: Declining Violence through Time among Prehispanic Farmers of the Pueblo Southwest. *American Antiquity* 79(3):444–464.

Kohler, Timothy A., Michael E. Smith, Amy Bogaard, Gary M. Feinman, Christian E. Peterson, Alleen Betzenhauser, Matthew Pailes, Elizabeth C. Stone, Anna Marie Prentiss, Timothy J. Dennehy, Laura J. Ellyson, Linda M. Nicholas, Ronald K. Faulseit, Amy Styring, Jade Whitlam, Mattia Fochesato, Thomas A. Foor, and Samuel Bowles
2017 Greater Post-Neolithic Wealth Disparities in Eurasia than in North America and Mesoamerica. *Nature* (doi:10.1038/nature24646).

Kohler, Timothy A., and Mark D. Varien (editors)
2012 *Emergence and Collapse of Early Villages: Models of Central Mesa Verde Archaeology*. University of California Press, Berkeley.

Koning, Daniel J., Gary A. Smith, and Scott Aby
2008 *Geologic Map of the El Rito Quadrangle, Rio Arriba County, New Mexico*. Open-file Map Series OF-GM 166. New Mexico Bureau of Geology and Mineral Resources, Socorro.

Kraemer, Paul M.
1976 New Mexico's Ancient Salt Trade. *El Palacio* 82(1):22–30.

Kremer, Michael
1993 Population Growth and Technological Change, One Million B.C. to 1990, *The Quarterly Journal of Economics* 108(3):681–716.

Kuckelman, Kristin A.
2006 Ancient Violence in the Mesa Verde Region. In *The Mesa Verde World: Explorations in Ancestral Pueblo Archaeology*, edited by D. Grant Noble, pp. 126–135. School of American Research Press, Santa Fe.
2008 An Agent-Centered Case Study of the Depopulation of Sand Canyon Pueblo. In *The Social Construction of Communities: Agency, Structure, and Identity in the Prehispanic Southwest*, edited by Mark D. Varien and James M. Potter, pp. 109–124. Altamira Press, New York.
2015 Cycles of Subsistence Stress, Warfare, and Population Movement in the Northern San Juan. In *The Archaeology of Food and Warfare*, edited by A. M. Vanderwarker and G. D. Wilson, pp. 107–132. Springer International, Switzerland.

Kuckelman, Kristin A. (editor)
2000 *The Archaeology of Castle Rock Pueblo: A Thirteenth-Century Village in Southwestern Colorado*. Available: http://www.crowcanyon.org/castlerock. Date of use: April 29, 2015.

Kulisheck, Jeremy
2005 *The Archaeology of Pueblo Population Change on the Jemez Plateau, A.D. 1200 to 1700: The Effects of Spanish Contact and Conquest*. Unpublished Ph.D. dissertation, Department of Anthropology, Southern Methodist University, Dallas.

Kurath, Gertrude P., and Antonio Garcia
1970 *Music and Dance of the Tewa Pueblos*. Research Records No. 8. Museum of New Mexico, Santa Fe.

Kvamme, Kenneth L., Miriam T. Stark, and William A. Longacre

1996 Alternative Procedures for Assessing Standardization in Ceramic Assemblages. *American Antiquity* 61(1):116–126.

Landels, John G.

1978 *Engineering in the Ancient World*. University of California Press, Berkeley.

Lange, Charles H., Jr.

1959 *Cochiti: A New Mexico Pueblo, Past and Present*. University of New Mexico, Albuquerque.

Larson, Dorothy, Kari L. Schleher, Ann F. Ramenofsky, Jonathan Van Hoose, and Jennifer Boyd Dyer

2017 Artifacts at San Marcos Pueblo. In *The Archaeology and History of Pueblo San Marcos: Change and Stability*, edited by Ann F. Ramenofsky and Kari L. Schleher, pg. 89–105. University of New Mexico Press, Albuquerque.

Laski, Vera

1959 *Seeking Life*. American Folklore Society, Philadelphia.

Lawrence, Robert

2005 *Sapawe Area Passport in Time Project. Preliminary Report of 2005 and 2006 Field Seasons*. Heritage Report No. 2005-02-011-B. NMCRIS Activity No. 104227. USDA, US Forest Service, Carson National Forest, El Rito Ranger District, Taos.

2009 *Sapawe Area Passport in Time: 2009*. Heritage Report No. 200S-02-011-E NMCRIS Activity No.108910. USDA, US Forest Service, Carson National Forest, El Rito Ranger District, Taos.

LeBlanc, Steven A.

1999 *Prehistoric Warfare in the American Southwest*. University of Utah Press, Salt Lake City.

Lee, Ronald Demos

1988 Induced Population Growth and Induced Technological Progress: Their Interaction in the Accelerating Stage. *Mathematical Population Studies* 1(3):265–288.

Lekson, Stephen H.

1984 *Great Pueblo Architecture of Chaco Canyon*. National Park Service, Washington, D.C.

2002 War in the Southwest, War in the World. *American Antiquity* 67(4):607–624.

Lepenies, Philipp

2016 *The Power of a Single Number: A Political History of GDP*. Columbia University Press, New York.

Lewton, Frederick L.

1912 *The Cotton of the Hopi Indians: A New Species of* Gossypium. Miscellaneous Collections 60(6):1–10. Smithsonian Institution, Washington, DC.

Liebmann, Matthew J., Joshua Farella, Christopher I. Roos, Adam Stack, Sarah Martini, and Thomas W. Swetnam

2016 Native American Depopulation, Reforestation, and Fire Regimes in the Southwest U.S., 1492–1900 C.E. *Proceedings of the National Academy of Sciences* 113(6):E696–E704.

Lightfoot, Dale R.

1990 *The Prehistoric Pebble-Mulched Fields of the Galisteo Anasazi: Agricultural Innovation and Adaptation to Environment*. Ph.D. dissertation, Department of Geography, University of Colorado, Boulder. University Microfilms, Ann Arbor.

1993 The Landscape Context of Anasazi Pebble-Mulched Fields in the Galisteo Basin, Northern New Mexico. *Geoarchaeology* 8:349–370.

1996 The Nature, History, and Distribution of Lithic Mulch Agriculture: An Ancient Technique of Dryland Agriculture. *The Agricultural History Review* 44(2): 206–222.

Lightfoot, Dale R., and Frank W. Eddy

1994 The Agricultural Utility of Lithic-Mulched Gardens: Past and Present. *GeoJournal* 34:425–437.

Lightfoot, Kent G.

1979 Food Redistribution among Prehistoric Pueblo Groups. *Kiva* 44(4):319–339.

Lightfoot, Ricky R.

1993 Abandonment Processes in Prehistoric Pueblos. In *Abandonment of Settlements and Regions: Ethnoarchaeological and Archaeological Approaches*, edited by Catherine M. Cameron and Steve A. Tomka, pp. 165–177. Cambridge University Press, Cambridge, United Kingdom.

Lightfoot, Ricky R., and Kristin A. Kuckelman

2001 A Case of Warfare in the Mesa Verde Region. In *Deadly Landscapes: Case Studies in Prehistoric Southwestern Warfare*, edited by Glen E. Rice and Steven A. LeBlanc, pp. 51–64. University of Utah Press, Salt Lake City.

Lindauer, Owen

1988 *A Study of Vessel Form and Painted Designs to Explore Regional Interaction of the Sedentary Period Hohokam*. Ph.D. dissertation, Department of Anthropology, Arizona State University, Tempe. Proquest Dissertations and Theses.

Lintz, Christopher
1991 Texas Panhandle-Pueblo Interactions from the Thirteenth Through the Sixteenth Century. In *Farmers, Hunters, and Colonists: Interaction between the Southwest and the Southern Plains*, edited by Katherine A. Spielmann, pp. 89–106. University of Arizona Press, Tucson.

Lipe, William D.
2010 Lost in Transit: The Central Mesa Verde Archaeological Complex. In *Leaving Mesa Verde: Peril and Change in the Thirteenth-Century Southwest*, edited by Timothy Kohler, Mark Varien, and Aaron Wright, pp. 262–284. University of Arizona Press, Tucson.

Lipe, William, and Michele Hegmon.
1989 *The Architecture of Social Integration at Prehistoric Pueblos*. Occasional Papers of the Crow Canyon Archaeological Center No. 1. University of Arizona Press, Tucson.

Lo Cascio, Elio, and Paolo Malanima
2009 GDP in Pre-Modern Agrarian Economies (1–1820 AD): A Revision of the Estimates. *Rivista di Storia Economica*, 25:391–419.

London, Gloria A.
1991 Standardization and Variation in the Work of Craft Specialists. In *Ceramic Ethnoarchaeology*, edited by William A. Longacre, pp. 182–204. University of Arizona Press, Tucson.

Longacre, William A.
1976 Population Dynamics at Grasshopper Pueblo. In *Demographic Anthropology: Quantitative Approaches*, edited by E. Zubrow, pp. 169–184. University of Texas Press, Austin.
1999 Standardization and Specialization: What's the Link? In *Pottery and People: A Dynamic Interaction*, edited by James M. Skibo and Gary M. Feinman, pp. 44–58. University of Utah Press, Salt Lake City.

Longacre, William A., Kenneth L. Kvamme, and Masashi Kobayashi
1988 Southwestern Pottery Standardization: An Ethnoarchaeological View from the Philippines. *Kiva* 53(2):101–112.

Lucas, Robert E.
1988 On the Mechanics of Economic Development. *Journal of Monetary Economics* 22:3–42.

Luebben, Ralph A.
1953 Leaf Water Site. In *Salvage Archaeology in the Chama Valley, New Mexico*, edited by Fred Wendorf, pp. 9–33. Monograph No. 17. School of American Research, Santa Fe.

Maddison, Angus
1998 *Chinese Economic Performance in the Long Run*. Development Centre Studies, Organization for Economic Cooperation and Development, Paris.

Malanima, Paolo
2005 Urbanisation and the Italian Economy during the Last Millennium. *European Review of Economic History* 9:97–122.
2014 Energy in History. In *The Basic Environmental History*, Vol. 4, edited by Mauro Agnoletti and Neri Serneri, pp. 1–29, Springer-Verlag, Berlin.

Malerba, Franco
1992 Learning by Firms and Incremental Technical Change. *Economic Journal*, 102:845–859.

Manning, Joseph I.
2018 *The Open Sea: The Economic Life of the Ancient Mediterranean World from the Iron Age to the Rise of Rome*. Princeton University Press, Princeton.

Marcus, Joyce, and Kent V. Flannery
1996 *Zapotec Civilization: How Urban Society Evolved in Mexico's Oaxaca Valley*. Thames and Hudson, New York.

Marshall, Michael P.
1995 *A Cultural Resource Survey for the U.S. Highway 285 Improvement Projects in the Ojo Caliente Valley, Rio Arriba and Taos Counties, New Mexico*. Research Report No. 111. Cibola Research Consultants, Albuquerque.

Marshall, Michael P., and Henry Walt
1984 *Rio Abajo: Prehistory and History of a Rio Grande Province*. New Mexico Historic Preservation Program, Santa Fe.
2007 *The Eastern Homeland of San Juan Pueblo: Tewa Land and Water Use in the Santa Cruz and Truchas Watersheds: An Archaeological and Ethnogeographic Study*. Prepared for Ohkay Owingeh (San Juan) Pueblo. Research Report No. 432. Cibola Rsearch Consultants, Corrales, New Mexico.

Mauney, J. R., and L. L. Phillips
1963 Influence of Daylength and Night Temperature on Flowering of *Gossypium*. *Botanical Gazette* 124:278–283.

Maxwell, Timothy D.
1994 Prehistoric Population Change in the Lower Rio Chama Valley, Northwestern New Mexico. Paper presented at the 59th annual meeting of the Society for American Archaeology, Anaheim.
1997 *A Survey of Portions of the El Rito and Ojo Caliente Drainages, Rio Arriba County, New Mexico*. Archaeology Notes No. 160. Office

of Archaeological Studies, Museum of New Mexico, Santa Fe.

2000 *Looking for Adaptation: A Comparative and Engineering Analysis of Prehistoric Agricultural Technologies and Techniques in the Southwest.* PhD dissertation, Department of Anthropology, University of New Mexico, Albuquerque. University Microfilms, Ann Arbor.

Maxwell, Timothy D., and Kurt F. Anschuetz

1992 The Southwestern Ethnographic Record and Prehistoric Agricultural Diversity. In *Gardens in Prehistory: The Archaeology of Settlement Agriculture in Greater Mesoamerica*, edited by Thomas W. Killion, pp. 35–68. University of Alabama Press, Tuscaloosa.

McCloskey, Donald N.

1976 Does the Past Have Useful Economics? *Journal of Economic Literature,* 14: 434–461.

McGregor, S.E.

1976 *Insect Pollination of Cultivated Crop Plants.* Agriculture Handbook No. 496. USDA, US Government Printing Office, Washington, DC.

McGuire, Joseph

1899 *Pipes and Smoking Customs of the American Aborigines*. Smithsonian Institution, Washington, DC.

McKenna, Peter J.

2015 *Cultural Resource Survey: Proposed Drinking Water Well Locality on Pueblo of Ohkay Owingeh Lands, New Mexico*. Cultural Resources Survey Report No. SJ15-254. NMCRIS No. 134481. USDI, Bureau of Indian Affairs, Southwest Regional Office, Albuquerque.

McKenna, Peter J., and Judith Miles

1996 Pecos Archaeological Survey 1996 Ceramic Typology: Field Manual. Ms. on file, Laboratory of Anthropology, Santa Fe.

Mera, Harry P.

1932 *Wares Ancestral to Tewa Polychrome.* Technical Series Bulletin No. 4. Laboratory of Anthropology, Santa Fe.

1933 *A Proposed Revision of the Rio Grande Glaze Paint Sequence*. Technical Series Bulletin No. 5. Archaeological Survey, Laboratory of Anthropology, Santa Fe.

1934 *A Survey of the Biscuit Ware Area in Northern New Mexico*. Technical Series Bulletin No. 6. Laboratory of Anthropology, Santa Fe.

1935 *Ceramic Clues to the Prehistory of North Central New Mexico.* Technical Series Bulletin No. 8. Laboratory of Anthropology, Santa Fe.

Mesa Verde Museum Association

1986 *Petroglyph Point Trail Guide*. Mesa Verde Museum Association, Cortez, and Mesa Verde National Park, Colorado.

Mick-O'Hara, Linda

1987 Worked Bone. In *Howiri: Excavation at a Northern Rio Grande Biscuit Ware Site*, edited by Denise Fallon and Karen Welling, pp. 81–90. Note No. 261B. Laboratory of Anthropology, Santa Fe.

Miller, John H.

2016 *A Crude Look at the Whole: The Science of Complex Systems in Business, Life, and Society.* Basic Books, New York.

Mills, Barbara J.

1995 The Organization of Protohistoric Zuni Ceramic Production. In *Ceramic Production in the American Southwest*, edited by Barbara J. Mills and Patricia L. Crown, pp. 200–230. University of Arizona Press, Tucson.

1996 The Social Context of Production in the American Southwest. In *Interpreting Southwesterly Diversity: Underlying Principles and Overarching Patterns*, edited by Paul R. Fish and J. Jefferson Reid, pp. 121–124. Anthropological Research Papers No. 48. Arizona State University, Tempe.

Mills, Barbara J., and Patricia L. Crown

1995 Ceramic Production in the American Southwest: An Introduction. In *Ceramic Production in the American Southwest*, edited by Barbara J. Mills and Patricia L. Crown, pp. 1–29. University of Arizona Press, Tucson.

Minar, C. Jill

2001 Skills and the Learning Process: The Conservation of Cordage Final Twist Direction in Communities of Practice. *Journal of Anthropological Research* 57:381–405.

Mindeleff, Victor

1891 A Study of Pueblo Architecture in Tusayan and Cibola. In *Eighth Annual Report of the Bureau of American Ethnology for the Years 1886–1887,* pp. 3–228. Bureau of American Ethnology, Washington DC.

Minnis, Paul E.

1985 *Social Adaptation to Food Stress: A Prehistoric Southwestern Example.* University of Chicago Press, Chicago.

Mokyr, Joel

2005 Long-Term Economic Growth and the History of Technology. In *Handbook of Economic Growth,* Vol. IB, edited by Philippe Aghion

Mokyr, Joel (continued)
and Steven Durlauf, pp. 1133–1176. Elsevier, Amsterdam.

Moore, James L.
1981 *Prehistoric Soil and Water Conservation in the Middle Rio Puerco Valley*. Unpublished Master's thesis, Department of Anthropology, University of New Mexico, Albuquerque.
2009 *Living on the Northern Rio Grande Frontier: Eleven Classic Period Pueblo Sites and an Early Twentieth-Century Spanish Site near Gavilan, New Mexico,* Vol. 1, Overview and Site Descriptions. Archaeology Notes 315. Office of Archaeological Studies, Museum of New Mexico, Santa Fe.

Morales, Thomas M.
1997 *Glazeware Pottery Production and Distribution in the Upper-Middle Rio Grande Valley.* Unpublished PhD dissertation, Department of Anthropology, University of New Mexico, Albuquerque.

Morris, Ian M.
2004 Economic Growth in Ancient Greece. *Journal of Institutional and Theoretical Economics* 160(4):709–742.
2010 *Why the West Rules—For Now.* Farrar, Strauss and Giroux, New York.
2013 *The Measure of Civilization: How Social Development Decides the Fate of Nations.* Princeton University Press, Princeton.

Motsinger, Thomas N.
1992 *The Rise and Fall of a Village Industry: Specialized Ceramic Production in Protohistoric New Mexico.* Unpublished Master's thesis, Department of Anthropology, Northern Arizona University, Flagstaff.
1997 Tracking Protohistoric Glazeware Specialization in the Upper Rio Grande Valley, New Mexico. *Kiva* 63:102–116.

Muehlberger, William R.
1960 *Precambrian Rocks of the Tusas Mountains, Rio Arriba County, New Mexico*. Guidebook to the Rio Chama County, 11th Field Conference, pp. 45–47. New Mexico Geological Society, Albuquerque.

Muenchrath, D. A., and R. J. Salvador
1995 Maize Productivity and Agroecology: Effects of Environment and Agricultural Practices on the Biology of Maize. In *Soil, Water, Biology, and Belief in Prehistoric and Traditional Southwestern Agriculture,* edited by H. W. Toll, pp. 303–333. Special Publication No. 2. New Mexico Archaeological Council, Albuquerque.

Munson, Marit K.
2002 *On Boundaries and Beliefs: Rock Art and Identity on the Pajarito Plateau*. PhD dissertation, Department of Anthropology, University of New Mexico, Albuquerque.

Naranjo, Tessie
1995 Thoughts on Migration by Santa Clara Pueblo. *Journal of Anthropological Archaeology* 14:247–250.
2008 Life as Movement: A Tewa View of Community and Identity. In *The Social Construction of Communities: Agency, Structure and Identity in the Prehispanic Southwest,* edited by Mark D. Varien and James M. Potter, pp. 251–262. Altamira Press, Lanham, Maryland.

Naroll, Raoul
1956 A Preliminary Index of Social Development. *American Anthropologist* 56:687–715.
1962 Floor Area and Settlement Population. *American Antiquity* 27(4):587–589.

Nelson, Kit, and Judith A. Habicht-Mauche
2006 Lead, Paint, and Pots. In *The Social Life of Pots: Glaze Wares and Cultural Dynamics in the Southwest A.D. 1250–1680,* edited by Judith A. Habicht-Mauche, Suzanne L. Eckert, and Deborah L. Huntley, pp. 197–215. University of Arizona Press, Tucson.

Nelson, Nels C.
1914 *Pueblo Ruins of the Galisteo Basin, New Mexico.* Anthropological Papers Vol. 15. American Museum of Natural History, New York.

Netting, Robert M.
1969 Ecosystems in Process: A Comparative Study of Change in Two West African Societies. In *Contributions to Anthropology: Ecological Essays,* edited by D. Damas, pp. 102–112. Queen's Printer, Ottawa.
1993 *Smallholders, Householders: Farm Families and the Ecology of Intensive, Sustainable Agriculture.* Stanford University Press, Stanford.

Nordbeck, S.
1971 Urban Allometric Growth. *Geografiska Annaler* 53:54–67.

North, Douglass C.
1994 Economic Performance through Time. *American Economic Review* 84(3): 359–368.

North, Douglass C., John Joseph Wallis, and Barry R. Weingast
2009 *Violence and Social Orders: A Conceptual Framework for Interpreting Recorded Human History.* Cambridge University Press, Cambridge, United Kingdom.

Ober, Josiah
2010 Wealthy Hellas. *Transactions of the American Philological Association* 140(2):241–286.
2015 *The Rise and Fall of Classical Greece*. Princeton University Press, Princeton.

O'Driscoll, Gerald P.
1977 *Economics as a Coordination Problem: The Contributions of Friedrich A. Hayek*. Sheed Andrews and McMeel, Kansas City.

Olsen, Bjønar
2010 *In Defense of Things: Archaeology and the Ontology of Objects*. Altamira Press, New York.

Orcutt, Janet D.
1991 Environmental Variability and Settlement Changes on the Pajarito Plateau, New Mexico. *American Antiquity* 56(2):315–332.
1999 Demography, Settlement, and Agriculture. In *The Bandelier Archaeological Survey*, Vol. 1, edited by Robert P. Powers and Janet D. Orcutt, pp. 219–308. USDI, National Park Service, Intermountain Region, Santa Fe.

Ortiz, Alfonso
1969 *The Tewa World, Space, Time, Being, and Becoming in a Pueblo Society*. University of Chicago Press, Chicago.
1972 Ritual Drama and the Pueblo World View. In *New Perspectives on the Pueblos*, edited by Alfonso Ortiz, pp. 135–161. University of New Mexico Press, Albuquerque.
1979 San Juan Pueblo. In *Southwest*, edited by A. Ortiz, pp. 278–295. Handbook of North American Indians. vol. 9, William C. Sturtevant, general editor. Smithsonian Institution, Washington, DC.
1994 The Dynamics of Pueblo Cultural Survival. In *North American Indian Anthropology: Essays on Society and Culture*, edited by R.J. DeMallie and Alfonso Ortiz, pp. 296–306. University of Oklahoma Press, Norman.

Ortman, Scott G.
2010a Evidence of a Mesa Verde Homeland for the Tewa Pueblos. In *Leaving Mesa Verde: Peril and Change in the Thirteenth-Century Southwest*, edited by Timothy A. Kohler, Mark D. Varien, and Aaron M. Wright, pp. 222–261. University of Arizona Press, Tucson.
2010b *Genes, Language and Culture in Tewa Ethnogenesis, A.D. 1150–1400*. Unpublished PhD dissertation, School of Human Evolution and Social Change, Arizona State University, Tempe.
2012 *Winds from the North: Tewa Origins and Historical Anthropology*. University of Utah Press, Salt Lake City.
2016a Discourse and Human Securities in Tewa Origins. In *The Archaeology of Human Experience*, edited by Michelle Hegmon, pp. 74–94. Archeological Papers Vol. 27. American Anthropological Association, Washington, DC.
2016b Uniform Probability Density Analysis and Population History in the Northern Rio Grande. *Journal of Archaeological Method and Theory* 23(1):95–126.
2016c Why All Archaeologists Should Care About and Do Population Estimates. In *Exploring Cause and Explanation: Historical Ecology, Demography, and Movement in the American Southwest*, edited by Cynthia Herhahn and Ann F. Ramenofsky, pp. 103–121. University Press of Colorado, Boulder.
2017 Uniform Probability Density Analysis and Population History: A Test Case at San Marcos. In *The Archaeology and History of Pueblo San Marcos: Change and Stability*, edited by Ann F. Ramenofsky and Kari M. Schleher, pp. 231–246. University of New Mexico Press, Albuquerque.

Ortman, Scott G., and Grant D. Coffey
2017 Settlement Scaling in Middle-Range Societies. *American Antiquity* 82(4):662–682.

Ortman, Scott G., Lily Blair, and Peter N. Peregrine
2018 The Contours of Cultural Evolution. In *The Emergence of Premodern States*, edited by Jerry A. Sabloff and Paula L. W. Sabloff, pp. 185–215. SFI Press, Santa Fe.

Ortman, Scott G., Andrew H. F. Cabaniss, Jennie O. Sturm, and Luis M. A. Bettencourt
2014 The Pre-History of Urban Scaling. *PLOS ONE* 9(2):e87902. doi:87910.81371/journal.pone.0087902.
2015 Settlement Scaling and Increasing Returns in an Ancient Society. *Science Advances* 1:1–8.

Ortman, Scott G., Kaitlyn E. Davis, Jose Lobo, Michael E. Smith, Luis M.A. Bettencourt, and Aaron Trumbo
2016 Settlement Scaling and Economic Change in the Central Andes. *Journal of Archaeological Science* 73:94-106.

Ossa, Alanna, Michael E. Smith, and José Lobo
2017 The Size of Plazas in Mesoamerican Cities and Towns: A Quantitative Analysis. *Latin American Antiquity* 28(4):457–475.

Pacey, Arnold
1991 *Technology in World Civilization: A Thousand-Year History*. The MIT Press, Cambridge, Massachusetts.
Paper, Jordan
1988 *Offering Smoke: The Sacred Pipe and Native American Religion*. University of Idaho Press, Moscow.
Parsons, Elsie Clews
1929 *The Social Organization of the Tewa of New Mexico*. Memoir No. 36. American Anthropological Association, Menasha, Wisconsin.
1932 Isleta, New Mexico. *47th Annual Report of the Bureau of American Ethnology for the Years 1929–1930*, pp. 193–466. Smithsonian Institution, Washington, D.C.
1936 *The Hopi Journal of Alexander M. Stephen*. Contributions to Anthropology, Vol. 23, Part 2. Columbia University Press, New York.
1939 *Pueblo Indian Religion*. 2 vols. University of Chicago Press, Chicago.
Pauketat, Timothy R.
1989 Monitoring Mississippian Homestead Occupation Span and Economy Using Ceramic Refuse. *American Antiquity* 54:288–310.
Peacock, D. P. S.
1982 *Pottery in the Roman World: An Ethnoarchaeological Approach*. Longman, London.
Peckham, Stewart L.
1979 When is a Rio Grande Kiva? In *Collected Papers in Honor of Bertha Pauline Dutton*, edited by Albert H. Schroeder, pp. 55–86. Papers of the Archaeological Society of New Mexico No. 4. Archaeological Society Press, Albuquerque.
Peregrine, Peter N., Carol R. Ember, and Melvin Ember
2004 Universal Patterns in Cultural Evolution: An Empirical Analysis Using Guttman Scaling. *American Anthropologist* 106(1):145–149.
Perez, Carlota
2002 *Technological Revolutions and Financial Capital: The Dynamics of Bubbles and Golden Ages*. Edward Elgar, London.
Picketty, Thomas
2014 *Capital in the Twenty-First Century*. Harvard University Press, Cambridge.
Pinker, Stephen
2011 *The Better Angels of our Nature: Why Violence Has Declined*. Penguin, New York.
Plog, Fred
1975 Demographic Studies in Southwestern Prehistory. In *Population Studies in Archaeology and Biological Anthropology: A Symposium*, edited by A. C. Swedlund, pp. 94–103. SAA Memoirs No. 30. Society for American Archaeology, Washington, D.C.
Plog, Stephen
1976 Measurement of Prehistoric Interaction Between Communities. In *The Early Mesoamerican Village*, edited by Kent V. Flannery, pp. 255–272. Academic Press, New York.
Poesen, J. W. A., and H. Lavee
1991 Effects of Size and Incorporation of Synthetic Mulch on Runoff and Sediment Yield from Interrills in a Laboratory Study with Simulated Rainfall. *Soil & Tillage Research*, 21(1991):209–223.
Polanyi, Karl
1944 *The Great Transformation*. Farrar & Rinehart, New York.
1977 *The Livelihood of Man*. Academic Press, New York.
Powell, Melissa S.
2002 *The Organization of Ceramic Production in the Upper Pecos Valley, New Mexico, A.D. 1200–1400*. Unpublished PhD dissertation, Department of Anthropology, University of New Mexico, Albuquerque.
Powers, Robert P., and Janet D. Orcutt
1999 Summary and Conclusions. In *The Bandelier Archaeological Survey*, Vol. 2, edited by Robert P. Powers and Janet D. Orcutt pp. 551–589. Professional Paper No. 57. Inter-mountain Cultural Resources Management, Santa Fe.
Powers, Robert P., and Janet D. Orcutt (editors)
1999 *The Bandelier Archaeological Survey*. Professional Paper No. 57. Intermountain Cultural Resource Management, Santa Fe.
Pryor, Frederick L.
1977 *The Origins of the Economy: A Comparative Study of Distribution in Primitive and Peasant Economies*. Academic Press, New York.
2005 *Economic Systems of Foraging, Agricultural, and Industrial Societies*. Cambridge University Press, New York.
Quigley, John M.
2009 Urbanization, Agglomeration, and Economic Development. In *Urbanization and Growth*, edited by Michael Spence, Patricia Clarke

Annez, and Robert M. Buckley, pp. 115–132. World Bank, Washington, D.C.

Ramenofsky, Ann F., and James K. Feathers

2004 Documents, Ceramics, Tree Rings, and Luminescence: Estimating Final Native Abandonment of the Lower Rio Chama. *Journal of Anthropological Research* 58:121–159.

Ramenofsky, Ann F., and Kari L. Schleher (editors)

2017 *The Archaeology and History of Pueblo San Marcos.* University of New Mexico Press, Albuquerque.

Ramenofsky, Ann F., Fraser D. Neiman, and Christopher D. Pierce

2009 Measuring Time, Population, and Residential Mobility from the Surface at San Marcos Pueblo, North Central New Mexico. *American Antiquity* 7(3):505–530.

Rands, Robert L., and Ronald L. Bishop

1980 Resource Procurement Zones and Patterns of Ceramic Exchange in the Palenque Region, Mexico. In *Models and Methods of Regional Exchange*, edited by Robert E. Fry, pp. 19–46. Archaeology Papers No. 1, Society for American Archaeology, Washington, D.C.

Rathje, William L.

1971 The Origin and Development of Lowland Classic Maya Civilization. *American Antiquity.* 36(3):275–285.

1972 Praise the Gods and Pass the Metates: A Hypothesis of the Development of Lowland Rainforest Civilizations in Mesoamerica. In *Contemporary Archaeology; A Guide to Theory and Contributions*, edited by Mark P. Leone, pp. 365–392. Carbondale, Illinois.

Raynor, Gilbert S., Eugene C. Ogden, and Janet V. Hayes

1972 Dispersion and Deposition of Corn Pollen from Experimental Sources. *Agronomy Journal* 64:420–427.

Reed, Lori S.

1990 X-Ray Diffraction Analysis of Glaze-Painted Ceramics from the Northern Rio Grande Region, New Mexico. In *Economy and Polity in Late Rio Grande Prehistory*, edited by Steadman Upham and Barbara D. Staley, pp. 90–149. University Museum Occasional Papers No. 16. New Mexico State University, Las Cruces.

Reed, Paul F.

1990 A Spatial Analysis of the Northern Rio Grande Region, New Mexico: Implications for Sociopolitical and Economic Development from A.D. 1325–1540. In *Economy and Polity in Late Rio Grande Prehistory*, edited by Steadman Upham and Barbara D. Staley, pp. 1–89. University Museum Occasional Papers 16. New Mexico State University, Las Cruces.

Reiter, Paul

1938 *The Jemez Pueblo of Unshagi, New Mexico.* UNM Bulletin, Monograph Series, Vol. 1, No. 4. University of New Mexico Press, Albuquerque.

Renfrew, Colin

1969 Trade and Culture Process in European Prehistory. *Current Anthropology* 10:151–169.

1977 Alternative Models Exchange and Spatial Distribution. In *Exchange System in Prehistory*, edited by T. Earle and J. E. Ericson, pp. 71–90. Academic Press, New York.

Rice, Prudence M.

1987 *Pottery Analysis: A Sourcebook.* University of Chicago Press, Chicago.

1991 Specialization, Standardization, and Diversity: a Retrospective. In *The Ceramic Legacy of Anna O. Shepard*, edited by Ronald L. Bishop and Fredrick W. Lange, pp. 257–279. University Press of Colorado, Boulder.

Robertson, Eugene C.

1988 *Thermal Properties of Rocks.* Open-File Report No. 88-441. USDI, US Geological Survey, Reston, Virginia. Available: https://pubs.usgs.gov/of/1988/0441/report.pdf.

Robinson, Joan

1953 The Production Function and the Theory of Capital. *The Review of Economic Studies*, 21:81–106.

Robinson, William J., and Richard L. Warren

1971 *Tree-ring Dates from New Mexico C-D, Northern Rio Grande Area.* Laboratory of Tree-Ring Research. University of Arizona, Tucson.

Romer, Paul M.

1986 Increasing Returns and Long-Run Growth. *Journal of Political Economy* 94:1002–1037.

1996 Why, Indeed, in America? Theory, History, and the Origins of Modern Economic Growth. *American Economic Review* 86:202–206.

Root, Matthew J.

1989 Stone Artifacts. In *Bandelier Archaeological Excavation Project: Research Design and Summer Sampling*, edited by Timothy A. Kohler, pp. 69–84. Reports of Investigations No. 61. Department of Anthropology, Washington State University, Pullman.

Root, Matthew J., and Douglas R. Harro
1993 Stone Artifacts. In *Papers on the Early Classic Period Prehistory of the Pajarito Plateau, New Mexico*, edited by Timothy A. Kohler and Angela R. Linse, pp. 43–59. Reports of Investigations No. 65. Department of Anthropology, Washington State University, Pullman.

Roper, Donna C.
1979 The Method and Theory of Site Catchment Analysis: A Review. *Advances in Archaeological Method and Theory* 2:119–140.

Rosen, Sherwin
1978 Substitution and the Division of Labor. *Economica* 45:235–250.

Rosenberg, Nathan
1968 Adam Smith, Consumer Tastes, and Economic Growth. *Journal of Political Economy*, 76:361–374.

Roux, Valentine
2003 Ceramic Standardization and Intensity of Production: Quantifying Degrees of Specialization. *American Antiquity* 68(4):768–782.

Ruscavage-Barz, Samantha M., and Elizabeth A. Bagwell
2006 Gathering Spaces and Bounded Places: The Religious Significance of Plaza-Oriented Communities in the Northern Rio Grande, New Mexico. In *Religion in the Prehispanic Southwest*, edited by Christine S. VanPool, Todd L. VanPool, and David A. Phillips, Jr., pp. 8 –101. Altamira Press, Lanham, Maryland.

Sabloff, Jeremy A.
2008 *Archaeology Matters: Action Archaeology in the Modern World*. Left Coast Press, Walnut Creek, California.
2010 Where Have You Gone, Margaret Mead? Anthropology and Public Intellectuals. *American Anthropologist* 113(3):408–416.

Sahlins, Marshall D.
1972 *Stone Age Economics*. Aldine, Chicago.

Samuelson, Paul A.
1947 *Foundations of Economic Analysis*. Harvard University Press, Cambridge, Massachusetts.
1977 A Modem Theorist's Vindication of Adam Smith. *American Economic Review* 67:42–49.

Samuelson, Paul A., and William D. Nordhaus
2004 *Economics*. McGraw-Hill, New York.

Sanders, William T., Jeffrey Parsons, and Robert S. Santley
1979 *The Basin of Mexico: Ecological Processes in the Evolution of a Civilization*. Academic Press, New York.

Santley, Robert S., Philip J. Arnold, and Christopher A. Pool
1989 The Ceramic Production System at Matacapan. *Journal of Field Archaeology* 16:107–132.

Schaafsma, Polly
1975 *Rock Art in New Mexico*. University of New Mexico Press, Albuquerque.
1985 Form, Content, and Function: Theory and Method in North American Rock Art Studies. *Advances in Archaeological Method and Theory* 8:237–278.
1992 Imagery and Magic: Petroglyphs at Comanche Gap, Galisteo Basin, New Mexico. In *Archaeology, Art, and Anthropology: Papers in Honor of J. J. Brody*, edited by R. A. Bice, M. S. Duran and D. T. Kirkpatrick, pp. 157–174. Archaeological Society of New Mexico, Albuquerque.
2000 *Warrior, Shield, and Star: Imagery and Ideology of Pueblo Warfare*. Western Edge Press, Santa Fe.

Schacht, Robert M.
1984 The Contemporaneity Problem. *American Antiquity* 49(4):678–695.

Scheick, Cherie L. (editor)
1996 *A Study of Pre-Columbian and Historic Uses of the Santa Fe National Forest: Competition and Alliance in the Northern Middle Rio Grande*, Vol. 1, The Archaeological and Historical Cultural Resources. SWAC Research Series No. 253. Southwest Archaeological Consultants, Santa Fe.

Scheidel, Walter
2008 In Search of Roman Economic Growth. *Princeton/Stanford Working Papers in Classics* No. 060808. Available at SSRN: https://ssrn.com/abstract=1214732 or http://dx.doi.org/10.2139/ssrn.1214732.

Scheidel, Walter, and Steve Friesen
2009 The Size of the Economy and the Distribution of Income in the Roman Empire. *Journal of Roman Studies* 99:191–252.

Schiffer, Michael B.
1987 *Formation Processes of the Archaeological Record*. University of New Mexico Press, Albuquerque.

Schillaci, Michael A., and Steven A. Lakatos
2016 Refiguring the Population History of the Tewa Basin. *Kiva*. 82(4):364–386.

Schleher, Kari L.
2010 *The Role of Standardization in Specialization of Ceramic Production at San Marcos Pueblo, New Mexico*. Unpublished PhD. Dissertation, University of New Mexico, Albuquerque.

2017 Learning and Production: The Northern Rio Grande Glaze Ware Community of Practice at San Marcos Pueblo. In *The Archaeology and History of Pueblo San Marcos*, edited by Ann F. Ramenofsky and Kari L. Schleher, pp. 107–127. University of New Mexico Press, Albuquerque.

Schleher, Kari L., and Jennifer E. Boyd
2005 Petrographic Analysis of Glaze-Painted Ceramics. In *Across the Caja del Rio Plateau III: Hunters and Farmers in the Northern Rio Grande*, edited by Peggy A Gerow and Patrick Hogan, pp. 153–165. Office of Contract Archaeology, University of New Mexico, Albuquerque.

Schleher, Kari L., and Suzanne L. Eckert
2012 Ceramic Chronology, Function, and Production at The Agua Fria School House Site. In *Pueblo at the Cold Water Place, P'O'Karige: Archaeological Investigation of The Agua Fria School House Site*, by Cherie L. Scheick, Glenda Deyloff, and Cortney A. Wands, pp. 7.1–7.110. Research Series No. 507F.3. Southwest Archaeological Consultants, Santa Fe.

Schleher, Kari. L., Deborah L. Huntley, and Cynthia L. Herhahn
2012 Glazed Over: Composition of Northern Rio Grande Glaze Ware Paints from San Marcos Pueblo. In *Potters and Communities of Practice: Glaze Paint and Polychrome Pottery in the American Southwest, A.D. 1250–1700*, edited by Linda S. Cordell and Judith A. Habicht-Mauche, pp. 97–106. University of Arizona Press, Tucson.

Schoeneberger, P.J., D.A. Wysocki, E.C. Benham, and W.D. Broderson (editors)
2002 *Field Book for Describing and Sampling Soils*, Version 2.0. Natural Resources Conservation Service, National Soil Survey Center, Lincoln, Nebraska.

Schroeder, Albert H., and Don S. Matson
1965 *A Colony on the Move: Caspar Castano de Sosa's Journal, 1590–1591*. The School of American Research, Santa Fe.

Schwindt, Dylan M., R. Kyle Bocinsky, Scott G. Ortman, Donna M. Glowacki, Mark D. Varien, and Timothy A. Kohler
2016 The Social Consequences of Climate Change in the Central Mesa Verde Region. *American Antiquity* 81(1):74–96.

Senhadji, A.
1999 Sources of Economic Growth: An extensive growth accounting exercise. IMF Working Paper WP/99/77.

Seymour, Deni
2015 Mobile Visitors to the Eastern Frontier Pueblos: An Archaeological Example from Tabira." *Plains Anthropologist* 60(233):4–39.

Shennan, Stephen
2002 *Genes, Memes and Human History: Darwinian Archaeology and Cultural Evolution*. Thames & Hudson, London.

Shepard, Anna O.
1936 The Technology of Pecos Pottery. In *The Pottery of Pecos*, Vol. 2, Part 2, edited by Alfred V. Kidder, pp. 389–587. Yale University Press, New Haven.
1942 *Rio Grande Glaze Paint Ware: A Study Illustrating the Place of Ceramic Technological Analysis in Archaeological Research*. Contributions to American Anthropology and History No. 39, Publication No. 528, pp. 129–262. Carnegie Institution, Washington, DC.
1965 Rio Grande Glaze-Paint Pottery: A Test of Petrographic Analysis. In *Ceramics and Man*, edited by Frederick R. Matson, pp. 62–87. Aldine, Chicago.

Silver, Morris
2007 Roman Economic Growth and Living Standards: Perception versus Evidence. *Ancient Society*, 37:191–252.

Silvertooth, J. C.
2001 *Agromonic Guidelines for Pima Cotton Production in Arizona*. Cooperative Extension No. AZ1242. University of Arizona, Tucson.

Simon, Julian
1986 Theory of Population and Economic Growth. Basic Blackwell, Oxford, United Kingdom.

Singer, Peter
1981 *The Expanding Circle: Ethics, Evolution and Moral Progress*. Princeton University Press, Princeton.

Sinopoli, Carla M.
1988 The Organization of Craft Production at Vijayanagara, South India. *American Anthropologist* 90:580–597.

Skinner, S. Allen
1965 A Survey of Field Houses at Sapawe, North Central New Mexico. *Southwestern Lore* 31(1):18–24.

Slifer, Dennis
1998 *Signs of Life: Rock Art of the Upper Rio Grande.* Ancient City Press, Santa Fe.

Smil, Vaclav
2008 *Energy in Nature and Society: General Energetics of Complex Systems.* MIT Press, Cambridge, Massachusetts.
2017 *Energy and Civilization: A History.* MIT Press, Cambridge, Massachusetts.

Smiley, Terah L., Stanley A. Stubbs, and Bryant Bannister
1953 *A Foundation for Dating of Some Late Archaeological Sites in the Rio Grande Area, New Mexico: Based on Studies in Tree-Ring Methods and Pottery Analyses.* University of Arizona Bulletin 24(3), Laboratory of Tree-Ring Research Bulletin No. 6. Laboratory of Tree-Ring Research, University of Arizona, Tucson.

Smith, Adam
1759 *Theory of Moral Sentiments,* first edition. Strand & Edinburgh, London.
1776 *An Inquiry into the Nature and Causes of the Wealth of Nations.* 1st edition, W. Strahan, London (books.google.com/books?id=C5dNAAAAcAAJ&pg=PP7#v=onepage&q&f=true)

Smith, Adam T.
2001 The Limitations of Doxa: Agency and Subjectivity from an Archaeological Point of View. *Journal of Social Archaeology* 1:155–171.

Smith, Michael E.
1987 Household Possessions and Wealth in Agrarian States: Implications for Archaeology. *Journal of Anthropological Archaeology* 6:297–335.

Smith, Michael E., Timothy Dennehy, April Kamp-Whittaker, Emily Colon, and Emily Harkness
2014 Quantitative Measures of Wealth Inequality in Ancient Central Mexican Communities. *Advances in Archaeological Practice* 2(4):311–323.

Smith, Michael E., Gary M. Feinman, Robert D. Drennan, Timothy Earle, and Ian Morris
2012 Archaeology as a Social Science. *Proceedings of the National Academy of Science of the U.S.A.* 109(20):7617–7621.

Smith, Susan J.
1998 AR-03-0-02-0460 (LA 114161) Pollen Analysis. In *Pre-Columbian Pueblo Agricultural Plots (AR-0-02-0460 [LA 114161] within the Proposed Las Clinicas Del Norte Special-Use Permit Parcel, El Rito Ranger District, Carson National Forest, Rio Arriba County, New Mexico,* by Kurt F. Anschuetz, pp. 73–84. Contribution II. Rio Grande Foundation for Communities and Cultural Landscapes, Santa Fe.
2006 San Juan Airport Pollen Analysis. In *Documentation of Pre-Columbian Pueblo Farmland Irrigation on the San Juan Pueblo Grant Near the San Juan Airport with the Geographic Scope of* New Mexico v. Abbott, by Kurt F. Anschuetz, Eileen L. Camilli, and Christopher Banet, pp. 7.1–7.40. Report prepared for USDI, Bureau of Indian Affairs, Southwest Regional Office, Albuquerque, and US Department of Justice, Indian Resources Section, Denver.
2007 The U.S. 89 Pollen Analysis and Regional Archaeobotanical Overview. In *Sunset Crater Archaeology. The History of a Volcanic Landscape. Environmental Analyses,* edited by Mark D. Elson, pp. 1–19. Anthropological Papers No. 33. Center for Desert Archaeology, Tucson.
2008 Pollen's Eye View of Archaeology on the Pajarito Plateau. In Analyses, edited by Bradley Vierra and Kari Schmidt, pp. 523–595. T*he Land Conveyance and Transfer Data Recovery Project: 7000 Years of Land Use on the Pajarito Plateau,* Vol. 3. LA-UR-07-6205. NMCRIS No. 107505. US Department of Energy, National Nuclear Security Administration, Los Alamos National Laboratory, Ecology and Air Quality Group, Los Alamos.
2009 San Ildefonso Pollen Analysis. Draft report in possession of author.
2012 Yunge Hills Archaeopalynology. In *Late-Pre-Columbian and Early Historic Period Pueblo Farming in the Yunge Hills Area of the San Juan Pueblo Grant,* by Eileen L. Camilli, Kurt F. Anschuetz, Susan J. Smith, and Christopher D. Banet, pp. 6.1–6.25. Report prepared for USDI, Bureau of Indian Affairs, Southwest Regional Office, Albuquerque, and US Department of Justice, Indian Resources Section, Denver. Ebert and Associates, Albuquerque.

Smith, Susan J., Eileen Camilli, Kurt F. Anschuetz, Bruce G. Phillips, and Christopher Banet
2012 Pollen Analysis from LA 118547, LA 105708, LA 105709, LA 105703, and LA 105704. Pre-Columbian Fields, Ojo Caliente Valley, New Mexico, May 2012. Draft report in possession of author.

Smith, Watson, Richard B. Woodbury, and Nathalie F. S. Woodbury
1966 *The Excavation of Hawikuh by Frederick Webb Hodge: Report of the Hendricks-Hodge*

Expedition. Contributions from the Museum of the American Indian, Heye Foundation. Museum of the American Indian, New York.

Snead, James E.
2008 *Ancestral Landscapes of the Pueblo World*. University of Arizona Press, Tucson.

Snead, James E., Winifred Creamer, and Tineke Van Zandt
2004 "Ruins of Our Forefathers": Large Sites and Site Clusters in the Northern Rio Grande. In *The Protohistoric Pueblo World, A.D. 1275–1600*, edited by E. Charles Adams and Andrew I. Duff, pp. 26–34. University of Arizona Press, Tucson.

Snow, David H.
1976 Artifacts from Pueblo Del Encierro. In *Archaeological Excavations at Pueblo Del Encierro, LA 70, Cochiti Dam Salvage Project, Cochiti, New Mexico, Final Report: 1964–1965 Field Seasons*, edited by David H. Snow, pp. D1–D66 and D16a–D16g. Laboratory of Anthropology Notes No. 78. Museum of New Mexico, Santa Fe.
1981 Protohistoric Rio Grande Pueblo Economics: A Review of Trends." In *The Protohistoric Period in the North American Southwest, AD 1450–1700*, edited by David A Wilcox and W. Bruce Masse, pp. 354–377. Anthropological Research Papers No. 24. Arizona State University, Tempe.

Soil Survey Division Staff
1993 *Soil Survey Manual*. USDA Handbook No. 18. US Government Printing Office, Washington, DC.

Solow, Robert M.
1956 A Contribution to the Theory of Economic Growth. *Quarterly Journal of Economics* 70:65–94.
1957 Technical Change and the Aggregate Production Function. *Review of Economics and Statistics*, 39: 312–320.
1997 *Learning from 'Learning by Doing': Lessons for Economic Growth*. Stanford University Press, Stanford.

Spangler, Jerry D.
2011 *Formal Site Documentation and Analysis of Visitor Impacts at Warrior Ridge (42DC1)*. Colorado Plateau Archaeological Alliance, Utah.

Speakman, Robert J., and Hector Neff
2005 *Laser Ablation-ICP-MS in Archaeological Research*. University of New Mexico Press, Albuquerque.

Speth, John D.
1991 Some Unexplored Aspects of Mutualistic Plains-Pueblo Food Exchange. In *Farmers, Hunters, and Colonists: Interaction between the Southwest and the Southern Plains*, edited by Katherine A. Spielmann, pp. 18–35. University of Arizona Press, Tucson.
2005 The Beginnings of Plains-Pueblo Interaction: An Archaeological Perspective from Southeastern New Mexico. In *Engaged Anthropology, Research Essays on North American Archaeology, Ethnobotany, and Museology*, edited by Michelle Hegmon and B. Sunday Eiselt, pp. 129–147. Anthropological Papers No. 94. Museum of Anthropology, University of Michigan, Ann Arbor.

Speth, John D., and Khori Newlander.
2012 Plains-Pueblo Interaction: A View from the "Middle." In *The Toyah Phase of Central Texas: Late Prehistoric Economic and Social Processes*, edited by Nancy A. Kenmotsu and Douglas K. Boyd, pp. 152–180. Texas A&M Press, College Station.

Spielmann, Katherine A.
1982 *Intersocietal Food Acquisition among Egalitarian Societies: An Ecological Study of Plains/Pueblo Interaction in the American Southwest*. Unpublished PhD dissertation, Department of Anthropology, University of Michigan, Ann Arbor.
1983 Late Prehistoric Exchange Between the Southwest and Southern Plains. *Plains Anthropologist* 28(102):257–272.
1991 Coercion or Cooperation? Plains-Pueblo Interaction in the Protohistoric Period. In *Farmers, Hunters, and Colonists: Interaction between the Southwest and the Southern Plains*, edited by Katherine A. Spielmann, pp. 36–50. University of Arizona Press, Tucson.
1994 Clustered Confederacies: Sociopolitical Organization in the Protohistoric Rio Grande. In *The Ancient Southwestern Community: Models and Methods for the Study of Prehistoric Social Organization*, edited by W. H. Wills and Robert D. Leonard, pp. 45–54. University of New Mexico Press, Albuquerque.
1998a Ritual Craft Specialists in Middle Range Societies. In *Craft and Social Identity*, edited by L. Cathy and Rita P. Wright, pp. 153–160. Archaeological Papers No. 8. American Anthropological Association, Arlington, Virginia.
1998b Ritual Influences on the Development of Rio Grande Glaze A Ceramics. In *Migration and Reorganization: The Pueblo IV Period in the American Southwest*, edited by Katherine A. Spielmann, pp. 253–261. Anthropological Research Papers No. 51. Arizona State University, Tempe.

Spielmann, Katherine A. (continued)
2002 Feasting, Craft Specialization, and the Ritual Mode of Production in Small-Scale Societies. *American Anthropologist* 104(1):195–207.
2004 Clusters Revisited. In *The Protohistoric Pueblo World, A.D. 1275–1600*, edited by E. Charles Adams and Andrew I. Duff, pp. 119–127. University of Arizona Press, Tucson.

Spielmann, Katherine A. (editor)
1991 *Farmers, Hunters, and Colonists: Interaction Between the Southwest and the Southern Plains.* University of Arizona Press, Tucson.
1998 *Migration and Reorganization: The Pueblo IV Period in the American Southwest.* Anthropological Research Papers No. 51. Arizona State University, Tempe.

Spier, Leslie
1924 Zuni Weaving Technique. *American Anthropologist* 26:64–85.

Staley, Barbara D.
1990 Production of Rio Grande Glaze-Paint Ceramics: Refining the Concepts of Standardization and Specialization. In *Economy and Polity in Late Rio Grande Prehistory*, edited by Steadman Upham and Barbara D. Staley, pp. 150–260. University Museum Occasional Papers No. 16. New Mexico State University, Las Cruces.

Stark, Barbara L.
1995 Problems in Analysis of Standardization and Specialization. In *Ceramic Production in the American Southwest*, edited by Barbara J. Mills and Patricia L. Crown, pp. 231–267. University of Arizona Press, Tucson.

Stark, Barbara L., and Alanna Ossa
2010 Origins and Development of Mesoamerican Marketing: Evidence from South-Central Veracruz, Mexico. In *Archaeological Approaches to Market Exchange in Ancient Societies*, edited by Chris Garraty and Barbara L. Stark, pp. 99–126. University Press of Colorado, Boulder.

Stark, Barbara L., Matthew A. Boxt, Janine Gasco, Rebecca B. González Lauck, Jessica D. Hedgepeth Balkin, Arthur A. Joyce, Stacie M. King, Charles L. F. Knight, Robert Kruger, Marc N. Levine, Richard G. Lesure, Rebecca Mendelsohn, Marx Navarro-Castillo, Hector Neff, Michael Ohnersorgen, Christopher A. Pool, L. Mark Raab, Robert M. Rosenswig, Marcie Venter, Barbara Voorhies, David T. Williams, and Andrew Workinger
2016 Economic Growth in Mesoamerica: Obsidian Consumption in the Coastal Lowlands. *Journal of Anthropological Archaeology* 41:263–282.

Steen, Charlie R.
1977 *Pajarito Plateau Archaeological Survey and Excavations.* Scientific Laboratory Report No. 77-4. Los Alamos National Laboratory, Los Alamos.
1982 *Pajarito Plateau Archaeological Surveys and Excavations.* Part II. Los Alamos National Laboratory, Los Alamos.

Stigler, George
1951 The Division of Labor Is Limited by the Extent of the Market. *Journal of Political Economy* 59:185–193.

Stone, Glenn Davis
1996 *Settlement Ecology: The Social and Spatial Organization of Kofyar Agriculture.* University of Arizona Press, Tucson.

Stubbs, Stanley A., and W. S. Stallings, Jr.
1953 *The Excavation of Pindi Pueblo, New Mexico.* Monograph No. 18. School of American Research and the Laboratory of Anthropology, Santa Fe.

Stull, William J.
1986 The Urban Economics of Adam Smith. *Journal of Urban Economics* 20:291–311.

Sundt, William M.
1984 Design Analysis of a Pure Variety of Santa Fe Black-on-white. In *Papers in Honor of Harry L. Hadlock*, edited by Nancy L. Fox, pp. 13–35. Paper No. 9. Archaeological Society of New Mexico, Albuquerque.

Sweet, Jill D.
2004 *Dances of the Tewa Pueblo Indians: Expressions of New Life.* School of American Research Press, Santa Fe.

Switzer, Ronald. R.
1969 *Tobacco, Cigarettes, and Pipes of the Prehistoric Southwest.* El Paso Archaeological Society Special Report, El Paso.

Teague, Lynn S.
1998 *Textiles in Southwestern Prehistory.* University of New Mexico Press, Albuquerque.

Temin, Peter
2006 The Economy of the Early Roman Empire. *Journal of Economic Perspectives* 20(1):133–151.
2012 *The Roman Market Economy.* Princeton University Press, Princeton.

Texas A & M Agrilife Extension Service
2016 How a Cotton Plant Grows. San Angelo, Texas. Adapted from a series of articles by Del Deterling for *Progressive Farmer*, 1982. http://sanangelo.tamu.edu/extension/agronomy/

agronomy-publications/how-a-cotton -plant-grows/.

Thibodeau, Anthony
1993 Miscellaneous Ceramic Artifacts from Arroyo Hondo Pueblo. In *The Pottery from Arroyo Hondo Pueblo, New Mexico: Tribalization and Trade in the Northern Rio Grande*, edited by Judith A. Habicht-Mauche. Arroyo Hondo Archaeological Series, Vol. 8. School of American Research Press, Santa Fe.

Tichy, Marjorie
1937 A Preliminary Account of the Excavation of Paa-Ko San Antonio, New Mexico. *New Mexico Anthropologist* 1:73–77.

Tjaden, Rex L.
1979 *Bordered Garden Plots and Field Houses Near Sapawe, North Central New Mexico: A Dry Farming Strategy.* Unpublished Master's thesis, Department of Anthropology, Arizona State University, Tempe.

Toll, H. Wolcott
1981 Ceramic Comparisons Concerning Redistribution in Chaco Canyon, New Mexico. In *Production and Distribution: A Ceramic Viewpoint*, edited by Hilary Howard and Elaine L. Morris, pp. 83–121. B.A.R. International Series, Oxford, England.
1990 A Reassessment of Chaco Cylinder Jars. In *Clues to the Past: Papers in honor of William M. Sundt*, edited by Meliha S. Duran and David T. Kirkpatrick, pp. 273–305 Archaeological Society of New Mexico Papers Vol. 16. Archaeological Society of New Mexico, Albuquerque.
1995 *An Analysis of Variability and Conditions of Cavate Structures in Bandelier National Monument.* Intermountain Cultural Resources Center Professional Paper No. 53. USDI, National Park Service, Washington, DC.

Toll, H. Wolcott, and Jessica A. Badner
2008 *Galisteo Basin Archaeological Sites Protection Act Site Assessment Project.* Office of Archaeological Studies, Santa Fe.

Towner, Ronald H., and Mathew W. Salzer
2013 Dendroclimatic Reconstructions of Precipitation for the Northern Rio Grande. In *From Mountain Top to Valley Bottom: Understanding Past Land Use in the Northern Rio Grande Valley, New Mexico*, edited by Bradley Vierra, pp. 54–68. University of Utah Press, Salt Lake City.

Trierweiler, William N.
1990 *Prehistoric Tewa Economy: Modeling Subsistence Production on the Pajarito Plateau.* Garland, New York.

Trigger, Bruce G.
2003 *Understanding Early Civilizations: A Comparative Study*. Cambridge University Press, New York.

Turner, B. L., II
1992 Summary and Critique: Comments by B. L. Turner II. In *Gardens in Prehistory: The Archaeology of Settlement Agriculture in Greater Mesoamerica*, edited by Thomas W. Killion, pp. 263–273. University of Alabama Press, Tuscaloosa.

Turner, Brian L., II, and Jeremy A. Sabloff
2012 Classic Period Collapse of the Central Maya Lowlands: Insights about Human-Environment Relationships for Sustainability. *Proceedings of the National Academy of Science of the U.S.A.* DOI: 10.1073/pnas.1210106109.

Upham, Steadman
1982 *Polities and Power: An Economic and Political History of the Western Pueblo.* Academic Press, New York.

Usher, Abbot P.
1954 *A History of Mechanical Inventions*. Dover, New York.

van der Leeuw, S. E.
1977 Towards a Study of the Economics of Pottery Making. In *Ex Horreo*, edited by B. L. Beck, R. W. Brant and W. Gruenman van Watteringe, pp. 68–76. University of Amsterdam, Amsterdam.

Van West, Carla R.
1994 Reconstructing Prehistoric Climatic Variability and Agricultural Production in Southwestern Colorado, A.D. 901–1300: A GIS Approach. In *Proceedings of the Anasazi Symposium, 1991*, edited by Art Hutchinson and Jack E. Smith, pp. 25–33. Mesa Verde Museum Association, Mesa Verde, Colorado.

van Zandt, Tineke
1999 Architecture and Site Construction. In *Bandelier Archaeological Survey*, edited by Robert P. Powers and Jane D. Orcutt, pp. 309–388. Intermountain Cultural Resource Management, Professional Paper No. 57. USDI, National Park Service, Washington, DC.

Varien, Mark D.
1999 *Sedentism and Mobility in a Social Landscape: Mesa Verde and Beyond.* University of Arizona Press, Tucson.

Varien, Mark D., and Barbara J. Mills
1997 Accumulations Research: Problems and Prospects for Estimating Site Occupation Span.

Varien, Mark D., and Barbara J. Mills (continued)
Journal of Archaeological Method and Theory 4:141–191.

Varien, Mark D., and Scott G. Ortman
2005 Accumulations Research in the Southwest United States: Middle-Range Theory for Big-Picture Problems. *World Archaeology* 37(1):132–155.

Varien, Mark D., Scott G. Ortman, Timothy A. Kohler, Donna M. Glowacki, and C. David Johnson
2007 Historical Ecology in the Mesa Verde Region: Results from the Village Project. *American Antiquity* 72(2):273–299.

Vaughan, C. David
2017 Metallurgy and Its Consequences in the New Mexico Colony. In *The Archaeology and History of Pueblo San Marcos*, edited by Ann F. Ramenofsky and Kari L. Schleher, pp. 185–204. University of New Mexico Press, Albuquerque.

Vierra, Bradley J., Larry Nordby, and Gerald Martinez
2003 Nake'muu: Village on the Edge. In *Anasazi Archaeology at the Millennium*, edited by Paul F. Reed, pp. 137–144. Proceedings of the Sixth Occasional Anasazi Symposium. Center for Desert Archaeology, Tucson.

Vint, James M.
2000 Ceramic Artifacts. In *The Bandelier Survey*, Vol. 2, edited by Robert P. Powers and Janet D. Orcutt, pp. 389–467. Intermountain Cultural Resource Management Professional Paper No. 57. USDI, National Park Service, Washington, DC.

Vivian, Gordon
2003 *Gran Quivira: Excavations in a 17*th *Century Jumano Pueblo*. Archaeological Research Series No. 8. USDI, National Park Service, Washington, DC. Originally published in 1979.

von Hippel, Eric, and Marcie Tyre
1995 How Learning by Doing Is Done: Problem Identification in Novel Process Equipment. *Research Policy*, 24:1–12.

Walker, Robert S., and Kim R. Hill
2014 Causes, Consequences, and Kin Bias of Human Group Fissions. *Human Nature* 25:465–475.

Walsh, Michael R.
1997 *Lines in the Sand: Competition and Territoriality in the Northern Rio Grande A.D. 1150–1325*. PhD Dissertation, University of California, Los Angeles. University Microfilms, Ann Arbor.
1998 Lines in the Sand: Competition and Stone Selection on the Pajarito Plateau, New Mexico. *American Antiquity* 63:573–593.
2000 Material Evidence for Social Boundaries on the Pajarito Plateau, New Mexico. *The Kiva* 65(3):197–213.

Walt, Henry
2014 *The Western Homeland of Ohkay Owingeh: The Use and Ancestral Occupation of the Chama Watershed*. Report prepared for Ohkay Owingeh Pueblo, Plaintiff in *New Mexico v. Aragon*.

Ware, John A.
2014 *A Pueblo Social History: Kinship, Sodality and Community in the Northern Southwest*. School for Advanced Research Press, Santa Fe.

Ware, John A., and Macy Mensel
1992 *The Ojo Caliente Project: Archaeological Test Excavations and a Data Recovery Plan for Cultural Resources along U.S. 285, Rio Arriba County, New Mexico*. Archaeology Notes No. 99. Office of Archaeological Studies. Museum of New Mexico, Santa Fe.

Warren, A. Helene
1969 Tonque: One Pueblo's Glaze Pottery Industry Dominated Middle Rio Grande Commerce. *El Palacio* 76 (2):36–42.
1976a The Pottery of Pueblo Del Encierro." In *Archaeological Excavations at Pueblo Del Encierro, LA 70, Cochiti Dam Salvage Project, Cochiti, New Mexico*, Final Report: 1964–1965 Field Seasons, edited by David H. Snow, pp. B1–B184. Laboratory of Anthropology Notes No. 78. Museum of New Mexico, Santa Fe.
1976b The Tempering Material and Glazes of Pueblo del Encierro and the Cochiti Area. In *Archaeological Excavations at Pueblo del Encierro, LA 70: Cochiti Dam Salvage Project, Cochiti, New Mexico*. Final Report: 1964–1965 Field Seasons, edited by David H. Snow, pp. B83–B169. Laboratory of Anthropology Notes No. 78. Museum of New Mexico, Santa Fe.
1979 The Glaze Paint Wares of the Upper Middle Rio Grande. In *Archaeological Investigations in Cochiti Reservoir, New Mexico*, Vol. 4, Adaptive Change in the Northern Rio Grande, edited by Jan V. Biella and Richard C. Chapman, pp. 187–216. Office of Contract Archaeology, Department of Anthropology, University of New Mexico, Albuquerque.

Webster, David A.
1976 *Defensive Earthworks at Becan, Campeche, Mexico: Implications for Maya Warfare*. Middle American Research Institute, New Orleans.

Webster, Laurie

1997 *Effects of European Contact in Textile Production and Exchange in the North American Southwest: A Pueblo Case Study.* PhD Dissertation. Department of Anthropology, University of Arizona, Tucson.

2000 The Economics of Pueblo Textile Production and Exchange in Colonial New Mexico. In *Beyond Cloth and Cordage: Current Approaches to Archaeological Textile Research in the Americas*, edited by Penelope Ballard Drooker and Laurie D. Webster, pp. 179–204. University of Utah Press, Salt Lake City.

2003 *Collecting the Weaver's Art: The William Claftin Collection of Southwestern Textiles.* Harvard University Press, Cambridge, Massachusetts.

2007 Ritual Costuming at Pottery Mound: The Pottery Mound Textiles in Regional Perspective. In *New Perspectives on Pottery Mound Pueblo*, edited by Polly Schaafsma. pp. 167–206. University of New Mexico Press, Albuquerque.

Weitzman, Martin

1970 Soviet Postwar Economic Growth and Capital-Labor Substitution. *American Economic Review* 60:676–692.

Welker, Eden A.

1995 The Pottery of Pueblo San Marcos. In *Of Pots and Rocks: Papers in Honor of A. Helene Warren*, edited by Meliha S. Duran and David T. Kirkpatrick, pp. 175–187. Archaeological Society of New Mexico Papers No. 21. Archaeological Society of New Mexico, Albuquerque.

1997 *Attributes of Aggregation at Pueblo San Marcos and Pecos Pueblo in the Northern Rio Grande of New Mexico.* PhD Dissertation, University of Colorado, Boulder.

Wendorf, Fred

1952 Excavations at Cuyamungue. *El Palacio* 59:265–266.

1953 Excavations at Te'ewi. In *Salvage Archaeology in the Chama Valley, New Mexico*, assembled by Fred Wendorf, pp. 34–93. Monograph No. 17. School of American Research, Santa Fe.

Wendorf, Fred (editor)

1953 *Salvage Archaeology in the Chama Valley, New Mexico.* Monographs No. 17. School of American Research, Santa Fe.

Wendorf, Fred, and Erik K. Reed

1955 An Alternative Reconstruction of Northern Rio Grande Prehistory. *El Palacio* 62(56):131–173.

Wendorf, Fred, and Roscoe Wilmeth

1952 Cuyamungue Field Notes. Ms. available at the Laboratory of Anthropology, Museum of New Mexico, Santa Fe. Artifact data tabulated by Kaitlyn Davis, December 2014–January 2015.

Wetherington, Ronald K.

1968 *Excavations at Pot Creek Pueblo.* Paper No. 6. Fort Burgwin Research Center, Taos.

Wetterstrom, Wilma

1976 *The Effects of Nutrition on Population Size at Pueblo Arroyo Hondo, New Mexico.* PhD dissertation, University of Michigan, Ann Arbor, University Microfilms International, Ann Arbor.

White, C. S., S. R. Loftin, and R. Aguilar

1995 Ecology of Cobble Mulch Gardens: Structures for Modification of Soil Moisture Dynamics. Ms. on file, Department of Biology, University of New Mexico, Albuquerque.

White, Carleton S., David R. Dreesen, and Samuel R. Loftin

1998 Water Conservation Through an Anasazi in Gardening Technique. *New Mexico Journal of Science* 38:21–278.

White, Leslie

1959 *The Evolution of Culture: The Development of Civilization to the Fall of Rome.* McGraw-Hill, New York.

Whiting, David

2015 *Plant Growth Factors: Temperature.* Garden Notes No. 143, revised. Colorado Master Gardener Program, Colorado State University Extension, Fort Collins.

Wilcox, David R.

1981 Changing Perspectives on the Protohistoric Pueblos, A.D. 1450–1700. In *The Protohistoric Period in the North American Southwest, A.D. 1450–1700*, edited by David R. Wilcox and W. Bruce Masse, pp. 378–409. Anthropological Research Papers No. 24. Arizona State University, Tempe.

1991 Changing Contexts of Pueblo Adaptations, A.D. 1250–1600. In *Farmers, Hunters and Colonists: Interaction between the Southwest and the Southern Plains*, edited by Katherine A. Spielmann, pp. 128–154. University of Arizona Press, Tucson.

Wilk, Richard R., and Lisa C. Cliggett

2007 *Economies and Cultures: Foundations of Economic Anthropology.* Westview Press, Boulder.

Wilson, Andrew

2002 Machines, Power and the Ancient Economy. *The Journal of Roman Studies*, 92:1–32.

Wilson, Lucy
1916 Excavations at Otowi, New Mexico. *El Palacio* 3(2):28–36.

Windes, Thomas C., and Peter J. McKenna
2006 The Kivas of Tsama (LA 908). In *Southwestern Interludes: Papers in Honor of Charlotte J. and Theodore R. Frisbie*, edited by Regge N. Wiseman, Thomas C. O'Laughlin and Cordelia T. Snow, pp. 233–253. Reports Vol. 32. Archaeological Society of New Mexico, Albuquerque.

Wiseman, Regge, and John A. Ware
1996 *The Gavilan Project: Testing Results and a Data Recovery Plan for Eleven Prehistoric and Historic Sites Along U.S. 285 Near Ojo Caliente, Rio Arriba County, New Mexico.* Archaeology Notes No. 194. Office of Archaeological Studies. Museum of New Mexico, Santa Fe.

Woosley, Anne I.
1980 Agricultural Diversity in the Prehistoric Southwest. *Kiva* 45:317–335.

Wozniak, Frank J.
1992 Ethnohistory of the Abiquiu Reservoir Area. In *History and Ethnohistory along the Rio Chama*, by Frank J. Wozniak, Meade F. Kemrer, and Charles M. Carrillo, pp. 1–65. Prepared by J. D. Shelberg and Ronald R. Kneebone for US Army Corps of Engineers Albuquerque District, in partial fulfillment of Contract No. DAWC47-84-C-0032. Copies available from US Army Corps of Engineers, Albuquerque District, Albuquerque.

Wright, Karen
2000 *Archaeobotanical Evidence of Cotton*, Gossypium hirsutum var. punctatum, *on the Southern Colorado Plateau.* Unpublished Master's thesis, Department of Anthropology, Northern Arizona University, Flagstaff.

Wrigley, E. A.
2013 Energy and the English Industrial Revolution. *Philosophical Transactions of the Royal Society A* 371:1–10.
2016 *The Path to Sustained Growth: England's Transition from an Organic Economy to an Industrial Revolution.* Cambridge University Press, Cambridge, United Kingdom.

Yang, Xiaokai, and Jeff Borland
1991 A Microeconomic Mechanism for Economic Growth. *Journal of Political Economy*, 99: 460–482.

Youn, Hyejin, Luís MA Bettencourt, José Lobo, Deborah Strumsky, Horacio Samaniego, and Geoffrey B. West
2016 Scaling and Universality in Urban Economic Diversification. *Journal of The Royal Society Interface* 13(114):20150937.

Young, Allyn
1928 Increasing Returns and Economic Growth. *Economic Journal* 38:527–542.

Index

ABSTRACT

Rio Grande pueblo societies took shape in the aftermath of a period of significant turmoil and migration in the thirteenth century CE. In the centuries that followed, the size of pueblo settlements, degree of aggregation, level of productive specialization, extent of inter-ethnic exchange, and overall social harmony increased to unprecedented levels. Economists recognize scale, agglomeration, the division of labor, international trade, and control of violence as important determinants of socioeconomic development in the modern world. To what extent is it productive to frame Rio Grande archaeology in these terms? What do we learn about contemporary Pueblo culture and its resiliency when Pueblo history is viewed through this lens? What do we learn about the determinants of socioeconomic development more generally? The papers in this volume take up these questions, documenting change through time in living conditions in the Northern Rio Grande, interpreting their significance, and considering their implications for theories of socio-economic development.

KEY WORDS: Archaeology, American Indians, Development, Economic Anthropology

RESUMEN

Las sociedades de los Pueblos del Rio Grande se formaron tras un periodo de gran turbulencia social y migratoria en el siglo 13 EC. En los siglos subsiguientes el tamaño de los asentamientos Puebleños, su grado de agregación, el nivel de especializaciòn, la intensidad de intercambio inter-ètnico, y en general la armonía social, aumentaron de una manera sin precedentes. Los economistas reconocen la población, la aglomeración, la division del trabajo, el comercio intra-regional, y la diminución de la violencia como importantes determinantes del desarrollo socieconómico contemporáneo. ¿Qué tan util resulta investigar la arqueología del Rio Grande con este marco de referencía analitico? ¿Qué se puede aprender sobre la cultura y resistencia de los Pueblos cuando su historia es vista a través de esta perspective? ¿Qué se puede aprender sobre las causas del desarrollo socieconómico de manera general cuando se examina el desarrollo socieconómico de sociedades antiguas? Los ensayos en este volumen acometén estas preguntas, documentando el cambio en las condiciones de vida en las comunidades del Norte del Rio Grande, interpretando el significado de estos cambios, y considerando sus consequencias para la construción de teorias sobre desarrollo socieconómico.

ANTHROPOLOGICAL PAPERS OF THE UNIVERSITY OF ARIZONA

1. **Excavations at Nantack Village, Point of Pines, Arizona**
   David A. Breternitz. 1959.
2. **Yaqui Myths and Legends**
   Ruth W. Giddings. 1959. Now in book form.
3. **Marobavi: A Study of an Assimilated Group in Northern Sonora**
   Roger C. Owen. 1959.
4. **A Survey of Indian Assimilation in Eastern Sonora**
   Thomas B. Hinton. 1959.
5. **The Phonology of Arizona Yaqui with Texts**
   Lynn S. Crumrine. 1961.
6. **The Maricopas: An Identification from Documentary Sources**
   Paul H. Ezell. 1963.
7. **The San Carlos Indian Cattle Industry**
   Harry T. Getty. 1963.
8. **The House Cross of the Mayo Indians of Sonora, Mexico**
   N. Ross Crumrine. 1964.
9. **Salvage Archaeology in Painted Rocks Reservoir, Western Arizona**
   William W. Wasley and Alfred E. Johnson. 1965.
10. **An Appraisal of Tree-Ring Dated Pottery in the Southwest**
    David A. Breternitz. 1966.
11. **The Albuquerque Navajos**
    William H. Hodge. 1969.
12. **Papago Indians at Work**
    Jack O. Waddell. 1969.
13. **Culture Change and Shifting Populations in Central Northern Mexico**
    William B. Griffen. 1969.
14. **Ceremonial Exchange as a Mechanism in Tribal Integration Among the Mayos of Northwest Mexico**
    Lynn S. Crumrine. 1969.
15. **Western Apache Witchcraft**
    Keith H. Basso. 1969.
16. **Lithic Analysis and Cultural Inference: A Paleo-Indian Case**
    Edwin N. Wilmsen. 1970.
17. **Archaeology as Anthropology: A Case Study**
    William A. Longacre. 1970.
18. **Broken K Pueblo: Prehistoric Social Organization in the American Southwest**
    James N. Hill. 1970.
19. **White Mountain Redware: A Pottery Tradition of East-Central Arizona and Western New Mexico**
    Roy L. Carlson. 1970.
20. **Mexican Macaws: Comparative Osteology**
    Lyndon L. Hargrave. 1970.
21. **Apachean Culture History and Ethnology**
    Keith H. Basso and Morris E. Opler, eds. 1971.
22. **Social Functions of Language in a Mexican-American Community**
    George C. Barker. 1972.
23. **The Indians of Point of Pines, Arizona: A Comparative Study of Their Physical Characteristics**
    Kenneth A. Bennett. 1973.
24. **Population, Contact, and Climate in the New Mexico Pueblos**
    Ezra B. W. Zubrow. 1974.
25. **Irrigation's Impact on Society**
    Theodore E. Downing and McGuire Gibson, eds. 1974.
26. **Excavations at Punta de Agua in the Santa Cruz River Basin, Southeastern Arizona**
    J. Cameron Greenleaf. 1975.
27. **Seri Prehistory: The Archaeology of the Central Coast of Sonora, Mexico**
    Thomas Bowen. 1976.
28. **Carib-Speaking Indians: Culture, Society, and Language**
    Ellen B. Basso, ed. 1977.
29. **Cocopa Ethnography**
    William H. Kelly. 1977.
30. **The Hodges Ruin: A Hohokam Community in the Tucson Basin**
    Isabel Kelly, James E. Officer, and Emil W. Haury, collaborators; Gayle H. Hartmann, ed. 1978.
31. **Fort Bowie Material Culture**
    Robert M. Herskovitz. 1978.
32. **Wooden Ritual Artifacts from Chaco Canyon, New Mexico: The Chetro Ketl Collection**
    R. Gwinn Vivian, Dulce N. Dodgen, and Gayle H. Hartmann. 1978.
33. **Indian Assimilation in the Franciscan Area of Nueva Vizcaya**
    William B. Griffen. 1979.
34. **The Durango South Project: Archaeological Salvage of Two Late Basketmaker III Sites in the Durango District**
    John D. Gooding. 1980.
35. **Basketmaker Caves in the Prayer Rock District, Northeastern Arizona**
    Elizabeth Ann Morris. 1980.
36. **Archaeological Explorations in Caves of the Point of Pines Region, Arizona**
    James C. Gifford. 1980.
37. **Ceramic Sequences in Colima: Capacha, an Early Phase**
    Isabel Kelly. 1980.
38. **Themes of Indigenous Acculturation in Northwest Mexico**
    Thomas B. Hinton and Phil C. Weigand, eds. 1981.
39. **Sixteenth Century Maiolica Pottery in the Valley of Mexico**
    Florence C. Lister and Robert H. Lister. 1982.
40. **Multidisciplinary Research at Grasshopper Pueblo, Arizona**
    William A. Longacre, Sally J. Holbrook, and Michael W. Graves, eds. 1982.
41. **The Asturian of Cantabria: Early Holocene Hunter-Gatherers in Northern Spain**
    Geoffrey A. Clark. 1983.
42. **The Cochise Cultural Sequence in Southeastern Arizona**
    E. B. Sayles. 1983.
43. **Cultural and Environmental History of Cienega Valley, Southeastern Arizona**
    Frank W. Eddy and Maurice E. Cooley. 1983.
44. **Settlement, Subsistence, and Society in Late Zuni Prehistory**
    Keith W. Kintigh. 1985.

45. **The Geoarchaeology of Whitewater Draw, Arizona**
Michael R. Waters. 1986.

46. **Ejidos and Regions of Refuge in Northwestern Mexico**
N. Ross Crumrine and Phil C. Weigand, eds. 1987.

47. **Preclassic Maya Pottery at Cuello, Belize**
Laura J. Kosakowsky. 1987.

48. **Pre-Hispanic Occupance in the Valley of Sonora, Mexico**
William E. Doolittle. 1988.

49. **Mortuary Practices and Social Differentiation at Casas Grandes, Chihuahua, Mexico**
John C. Ravesloot. 1988.

50. **Point of Pines, Arizona: A History of the University of Arizona Archaeological Field School**
Emil W. Haury. 1989.

51. **Patarata Pottery: Classic Period Ceramics of the South-central Gulf Coast, Veracruz, Mexico**
Barbara L. Stark. 1989.

52. **The Chinese of Early Tucson: Historic Archaeology from the Tucson Urban Renewal Project**
Florence C. Lister and Robert H. Lister. 1989.

53. **Mimbres Archaeology of the Upper Gila, New Mexico**
Stephen H. Lekson. 1990.

54. **Prehistoric Households at Turkey Creek Pueblo, Arizona**
Julie C. Lowell. 1991.

55. **Homol'ovi II: Archaeology of an Ancestral Hopi Village, Arizona**
E. Charles Adams and Kelley Ann Hays, eds. 1991.

56. **The Marana Community in the Hohokam World**
Suzanne K. Fish, Paul R. Fish, and John H. Madsen, eds. 1992.

57. **Between Desert and River: Hohokam Settlement and Land Use in the Los Robles Community**
Christian E. Downum. 1993.

58. **Sourcing Prehistoric Ceramics at Chodistaas Pueblo, Arizona: The Circulation of People and Pots in the Grasshopper Region**
María Nieves Zedeño. 1994.

59. **Of Marshes and Maize: Preceramic Agricultural Settlements in the Cienega Valley, Southeastern Arizona**
Bruce B. Huckell. 1995.

60. **Historic Zuni Architecture and Society: An Archaeological Application of Space Syntax**
T. J. Ferguson. 1996.

61. **Ceramic Commodities and Common Containers: Production and Distribution of White Mountain Red Ware in the Grasshopper Region, Arizona**
Daniela Triadan. 1997.

62. **Prehistoric Sandals from Northeastern Arizona: The Earl H. Morris and Ann Axtell Morris Research**
Kelley Ann Hays-Gilpin, Ann Cordy Deegan, and Elizabeth Ann Morris. 1998.

63. **Expanding the View of Hohokam Platform Mounds: An Ethnographic Perspective**
Mark D. Elson. 1998.

64. **Great House Communities Across the Chacoan Landscape**
John Kantner and Nancy M. Mahoney, eds. 2000.

65. **Tracking Prehistoric Migrations: Pueblo Settlers among the Tonto Basin Hohokam**
Jeffery J. Clark. 2001.

66. **Beyond Chaco: Great Kiva Communities on the Mogollon Rim Frontier**
Sarah A. Herr. 2001.

67. **Salado Archaeology of the Upper Gila, New Mexico**
Stephen H. Lekson. 2002.

68. **Ancestral Hopi Migrations**
Patrick D. Lyons. 2003.

69. **Ancient Maya Life in the Far West Bajo: Social and Environmental Change in the Wetlands of Belize**
Julie L. Kunen. 2004.

70. **The Safford Valley Grids: Prehistoric Cultivation in the Southern Arizona Desert**
William E. Doolittle and James A. Neely, eds. 2004.

71. **Murray Springs: A Clovis Site with Multiple Activity Areas in the San Pedro Valley, Arizona**
C. Vance Haynes, Jr., and Bruce B. Huckell, eds. 2007.

72. **Ancestral Zuni Glaze-Decorated Pottery: Viewing Pueblo IV Regional Organization through Ceramic Production and Exchange**
Deborah L. Huntley. 2008.

73. **In the Aftermath of Migration: Renegotiating Ancient Identity in Southeastern Arizona**
Anna A. Neuzil. 2008.

74. **Burnt Corn Pueblo, Conflict and Conflagration in the Galisteo Basin, A.D. 1250–1325**
James E Snead and Mark W. Allen. 2011.

75. **Potters and Communities of Practice: Glaze Paint and Polychrome Pottery in the American Southwest, A.D. 1250–1700**
Linda S. Cordell and Judith Habicht-Mauche, eds. 2012.

76. **Los Primeros Mexicanos: Late Pleistocene and Early Holocene People of Sonora**
Guadalupe Sánchez. 2015.

77. **The Ceramic Sequence of the Holmul Region, Guatemala**
Michael G. Callaghan and Nina Neivens de Estrada. 2016.

78. **The Winged: An Upper Missouri River Ethno-Ornithology**
Kaitlyn Chandler, Wendi Field Murray, María Nieves Zedeño, Samrat Clements, Robert James. 2016.

79. **Seventeenth-Century Metallurgy on the Spanish Colonial Frontier: Pueblo and Spanish Interactions**
Noah H. Thomas. 2018.

80. **Reframing the Northern Rio Grande Pueblo Economy**
Scott G. Orman, ed. 2019.